ROBERTA HECK MINISTRIES PRESENTS

"BIBILICAL ANSWERS TO LIFE'S PRESSING PROBLEMS"

"GOD'S WORD, YOUR ANSWER FOR EVERY SEASON OF LIFE"

DAILY DEVOTIONALS

REV. DR. ROBERTA M. HECK, CHAPLAIN

"Scripture quotations are from the ESV® Bible (The Holy Bible, English Standard Version®), copyright © 2001 by Crossway, a publishing ministry of Good News Publishers. Used by permission. All rights reserved."

"Scripture quotations taken from The Holy Bible, New International Version® NIV® Copyright © 1973, 1978, 1984, 2011 by Biblica, Inc. Used with permission. All rights reserved worldwide."

"Scripture quotations are taken from the Holy Bible, New Living Translation, Copyright © 1996, 2004, 2015 by Tyndale House Foundation. Used by permission of Tyndale House Publishers, Inc., Carol Stream, Illinois 60188. All rights reserved."

Scripture taken from the New King James Version®. Copyright © 1982 by Thomas Nelson. Used by permission. All rights reserved.

"The Holy Bible, Berean Standard Bible, BSB Copyright ©2016, 2018 by Bible Hub Used by Permission. All Rights Reserved Worldwide."

The Holy Bible, King James Version KJV. Used by permission. All Rights reserved.

Biblical Answers to Life's Pressing Problems – God's Word, Your Answer, For Every Season of Life
Copyright © 2025 by Roberta M. Heck
Published by RnRH Publishing, LLC
Jackson, NJ 08527

ISBN 979-8-9934414-0-5 (eBook)
ISBN 979-8-9934414-1-2 (paperback)
ISBN 979-8-9934414-2-9 (hardcover)

All rights reserved. No part of this publication may be reproduced, stored in a retrieval system, or transmitted in any form or by any means –electronic, mechanical, digital, photocopy, recording, or any other—except for brief quotations in printed reviews, without the prior permission of the publisher.

Also by Rev. Dr. Roberta M. Heck

After The Storm Is Over – A Collection of Poems

The Dawn of A New Day – Poems of Insight and Awareness

One With God – A Spiritual Revelation

Changes of the Mind – Thoughts with Sober Conclusions

From Hell to Salvation – One Girl's Journey

Please visit www.robertaheckministries.org for additional resources. New resources are added on a regular basis to help you on your faith journey.

DEDICATION ~ TO ALMIGHTY GOD

To the One who is the Answer before the question is ever asked:

We dedicate this devotional book to You, Almighty God ~ our Creator, our Redeemer, our Sustainer, and our Ever-Present Help in times of trouble.

Lord, every page of this book is a testament to Your unfailing love and Your living Word. Without You, there would be no wisdom to offer, no hope to extend, and no truth to proclaim. You are the source of every solution, the healer of every wound, and the light in every dark place. You are not only the God of the mountaintop but also the faithful guide in every valley.

We honor You as the Author of all life and the Architect of eternal truth. It is by Your Spirit that hearts are transformed, minds renewed, and lives made whole. May this work serve as a tool in Your hands. A humble offering meant to point every reader back to You, the One true Answer to every pressing problem we face.

Let every word written be saturated with Your presence and guided by Your truth. Let the discouraged find hope, the confused find clarity, the lost find direction, and the broken find healing. We surrender this work to Your purpose and pray that You use it to draw many into deeper intimacy with You.

This is not just a Devotional ~ it is an offering of worship.

This is not just a book ~ it is a vessel of Your truth.

This is not just our work ~ it is Yours, for Your glory alone.

"For from Him and through him and for Him are all things. To Him be the glory forever! Amen." Romans 11:36 (NIV)

Father God, We thank You for the privilege of serving You through the written word. Every thought, every prayer, every message in this book is for Your glory and Your purpose. May it never point to us but always direct hearts to You. Breathe life into every page, and may Your Holy Spirit minister deeply to each reader.

Use this devotional as a divine instrument to meet people right where they are and lead them closer to You. May Your truth break chains, Your love bring peace, and Your presence be known in every chapter.

We give this work back to You as a holy offering. In Jesus' mighty name we pray, Amen and To God Be The Glory ~ Always and Forever!

INTRODUCTION

Life is full of questions. Some are small and pass with time, but others linger. Questions about purpose, suffering, relationships, decisions, and the unknowns of tomorrow. In these moments, we often search for clarity, comfort, and direction. Thankfully, God's Word is not silent. The Bible is not just an ancient book but a living guide, filled with divine wisdom that speaks to the very heart of life's pressing problems.

This devotional was prayerfully created to remind you that no matter what you face, God's Word holds the answers. Each day, as you read these pages, you will find scriptures, reflections, and prayers designed to help you navigate challenges, renew your faith, and draw closer to the One who holds all wisdom.

You are not alone in your struggles, and you don't have to figure life out on your own. God has provided His Word as a lamp to your feet and a light to your path (Psalm 119:105). As you journey through this devotional, may your heart be encouraged, your questions met with truth, and your life transformed by the timeless promises of God.

[16] All scripture is given by inspiration of God, and is profitable for doctrine, for reproof, for correction, for instruction in righteousness:

[17] That the man of God may be perfect, thoroughly furnished unto all good works. 2 Timothy 3:16-17 KJV

Heavenly Father, we give thanks to you for giving us Your Word, a steady anchor in a world filled with uncertainty. As we open these pages, open our hearts. Teach us, guide us, and give us the wisdom to apply Your truth to life's pressing problems. Remind us that no challenge is too great and no question too complicated when we place it in Your hands. May this devotional lead us closer to You and help us live with faith, peace, and purpose.

In Jesus' name, Amen and To God be The Glory!

Table of Contents

INTRODUCTION 1

JANUARY INTRODUCTION 20

    JANUARY 1. - "A NEW YEAR'S BLESSING FOR FAMILY AND FRIENDS" 22

    JANUARY 2. - "FAITH IS LETTING GO AND LETTING GOD" 24

    JANUARY 3 - "NOT MY RESPONSIBILITY 25

    JANUARY 4. - "YOUR DREAMS DO NOT HAVE AN EXPIRATION DATE ~ TRY AGAIN" 27

    JANUARY 5. - "YOUR GREATEST PROJECT IN LIFE ~ IS YOU" 29

    JANUARY 6. - "BE THE ONE WITH A GOD GIVEN PURPOSE" 31

    JANUARY 7. - TWO THINGS YOU WILL NEVER HAVE TO CHASE - "TRUE FRIENDS AND TRUE LOVE" 33

    JANUARY 8. - "YOU DESERVE THE LOVE YOU GIVE" 35

    JANUARY 9. - "FAITH IS LETTING GO AND LETTING GOD" 37

    JANUARY 10. - "NEVER LET ANYONE INFLUENCE WHO YOU WORSHIP" 38

    JANUARY 11. - "THAT'S WHEN YOU KNOW YOU'VE HEALED" 39

    JANUARY 12. - "TRUST GOD AND NOT YOUR MINDSET" 41

    JANUARY 13. - "TRUST GODS PLAN" 42

    JANUARY 14. - "YOU ARE A CHILD OF GOD" 43

    JANUARY 15.- "WOMAN OF GOD" 44

    JANUARY 16.- "BE A BLESSING ~ SPEAK LIFE OVER PEOPLE" 45

    JANUARY 17. - "GRACE ~ MERCY ~ BLESSINGS" - The True Meaning of Grace, Mercy, and Blessings 46

    JANUARY 18.- "GOD WILL NEVER LEAVE YOU ALONE" 48

    JANUARY 19.- "LENDING TO THE LORD" 49

    JANUARY 20.- "CHOOSING PEACE OVER DISRESPECT" 50

JANUARY 21. - "IT'S NOT PERSONAL, IT'S PURPOSEFUL" 52

JANUARY 22. - "FIVE REASONS TO TRUST GOD" 54

JANUARY 23. - "CHOOSING LOVE OVER SEPARATION" 56

JANUARY 24. - "PEOPLE WHO DON'T CLAP WHEN YOU WIN" 58

JANUARY 25. - "WHEN YOU GIVE UP ~ THE HOLY SPIRIT LIFTS YOU UP" 60

JANUARY 26. - "FROM MY LIPS TO GODS' EARS ~ THANK YOU PRAYER" 61

JANUARY 27. - "HERE BY THE GRACE OF GOD" 63

JANUARY 28. - "TEARS OF THE HEART -THANK YOU FATHER" 65

JANUARY 29. - "HAVE YOU EVER AGREED WITH SOMEONE JUST SO THEY'D SHUT UP" 67

JANUARY 30. - "IT'S OK NOT TO BE OK ~ JUST CONTINUE TO BELIEVE IN GODS' WORDS" 69

JANUARY 31. - "WHEN YOU REALIZE YOU HAVE IT ALL IN JESUS ~YOU HAVE PEACE" 70

FEBRUARY INTRODUCTION 71

FEBRUARY 1. - "FROM THE HEAD TO THE HEART~ THE MIRACLE OF GODS WORDS" 72

FEBRUARY 2. - "THERE IS POWER IN SILENCE" 73

FEBRUARY 3. - "FROM MY LIPS TO GODS' EARS ~ MY PRAYER TO YOU" 75

FEBRUARY 4. - "BLOCKD BY GODS' GRACE" 76

FEBRUARY 5. - "I DECLARE ~ I AM A WARRIOR OF GOD" 78

FEBRUARY 6. - "NO LOYALTY FOUND ~ GUARDING YOUR HEART FROM THE NARCISSIST" 79

FEBRUARY 7. - "GOD IS PREPARING YOU" 81

FEBRUARY 8. - "SOME PEOPLE ARE LIKE THERAPY ~ THEY ENLIGHTEN YOUR LIFE" 83

FEBRUARY 9. - "THE DIFFERENCE BETWEEN JESUS AND RELIGIONS ~ HE WASHES DIRTY FEET" 84

FEBRUARY 10. - "THANK YOU FATHER FOR ALL YOUR BLESSINGS" 86

FEBRUARY 11. - "FATHER I'M TRULY GRATEFUL" 87

FEBRUARY 12. - "YOU CAN BELIEVE WHATEVER YOU PLEASE ~ GOD GAVE YOU FREEWILL" 88

FEBRUARY 13. - "MIRACLES HAPPENS ~ DO YOU HAVE FAITH" 89

FEBRUARY 14. - "A PHYSICAL PRAYER ~ FROM HEAD TO FEET" 90

FEBRUARY 15. - "GODS CONTINUOUS PROTECTION" 93

FEBRUARY 16. - "DO NOT BE ANXIOUS ABOUT ANYTHING" 95

FEBRUARY 17. - "ENJOY THE LITTLE THINGS IN LIFE" 97

FEBRUARY 18. - "NOT EVERY RESPONSE NEEDS A REACTION" 98

FEBRUARY 19. - "WARRIORS IN FAITH" 100

FEBRUARY 20. - "WAIT ON THE LORD" 102

FEBRUARY 21. - "TIME, YOUR HEART, AND YOUR BEHAVIOR DECIDES YOUR DESTINY" 104

FEBRUARY 22. - "THERE'S MORE TO LIFE ~ THERE IS PURPOSE AND THERE IS A CALLING" 106

FEBRUARY 23. - "THE LORD EQUIPS" 108

FEBRUARY 24. - "WATCH AND LEARN" 110

FEBRUARY 25. - "THE SIMPLE FACT THAT YOU CARE ~ MAKES YOU MORE THAN ENOUGH" 111

FEBRUARY 26. - "THIS MOMENT RIGHT NOW IS WHAT'S MOST IMPORTANT" 112

FEBRUARY 27. - "LAUGH, LOVE, LIVE" 114

FEBRUARY 28. - "IT'S OK TO BELIEVE" 115

FEBRUARY 29. (LEAP YEAR) - "THEIR ACTION REFLECT HUMANITY ~ NOT YOURS" 116

MARCH INTRODUCTION 118

MARCH 1. - "SOME PEOPLE WILL TEACH YOU HOW NOT TO BE" .. 120

MARCH 2. - "SHOW RESPECT WHEN I'M NOT AROUND.................... 122

MARCH 3. - "FROM MY LIPS TO GODS' EARS ~ FOR BY YOU AND THROUGH YOUR GRACE, I THANK YOU FATHER" 123

MARCH 4. - "FOUR REASONS YOU CAN SMILE TODAY AND EVERYDAY".. 124

MARCH 5. - "THE HAPPIEST PEOPLE IN LIFE ARE GIVERS NOT TAKERS".. 126

MARCH 6. - "HATE NO ONE ~ IT'S BEST TO FORGIVE" 128

MARCH 7. - "TIME DECIDES WHO YOU MEET ~ BEHAVIOR DECIDES WHO STAYS"... 130

MARCH 8. - "HIS NAME IS JESUS" 132

MARCH 9. - "STANDING WITH GOD" 134

MARCH 10. - "LIFTING THE VEIL" 136

MARCH 11. - "GOD PROTECTS ME" 138

MARCH 12. - "GOD HAS IT ALL IN CONTROL" 139

MARCH 13. - "LIVE BY WHAT YOU GET ~ MAKE LIFE BY WHAT YOU GIVE" 141

MARCH 14. - "THE FULL ARMOR OF GOD"... 142

MARCH 15. - "FORGIVE AND MOVE ON"... 144

MARCH 16. - "KEEP YOUR MIND ON WHAT IS TRUE ~ PURE ~ RIGHT" Philippians 4:8 (KJV) 145

MARCH 17. - "FASTING FROM PEOPLE IS ALSO IMPORTANT" 147

MARCH 18. - "FAMILY IS NOT ALWAYS ABOUT BLOOD" 149

MARCH 19. - "JESUS ~ THE ONLY ONE WHO QUALIFIES" 150

MARCH 20. - "DON'T BE DISCOURAGED" 152

MARCH 21. - "HOW MANY SCARS ARE JUSTIFIED OUT OF LOVE" .. 153

MARCH 22. - "LOYALTY vs COMMON SENSE"...................................... 155

MARCH 23. - "THE CHOICE IS YOURS" 157

MARCH 24. - "CHANGE STARTS WITH YOU" 159

MARCH 25. - "STOP PLAYING CHURCH"... 161

MARCH 26. - "GOD DON'T CONDEMN" 162

MARCH 27. - "LOVE THEM ENOUGH TO TELL THEM THE WHOLE TRUTH" 163

MARCH 28. - "HOW TO PLAY THE LONG GAME" 165

MARCH 29. - "WHEN YOU ARE MADE TO FEEL UNWANTED ~ LEAVE or STAY" 166

MARCH 30. - "HUMBLE ENOUGH ~ WHEN YOU SERVE SOMEONE WHOSE HURT YOU" 168

MARCH 31. - "A TOUGH LESSON ~ LOVE YOUR ENEMIES" 169

APRIL INTRODUCTION 170

APRIL 1. - "A TIME FOR CHANGE" 172

APRIL 2. - "GUARDING YOUR CIRCLE" 174

APRIL 3. - "GOD CAME DOWN TO US ~ GOOD FRIDAY" 176

APRIL 4. - "A HOUSE IS NOT A HOME WITHOUT GOD IN IT" 178

Inspired by Joshua 24:15 (KJV) 178

APRIL 5. - "THREE MEN, THREE CROSSES, ONE HILL 180

APRIL 6. - "WHEREVER I AM GOD IS" 182

APRIL 7. - "CHOOSE ~ FAITH OR FEAR" 184

APRIL 8. - "YOU'RE ALWAYS SAFE WITH GOD" 185

When You Journey with God, You Reach Your Destination 185

APRIL 9. - "SOMETHING BEST REMEMBERED" 186

APRIL 10. - "WHAT MUST WE DO ~ TO DO THE WORK GOD REQUIRES" Inspired by John 6:28–29, 40 (KJV) 188

APRIL 11. - "I AM NOT ASHAMED TO SAY I STAND WITH THE LORD" 190

APRIL 12. - "WHEN YOU RECOGINZE YOUR WORTH" 192

APRIL 13. - "MARRIAGE IS NOT ONLY ABOUT LOVE ~ IT TAKES COMMITMENT" 194

APRIL 14. - "LEAVE SOMETHING THAT'S LASTING" 196

APRIL 15. - "HE HEARD WHAT YOU DIDN'T" 197

- APRIL 16. - "THE LORD WON'T HOLD IT AGAINST YOU ~ FINDING GRACE IN YOUR MESS" 198
- APRIL 17. - "WORRY ~ SOLVES NOTHING" 199
- APRIL 18. - "BLOOM IN GRACE" 200
- APRIL 19. - "DON'T LET REGRET HOLD YOU BACK" 201
- APRIL 20. - "THREE TRUTHS OF LIFE" 202
- APRIL 21. - "LIVING IN THE LIGHT OF GLORY" 203
- APRIL 22. - "LOVE WITHOUT CONDITIONS" 205
- APRIL 23. - "GOD IS GOOD ALL THE TIME" 207
- APRIL 24. - "A PRAYER FOR THE STRUGGLING" 209
- APRIL 25. - "THE WISDOM OF SILENCE" 211
- APRIL 26. - "FAITH BEYOND LOGIC" 213
- APRIL 27. - "TEN SIMPLE BLESSINGS ~ ONE FAITHFUL GOD" 215
- APRIL 28. - "ONLY ASK OF THE FATHER" 217
- APRIL 29. - "THE PURPOSE GOD CALLED YOU ~ TO WIN SOULS NOT ARGUMENTS" 219
- APRIL 30. - "SNATCHED BY GRACE ~ WHEN JESUS GRABBED ME" 221
- MAY INTRODUCTION 223
  - MAY 1. - "BOUNDARIES AND PEACE ~ CHOOSING TO LET GO" 225
  - MAY 2. - "UNBREAKABLE STRENGTH" 227
  - MAY 3. - "STANDING IN THE GAP ~ MY PRAYER FOR FAMILY" 229
  - MAY 4. - "LETTING GO AND LETTING GOD" 231
  - MAY 5. - "MY GOD IS GOOD ALL THE TIME" 233
  - MAY 6. - "LOVE YOURSELF A LITTLE EXTRA ~ GIVE YOURSELF GRACE" 235
  - MAY 7. - "SOME BATTLES ARE BETTER LEFT TO THE LORD" 237
  - MAY 8. - "THE CALLING ATTRACTS THE ATTACK ~ BUT YOU HAVE AUTHORITY" 239
  - MAY 9. - "MAKING THE NAME OF JESUS KNOWN" 241

MAY 10. - "A MOTHER'S DAY PRAYER" 243

MAY 11. - "SITTING WITH THE BROKEN" 245

MAY 12. - "HOW TO SURRENDER TO GOD'S WILL" 247

MAY 13. - "GOD STILL USES THE BROKEN" 250

MAY 14. - "LOVING ~ FORGIVING ~ LETTING GO" 252

MAY 15. - "CONFORMED TO HIS IMAGE" 254

MAY 16. - "YOU CAN'T BE BOTH THE BRIDE AND THE SIDE CHICK" 256

MAY 17. - "YOU CAN'T HAVE IT BOTH WAYS" 258

MAY 18. - WHEN EVERYTHING FALLS APART ~ TRUST GOD 260

MAY 19. - "WHEN GOD RELOCATES YOU FOR GROWTH" 262

MAY 20. - "DON'T BE IMPRESSED BY STATUS ~ BE MOVED BY CHARACTER" 264

MAY 21. - "THE STRENGTH BEHIND THE SMILE" 266

MAY 22. - "SUBMITTING TO THE FULL CONUSEL OF GOD" 268

MAY 23. - "WILLING TO DINE ~ BUT NOT SERVE" 270

MAY 24. - "BREAKING WHAT RUNS IN THE FAMILY" 272

MAY 25. - "WHEN THE BACKSLIDER RETURNS ~ CHECK YOUR HEART" 274

MAY 26. - "LET THE LION ROAR ~ IT WILL DEFEND ITSELF" 276

MAY 27. - "FAITHFULNESS OVER POPULARITY" 278

May 28. - "LET THEM THINK YOU DON'T KNOW" 280

MAY 29. - "NOTHING IS OUT OF HIS CONTROL" 282

MAY 30. - "GOD IS NOT THROUGH WITH ME YET" 284

MAY 31. - "KNOW YOUR WORTH ~ WALK IN GOD'S VALUE" 286

JUNE INTRODUCTION 288

JUNE 1. - "YES, I'M CHANGED ~ THE OLD ME WAS TOO WEAK" 290

JUNE 2. - "TRUST THE TRANSITION" 292

JUNE 3. - "WHAT TRIED TO BREAK ME ~ BUILT ME" 294

JUNE 4. - "YOU ARE THE ANSWER" 296

JUNE 5. - "WHAT TRULY MATTERS" 298

JUNE 6. - "UNSHAKABLE PEACE" 300

JUNE 7. - "GRASPING AIR ~ THE FUTILITY OF RESISTING GODS PLAN 302

JUNE 8. - "WHO TO STAY CLOSE TO" 304

JUNE 9. - "THE POWER OF STEPPING AWAY" 306

JUNE 10. - "GRATEFUL FOR EVERYTHING ~ ENTITLED TO NOTHING" 308

JUNE 11. - "NEVER STOP DOING GOOD" 310

JUNE12. - "GOD CALLS THE UNLIKELY" 313

JUNE 13. - "YES, I'M THAT KIND OF FRIEND 315

JUNE 14. - "THE STATE OF CONTENTMENT" 317

JUNE 15. - "REMEMBER Ephesians 4:26–27 ~ DON'T GIVE THE DEVIL OPPORTUNITY" 319

JUNE 16. - "REMEMBER PROVERBS 29:16 ~ THE DOWNFALL OF EVIL" 321

JUNE 17. - "GUARDING A GOOD HEART WITHOUT HARDENING IT" 323

JUNE 18. - "FROM A TRAP HOUSE TO THE CHURCH HOUSE" 325

JUNE 19. - "LET GOD LEAD ~ NOT YOUR EMOTIONS" 327

JUNE 20. - "WHEN THE BATTLE BEGINS" 329

JUNE 21. - "IN RECOGNITION TO OUR FATHERS ~ ON FATHERS DAY" 331

JUNE 22. - "LOOKING BACK TO MOVE FORWARD" 333

JUNE 23. - "FAITH THAT BUILDS" 335

JUNE 24. - "REMEMBERING YOUR WORTH IN CHRIST" 337

JUNE 25. - "LET THEM TALK ~ STAY TRUE TO GOD'S PATH" 339

JUNE 26. - "LETTING GO OF WHAT YOU CAN'T CONTROL" 341

JUNE 27. - "THE WHOLE TRUTH OF THE GOSPEL" 343

JUNE 28. - "SURROUNDED AND COVERED" 345

JUNE 29. - "TUSTING THE UNSEEN PLAN" 347

JUNE 30. - "WHEN DISRESPECT BECOMES YOUR ANSWER" 349

JULY INTRODUCTION 351

JULY 1. - "A WOMAN WHO SHAKES THE KINGDOM OF DARKNESS" 353

JULY 2. - "THE GIFT OF GODLY FRIENDSHIP AND BROTHERHOOD" 355

JULY 3. - "VICTORY ON MY KNEES IN PRAYER" 357

JULY 4. - "LETTING GO TO WALK THROUGH" 360

JULY 5. - "FORGIVENESS ~ THE KEY TO FREEDOM" 362

JULY 6. - "DON'T YOU DARE GIVE UP" 364

JULY 7. - "THE STRENGTH OF SILENCE" 366

JULY 8. - "TRUE RICHES ~ TRUE WISDOM ~ TRUE KINDNESS 368

JULY 9. - "SEEING GODS LOVE IN EVERYTHING" 370

JULY 10. - "BLESSED BEYOND WHAT WE DESERVE" 372

JULY 11. - "CHASING GOD ABOVE ALL ELSE" 374

JULY 12. - "STRENGTH FORGED THROUGH GOD" 376

JULY 13. - "ONCE YOU GET A TASTE OF PEACE" 378

JULY 14. - "SMILE AND REJOICE" 380

JULY 15. - "I WILL NOT TOLERATE WHAT I DID IN THE PAST" 382

JULY 16. - WHEN THE STORM CLEARS THE WAY" 384

JULY 17. - "WITHOUT LOVE ~ WITHOUT DREAMS ~ WITHOUT GOD 386

JULY 18. - "ITS NOT HOW MUCH SCRIPTURE YOU KNOW ~ IT'S HOW MUCH SCRIPTURE YOU LIVE" 389

JULY 19. - "FROM MY LIPS TO GODS EAR ~ FAMILY" 391

JULY 20. - "MORE THAN PAPER ~ BUILDING A MARRIAGE THAT LASTS" 393

JULY 21. - "THE PAIN OF GRIEF ~ IT'S LIKE HAVING BROKEN RIBS" 395

JULY 22. - "THE LORD WILL FIGHT FOR YOU" 397

JULY 23. - "IF NOT NOW WHEN ~ THE TIME IS NOW" 399

JULY 24. - "TRUST ~ LOVE ~ AND TRUTH IN A BROKEN WORLD" .. 401

JULY 25. - "LIFE HAS TWO RULES ~ ALL INVOLVING NEVER QUIT" 403

JULY 26. - "LIVING WITH OLD AGE ~ A BLESSING TO BE HERE" ... 405

JULY 27. - "SATURATED IN HIS WORD" 407

JULY 28. - "STAND FIRM ON GODS TRUTH ~ NOT CULTURE" 409

JULY 29. - "IMAGINE THIS…" 411

JULY 30. - "ARE YOU UNKNOWINGLY DRIFTING AWAY FROM GOD" 413

JULY 31. - "WHERE DID THE TIME GO" 415

AUGUST INTRODUCTION 417

AUGUST 1. - "BULLYING IS NOT OK ~ ESPECIALLY IN SCHOOLS" ... 419

AUGUST 2. - "JESUS ~ THE SOURCE OF TRUE LIFE" 421

AUGUST 3. - "FEAR NOT ~ FOR GOD IS WITH YOU" 423

AUGUST 4. - "SOMETHINGS ARE NOT ACCEPTABLE ~ ESPECIALLY FOR LOVE" 425

AUGUST 5. - "WHEN YOU HAVE GOD ~ YOU HAVE EVERYTHING" . 427

AUGUST 6. - "DON'T IGNORE THE SIGNS OF DISCERNMENT" 430

AUGUST 7. - "A GOAL WITHOUT A PLAN IS JUST A WISH" 432

AUGUST 8. - "THE GIFT OF A TRUE FRIEND" 434

AUGUST 9. - "JOY KEEPS YOU YOUNG" 436

AUGUST 10. - "YOU CAN NOT PICK UP WHILE YOU'RE STILL HOLDING" 438

AUGUST 11. - "ACCOUNTABILITY AS A MIRROR OF THE HEART" .. 440

AUGUST 12. - "YOU CANNOT BREAK A PERSON WHO GETS THEIR STRENGTH FROM GOD" 442

AUGUST 13. - "CURSES TURNED INTO BLESSINGS" 444

AUGUST 14. - "DO UNTO OTHERS AS YOU WOULD HAVE THEM TO DO UNTO YOU" 446

AUGUST 15. - "GOD NEVER SENDS YOU OUT ALONE" 448

AUGUST 16. - "ANXIETY AND CONFUSION IS NOT JESUS WAY" ... 450

AUGUST 17. - "LOVE BEYOND MISTAKES" 452

AUGUST 18. - "JESUS TURNS DELAYS INTO PROGRESS" 454

AUGUST 19. - "IT'S BETWEEN YOU AND GOD ~ ANYWAY" 456

AUGUST 20. - "A TEACHABLE SPIRIT 458

AUGUST 21. - "BE THANKFUL FOR TODAY" 460

AUGUST 22. - "BE THE RAINBOW INSTEAD OF THE CLOUD" 462

AUGUST 23. - "BE THE REASON" 464

AUGUST 24. - "BELIEVE IT AND RECEIVE IT" 466

AUGUST 25. - "LIVING UP TO WHAT GOD PUT IN YOU" 468

AUGUST 26. - "HUMILITY IN A WORLD OF ENTITLEMENT" 470

AUGUST 27. - "BIBLE EMERGENCY NUMBERS" 472

AUGUST 28. - "IF OPPORTUNITY DOES NOT KNOCK ~ BUILD A DOOR" 475

AUGUST 29. - "REST IN GODS ASSURANCE" 477

AUGUST 30. - "SOME SITUATIONS GOD WANTS TO CHANGE YOUR HEART" 479

AUGUST 31. - "TRUE CHARACTER" 481

SEPTEMBER INTRODUCTION 483

SEPTEMBER 1. - "PERFECT LOVE CAST OUT FEAR" 485

SEPTEMBER 2. - "FEED YOUR MIND HOPE" 487

SEPTEMBER 3. - "WE FALL DOWN ~ BUT WE GET BACK UP AGAIN" 488

SEPTEMBER 4. - "LOVE IN ACTION" 490

SEPTEMBER 5. - "MY STRENGTH IN CHRIST ALONE" 492

SEPTEMBER 6. - "GOD IS LOVE" 494

SEPTEMBER 7. - "DON'T GET YOUR ROLE TWISTED" 496

SEPTEMBER 8. - "BETTER OR BITTER ~ WHAT'S YOUR CHOICE".. 498

SEPTEMBER 9. - "THE MIRACLE OF CONTINOUS PRAYER" 500

SEPTEMBER 10. - "HONORING GOD WITH SUBSTANCE" 502

SEPTEMBER 11. - "OVERCOMING THE VOICES OF DOUBT" 504

SEPTEMBER 12. - "THE LORD'S STOREHOUSE OF BLESSINGS"...... 506

SEPTEMBER 13. - "YOU ARE MY BELOVED"...................................... 508

SEPTEMBER 14. - "DO GOOD THNGS WHETHER OTHERS NOTICE OR NOT" 510

SEPTEMBER 15. - "DON'T BE BLIND" 512

SEPTEMBER 16. - "YOUR FUTURE IN GODS HANDS" 514

SEPTEMBER 17. - "DON'T JUDGE BY YOUR PAST" 516

SEPTEMBER 18. - "DON'T LET SMALL MINDS DECIEVE YOU" 518

SEPTEMBER 19. - "NOT ON YOUR TERMS"... 520

SEPTEMBER 20. - "DON'T QUIT ~ GOD IS ON YOUR SIDE" 522

SEPTEMBER 21. - "GOD SEES, GOD HEARS, GOD DELIVERS"........... 524

SEPTEMBER 22. - "EITHER WAY WE WIN WITH JESUS"................... 526

SEPTEMBER 23. – "THE SPIRIT OF ESTER ~BOLD AND COURAGEOUS" 528

SEPTEMBER 24. - "GRACE FOR OUR HUMAN MISTAKES" 530

SEPTEMBER 25. - "FEAR NOT ~ FOR GOD IS WITH YOU"...................532

SEPTEMBER 26. - "FINISH EACH DAY AND BE DONE WITH IT" 534

SEPTEMBER 27. - "FOCUS AND BUILD ON YOUR STRENGTHS" 536

SEPTEMBER 28. - "HOW CRITICIZING YOUR KIDS AFFECT THEM" 538

SEPTEMBER 29. - "FORGIVE AS YOU WOULD LIKE TO BE FORGIVEN" 540

SEPTEMBER 30. - "DOING FREEDOM ~ LIKING HAPPINESS"...........542

OCTOBER INTRODUCTION 544

OCTOBER 1. - "LETTING GO AND LETTING GOD" 546

OCTOBER 2. - "THERE IS NO SCRIPT FOR PRAYER ~ IT MUST COME FROM THE HEART" 548

OCTOBER 3. - "BREAKING GENERATIONAL CURSES" 550

OCTOBER 4. - "GOD'S GRACE IS SUFFICIENT ~ AND I'M GRATEFUL" 552

OCTOBER 5. - "GIVE YOURSELF PERMISSION TO WALK AWAY" 554

OCTOBER 6. - "WALKING IN GOD'S POWER~LOVE~AND A SOUND MIND" 556

OCTOBER 7. - "GOD WILL FIGHT YOUR BATTLES ~ REPAY EVIL WITH GOOD" 558

OCTOBER 8. - "STAND WITH THE WINNER ~ THE LORD" 560

OCTOBER 9. - "TRUST GOD'S PROCESS OF TRANSFORMATION".... 562

OCTOBER 10. - "PUT YOUR TRUST IN JESUS" 564

OCTOBER 11. - "TRANSFORMATION OVER INFORMATION" 566

OCTOBER 12. - "HOW OFTEN DO YOU TELL GOD HE IS THE GREATEST ~ HOW OFTEN" 568

OCTOBER 13. - "HOW MANY SCARS IS ENOUGH" 570

OCTOBER 14. - "I AM WHO I AM" 572

OCTOBER 15. - "FORGIVING MY PAST SELF" 574

OCTOBER 16. - "MONEY ~ DOES IT MAKE THE MAN" 576

OCTOBER 17. - "NEVER FORGET HOW FAR THE LORD HAS BROUGHT YOU" 578

OCTOBER 18. - "IF MY PEOPLE PRAY" 579

OCTOBER 19. - "I AM NOT LIKE EVERYONE ELSE ~ I'M JUST ME" . 581

OCTOBER 20. - "BELIEVE ~ BE PATIENT ~ NEVER GIVE UP" 583

OCTOBER 21. - "A LIFE THAT TOUCHES OTHERS" 585

OCTOBER 22. - "FROM MY LIPS TO GODS' EARS ~ WISHING YOU A BLESSED DAY" 587

OCTOBER 23. - "LIVING WITH JOY IN THE PRESENT MOMENT"... 589

OCTOBER 24. - "A GOD-LIKE HEART" 591

OCTOBER 25. - "IN ONE WORD ~ BLESSED" 593

OCTOBER 26. - "THE BEAUTY THAT LAST FOREVER" 595

OCTOBER 27. - "IMPERFECT BUT IMPACTFUL" 597

OCTOBER 28. - "GUARDING YOUR HEART AGAINST BETRAYAL".. 599

OCTOBER 29. - "STRENGTH IS QUIET TEARS" 601

OCTOBER 30. - "THE ART OF SAYING NO" 603

OCTOBER 31. - "LIVING IN INTEGRITY AMID MISUNDERSTANDING" 605

NOVEMBER INTRODUCTION 607

NOVEMBER 1. - "GUARDING THE BALANCE OF YOUR LIFE" 609

NOVEMBER 2. - "LESSONS IN THE HARD PLACES"............................ 611

NOVEMBER 3. - "EVERY REJECTION OPENS THE DOOR TO GOD'S REDIRECTION" 614

NOVEMBER 4. - "LIFE IS SHORT ~ ENJOY IT" 616

NOVEMBER 5. - "SPEND YOUR TIME ON THOSE WHO LOVE YOU UNCONDITIONALLY"..618

NOVEMBER 6. - "LOVE YOURSELF A LITTLE EXTRA RIGHT NOW" 621

NOVEMBER 7. - "WHY LOYALTY COST MORE THAN IT GIVES" 623

NOVEMBER 8. - "CARING IS ENOUGH" 625

NOVEMBER 9. - "A LIFE THAT INSPIRES"..627

NOVEMBER 10. - "FROM BROKEN PIECES TO A MAJOR COMEBACK" 629

NOVEMBER11. - "THIS PLACE IS NOT WHERE MY STORY BEGAN OR WHERE IT WILL END" 631

NOVEMBER 12. - "LIFE IS TOO SHORT ~ MAKE THE MOST OF EVERYDAY".. 633

NOVEMBER 13. - "STANDING ON THE PROMISE OF GOD'S PRESENCE" 635

NOVEMBER 14. - "RAISE THE RENT AND KICK THEM OUT"............ 637

NOVEMBER 15. - "DON'T BE DEFINED BY OTHERS".........................640

NOVEMBER 16. - "NEVER JUDGE SOMEONE BASED ON A SEASON" 642

NOVEMBER 17. - "NEVER LET THE PAST IMPRISON YOU"............... 644

NOVEMBER 18. - "THE POWER OF ONE SMALL PRAYER"................ 646

NOVEMBER 19. - "LEARN TO ACCEPT BOTH TRUTHS"..................... 648

NOVEMBER 20. - "NO WEAPON FORMED AGAINST ME SHALL PROSPER"..650

NOVEMBER 21. - "RESTORING HONOR AND REVERENCE"............. 652

NOVEMBER 22. - "REALIZING YOUR WORTH"................................... 654

NOVEMBER 23. - "TEARS OF THE SOUL".. 656

NOVEMBER 24. - "SOME PEOPLE ARE JUST A CHAPTER ~ NOT THE ENTIRE STORY 658

NOVEMBER 25. - "THE POWER OF PERSISTENCE AND CONSISTENCY" 660

NOVEMBER 26. - "A HEART OVERFLOWING WITH GRATITUDE ~ THANKSGIVING BLESSINGS" 662

NOVEMBER 27. - "LOVING YOURSELF GOD'S WAY"........................ 664

NOVEMBER 28. - "GUARDING OUR WORDS AND OUR LOYALTIES" 666

NOVEMBER 29. - "THE STRENGTH AND ANOINTING OF THE LORD" 668

NOVEMBER 30. - "MOTIVATION AND GOOD HABITS"...................... 670

DECEMBER INTRODUCTION 672

DECEMBER 1. - "THE POWER OF PLANTING A SEED"...................... 674

DECEMBER 2. - "PURPOSE IN THE PAIN".. 676

DECEMBER 3. - "THE FOOL AND THE PRUDENT"............................. 678

DECEMBER 4. - "PRUNE THOSE LIMBS FOR PEACE AND GROWTH" 680

DECEMBER 5. - "BEING STUCK WHERE YOU DON'T BELONG IS PAINFUL" 682

DECEMBER 6. - "THE SPIRIT WHO INTERCEDED FOR US" 684

DECEMBER 7. - "SAVED BY A THREAD" 686

DECEMBER 8. - "RAIN ONLY MATTERS IF THERE ARE SEEDS IN THE GROUND" 688

DECEMBER 9. - "PRIORITIZING PEACE AND REST IN GOD" 690

DECEMBER 10. - "MY EMERGENCY CONTACT IS JESUS" 692

DECEMBER 11. - "THERE IS NO SUCH THING AS A HOPELESS SITUATION" 694

DECEMBER 12. - "WHY THEY DON'T ASK YOUR SIDE" 696

DECEMBER 13. - "THE LOVE YOU DESERVE" 698

DECEMBER 14. - "WHEN YOU ACTUALLY MATTERS" 700

DECEMBER 15. - "SOMETIMES HAPPINESS IS JUST DOING YOU" . 702

DECEMBER 16. - "SOMEONE WHO WILL BE THER FOR US" 704

DECEMBER 17. - "STANDING IN OUR TRUTH" 706

DECEMBER 18. - "COMING OUT STRONGER" 708

DECEMBER 19. - "FROM MY LIPS TO GOD'S EARS ~ A PRAYER OF HOPE" 710

DECEMBER 20. - "YOU CAN GIVE KNOWLEDGE ~ BUT YOU CAN'T MAKE THEM THINK" 712

DECEMBER 21. - "RECOGNIZING TRUE ENEMIES AND GOD' FAITHFULNESS" 714

DECEMBER 22. - "DISCERNMENT IN FRIENDSHIP" 716

DECEMBER 23. - "HOW WOULD YOU DEFINE THE POOREST PERSON" 718

DECEMBER 24. - "RECOGNIZING OUR BLESSINGS" 720

DECEMBER 25. - "O HOLY NIGHT ~ CHRIST THE SAVIOR IS BORN" 722

DECEMBER 26. - "THIS IS THE TIME OF YEAR TO JUST STOP AND TAKE A PAUSE" 724

DECEMBER 27. - "THIS LITTLE LIGHT OF MINE ~ I'M GONNA LET IT SHINE" 726

DECEMBER 28. - "THE BLESSING OF LOW MAINTENANCE FRIENDS" 728

DECEMBER 29. - "WILL YOU PUT ON THE FULL ARMOR OF GOD" 730

DECEMBER 30. - "THE BATTLES NOT YOURS IT'S THE LORDS" 732

DECEMBER 31. "FOR GOD BLESSES US TO BE A BLESSING TO OTHERS ~ IF ONLY WE WOULD" 734

JANUARY INTRODUCTION

As we step into a brand-new year, many of us carry questions, uncertainties, and burdens from the past, along with hopes and dreams for what lies ahead. Life is full of challenges that press on our minds and hearts. Questions about purpose, direction, relationships, finances, health, and inner peace. In these moments, we often search for answers in all the wrong places, overlooking the one source that has never failed: God's Word.

This month's devotional, Biblical Answers to Life's Pressing Problems, is designed to remind you that no matter what you're facing, God has already provided the wisdom, comfort, and instruction you need. The Bible isn't just a book of ancient stories, it's a living, breathing guide for everyday life. Within its pages, we find God's promises, His warnings, His encouragement, and His unwavering truth.

Throughout the month of January, as we set the tone for the year ahead, each day you'll discover a short, practical devotion rooted in Scripture. These reflections will point you back to God's Word for direction as you navigate life's uncertainties. Whether you're struggling with fear, facing temptation, seeking peace, or needing clarity, God's Word holds the answers.

My prayer is that as you walk through these daily readings, you won't just find temporary encouragement, but lasting confidence in knowing that God's truth speaks directly to the pressing problems you face. Let's start this year anchored in His promises, standing on His Word, and trusting His answers.

"Your word is a lamp to my feet and a light to my path." Psalm 119:105 (ESV)

Father, as we enter this new year, we surrender our worries, questions, and struggles to You. Remind us daily that Your Word holds the answers we seek. Open our hearts and minds to receive Your truth and give us the courage to trust You completely. Let this month be the beginning of deeper faith, renewed hope, and clear direction. In Jesus' name, Amen and To God Be The Glory!

JANUARY 1. - "A NEW YEAR'S BLESSING FOR FAMILY AND FRIENDS"

As one-year closes and another begins, we are reminded of the faithfulness of God who has carried us through every season. The phrase "New Year's Blessings" is more than a simple greeting; it is a declaration of God's goodness and a prayer of hope over the lives of those we hold dear.

When we speak blessings into the new year, we are inviting God's presence to shape our days ahead. Blessings are not mere wishes; they are spiritual declarations rooted in faith, declaring that love, health, peace, and joy will flow from the heart of God into the lives of His people.

For our families and friends, this means asking God to touch their hearts with His love, strengthen their bodies with His health, calm their homes with His peace, and fill their lives with His joy. It also means trusting that His power will guide their steps, His presence will hold them steady, His eyes will watch over them, and His wisdom will instruct them in every decision.

The new year is not promised to be free of trials, but with God's hand upon us, we can face it with confidence. Each sunrise is another opportunity to walk in His grace, to see His mercies made new, and to lean on His everlasting arms.

"The Lord bless you and keep you; the Lord make his face shine upon you and be gracious to you; the Lord turn his face toward you and give you peace." Numbers 6:24-26 (NIV)

Heavenly Father, as we step into this new year, we pause to thank You for the gift of life, for family, for friends, and for Your unfailing love. Lord, we ask You to bless our loved ones with love in their hearts, strength in their bodies, peace in their homes, and joy in their lives. Guide us with Your power, hold us with Your presence, watch over us with Your eyes, and teach us with Your wisdom. May this year be a testimony of Your faithfulness and a journey that draws us closer to You. In Jesus' name, Amen and To God Be The Glory!

JANUARY 2. - "FAITH IS LETTING GO AND LETTING GOD"

Faith isn't just believing God can make it happen, it's trusting Him enough to let go. True faith means surrendering our grip on the outcome and allowing God to lead, even when the road ahead is uncertain. It takes courage to release our own plans, timelines, and desires, but that's exactly where God meets us with His peace, His power, and His purpose.

Sometimes we try to control everything because we're afraid of what might happen if we don't. But faith is not about having all the answers; it's about trusting the One who does. When we let God take control, we find strength in His sovereignty, not in our strategies. We learn that His ways are always higher, His timing always perfect, and His love never fails.

Letting God take control doesn't mean we stop caring. It means we stop carrying what was never ours to bear. He invites us to cast our cares on Him, to trust Him with the unknown, and to walk by faith, not by sight.

"Trust in the Lord with all your heart and lean not on your own understanding; in all your ways submit to him, and he will make your paths straight." Proverbs 3:5–6 (NIV)

Heavenly Father, I thank You for being trustworthy even when life feels uncertain. I confess that I sometimes try to control things out of fear. Give me the courage to surrender; to let go and let You take control. Help me walk in faith, believing that You are guiding my steps, even when I cannot see the way. Lead me according to Your will and remind me that Your plan is always better than mine. I trust You, Lord. In Jesus' name I pray.

Amen and To God Be The Glory!

JANUARY 3 - "NOT MY RESPONSIBILITY

There's a powerful freedom that comes from realizing you are not responsible for the version of yourself that others have imagined.

In a world full of assumptions, projections, and opinions, people will often form images of you that have little to do with truth. Sometimes, they base those images on your past. Other times, it's on their own insecurities, fears, or unmet expectations. And when those ideas don't match who you really are or who you are becoming in Christ, they may become disappointed, angry, or judgmental.

But here's the truth: God never asked you to live for their version of you.

He calls you to walk in His truth, not their imagination.

Jesus Himself was misunderstood, misrepresented, and even rejected. Not because of who He was, but because of who people expected Him to be. Some wanted a military leader. Others wanted a political savior. But Jesus stayed committed to the Father's purpose, not people's projections.

When you try to constantly explain, defend, or reshape yourself to fit everyone's idea of you, you end up losing your identity and peace. Instead, focus on who God says you are. That's where your responsibility lies.

THINK ON THIS: Who God knows you to be is more important than who people think you are. Keep growing. Keep healing. Let their version fall away — it's not your responsibility.

"For do I now persuade men, or God? or do I seek to please men? for if I yet pleased men, I should not be the servant of Christ." Galatians 1:10 (KJV)

Heavenly Father, thank You for reminding me that I am not responsible for the false image's others create of me. Help me to walk in truth, not performance. Teach me to find my identity in You alone and not in the opinions or expectations of others. Give me the strength to release the need to be understood by everyone, and the confidence to keep growing in the image of Christ. In Jesus' name, Amen and To God Be The Glory!

JANUARY 4. - "YOUR DREAMS DO NOT HAVE AN EXPIRATION DATE ~ TRY AGAIN"

Sometimes life delays what God has placed in your heart. Time passes, doors close, and discouragement creeps in. You may begin to wonder if you missed your moment. If the dream you once held is now too far gone. But here's the truth: God is not limited by time, and neither are His promises.

Just because it hasn't happened yet doesn't mean it won't. God doesn't throw away what He plants in you. That dream, vision, or calling may be buried under disappointment, fear, or years of waiting, but it is not dead.

Joseph waited years in prison before his dream came to pass. Sarah waited decades before she held Isaac in her arms. David was anointed as king but went back to tending sheep and fighting battles long before the crown ever touched his head.

Delays are not denials. Detours are not dead ends. When God breathes life into something, it still has power, no matter how much time has passed. If He placed the dream in your heart, don't count yourself out. You're not too old, too late, or too far behind.

Try again. Trust again. Hope again. Because your dream, in God's hands, has no expiration date.

THINK ON THIS: What dream have you let go of because you thought it was too late? God says, "It's still alive. Try again."

"For the vision is yet for an appointed time, but at the end it shall speak, and not lie: though it tarry, wait for it; because it will surely come, it will not tarry." Habakkuk 2:3 (KJV)

Heavenly Father, thank You for reminding me that delay is not defeat. Help me to trust Your perfect timing. Breathe fresh life into the dreams I've laid down or forgotten. Give me the courage to try again, the strength to endure, and the faith to believe that what You have promised will come to pass. In Jesus' name, Amen and To God Be The Glory!

JANUARY 5. - "YOUR GREATEST PROJECT IN LIFE ~ IS YOU"

We often pour our time, effort, and love into others, into careers, goals, and responsibilities. Yet we forget that one of the most important assignments God has given us is ourselves.

You are the greatest project you'll ever work on. Not because you're flawed beyond repair, but because you're valuable beyond measure. You are God's handiwork, being shaped daily into something beautiful, meaningful, and strong. Growth isn't always visible, and healing doesn't happen overnight. But every prayer, every surrender, every step forward, even the small one's matter.

Taking your time isn't a sign of weakness; it's a reflection of grace. God is not in a rush with your life. He is patient, intentional, and deeply involved in your process. So, give yourself permission to grow slowly, to rest when needed, to forgive your mistakes, and to celebrate progress instead of perfection.

You are becoming what the Lord intended for you to be. And that journey is sacred.

"For we are God's masterpiece. He has created us anew in Christ Jesus, so we can do the good things he planned for us long ago." Ephesians 2:10 (NLT)

Heavenly Father, I thank You for reminding me that I am Your masterpiece. Help me to see myself the way You see me. Not as a problem to fix, but as a work in progress shaped by Your love. Teach me to be patient with the process, to trust Your timing, and to honor the journey. May I not rush what You are carefully building in me. Give me the strength to keep growing, the grace to rest when needed, and the faith to know that You are always working in me and through me. In Jesus' name I pray.

Amen and To God Be The Glory!

JANUARY 6. - "BE THE ONE WITH A GOD GIVEN PURPOSE"

In a world that often values being right over being kind, God calls us to a higher standard. To be the ones who nurture, build, understand, and forgive. Jesus modeled this perfectly. He didn't just pass through people's lives, He changed them. He healed the broken, forgave the sinner, and restored the weary.

To nurture means to care for the growth of someone else, emotionally, spiritually, even physically. To build means to leave someone stronger, not more broken. To understand is to listen before speaking. To forgive is to reflect the grace God has shown you. And in all these things, the goal is simple: leave people better than you found them.

This isn't always easy. It requires humility, patience, and love, the fruit of the Holy Spirit. When we choose to be a builder rather than a breaker, we reflect the heart of God. We become instruments of His peace, carriers of His compassion, and reflections of His mercy.

When you walk into a room, may healing walk in with you. When someone leaves your presence, may they feel lighter, loved, and seen. Choose to be the one who nurtures and builds, who understands and forgives. Not because others deserve it, but because you have been transformed by the One who first loved you.

"So then, let us pursue what makes for peace and for mutual upbuilding." Romans 14:19 (ESV)

My Heavenly Father, I thank You for Your constant love, patience, and forgiveness. Help me to be more like You. Someone who nurtures the hurting, builds up the broken, understands without judgment, and forgives freely. Teach me to see others through Your eyes and to leave every person better than I found them. Let my presence carry Your peace and kindness, and may my words and actions bring healing and hope. In Jesus' name I pray.

Amen and To God Be The Glory!

JANUARY 7. - TWO THINGS YOU WILL NEVER HAVE TO CHASE - "TRUE FRIENDS AND TRUE LOVE"

In a world that often makes you feel like you have to earn love and prove your worth, this truth brings peace: real friendship and true love don't have to be chased, they stay.

Godly relationships are not built on performance, pressure, or pretending. They are rooted in loyalty, truth, and love. The kind that reflects the heart of God. A true friend will walk with you through the highs and the lows. True love will not make you question your value. They are drawn to your soul, not your status.

Jesus is the greatest example of both. He never made us chase Him. He came to us. He loved us first, fully, freely, and faithfully. And when He connects you to people who reflect His love, those friendships and relationships will carry that same spirit.

You won't have to beg them to stay, explain your worth, or chase their approval. Real love recognizes you. Real friendship shows up and stays.

So, stop running after what God never meant for you to chase. What is true will stand. What is from Him will remain.

FOOD FOR THOUGHT: If it's from God, it won't run from you. Trust Him to send the people who are meant to walk with you. No chasing required.

"A man that hath friends must shew himself friendly: and there is a friend that sticketh closer than a brother." Proverbs 18:24 (KJV)

Heavenly Father, thank You for reminding me that I don't have to chase what's real. Help me to release the need to prove myself to people You never assigned to my life. Send relationships that reflect Your heart; faithful, honest, and anchored in love. Teach me to be the kind of friend and person who also gives that kind of love. In Jesus' name.

Amen and To God Be The Glory!

JANUARY 8. - "YOU DESERVE THE LOVE YOU GIVE"

So often, we pour our hearts into others. Encouraging them, praying for them, forgiving them, showing up for them, and yet we neglect to extend that same grace to ourselves. We give love freely, yet question whether we are worthy of it in return. But here's the truth: you are just as deserving of the love, kindness, patience, and compassion that you so generously give to others.

God doesn't call us to love others while abandoning ourselves. In fact, Jesus said, "Love your neighbor as yourself" (Mark 12:31). That command assumes that loving yourself is not only allowed, but also essential. Loving yourself isn't prideful; it's recognizing your worth as someone created in God's image and deeply loved by Him.

The love you keep giving often without measure or condition is beautiful. But it's time to reflect that love inward too. Give yourself permission to heal, to rest, to be forgiven, and to be loved, not just by others, but by yourself and by God. You are loved, deeply and completely, by the One who created you. Let that truth sink in. And as you share love with others, remember to receive it for yourself as well.

"We love because He first loved us." 1 John 4:19 (NIV)

Father God, I thank You for loving me first, without condition and without limits. Help me to see myself through Your eyes; worthy, valuable, and loved. Teach me to extend the same love to myself that I so easily give to others. Heal the parts of me that feel undeserving. Replace my self-criticism with grace and my doubts with truth. Let Your love fills me so deeply that it overflows in every direction, including inward. In Jesus' name I pray.

Amen and To God Be The Glory!

JANUARY 9. - "FAITH IS LETTING GO AND LETTING GOD"

Faith isn't just believing God can make it happen, it's trusting Him enough to let go. True faith means surrendering our grip on the outcome and allowing God to lead, even when the road ahead is uncertain. It takes courage to release our own plans, timelines, and desires, but that's exactly where God meets us with His peace, His power, and His purpose.

Sometimes we try to control everything because we're afraid of what might happen if we don't. But faith is not about having all the answers; it's about trusting the One who does. When we let God take control, we find strength in His sovereignty, not in our strategies. We learn that His ways are always higher, His timing always perfect, and His love never fails.

Letting God take control doesn't mean we stop caring. It means we stop carrying what was never ours to bear. He invites us to cast our cares on Him, to trust Him with the unknown, and to walk by faith, not by sight.

"Trust in the Lord with all your heart and lean not on your own understanding; in all your ways submit to him, and he will make your paths straight." Proverbs 3:5–6 (NIV)

Heavenly Father, I thank You for being trustworthy even when life feels uncertain. I confess that I sometimes try to control things out of fear. Give me the courage to surrender; to let go and let You take control. Help me walk in faith, believing that You are guiding my steps, even when I cannot see the way. Lead me according to Your will and remind me that Your plan is always better than mine. I trust You, Lord. In Jesus' name I pray.

Amen and To God Be The Glory!

JANUARY 10. - "NEVER LET ANYONE INFLUENCE WHO YOU WORSHIP"

It's easy to let the opinions, judgments, or even silent stares of others influence how we worship God. But here is a truth that will set you free: they did not die for you, Jesus did. Their approval did not and cannot save your soul. Their acceptance cannot heal your brokenness. Their opinions cannot redeem your life. Only Jesus Christ, through His sacrifice on the cross, made a way for you to stand forgiven, free, and loved.

Your worship is personal. It is not for or to them, it is for the One who laid down His life for you. So, whether you lift your hands, sing off-key, kneel in reverence, or simply close your eyes in quiet surrender, do it for Him. Let your worship be bold, unashamed, and completely focused on the One who gave everything for you.

"I have been crucified with Christ and I no longer live, but Christ lives in me. The life I now live in the body, I live by faith in the Son of God, who loved me and gave himself for me." Galatians 2:20 (NIV)

Heavenly Father, thank You for the sacrifice of Your Son, Jesus Christ. Thank You that His love for me was proven on the cross. Help me to worship You with boldness and truth, without fear of judgment from others. Remind me that no one else's opinion holds the power to define my worth or dictate my worship. You alone are worthy. Teach me to worship You freely, fully, and without apology, because only You died for me, and only You deserve the honor and praise. In Jesus' Name I pray.

Amen and To God Be The Glory!

JANUARY 11. - "THAT'S WHEN YOU KNOW YOU'VE HEALED"

There is a quiet moment in the journey of healing where you revisit the chapters of your past, and something has changed, the pain no longer stings. The memories that once broke you now simply remind you how far God has brought you. That moment is sacred. It's the evidence of restoration. It's the sign that God didn't just bring you through, He brought you out and left the pain in the ashes.

Tears aren't weaknesses, they are a sign of release. When the story that used to make you weep now brings peace, it's a sure sign that the Healer has done His work.

God specializes in heart-work. He sees what no one else can see and heals what no one else can touch. You may still carry the memory, but you're no longer burdened by the weight of it. That's healing. That's grace.

If you can tell your story without tears, it's not that the pain didn't happen — it's that God has turned it into peace. And that, dear soul, is a miracle.

"He heals the brokenhearted and binds up their wounds." Psalm 147:3 (NIV)

Heavenly Father, I thank You for being my Healer. Thank You for staying with me through every broken moment and never letting go. The tears I once cried, You caught in Your hands. The wounds I carried, You gently bound. I give You glory for the healing that has come, for the strength to remember without breaking, and for the peace that now guards my heart. I trust You with every part of my story. The past, present, and future. Keep working in me, and let my healing be a testimony of Your faithfulness. In Jesus' name I pray, Amen and To God Be The Glory!

JANUARY 12. - "TRUST GOD AND NOT YOUR MINDSET"

There's something in us that craves control. We love to map out our lives, write the script, and plan every detail. But what if God's plan for you is so much greater than what your mind can even imagine? What if your best-laid plans are actually holding you back from the abundant life He's preparing for you?

The truth is you have no idea what God has prepared for you. You see the present moment, He sees the full picture. You see obstacles, He sees opportunities. You see delays, He sees divine timing. That's why He gently reminds us in His Word to stop striving, stop overthinking, and simply trust Him.

When we let go of our plans, we make room for His. And His plans? They're not ordinary, they're extraordinary. They're filled with purpose, provision, peace, and blessings beyond anything you could orchestrate on your own. So, breathe. Release the need to figure it all out. Gods got it and He's got you.

"But as it is written: 'What no eye has seen, what no ear has heard, and what no human mind has conceived'—the things God has prepared for those who love him." 1 Corinthians 2:9 (NIV)

Father God, please forgive me for the times I've clung so tightly to my own plans that I left no room for Yours. I confess that I don't always understand what You're doing, but today, I choose to trust You. I believe that what You've prepared for me is greater than what I could ever imagine. Help me to surrender my timeline, my expectations, and my fears. Teach me to rest in the assurance that You are working behind the scenes, arranging every detail for my good and Your glory. I may not see it yet, but I trust that it's coming. In Jesus' name, Amen and To God Be The Glory!

JANUARY 13. - "TRUST GODS PLAN"

Life doesn't always go the way we expect. Disappointments, delays, and detours can leave us feeling uncertain and questioning what's next. But even when life feels confusing, God's Word gives us an unshakable promise:

This verse reminds us that even when we can't see the whole picture, God already has it drawn out. His plans are filled with hope, not harm. His future for you is good, even if the present feels heavy. You may be walking through a season of uncertainty or pain, but don't mistake your current situation for your final destination.

God is working, even in the waiting. His timing is perfect. His purpose is greater than your present struggle. Trust that His plans for your life are not forgotten, they are unfolding, step by step.

"For I know the plans I have for you," declares the Lord, "plans to prosper you and not to harm you, plans to give you hope and a future." Jeremiah 29:11 (NIV)

Heavenly Father, I thank You for the promise of Jeremiah 29:11. Even when I can't see what's ahead, I trust that Your plans for me are good. Help me to surrender my worries and doubts to You. Give me the faith to believe that You are guiding my life, even when the path feels uncertain. Fill my heart with hope, knowing that You have prepared a future full of peace, purpose, and blessings. I trust You with every detail of my life. In Jesus' name, Amen and To God Be The Glory!

JANUARY 14. - "YOU ARE A CHILD OF GOD"

You are not here by accident. You were not a mistake, a coincidence, or an afterthought. You are a child of God. Fearfully and wonderfully made, handcrafted by the Creator of the universe. Before God ever formed you in your mother's womb, He knew you. He set you apart. He called you His own.

You are precious in His sight, not because of anything you've done, but simply because of who you are, His. There is no one else with your fingerprint, your voice, or your purpose. You carry the divine imprint of heaven. When the world tries to tell you that you're not enough, remember who called you by name; God did.

When you question your worth, look to the cross. That's where your value was proven once and for all. You are deeply loved. You matter. And you belong to the One who makes no mistakes.

"I praise you because I am fearfully and wonderfully made; your works are wonderful; I know that full well." Psalm 139:14 (NIV)

Heavenly Father, I thank You for creating me with purpose and love. Remind me daily that I am Your child. Fearfully and wonderfully made. When doubts creep in, help me see myself through Your eyes. Let me walk in confidence, knowing that I am chosen, known, and cherished by You. Thank You for the unique calling You've placed on my life. Use me for Your glory, and let my life reflect the beauty of being Yours. In Jesus' name I pray.

Amen and To God Be The Glory!

JANUARY 15.- "WOMAN OF GOD"

To be called a Woman of God is not just a title. It is a calling, a way of life, and a reflection of who you are in Christ. A woman of God walks in wisdom, grace, humility, and strength. She is not perfect, but she is purposeful. Her life is rooted in faith, guided by the Holy Spirit, and marked by love.

In a world that often defines women by appearance, status, or achievements, a woman of God is defined by her relationship with her Creator. She seeks to honor Him in her words, actions, and choices. She loves deeply, serves faithfully, prays fervently, and trusts God boldly.

Being a woman of God doesn't mean you'll always feel strong. It means you lean on the One who is. It means you keep showing up, even when life is hard, and you keep trusting God's plan, even when it doesn't make sense.

"Charm is deceptive, and beauty is fleeting; but a woman who fears the Lord is to be praised." Proverbs 31:30 (NIV)

Our Father In Heaven, thank You for calling me to be a woman of God. Help me to walk in Your truth, to live with purpose, and to be a light in the world around me. Strengthen me when I'm weak, guide me when I'm unsure, and fill me with Your Spirit daily. May my life be a reflection of Your love and grace. I surrender my heart and my will to You. Use me for Your glory. In Jesus' name I pray.

Amen and To God Be The Glory!

JANUARY 16.- "BE A BLESSING ~ SPEAK LIFE OVER PEOPLE"

There is power in the words we speak. As believers, we are called not only to live a life that reflects Christ but also to speak words that give life, hope, and encouragement. In a world filled with negativity and criticism, your voice can be the one that uplifts, heals, and restores. Every conversation is an opportunity to bless someone, not just with material things, but with words that breathe life into their spirit.

Your words carry weight. They can either tear someone down or build someone up. When you choose to speak life over others reminding them of their worth, pointing them back to God's promises, and calling out the gold in them you become a vessel of God's grace and love. Even a simple word of encouragement can change someone's day or even their life.

So today, be intentional. Choose to be a blessing. Whether it's a kind message, a prayer, or a gentle reminder of God's love, speak life.

"The tongue has the power of life and death, and those who love it will eat its fruit." Proverbs 18:21 (NIV)

Father in Heaven, thank You for the gift of speech and the power You have placed in my words. Help me to use my tongue to build up and not tear down. Teach me to be sensitive to the needs of those around me, that I may speak life, encouragement, and truth into their hearts. Let my words reflect Your love, kindness, and grace. Use me to be a blessing today and every day. In Jesus' name, Amen and To God Be The Glory!

JANUARY 17. - "GRACE ~ MERCY ~ BLESSINGS" - The True Meaning of Grace, Mercy, and Blessings

We often hear the words grace, mercy, and blessings in our daily walk with God, but do we truly understand the depth of what they mean?

Grace is God giving us what we don't deserve. It's unearned, unmerited favor. It's the love that covered our sins through the sacrifice of Jesus.

Mercy is God not giving us what we do deserve. It is His compassionate withholding of judgment, even when we've failed.

Blessings are the tangible and intangible gifts from God. Peace in the storm, provision in lack, strength in weakness, and every good and perfect thing He chooses to give.

When we understand the beauty of grace and mercy, we begin to live lives marked by gratitude, humility, and worship. And when we recognize our blessings, we stop complaining about what we lack and start thanking God for what we have.

We are not saved because we were good enough—we are saved because He is good. His grace covers our past, His mercy meets us in our present, and His blessings flow into our future.

"Let us then approach God's throne of grace with confidence, so that we may receive mercy and find grace to help us in our time of need." Hebrews 4:16 (NIV)

Father God, thank You for Your amazing grace, endless mercy, and abundant blessings. I know I am not worthy, yet You love me still. Help me to never take for granted the price You paid for me. Teach me to walk in humility, knowing that every good thing in my life is a result of Your favor. May I extend grace and mercy to others just as freely as You have extended it to me. In Jesus' name I pray. Amen and To God Be The Glory!

JANUARY 18.- "GOD WILL NEVER LEAVE YOU ALONE"

Life has a way of making us feel isolated, especially in seasons of hardship, heartbreak, or uncertainty. But no matter what you're facing, whether it's a storm of grief, a test of faith, or a moment of weakness, God promises that you are never alone.

His presence isn't based on your performance or your feelings. He's not a distant observer; He's an ever-present help. God walks with you through every valley, stands by you in every fire, and carries you through every storm. Even when people walk away or life feels silent, He is there.

You may not always see His hand, but you can trust His heart. He is Immanuel, God with us. The One who never sleeps, never forgets, and never abandons.

"Be strong and courageous. Do not be afraid or terrified because of them, for the Lord your God goes with you; He will never leave you nor forsake you." Deuteronomy 31:6 (NIV)

Dear Lord, thank You for the promise of Your constant presence. When I feel alone, remind me that You are with me. Help me to rest in the truth that no matter what I face, I will never walk alone. Strengthen my faith when fear tries to creep in and help me to feel Your nearness in every moment. I trust You to guide, comfort, and protect me. In Jesus' name I pray.

Amen and To God Be The Glory!

JANUARY 19.- "LENDING TO THE LORD"

Kindness is not just an act; it's a reflection of God's heart. When we show compassion to those in need, we do more than offer help; we honor God Himself. Scripture tells us that our generosity toward the poor is seen and remembered by the Lord, as if we are giving directly to Him.

This verse is a powerful reminder that acts of kindness do not go unnoticed. Whether it's feeding the hungry, encouraging someone in need, or simply being present for the hurting, our love for others becomes an offering to God. He doesn't just see the action, He honors it. And He promises to repay what we give, not always in material ways, but with peace, joy, and His divine favor.

We don't give to get; we give because it's the heart of Christ. When we extend His love to others, we become His hands and feet in a broken world.

"Whoever is kind to the poor lends to the Lord, and He will reward them for what they have done." Proverbs 19:17 (NIV)

Heavenly Father, I thank You for the opportunity to serve others as an act of worship to You. Teach me to see the poor and the hurting through Your eyes, and that's with compassion, love, and dignity. Give me a generous heart, not looking for reward, but simply desiring to please You. Use me to be a vessel of Your kindness in the lives of those who need it most. In Jesus' name I pray.

Amen and To God Be The Glory!

JANUARY 20.- "CHOOSING PEACE OVER DISRESPECT"

There comes a time in life when we are faced with hard choices. Not out of bitterness or pride, but out of obedience to God and love for ourselves. God calls us to love others, but never at the cost of our peace, dignity, or spiritual well-being. Disrespect is not a fruit of the Spirit, and when someone consistently dishonors your God-given value, it's okay to step back.

Adjusting your life to someone's absence doesn't mean you hate them. It means you love yourself enough to honor your boundaries. Healthy boundaries are not walls of bitterness; they are gates of wisdom. God's Word reminds us that peace is a gift, and we are called to pursue it:

Notice the phrase "as far as it depends on you." God never asks us to tolerate emotional abuse or constant dishonor. When peace requires you to step away, you're not being cruel, you're being wise.

Sometimes, God removes people from your life not to punish them, but to protect you. Respect is a basic form of love. When it's not present, distance may be necessary. Not out of revenge, but out of reverence for the temple that you are.

"If it is possible, as far as it depends on you, live at peace with everyone." Romans 12:18 (NIV)

Heavenly Father, I thank You for the wisdom to recognize when someone's presence is no longer healthy for my life. Help me to value peace over chaos, and discernment over guilt. Strengthen me to set godly boundaries without shame and give me courage to walk away from disrespect without bitterness. Teach me to love others from a distance if needed, and to always guard my heart as Your Word instructs. May I honor You by honoring myself.

In Jesus' name, Amen and To God Be The Glory!

JANUARY 21. - "IT'S NOT PERSONAL, IT'S PURPOSEFUL"

There are times in life when the enemy's attacks seem relentless. When discouragement, betrayal, loss, or hardship feels almost targeted. You may wonder, "Why me?" But what if the answer is not about you, at least not in the way you think?

It's not personal. It's purposeful.

The enemy doesn't attack you because you're weak; he attacks you because of the purpose and power within you. Satan isn't threatened by who you were, he's threatened by who you're becoming. The calling on your life, the anointing God has placed in you, and the impact you're destined to make are what draw the enemy's attention. Just like Joseph, David, Job, and even Jesus, your trials often reveal the weight of your purpose.

Joseph's brothers didn't hate him, they hated the dream inside him. David wasn't pursued by Saul because he was a boy with a harp, but because he was a king in the making. The attacks are not proof that you're doing something wrong; they are often confirmation that you are walking in God's plan.

Don't take it personally—stand in your purpose.

"The thief comes only to steal and kill and destroy. I came that they may have life and have it abundantly." John 10:10 (ESV)

Heavenly Father, thank You for reminding me that the attacks I face are not a reflection of my worthlessness but of my worth to Your Kingdom. Help me not to grow bitter, but to stand boldly in the purpose You've placed within me. Strengthen me when I feel weary and remind me what the enemy means for evil, You will turn for good. I trust You with my pain, my path, and my purpose. In Jesus' name, amen. Amen and To God Be The Glory!

JANUARY 22. - "FIVE REASONS TO TRUST GOD"

Trusting God can be hard when life feels uncertain or overwhelming. But time and time again, the Bible reminds us that God is trustworthy. Not just in theory, but in practice. When doubts creep in, hold tight to these five reasons to trust Him fully:

1. God is Faithful Even when we fall short, God remains consistent. His promises never fail. "Know therefore that the Lord your God is God; he is the faithful God, keeping his covenant of love..." Deuteronomy 7:9 (NIV)

2. God is in Control Nothing surprises Him. Even the storms of life are under His authority. "The Lord has established his throne in the heavens, and his kingdom rules over all." Psalm 103:19 (NIV)

3. God Has a Plan Even when we can't see the full picture, God is working for our good." 'For I know the plans I have for you,' declares the Lord, 'plans to prosper you and not to harm you, plans to give you a future and a hope.'" Jeremiah 29:11 (NIV)

4. God Cares Deeply for You, You are not forgotten. God sees you and is concerned with every detail of your life. "Cast all your anxiety on him because he cares for you." 1 Peter 5:7 (NIV)

5. God Gave His Son The ultimate proof of His love and trustworthiness is Jesus. If He gave us His best, surely He will take care of everything else. "He who did not spare his own Son, but gave him up for us all—how will he not also... graciously give us all things?" Romans 8:32 (NIV)

"Trust in the Lord with all your heart and lean not on your own understanding; in all your ways submit to him, and he will make your paths straight." Proverbs 3:5–6 (NIV)

Heavenly Father, thank You for being the God I can trust. Even when life is hard and my heart is heavy, You remain faithful, loving, and in control. Help me to surrender my fears and lean not on my own understanding. Teach me to rest in Your promises and walk in the confidence of Your care. You have never failed me, and I believe You never will. In Jesus' name I pray.

Amen and To God Be The Glory!

JANUARY 23. - "CHOOSING LOVE OVER SEPARATION"

"The question is Not "Why would a loving God send anyone to hell ~ The question is Why would anyone choose hell over a loving God."

The love of God is immeasurable, unchanging, and freely offered to all. Yet, He has also given us the sacred gift of choice. God doesn't force His love upon us; He invites us into it. Hell is not a place God eagerly sends people to; it is the tragic result of a heart that continually rejects Him.

God desires that none should perish but that all should come to repentance (2 Peter 3:9). But love demands freedom, and that freedom means we can say no to Him. The real tragedy is not that God sends people away, but that some willingly choose to live without Him, now and for eternity.

Heaven is not a reward for the perfect. It's the home prepared for those who have said yes to the One who paid the ultimate price for their soul. Jesus did not come to condemn the world, but to save it (John 3:17). The doors to grace are open. The cross is proof. The question we must ask is not about God's love, but about our response to it.

"For God so loved the world that he gave his one and only Son, that whoever believes in him shall not perish but have eternal life." John 3:16 (NIV)

Heavenly Father, thank You for loving me so deeply that You gave Your Son to rescue my soul. Forgive me for the times I've doubted or rejected Your love. Help me to choose You daily. Not out of fear of separation, but out of gratitude for Your nearness. Soften my heart to Your truth and give me courage to lead others to Your grace. May my life reflect the joy of someone who has chosen eternal life with You. In Jesus' name I pray. Amen and To God Be The Glory!

JANUARY 24. - "PEOPLE WHO DON'T CLAP WHEN YOU WIN"

In life, not everyone who walks with you is for you. Some people smile in your presence but silently compete in your absence. It can be painful to discover that those closest to you are silent during your moments of success. But discernment is a gift from God. He gives wisdom to recognize those who truly celebrate your victories and those who only applaud when you fall.

Paying close attention to who rejoices when you win reveals the posture of their heart. God calls us to rejoice with those who rejoice (Romans 12:15), yet jealousy, insecurity, and hidden bitterness often block people from doing so. While we are not called to judge their hearts, we are called to guard ours. Recognizing silence in your winning season helps you make healthy decisions about your circle in your growing season.

Even Jesus experienced this. He was betrayed by someone in His inner circle. That's why spiritual maturity involves knowing when to love people from a distance and when to keep pressing forward without waiting for their applause. God's approval is worth far more than human recognition. Let the quiet from others push you closer to the One who always celebrates your growth.

"A friend loves at all times, and a brother is born for adversity." Proverbs 17:17 (NIV)

Father in Heaven, please give me the eyes to see clearly and the heart to discern wisely. Help me recognize the people You've placed in my life for purpose and give me the strength to let go of those who cannot celebrate the blessings You've given me. Teach me not to chase applause but to remain anchored in Your approval. Help me rejoice in others' victories and trust You with mine. In Jesus' name I pray. Amen and To God Be The Glory!

JANUARY 25. - "WHEN YOU GIVE UP ~ THE HOLY SPIRIT LIFTS YOU UP"

There are moments when the weight of life becomes too much. When weariness sets in, hope fades, and giving up seems like the only option. But it's in these moments that the Holy Spirit gently whispers strength to your soul. He reminds you that you are not alone and breathes fresh courage into your spirit. The Holy Spirit is our Helper, our Comforter, and our Strength when we have none left.

When your heart is overwhelmed, the Spirit steps in. Not always with loud thunder, but often with quiet reassurance. He lifts you when you can't lift yourself, speaks peace when your thoughts are chaotic, and intercedes for you when you don't know how to pray. You may feel like giving up, but the Spirit of God within you will not let you fall.

"Likewise, the Spirit also helps in our weaknesses. For we do not know what we should pray for as we ought, but the Spirit Himself makes intercession for us with groanings which cannot be uttered." Romans 8:26 (NKJV)

Dear God in Heaven, I thank you for the Holy Spirit. For being my strength when I am weak and my hope when I feel hopeless. When I want to give up, lift me with Your power. Speak to my heart and calm my anxious thoughts. Remind me that I'm never walking alone and that You are working, even when I can't see it. Fill me with Your presence and give me the courage to keep going. This I pray In Jesus' name. Amen and To God Be The Glory!

JANUARY 26. - "FROM MY LIPS TO GODS' EARS ~ THANK YOU PRAYER"

Life is a series of seasons. Some are marked by joy and victory, others by pain and uncertainty. But one truth remains constant: God never changes, and He never leaves. In our highest moments, He rejoices with us. In our lowest valleys, He holds us close.

We often acknowledge God when we are in trouble, crying out for help and comfort. But how often do we thank Him in good times? And more importantly, how often do we recognize that He was also the one sustaining us when things were falling apart?

David, in the Psalms, often reflected on God's presence in every season of life. He didn't just praise God when he won battles. He also worshipped in caves, in exile, and even after personal failure. Why? Because he knew God was there all along.

Gratitude isn't only for the mountaintop moments. It's also for the strength He gave when you thought you couldn't make it. It's for peace in the storm, the whisper in the silence, and the unseen hand that held you up.

No matter where you are today. Whether life is going well or everything feels like it's falling apart, know this: God is with you, and He always has been.

"The Lord himself goes before you and will be with you; he will never leave you nor forsake you. Do not be afraid; do not be discouraged." Deuteronomy 31:8 (NIV)

Father God, I thank You for being my constant in a world that changes so quickly. Thank You for walking with me through the highest moments of joy and the darkest valleys of pain. Forgive me for the times I failed to see Your hand when things were hard or forgot to thank You when life was good. I trust that no matter where I go, You will be with me. Help me live each day with gratitude for Your presence and faithfulness. In Jesus' name I pray. Amen and To God Be The Glory!

JANUARY 27. - "HERE BY THE GRACE OF GOD"

Life has a way of wearing us down with its trials, disappointments, and detours. The path isn't always straight, and it's rarely smooth. We've all faced battles that no one knew about. We've cried tears that never got noticed. We've carried weights that felt too heavy and yet, here we are.

Not because we were the strongest. Not because we always knew what to do. But because God's grace never let go of us.

Grace is not the absence of hardship; it's the presence of God in the middle of it. When the road was too rough, His grace sustained you. When your strength ran out, His power showed up. Every scar you carry is proof that the enemy tried but failed. Because God's grace covered what you couldn't control and healed what you couldn't fix.

You're not here by accident. You are living proof of what the grace of God can do.

"But he said to me, 'My grace is sufficient for you, for my power is made perfect in weakness.' Therefore I will boast all the more gladly about my weaknesses, so that Christ's power may rest on me." 2 Corinthians 12:9 (NIV)

Heavenly Father, I thank You for walking with me through every storm and valley. The road hasn't been easy, but Your grace has been more than enough. When I was weak, You were my strength. When I was lost, You were my guide. Help me never to forget that I am here because of You and not my own doing. Keep me humble, grateful, and aware that Your grace is still carrying me. I trust You with the road ahead just as I thank You for the road behind me. In Jesus' name I pray.

Amen and To God Be The Glory!

JANUARY 28. - "TEARS OF THE HEART -THANK YOU FATHER"

There are moments in life when pain goes deeper than words. When sorrow doesn't show up on your face but lives quietly in your soul. These are the tears that never fall from your eyes, yet they soak every part of your spirit. You smile on the outside, but inside, you're aching in places no one can see.

God sees those hidden tears. He understands the silent cries and the pain that you can't put into words. Scripture reminds us that God doesn't just notice our tears. He collects them. Every unspoken heartache, every silent disappointment, every quiet surrender has touched the heart of your Heavenly Father.

You are not alone in your pain. He is near to the brokenhearted and saves those who are crushed in spirit. He's not intimidated by your sorrow. He welcomes it, and He offers peace in exchange. Though others may not understand, God knows. And His comfort reaches into the deepest places where even your loudest pain has no voice.

"You keep track of all my sorrows. You have collected all my tears in your bottle. You have recorded each one in your book." Psalm 56:8 (NLT)

Heavenly Father, You see the pain I try to hide. You know the tears I cry in silence, the ones that never reach my eyes but flood my soul. Thank You for being a God who is near, who understands, who never turns away from my sorrow. Heal the places in me that feel too broken to speak of. Give me strength to keep going and peace that surpasses understanding. Let Your presence cover every wound and comfort every silent cry. In Jesus' name I pray.

Amen and To God Be The Glory!

JANUARY 29. - "HAVE YOU EVER AGREED WITH SOMEONE JUST SO THEY'D SHUT UP"

There are moments in life when, out of sheer exhaustion, frustration, or the desire to avoid conflict, we find ourselves nodding in agreement. Not because we believe what's being said, but simply because we want the conversation to end. It's not that we're dishonest, but sometimes, silence feels like the path of least resistance.

While it may bring momentary peace, this habit can slowly erode our integrity, peace of mind, and even relationships. The Bible encourages us not to simply seek peace through avoidance, but through wisdom and truth spoken in love.

Agreeing just to end a conversation may feel like a shortcut to peace, but real peace comes from maturity in Christ. Where truth is shared in love, not suppressed for comfort. Sometimes, silence is wise. Other times, silence can be a missed opportunity for growth, clarity, or needed correction. The Holy Spirit gives us discernment to know the difference.

When we lean on God, we don't have to trade authenticity for convenience. He equips us to speak up when it matters and to stay silent when it's wise. Peace that costs your voice may not be peace at all.

"Instead, speaking the truth in love, we will grow to become in every respect the mature body of him who is the head, that is, Christ." Ephesians 4:15 (NIV)

Heavenly Father, please give me the courage to speak truth in love and the wisdom to know when silence is strength. Help me not to trade honesty for temporary comfort. Teach me to honor You in my conversations, and to seek peace that is rooted in truth, not avoidance. Guard my heart from people-pleasing and help me walk in integrity. May my words reflect Your grace, and may my silence be Spirit-led. In Jesus' name I pray.

Amen and To God Be The Glory!

JANUARY 30. - "IT'S OK NOT TO BE OK ~ JUST CONTINUE TO BELIEVE IN GODS' WORDS"

Life brings seasons when we don't feel strong, hopeful, or even functional. In those moments, it's easy to feel like we're failing spiritually. But here's the truth: it's OK not to be OK. God never asked us to have it all together. He simply asks us to trust Him.

Even in our lowest moments, God remains steady. His love isn't based on our mood, performance, or strength. When you feel broken, anxious, or overwhelmed, God draws near. He welcomes our honesty, and He meets us right there in the middle of our mess.

Your brokenness is not a disqualification; it's an invitation to lean deeper into God's grace. Trusting Him doesn't always mean smiling through the pain. It means believing He's still working even when you can't see the way forward. Faith doesn't require perfection, only surrender.

"The Lord is close to the brokenhearted and saves those who are crushed in spirit." Psalm 34:18 (NIV)
Heavenly Father, I thank You for reminding me that it's OK not to be OK. When I'm overwhelmed, help me to trust that You are near. When I feel weak, remind me that Your strength is made perfect in my weakness. Even in the dark moments, I believe You are working for my good. Teach me to rest in Your promises and to surrender my fears into Your hands. In Jesus' name I pray.

Amen and To God Be The Glory!

JANUARY 31. - "WHEN YOU REALIZE YOU HAVE IT ALL IN JESUS ~YOU HAVE PEACE"

In a world that constantly pressures us to perform, compete, and prove our worth, true peace can feel out of reach. But the peace that comes from Jesus is different. It's not based on achievement, recognition, or validation from others. It's rooted in knowing that in Him, we are already enough.

You don't have to strive to earn God's love. You don't have to prove your value or qualify for His grace. When you rest in your identity as a child of God, you discover a peace that surpasses understanding. A peace that settles your soul and silences the noise of the world.

Jesus is the source of our peace. He is our provider, our identity, and our victory. When we realize that He is all we need, we stop striving and start resting. There's nothing more to prove, only love to receive.

"You will keep in perfect peace those whose minds are steadfast, because they trust in you." Isaiah 26:3 (NIV)

Lord Jesus, I thank You for being all I need. In a world full of pressure and expectations, help me to find peace in Your presence. Remind me that I don't have to prove my worth, because I am already loved, chosen, and accepted by You. Quiet my heart and keep my mind focused on You. Fill me with the peace that only You can give. In Your name.

Amen and To God Be The Glory!

FEBRUARY INTRODUCTION

As we enter the month of February, our hearts naturally turn toward the theme of love. The world celebrates love in many forms this month, but as believers, we know that true love, that unfailing, unconditional, and everlasting kind of love comes only from God. Yet love is not the only answer God provides in His Word. Throughout Scripture, we find guidance, strength, peace, and clarity for every pressing problem we face. Whether it's heartache, confusion, fear, or uncertainty, God's Word speaks directly to the deepest needs of our lives.

This month, as we journey through Biblical Answers to Life's Pressing Problems, let us be reminded that we are never left without direction. God's promises are not vague hopes but solid, unshakable truths we can cling to in every season. His Word answers the hard questions, quiets the anxious heart, and provides light in the darkest moments.

"Your word is a lamp to my feet and a light to my path." Psalm 119:105 (NKJV)

Heavenly Father, thank You for the gift of Your Word. In a world full of uncertainty and challenges, Your truth is our foundation and our guide. As we open our hearts to these devotionals this month, help us to find the answers we need, the peace we seek, and the love that only You can give. Strengthen our faith, quiet our fears, and remind us that no problem is greater than Your power. In Jesus' name, Amen and To God Be The Glory.

FEBRUARY 1. - "FROM THE HEAD TO THE HEART~ THE MIRACLE OF GODS WORDS"

There is something truly miraculous that happens when God's Word travels from our head to our heart. It's one thing to know about Scripture, but it's another thing to live it, to feel it, and to let it transform every corner of our lives. The mind can memorize, but the heart believes, surrenders, and obeys.

When God's Word moves beyond intellectual understanding into the core of who we are, it becomes alive and active. It shapes our desires, renews our thoughts, and gives us strength we didn't know we had. It comforts us in sorrow, convicts' us in sin, and ignites a deeper intimacy with our Savior.

This heart-deep connection with Scripture isn't automatic, it's the work of the Holy Spirit. As we read the Bible with humility and expectation, He opens our eyes and softens our hearts. It's in that sacred space that the miracle unfolds: we no longer just read the Word, we are changed by it.

"I have hidden your word in my heart that I might not sin against you." Psalm 119:11 (NIV)

Heavenly Father, thank You for the gift of Your living Word. I ask that You move it from my mind into my heart. Let it not just be something I study, but something that transforms me. Open my heart to truly believe, obey, and trust what You have spoken. Let Your Word shape my thoughts, my choices, and my walk with You. May it take root deep within and bear fruit in every area of my life, In Jesus' precious name.

Amen and To God Be The Glory!

FEBRUARY 2. - "THERE IS POWER IN SILENCE"

"Don't waste words on people who deserve your silence. Sometimes the most powerful thing you can say is nothing."

This phrase is not about pride or revenge, it's about wisdom, restraint, and guarding your peace. There are moments in life when words can do more harm than good. In emotionally charged situations, silence is not weakness; it is spiritual maturity.

Jesus Himself modeled this. When accused and insulted, He often chose silence over defense. Why? Because His identity and purpose were rooted in the Father, not in the opinions of people. There is strength in holding your tongue, especially when provoked.

Some people aren't ready to hear the truth, and others may twist your words. Instead of engaging in every conflict, ask yourself: Will this conversation bring peace, or just fuel division? When your silence is led by discernment and humility, it speaks louder than any argument.

"Even a fool is considered wise if he keeps silent and discerning when he holds his tongue." Proverbs 17:28 (BRB)

Dear Lord, give me the wisdom to know when to speak and when to stay silent. Help me not to waste my words on arguments that lead nowhere or on people who seek only to provoke. Teach me to trust You in those quiet moments, knowing that You are my defender. Let my silence be led by Your Spirit, full of grace, strength, and peace, In Jesus' name.

Amen and To God Be The Glory!

FEBRUARY 3. - "FROM MY LIPS TO GODS' EARS ~ MY PRAYER TO YOU"

There are seasons in life when our hearts are full of desires. Not for fame or riches alone, but for the kind of strength that sustains, the wisdom that guides, the courage to face the unknown, prosperity that brings peace, and blessings that overflow into others' lives. It is not wrong to ask God for these things. In fact, when our motives are aligned with His will, He delights in giving good gifts to His children.

In moments of weariness, we need His strength. In decisions, His wisdom. In uncertainty, His courage. In need, His provision. And in everything, His blessing. But all these flows not from our striving, but from our abiding.

Let your prayer rise in faith, knowing that God is not distant. He is close, able, and willing to meet every need. Seek Him first, and all these things will be added to you.

"If any of you lacks wisdom, let him ask of God, who gives to all liberally and without reproach, and it will be given to him." James 1:5 (NKJV)

Heavenly Father, I come to You with a heart that longs for more of You. I ask for strength to endure the battles I face, for wisdom to make decisions that honor You, for prosperity not just for myself but so I may be a blessing to others, for courage to stand firm in faith when the world pushes back, and for Your blessings to pour over every area of my life. Help me to walk in obedience and humility, always seeking Your face. Thank You for being a God who hears and provides, I pray In Jesus' name.

Amen and To God Be The Glory!

FEBRUARY 4. - "BLOCKD BY GODS' GRACE"

There are moments in life when it feels like everything is being thrown at us. Confusion, discouragement, temptation, betrayal, fear. These aren't just coincidences or bad days; they're spiritual attacks meant to break us down. But take heart: the enemy is throwing everything that he can at you, but God is blocking it.

The reason you're still standing, still believing, still holding on isn't because the attacks stopped. It's because God's hand has been shielding you from the full force of what the enemy planned. Many darts were aimed your way, but God didn't allow them to destroy you. Some of what you never saw could have taken you out, but divine protection stood in the gap.

You may feel tired, but you are still covered. You may feel shaken, but you are still secure. God isn't just watching your battle; He's fighting for you.

"No weapon formed against you shall prosper, and every tongue which rises against you in judgment You shall condemn. This is the heritage of the servants of the Lord, and their righteousness is from Me," says the Lord. Isaiah 54:17 (NKJV)

Heavenly Father, I thank You for being my protector and my shield. Thank You for blocking what the enemy sent to harm me, things I saw and things I didn't. When I am weary, remind me that I'm not fighting alone. Strengthen me in the moments of weakness and help me to walk confidently in the knowledge that Your covering surrounds me. No matter what the enemy sends, I trust that You are greater and that Your purpose for my life will prevail. In Jesus' name I pray.

Amen and To God Be The Glory!

FEBRUARY 5. - "I DECLARE ~ I AM A WARRIOR OF GOD"

I declare, I am a warrior of God. I don't fight with fists or fear. I fight with faith, with truth, with righteousness, and with the power of the Holy Spirit. I may face battles, but I do not back down, because the Lord goes before me. I am clothed in the armor of God, called for purpose, and covered by His grace.

Being a warrior of God doesn't mean we won't feel fear. It means we fight through it, knowing who goes with us. Every spiritual battle we face is not fought alone. God equips us with His armor: truth, righteousness, peace, faith, salvation, and the Word. Our strength isn't in our own power but in His. As warriors, we don't just survive, we overcome. We advance in faith, speak boldly in truth, and walk forward even when we feel weak. You were not made to shrink. You were made to stand.

"Finally, be strong in the Lord and in his mighty power. Put on the full armor of God, so that you can take your stand against the devil's schemes." Ephesians 6:10-11 (NIV)

Heavenly Father, I thank You for calling me to be more than a conqueror. Please, remind me daily that I am Your warrior, clothed in Your armor and strengthened by Your Spirit. When the enemy tries to shake me, help me to stand firm in faith. When I feel weak, fill me with courage. I declare that I will walk in Your authority, fight with Your truth, and rest in Your victory. In Jesus' mighty name.

Amen and To God Be The Glory!

FEBRUARY 6. - "NO LOYALTY FOUND ~ GUARDING YOUR HEART FROM THE NARCISSIST"

Narcissists often present themselves with charm, confidence, and even spiritual words. But beneath the surface lies a heart driven by self-interest, manipulation, and deceit. One of the most painful lessons we can learn is that narcissists have no true loyalty to anyone but themselves. Their words are empty when their actions serve only their own agenda.

The Bible warns us not to be blind to such behavior. We are called to love, yes, but also to discern. Scripture teaches that trust must be earned and not freely given to those who consistently show dishonesty, betrayal, and pride. Narcissists often use your compassion as a tool and your forgiveness as a loophole to keep manipulating you.

God calls us to guard our hearts (Proverbs 4:23) and to be wise as serpents and harmless as doves (Matthew 10:16). Loyalty is the fruit of love, not control. A narcissist's inability to remain loyal reflects a deeper spiritual brokenness they refuse to confront. It's not your job to fix them, it's your responsibility to protect your peace.

Let this be your encouragement: you are not being unloving by setting boundaries. You are being biblical. Seek relationships that reflect the heart of Christ truth, trust, and selfless love.

"People may cover their hatred with pleasant words, but they're deceiving you. They pretend to be kind, but don't believe them. Their hearts are full of many evils." Proverbs 26:24–25 (NLT)

Heavenly Father, give me discernment to recognize those who do not have my best interest at heart. Teach me to guard my spirit and to seek wisdom in every relationship. Help me release toxic connections and walk in truth and freedom. May I never confuse manipulation for love or loyalty. Strengthen my heart to trust You above all and lead me into relationships that honor You. In Jesus' name I pray.

Amen and To God Be The Glory!

FEBRUARY 7. - "GOD IS PREPARING YOU"

There are seasons in life when you may feel hidden, delayed, or even forgotten. But God is not overlooking you, He's preparing you. Just as a seed must be buried before it blooms, preparation often happens in private beneath the surface. What feels like waiting is actually working rebuilding you. God is building your character, strengthening your faith, and aligning the right people and opportunities.

God never wastes a moment. Even in the silence, He's shaping you for something greater than you can imagine. David was an anointed king long before he ever sat on the throne. Joseph endured the pit and the prison before the palace. Jesus spent thirty quiet years before His three-year ministry. Try to remember that preparation seasons are not punishment, they are proof of God's intentional plan.

So don't rush the process. Trust that the God who called you is equipping you. You're not stuck, you're being strengthened. You're not behind, you're being built. God is preparing you for what He's already prepared for you.

"And we know that in all things God works for the good of those who love him, who have been called according to his purpose." Romans 8:28 (NIV)

Heavenly Father, thank You for the season of preparation. Even when I don't understand it, help me to trust that You are working behind the scenes for my good. Strengthen my patience, deepen my faith, and align my steps with Your purpose. Let me not grow weary in the waiting but be expectant. Knowing You are faithful to complete what You started. In Jesus' name.

Amen and To God Be The Glory!

FEBRUARY 8. - "SOME PEOPLE ARE LIKE THERAPY ~ THEY ENLIGHTEN YOUR LIFE"

God often uses people as vessels of healing, comfort, and joy. There are individuals in our lives who feel like therapy. Not because they fix our problems, but because their presence brings peace, laughter, and light to our souls. They listen without judgment, speak with wisdom, and love with sincerity. These people are gifts from God.

In a world filled with stress, anxiety, and isolation, God reminds us that joy can be found in relationship. Sometimes, He doesn't change our circumstances, but He sends someone to help carry the weight. Their words are soothing, their encouragement is uplifting, and their presence is a reminder that we are not alone.

Treasure the people who bring joy into your life. And more importantly, strive to be that kind of person for others. A gentle spirit, a listening ear, a joyful heart. These are healing tools God uses through us. Never underestimate the power of simply showing up with kindness and love.

"A cheerful heart is good medicine, but a crushed spirit dries up the bones." Proverbs 17:22 (NIV)

Dear Lord, I thank You for the people You've placed in my life who bring joy and comfort to my heart. They are a reflection of Your love and goodness. Help me to appreciate them and to be that same light to others. Teach me to listen with compassion, speak with encouragement, and love with joy. May I be a source of healing, just as others have been for me. In Jesus' name.

Amen and To God Be The Glory!

FEBRUARY 9. - "THE DIFFERENCE BETWEEN JESUS AND RELIGIONS ~ HE WASHES DIRTY FEET"

Religion often builds walls where Jesus built bridges. Where religion shames, Jesus shows compassion. Where religion points fingers, Jesus stretches out His hands. Religion says, "You're too dirty to be near God." But Jesus kneels down and says, "Let me wash your feet."

In John 13, on the night He was betrayed, Jesus knelt before His disciples, including the one who would deny Him and the one who would betray Him. He removed His outer garments, wrapped a towel around His waist, poured water into a basin, and began to wash their feet.

Jesus didn't wait for them to clean themselves up. He met them in their dirt. Religion focuses on appearances, rules, and performance. Jesus focuses on the heart. He came not to condemn, but to save. He touched the untouchable, welcomed the rejected, and forgave the fallen.

If you feel too unworthy, too far gone, too dirty, just remember this: Jesus is not ashamed of your feet. He kneels, not in judgment, but in grace. He restores your dignity not by demanding your perfection, but by offering His own.

"After that, He poured water into a basin and began to wash His disciples' feet, drying them with the towel that was wrapped around Him." John 13:5 (NIV)

Lord Jesus, I thank You for being so different from what this world sometimes calls religion. When others reject or shame me for my flaws, You draw me closer. You see my dirt, my failures, my brokenness, and yet, You still kneel to wash my feet. Help me to receive Your grace fully and freely. And may I extend that same grace to others, not with condemnation, but with compassion. Thank You for loving me as I am, and for transforming me with Your love. In Jesus name I pray.

Amen and To God Be The Glory!

FEBRUARY 10. - "THANK YOU FATHER FOR ALL YOUR BLESSINGS"

There is a beautiful peace that comes when we pause and simply say, "Thank You, God." In the midst of busy days and uncertain moments, recognizing God's hand in our lives draws us closer to Him. When we take time to thank Him not just for what we have, but for how He's made our lives more meaningful, our perspective changes.

God doesn't just bless us with things, He blesses us with purpose, with love, with relationships, and with His constant presence. Our families, our health, our daily breath, even the trials that shape us. Are woven into the story of His faithfulness.

The blessings may not always be loud or dramatic. Sometimes there are quiet moments at the dinner table, laughter in the living room, strength during hardship, or peace in the storm. God is always working, always giving, always loving.

"The Lord bless you and keep you; the Lord make His face shine on you and be gracious to you; the Lord turn His face toward you and give you peace." Numbers 6:24–26 (NIV

Heavenly Father, I thank You for blessing me and my family in ways seen and unseen. Thank You for Your grace that covers us, Your love that sustains us, and Your presence that makes our lives more meaningful. Teach us to always be grateful, even in the small things. May our home be a place where You are honored and where love flows freely. We give You all the glory, for every good and perfect gift that comes from You. In Jesus' name, Amen and To God Be The Glory!

FEBRUARY 11. - "FATHER I'M TRULY GRATEFUL"

Sometimes we look around and see others with more. More space, more comfort, more abundance, and we forget to thank God for the basic blessings He so faithfully has provided to us. A roof over your head may seem ordinary, but it's a sign of God's love and provision. Shelter means protection from storms, a place to rest, and a quiet reminder that God sees and sustains you.

Even when life feels overwhelming or when complaints want to rise in our hearts, may we be humble enough to say, "God, forgive me. I didn't mean to overlook what You've already done."

Lord, forgive me if I've ever complained, compared, or acted ungrateful. Help me see Your hand in the little things and recognize that even the simplest blessings are miracles from You. Grow in me a heart of contentment and a spirit of gratitude.

"But godliness with contentment is great gain. For we brought nothing into the world, and we can take nothing out of it. But if we have food and clothing, we will be content with that." 1 Timothy 6:6–8 (NIV)

Dear God, Thank You for the roof over my head. It may not be a palace, but it is a place of peace, a place You've provided out of love and mercy. Thank You for sheltering me, for giving me somewhere to lay my head each night. I know there are many without this gift, so today I pause to say thank You. In Jesus' name, Amen and To God Be The Glory!

FEBRUARY 12. - "YOU CAN BELIEVE WHATEVER YOU PLEASE ~ GOD GAVE YOU FREEWILL"

In a world full of opinions, beliefs, and personal truths, many people choose to live how they want, ignoring the reality of eternity. But truth isn't based on what we feel, it's based on God's Word. Hell is real. It's not just a metaphor or a distant concept. It's eternal separation from God, filled with torment and regret. And while people may choose not to believe it, that doesn't make it any less true.

But here's the good news: Jesus saves. He came not to scare us with hell, but to rescue us from it. His love is so deep, so fierce, that He gave His life so we wouldn't have to face the fire of eternal death. We get to choose life or death, light or darkness, truth or denial. Just know that death is real. Hell is hot. Eternity is long. And Jesus still saves.

Jesus, thank You for the cross. Thank You for dying so I wouldn't have to be separated from You. Forgive me for the times I've taken that sacrifice for granted. Help me live with eternity in mind and share Your truth with love and urgency. You are the way, the truth, and the life, and Father, I choose You.

"For the wages of sin is death, but the gift of God is eternal life in Christ Jesus our Lord." Romans 6:23 (NIV)
Father God, I thank You for speaking the truth, even when it's hard to hear. I know this life is short, but eternity, is forever. I don't want to live in ignorance or pride. Please, open my heart to the full truth of Your Word. Remind me daily that hell is not just a warning, but a real place that You desperately want to save us from. In Your holy name, Amen and To God Be The Glory!

FEBRUARY 13. - "MIRACLES HAPPENS ~ DO YOU HAVE FAITH"

There is incredible power in faith. Faith is not about seeing first and then believing; it's about trusting God's power even when you can't yet see the outcome. Time and time again throughout the Bible, we see miracles unfold simply because someone dared to believe.

The blind received sight, the sick was healed, the dead were raised. Not because of human ability, but because of unwavering faith in a God who is still in the miracle-working business. Faith is the key that unlocks the impossible. It invites God into situations that look hopeless and allows His power to turn them around.

Whatever you're facing today, whether it's an illness, a broken relationship, financial hardship, or an overwhelming obstacle, please remember, miracles happen when you have faith. Even faith the size of a mustard seed can move mountains.

"Jesus said to him, 'If you can believe, all things are possible to him who believes.'" Mark 9:23 (NKJV)

Heavenly Father, I thank You for being the God of miracles. Even when my situation feels impossible, remind me that nothing is impossible with You. Strengthen my faith, Lord. Help me to trust You completely, even when I can't see the way forward. I believe that You can heal, restore, provide, and make a way where there seems to be no way. I stand on Your promises today, expecting miracles to unfold in my life. In Jesus' name I pray.

Amen and To God Be The Glory!

FEBRUARY 14. - "A PHYSICAL PRAYER ~ FROM HEAD TO FEET"

Prayer is not only spoken, but it can also be felt. Throughout Scripture, we are reminded that our bodies are temples of the Holy Spirit (1 Corinthians 6:19-20). What better way to align ourselves with God than to physically pray, inviting Him to touch every part of us from our thoughts to our steps.

As you pray, gently place your hand on each part of your body, surrendering it to God. This physical prayer is a reminder that every part of you belongs to Him, and you are inviting His divine guidance, protection, and purpose over your life.

*Touch your Head:

"Lord, I surrender my mind to You. Renew my thoughts. Let me think with clarity, wisdom, and humility. Remove every lie of the enemy and fill me with Your truth."

Scripture: "Do not conform to the pattern of this world, but be transformed by the renewing of your mind." Romans 12:2 (NIV)

*Touch your Eyes:

"God, anoint my eyes. Help me see the world and people the way You see them. Open my eyes to Your truth and keep me from deception."

*Touch your Ears:

"Lord, help me to hear Your voice above all others. Silence every voice that speaks fear, doubt, and confusion."

*Touch your Mouth:

"Father, use my words for Your glory. Let me speak life, encouragement, and truth. Guard my tongue from gossip, anger, and negativity."

*Touch your Heart:

"Lord, purify my heart. Fill it with love, compassion, and courage. Heal any wounds and remove bitterness or unforgiveness."

Scripture: "Create in me a pure heart, O God, and renew a steadfast spirit within me." Psalm 51:10 (NIV)

*Touch your Hands:

"God, bless the work of my hands. Let them serve others, build Your kingdom, and reflect Your kindness and strength."

*Touch your Feet:

"Lord, order my steps. Lead me away from temptation and guide me along the path of righteousness. Help me walk in obedience and purpose."

Scripture: "The steps of a good man are ordered by the Lord, and He delights in his way." Psalm 37:23 (NKJV)

Take a few moments to breathe, reflect, and walk forward with the confidence that God has touched every part of your life.

Heavenly Father, I thank You for this body, fearfully and wonderfully made by Your hands. I surrender every part of me to You today. My mind, my eyes, my ears, my mouth, my heart, my hands, and my feet. Shape me, lead me, and use me for Your glory. Order my steps and let me walk in alignment with Your will. Wherever I go, let Your presence go before me.

In Jesus' mighty name, I pray.

Amen and To God Be The Glory!

FEBRUARY 15. - "GODS CONTINUOUS PROTECTION"

Life is filled with uncertainty. The world may seem chaotic, unpredictable, and even dangerous at times. But as believers, we stand on the unshakable truth that God's protection is not temporary or situational, it is continuous. His watchful eyes never turn away. His hand never weakens. His presence never leaves us vulnerable.

The enemy may plot, people may fail us, and storms may rise, but the covering of God surrounds His children day and night. He protects us from dangers seen and unseen. Sometimes we're aware of His intervention, and other times we walk through life completely unaware of the traps and harm He's already blocked on our behalf.

This doesn't mean life will be free from hardship, but it does mean that even in trials, we are sheltered. His protection is not just physical, it is emotional, spiritual, and mental. God guards our hearts, shields our minds, and preserves our souls.

Let this truth sink deep into your spirit: God's protection is now and forevermore. He doesn't take breaks. He doesn't sleep. He doesn't grow weary. You are always covered under His care.

"The Lord will keep you from all harm, He will watch over your life; the Lord will watch over your coming and going both now and forevermore." Psalm 121:7-8 (NIV)

Heavenly Father, I thank You for being my constant protector. Even when I am unaware, You are shielding me, guiding me, and covering me from harm. I rest in the truth that You never sleep, and Your watchful eye is always upon me. Guard my heart, my mind, and my life. Surround me with Your angels, block the schemes of the enemy, and let me walk in peace knowing I am safe under Your mighty hand. Strengthen my faith to trust in Your continuous protection, today and every day. In Jesus' name I pray.

Amen and To God Be The Glory!

FEBRUARY 16. - "DO NOT BE ANXIOUS ABOUT ANYTHING"

Worry has a way of creeping into our hearts, robbing us of joy and peace. The cares of life, whether it's finances, health, relationships, or uncertainty about the future. It can easily overwhelm us if we aren't careful. But God's Word reminds us that we don't have to carry these burdens alone.

Paul's words to the Philippians are both a command and a promise. He tells us to be careful about nothing; meaning don't allow anxiety to rule over your heart. Instead, take your concerns to God through prayer and supplication, and with thanksgiving. Notice the emphasis on gratitude, even as we bring our requests. Thanksgiving shifts our focus from fear to faith.

And here's the beautiful promise: when we lay our concerns at God's feet, His peace, a peace that passes all understanding will guard our hearts and minds. It's not the kind of peace that the world can offer. It's not dependent on changing circumstances. It's a divine, unexplainable calm that only our Christ can provide.

Today, let go of the weight you've been carrying. Speak to your Heavenly Father. Be honest about your fears, your needs, your doubts, and thank Him for all He's already done. As you do, allow His peace to flood over your heart and mind.

REMEMBER:

"Be careful for nothing; but in everything by prayer and supplication with thanksgiving let your requests be made known unto God. And the peace of God, which passeth all understanding, shall keep your hearts and minds through Christ Jesus." Philippians 4:6-7 (KJV)

Heavenly Father, Thank You for the precious promise of Your peace. I confess that too often, I allow worry to control my thoughts. Today, I lay every burden, every fear, and every anxious thought at Your feet. I ask that You replace my worry with faith, my fear with peace, and my doubt with trust. Thank You for hearing my prayers and for the peace that surpasses all understanding. Guard my heart and my mind through Christ Jesus. In His holy name, I pray. Amen and To God Be The Glory!

FEBRUARY 17. - "ENJOY THE LITTLE THINGS IN LIFE"

In the busyness of life, it's easy to overlook the small ordinary moments. The laughter shared at the dinner table, the quiet cup of coffee in the morning, the simple text from a friend saying they care. But one day, we will look back and realize those "little things" were actually the big things. They were the moments that shaped us, comforted us, and reminded us of God's goodness.

God is often found in the quiet, simple places. He doesn't always show up with lightning and thunder. Sometimes, He whispers through a cool breeze or smiles through the face of a loved one. If we rush through life always waiting for the next big achievement, we might miss the daily blessings that are building a beautiful life.

Each day is a gift. Every small moment, every quiet blessing is part of God's perfect design for our lives. So slow down, breathe, and enjoy the little things for they are far greater than they seem.

"This is the day which the Lord hath made; we will rejoice and be glad in it." Psalm 118:24 (KJV)
Heavenly Father, thank You for the simple, quiet blessings You pour into my life every day. Help me not to rush past them or take them for granted. Teach me to pause, to rejoice in the little things, and to recognize Your hand in them all. One day, when I look back, I want to remember a life full of love, laughter, and gratitude for even the smallest gifts. Open my eyes and heart to enjoy today. In Jesus' name I pray.

Amen and To God Be The Glory!

FEBRUARY 18. - "NOT EVERY RESPONSE NEEDS A REACTION"

In a world that constantly demands our attention and opinions, it's easy to believe we must react to everything. To every word spoken, every situation that arises, every offense that comes our way. But wisdom teaches us otherwise. There is power in restraint, peace in silence, and clarity in observation.

Sometimes, the greatest strength is not in what we say but in what we choose not to say. It's in the pause, that sacred moment where we allow God to guide our thoughts instead of reacting in emotion. When we sit back and observe, we often see the bigger picture. We notice the motives, the distractions, and the traps the enemy sets to steal our peace.

The Bible reminds us of the value of self-control and the wisdom of silence:

"He that is slow to wrath is of great understanding: but he that is hasty of spirit exalteth folly." Proverbs 14:29 (KJV)

Quick reactions often come from pride or insecurity, but patience and observation come from a heart that trusts God. You don't have to respond to every insult, defend yourself in every situation, or correct every misunderstanding. Sometimes, it's better to be quiet, watch, and let God work on your behalf.

Today, ask God to help you resist the urge to react and instead respond with wisdom, or not respond at all. The battle is often won, not in loud reactions, but in quiet confidence.

Father, teach me to be still in moments where my emotions want to take over. Help me to sit back and observe with the eyes of wisdom, rather than react out of frustration or pride. Remind me that You are in control and that I don't have to respond to every situation. Give me peace in the pause and clarity in the silence. In Jesus' name I pray.

Amen and To God Be The Glory!

FEBRUARY 19. - "WARRIORS IN FAITH"

Walking with Christ is not for the faint of heart. The Bible never promises a life free from struggle, but it does promise that we have everything we need to stand strong. As believers, we are called to be warriors in faith, not spectators. We may not fight with swords or shields, but our battles are real. We fight battles against doubt, fear, temptation, and the schemes of the enemy.

A warrior in faith doesn't shrink back when life gets hard. They press forward, even when they feel weak, because they know their strength comes from the Lord. They stand on God's promises, pray with boldness, and trust that victory belongs to Him.

Being a warrior in faith means believing God's Word even when circumstances seem impossible. It means standing when others fall, hoping when others doubt, and fighting in prayer when giving up feels easier. Your armor is the Word of God. Your weapon is prayer. Your victory is secured through Christ.

Remember, you are not fighting alone. God goes before you. He surrounds you. And He equips you with everything you need to overcome. Even with your Partner, so choose wisely.

"For we walk by faith, not by sight." 2 Corinthians 5:7 (KJV)

Father, we thank You for calling us to be a warrior in faith. Even when we feel weak, remind us that Your strength is made perfect in our weakness. Teach us to stand with our chosen Partner on Your promises, to walk by faith, and to fight the battles of life with courage and trust in You. We declare that we are more than a conqueror through Christ Jesus. Strengthen our hearts and help us to be bold in our faith. In Jesus' name we pray.

Amen and To God Be The Glory!

FEBRUARY 20. - "WAIT ON THE LORD"

Waiting on the Lord is one of the greatest acts of faith a believer can display. It is not a passive or idle wait, but a posture of trust, surrender, and expectation. While the world rushes and worries, God's people are called to rest in His perfect timing.

Waiting often feels uncomfortable. It tests our patience, our understanding, and our will. We may wonder, "Has God forgotten me?" or "Why is this taking so long?" But God's delays are not His denials. His timing is not only perfect, but also protective. Sometimes, He makes us wait because He is preparing the blessing for us. Other times, He makes us wait because He is preparing us for the blessing.

Like the eagle that soars high above the storm, those who wait on the Lord find renewed strength. They rise above anxiety, doubt, and fear. Their spiritual endurance grows, and their faith deepens.

If you are in a season of waiting today, take heart. God sees you. He has not forgotten your prayers. Trust His timing, lean into His promises, and allow Him to strengthen you in the process.

"But they that wait upon the Lord shall renew their strength; they shall mount up with wings as eagles; they shall run, and not be weary; and they shall walk, and not faint." Isaiah 40:31 (KJV)

Heavenly Father, I thank You for being a God who never leaves me nor forsakes me. Teach me to wait on You with a heart full of faith, not frustration. Strengthen me in my weakness and renew my spirit as I trust in Your perfect timing. Help me to soar above doubt and discouragement like the eagle. I believe that what You have for me is worth the wait. In Jesus' name I pray.

Amen and To God Be The Glory!

FEBRUARY 21. - "TIME, YOUR HEART, AND YOUR BEHAVIOR DECIDES YOUR DESTINY"

Every day we make decisions. Some small, some life-changing, but all of them shape the direction of our lives. Your destiny isn't determined by luck or chance; it's shaped by how you manage your time, the posture of your heart, and the choices seen through your behavior.

Time is one of the most precious gifts God has given us. How we spend it reflects what we value. Are we wasting hours on things that don't matter, or investing in what builds our faith and character?

Your heart is the wellspring of your life. Proverbs 4:23 (NIV) reminds us, "Above all else, guard your heart, for everything you do flows from it." If your heart is filled with bitterness, fear, or pride, your destiny will reflect that. But if it's filled with love, humility, and trust in God, your destiny will align with His promises.

Behavior is the outward evidence of what's happening inside you. Our actions, words, and choices paint the picture of who we truly are. You cannot walk into a blessed destiny while practicing disobedience, pride, or carelessness. But when your behavior reflects faith, obedience, and integrity, you are sowing seeds that will reap a harvest of God's best.

Together, your time, your heart, and your behavior form a pathway to your destiny. Choose wisely and allow God to lead each step. For he that soweth to his flesh shall of the flesh reap corruption; but he that soweth to the Spirit shall of the Spirit reap life everlasting. And let us not be weary in well doing: for in due season we shall reap, if we faint not." Galatians 6:8-9 KJV

"Be not deceived; God is not mocked: for whatsoever a man soweth, that shall he also reap. Galatians 6:7 (KJV)

Heavenly Father, thank You for the gift of time, for the ability to examine my heart, and for the strength to walk in Your ways. Help me to be mindful of how I spend my days. Search my heart, Lord, and cleanse it of anything that does not honor You. Let my behavior reflect Your love, grace, and truth. I know that my destiny is not an accident but the fruit of my daily choices. Guide me, Lord, so that my time, my heart, and my actions align with Your will. In Jesus' name, I pray.

Amen and To God Be The Glory!

FEBRUARY 22. - "THERE'S MORE TO LIFE ~ THERE IS PURPOSE AND THERE IS A CALLING"

Life can often feel like a cycle of routines, responsibilities, and at times, unanswered questions. But the truth is, there's more to life than simply existing. You were created with divine intention. There is a purpose written over your life, and there is a calling uniquely designed for you. You were not created to simply exist. God designed you with purpose and placed a calling on your life. Even when life feels ordinary or uncertain, just know that there is more, a lot more to discover, more to become, and more to do for His glory.

God never makes mistakes. Long before you took your first breath, He had a plan for you. A plan not just for survival, but for impact. You are not here by accident. You are part of His grand design, equipped with gifts, experiences, and a future that holds meaning beyond what you may see right now. You carry purpose because the Creator Himself shaped you with intention. Your gifts, your story, even your struggles. All of it can be used for His plan. Trust that your life holds meaning, and your calling will unfold as you walk in obedience, one faithful step at a time.

When life feels mundane or discouraging, remember you carry purpose. You are called to love, to serve, to grow, and to reflect God's light in a dark world. Don't let fear, failure, or distractions convince you otherwise. Your calling isn't always loud or obvious. Sometimes, it unfolds in quiet faithfulness, in small acts of obedience, and in moments when you choose to believe God has more in store.

"For we are God's handiwork, created in Christ Jesus to do good works, which God prepared in advance for us to do." Ephesians 2:10 (NIV)

Father, I thank You for reminding me that there's more to life than what I see. You have called me, You have equipped me, and You have given my life purpose. Even when I feel lost or uncertain, help me to trust that You are guiding my steps. Reveal the purpose You've placed within me and give me the courage to walk in my calling. I believe there is more, and I surrender my life to Your perfect plan. You have called me, You have a purpose for me, and You are working in me. Help me to walk in that purpose daily and trust Your plan for my life. In Jesus name I pray.

Amen and To God Be The Glory!

FEBRUARY 23. - "THE LORD EQUIPS"

There is great comfort in knowing that when God calls us to walk with Him, He doesn't leave us unprepared or unequipped. He supplies everything we need. Strength for the journey, wisdom for the decisions, peace for the storms, and grace for the failures. You were never expected to do life alone or in your own strength.

Sometimes we look at what's ahead and feel inadequate. We question if we have what it takes. The truth is, we don't, not in ourselves. But the beauty of walking with the Lord is that He doesn't ask us to rely on ourselves. He equips us. He fills in our weaknesses. He provides. He sustains.

Notice the promise: God Himself works in you, making you complete for every good work. You don't have to strive to be "enough", He is enough. You don't have to fear being unprepared, He equips. He gives you the tools, the strength, and the courage to follow Him faithfully.

"Now may the God of peace make you complete in every good work to do His will, working in you what is well pleasing in His sight, through Jesus Christ." Hebrews 13:20-21 (NKJV)

Heavenly Father, thank You that You never call me to walk this life alone or in my own strength. You are my source, my provider, and the One who equips me for every step. When I feel weak or unprepared, remind me that You are working within me, making me complete for Your purpose. Help me trust that You have already given me everything I need to walk with You. Strengthen my faith, Lord, and lead me each day in Your will. In Jesus' name, I pray.

Amen and To God Be The Glory!

FEBRUARY 24. - "WATCH AND LEARN"

Life has a way of teaching us valuable lessons, If we are willing to slow down, observe, and learn. So often, we rush into situations with assumptions or pride, missing the wisdom that comes simply by watching. God, in His grace, calls us not only to act but to observe. To watch how He moves, how others live, and how His Word unfolds in real life.

Jesus Himself told His disciples to watch and learn. He didn't just lecture them with words; He demonstrated love, humility, patience, and power. He showed them how to pray, how to serve, and how to trust God even in trials. If we desire wisdom, sometimes the greatest thing we can do is quiet our mouths, open our eyes, and watch.

A wise heart is teachable. It listens. It watches. It learns. But the fool talks over wisdom and stumbles. Today, let's choose the posture of humility. To be watchful students in God's classroom of life.

"The wise in heart will receive commandments: but a prating fool shall fall." Proverbs 10:8 (KJV)

Heavenly Father, please help me to slow down and open my eyes. Help me to watch and learn. To observe Your hand at work, to notice the lessons You are teaching through life's moments, and to humbly receive wisdom. Guard me from pride and haste. Give me a heart that listens and eyes that see. Thank You for being patient with me as I grow. In Jesus' name, Amen and To God Be The Glory!

FEBRUARY 25. - "THE SIMPLE FACT THAT YOU CARE ~ MAKES YOU MORE THAN ENOUGH"

In a world that measures worth by achievements, possessions, or popularity, it's easy to feel like we're not enough. But God reminds us that our value isn't tied to performance, it's rooted in love. To simply care, to show kindness, compassion, and a willing heart makes you more than enough in the eyes of God.

Caring reflects the heart of Jesus. He didn't seek fame or applause; He cared for the broken, the forgotten, and the lost. His love was simple, pure, and powerful. When you care, when you love without expecting anything in return, you are walking in His footsteps and that makes you more than enough.

You don't have to be perfect. You don't have to have all the answers. Your simple acts of care carry eternal value. Love, expressed through simple care, is what holds everything together. It completes us in ways the world never could.

"And above all these things put on charity, which is the bond of perfectness." Colossians 3:14 (KJV)

Father, I give thanks to you for reminding me that I don't have to strive to be enough. Help me to simply care and to love others as You love me. Let my compassion reflect Your heart and let my simple acts of kindness bring You glory. When I feel inadequate, I remind myself that love is what truly matters. With You, I am more than enough. In Jesus' name I pray.

Amen and To God Be The Glory!

FEBRUARY 26. - "THIS MOMENT RIGHT NOW IS WHAT'S MOST IMPORTANT"

Life has a way of pulling our attention in every direction. From regrets from the past, worries about the future, endless to-do lists. But in the midst of it all, God gently reminds us that this moment, right now, is what matters most. This is the only time we are guaranteed. This moment is where God meets us, speaks to us, and works within us.

It's easy to get stuck replaying yesterday's failures or anxiously trying to control tomorrow. But Scripture encourages us to focus on today, on the present moment where God's grace is available and His presence is near.

God made this day, this hour, this very moment. It's not by accident that you're here, reading these words, breathing this breath. Whatever happened yesterday is behind you, and tomorrow is in God's hands. But right now, you have the opportunity to praise Him, to trust Him, to love others, and to choose faith over fear.

So, take a deep breath. Let go of the past. Stop worrying about what's ahead. Fix your eyes on Jesus and embrace the gift of this moment. That's where His power, His peace, and His purpose for you are found.

"This is the day which the Lord hath made; we will rejoice and be glad in it." Psalm 118:24 (KJV)

Heavenly Father, thank You for the gift of this moment. Help me not to waste it by living in the past or fearing the future. Teach me to be present, to see Your hand at work in my life right now. Give me peace that surpasses all understanding and help me to rejoice in today, knowing that You are with me. I choose to trust You in this moment and every moment to come. In Jesus' name I pray.

Amen and To God Be The Glory!

FEBRUARY 27. - "LAUGH, LOVE, LIVE"

God never intended for life to be lived in constant stress, fear, or sorrow. Yes, there will be trials, but He also gives us the gift of joy, love, and abundant life. We are called to laugh. To find joy even in simple moments. We are called to love. To reflect His heart to those around us. And we are called to truly live. Not just survive but embrace life with hope and purpose.

Too often, we get so caught up in our responsibilities, worries, or regrets that we forget to simply enjoy life as God intended. But the truth is, laughter is healing, love is powerful, and life is precious.

Jesus came so we could live. Not weighed down by the world, but free, full of joy, love, and purpose. So, laugh freely, love deeply, and live fully, knowing each day is a blessing from God.

"I am come that they might have life, and that they might have it more abundantly." John 10:10 (KJV)

Father in Heaven, I truly thank You for the gift of life. Teach me to laugh even when days are hard, to love without hesitation, and to truly live the life You've given me. Remind me that joy is a gift from You and love is the greatest command. Help me not just to exist, but to live abundantly in Your grace. In Jesus' name I pray.

Amen and To God Be The Glory!

FEBRUARY 28. - "IT'S OK TO BELIEVE"

In a world filled with doubt, fear, and disappointment, believing can feel risky. Many of us have been let down by people, by circumstances, or by life itself. But God invites us to set aside fear and disappointment and believe again. Believe in His promises, believe in His love, believe in His power to work in our lives.

It's OK to believe even when the world calls it foolish. It's OK to believe even when you've been hurt. Belief isn't about ignoring reality; it's about trusting that God is greater than the obstacles, stronger than the storm, and faithful to His Word.

Belief is the doorway to miracles, hope, and peace. It's OK to believe not in your own strength, but in the One who holds your life in His hands. Today, let go of fear, lift your eyes to heaven, and simply believe.

"Jesus said unto him, If thou canst believe, all things are possible to him that believeth." Mark 9:23 (KJV)

Father God, thank You for reminding me that it's OK to believe. I confess that fear and disappointment have sometimes held me back. But today, I choose to believe in You, in Your promises, in Your goodness, and in Your faithfulness. Strengthen my faith, Lord, and help me to trust You more every day. In Jesus' name.

Amen and To God Be The Glory!

FEBRUARY 29. (LEAP YEAR) - "THEIR ACTION REFLECT HUMANITY ~ NOT YOURS"

There are moments in life when people will hurt us. Not always with evil intentions, but sometimes because of their own brokenness, pain, confusion, or spiritual immaturity. Whether it's betrayal, neglect, misunderstanding, or mistreatment, we often internalize the pain and begin to believe that the actions of others are a reflection of our worth. But the truth is this: what they believe, what they do, and what they caused you to endure does not testify to your priority testifies to their humanity.

It's human nature to seek affirmation, to want to be seen, valued, and prioritized. So, when others fail to treat us in a way that honors our value, it can leave deep emotional wounds. But here is the freeing truth, your value was never tied to their behavior. Their failure to love you well, to recognize your worth, or to treat you justly, says more about the state of their soul than it ever says about yours.

Jesus understood this more than anyone. He was despised, rejected, betrayed by His own disciples, and crucified by the very ones He came to save. Yet He never lost sight of His identity. He didn't allow their actions to redefine His purpose or worth. Instead, He saw them through the lens of compassion and mercy: "Father, forgive them; for they know not what they do…" (Luke 23:34, KJV).

This is not a call to tolerate abuse or to excuse wrongdoing, but rather to release yourself from the burden of thinking it was your fault. It's an invitation to rise above resentment by understanding that people often act from a place of brokenness, not always malice. Recognizing their humanity allows you to walk in freedom, not bitterness.

God has not forgotten you. He knows your name. He sees your wounds. And He will deal justly with all things in His time. Your identity is rooted in who He says you are, not in how others have treated you.

"For the Lord seeth not as man seeth; for man looketh on the outward appearance, but the Lord looketh on the heart." 1 Samuel 16:7 (KJV)

Heavenly Father, thank You for reminding me that my worth is not determined by how others treat me, but by the truth of who I am in You. Help me to release the pain caused by others and not internalize their actions as a reflection of my value. Give me discernment to recognize the brokenness in others without carrying the burden of their behavior on my shoulders. Teach me to walk in grace, rooted in Your love, and to extend the same mercy You've shown me. May I never lose sight of my identity as Your beloved child. In Jesus' name, I pray.

Amen and To God Be The Glory!

MARCH INTRODUCTION

As we step into the month of March, we are reminded that life often presents us with challenges that seem overwhelming. Questions fill our minds about our future, our purpose, our relationships, and even our faith. But God, in His wisdom and love, has not left us without answers. His Word remains our steady guide, offering direction, comfort, and hope for every situation we face.

March is often seen as a transitional month, where winter begins to fade, and signs of new life start to bloom. In the same way, God can bring new beginnings in the middle of our struggles. Whatever pressing problem you are carrying today, be it worry, fear, doubt, grief, or uncertainty. Let this month be a reminder that God is already working behind the scenes, providing answers and solutions through His living Word.

Let us draw nearer to Him daily through these devotionals. His promises are unchanging, His guidance is sure, and His love is constant.

"Call unto me, and I will answer thee, and shew thee great and mighty things, which thou knowest not." Jeremiah 33:3 (KJV)

Heavenly Father, as we enter the month of March, we bring our hearts, questions, and burdens before You. Thank You for being a God who hears us and provides answers in our time of need. Open our eyes to see Your truth, open our hearts to receive Your peace, and guide our steps according to Your Word. May these devotionals remind us daily that You are our source of hope and clarity. In Jesus' name we pray.

Amen and To God Be The Glory!

MARCH 1. - "SOME PEOPLE WILL TEACH YOU HOW NOT TO BE"

In life, not every lesson comes wrapped in kindness or good intentions. Sometimes, the most valuable lessons come from observing what not to do. The bitterness of betrayal, the sting of harsh words, the disappointment of broken promises. These experiences shape us, not by example, but by contrast. They teach us how not to treat others. They show us how not to carry ourselves.

God uses every person and every moment for our growth, even the difficult ones. Instead of becoming bitter or resentful, we can choose to let those moments refine us. We can say, "Because I know how that made me feel, I will never do that to someone else." The negative behavior of others becomes the boundary lines for the person God is molding us to be.

Jesus Himself warned us to be discerning, to observe, and to learn, even from the darkness of this world.

Let the actions of others, both good and bad, sharpen your character. When someone shows you selfishness, choose generosity. When they show cruelty, choose compassion. When they show pride, choose humility.

"Do not be overcome by evil but overcome evil with good." Romans 12:21 (NIV)

Heavenly Father, I thank You for using every experience, even the painful ones to teach me. Help me to learn not only from the good examples but also from the bad. When I see pride, teach me humility. When I see bitterness, teach me grace. When I see cruelty, teach me kindness. I choose to overcome evil with good. Mold me into the person You desire me to be, even through the difficult lessons. In Jesus' name I pray.

Amen and To God Be The Glory!

MARCH 2. - "SHOW RESPECT WHEN I'M NOT AROUND

True character isn't revealed by how we act when someone is watching, but by how we speak and behave when they're not present. To show respect when someone isn't around reflects integrity, honor, and love. It means we don't engage in gossip, slander, or disrespectful talk behind closed doors. Instead, we build others up even in their absence.

God calls us to live with consistency and sincerity. Showing respect behind someone's back, is as important as showing it to their face. It builds trust, reflects Christ, and guards our own hearts from bitterness and deceit. Our words have the power to tear down or to honor, even when no one else hears them but God.

The Bible reminds us of the power of our words and actions, especially when no one else is holding us accountable but God.

"Do not speak evil against one another, brothers. The one who speaks against a brother or judges his brother, speaks evil against the law and judges the law." James 4:11 (ESV)

Heavenly Father, please help me to be a person of integrity. Someone who speaks with love, kindness, and respect, whether others are present or not. Guard my heart from gossip and negativity. Teach me to honor others in their absence, to lift them up, and to reflect Your character through my words and actions. Let my life be consistent publicly and privately. And may everything I do bring glory to You. In Jesus' name, Amen and To God Be The Glory!

MARCH 3. - "FROM MY LIPS TO GODS' EARS ~ FOR BY YOU AND THROUGH YOUR GRACE, I THANK YOU FATHER"

When we pause to reflect on the goodness of God, it becomes clear that everything we have, everything we've overcome, and everything we hope for is by Him and through Him. It is not by our strength, but by His grace. It is not by our wisdom, but by His guidance. Every open door, every blessing, every moment of peace is because of His loving hand at work in our lives.

When we truly recognize that everything we have is by Him and through Him, gratitude naturally flows from our hearts. Even in the hard seasons, we can give thanks, knowing God is still working, still providing, still loving us beyond measure.

The Apostle Paul reminds us that all things exist by God, through God, and for God. Our lives are a living testimony of His goodness.

"For from him and through him and for him are all things. To him be the glory forever! Amen." Romans 11:36 (NIV)

Heavenly Father, by You and through You, I stand today. I thank You for Your grace, Your mercy, and all You've done for me. Every blessing I've received, every trial You've carried me through, and every moment of peace has come from Your hand. Help me to never take Your goodness for granted. I surrender my life to You, for all things are by You, through You, and for You. In Jesus' name I pray.

Amen and To God Be The Glory!

MARCH 4. - "FOUR REASONS YOU CAN SMILE TODAY AND EVERYDAY"

No matter how heavy life feels or how many burdens weigh on your heart, today, right now you have a reason to smile. His name is Jesus.

You can smile because Jesus died, not just a tragic death, but a victorious one because He rose arose from the dead and broke the chains of sin and death forever.

You can smile because He forgives every mistake, every failure, every shortcoming is covered by His grace.

You can smile because He heals your heart, your body, your mind, and your past.

And you can smile because He loves perfectly, unconditionally, and eternally.

The world may offer temporary reasons for happiness, but Jesus gives us eternal reasons for joy. His love is constant, His forgiveness is complete, His healing is available, and His sacrifice secured our salvation.

So even when circumstances try to rob your joy, remember this truth: You have a reason to smile today, and His name is Jesus!

"The Lord has done great things for us, and we are filled with joy." Psalm 126:3 (NIV)

Heavenly Father, I thank You for giving me a reason to smile today. Thank You for sending Jesus, who died for me, forgives me, heals me, and loves me beyond measure. Help me to hold on to that truth when life feels heavy. Let joy rise up in my heart, not because of circumstances, but because of who You are. In Jesus' name I pray.

Amen and To God Be The Glory!

MARCH 5. - "THE HAPPIEST PEOPLE IN LIFE ARE GIVERS NOT TAKERS"

There's a quiet joy that comes from living life with open hands and an open heart. The world often tells us that happiness is found in getting more. More success, more money, and more recognition. But God's Word reminds us that true happiness comes from giving. Giving our time, our love, our resources, and our encouragement.

When we live to give, we reflect the very nature of God Himself. He is the ultimate Giver of life, love, grace, and salvation. And when we follow His example, we experience a joy that material things can never provide. Givers walk through life with peace, fulfillment, and a sense of purpose. Takers may gain temporarily, but they often find themselves empty in the end.

The happiest people in life understand that giving isn't just about material things. It's about kindness, compassion, and lending a helping hand when someone needs it. It's about speaking life, offering encouragement, and sowing seeds of love wherever you go.

"It is more blessed to give than to receive." Acts 20:35 (NIV)

Heavenly Father, thank You for being the ultimate Giver in my life. You have given me breath, love, and the greatest gift of all, and that's salvation through Jesus Christ. Lord, help me to live with a generous heart. Teach me to give not only of my resources but also my time, my love, and my kindness. May I reflect Your love in all that I do. And as I give, fill my heart with the joy and peace that only comes from You. In Jesus' name I pray.

Amen and To God Be The Glory!

MARCH 6. - "HATE NO ONE ~ IT'S BEST TO FORGIVE"

In life, people will disappoint us, betray us, and hurt us sometimes deeply. The natural response may be to hold on to anger, resentment, or even hatred. But as followers of Christ, we are called to a higher way, the way of forgiveness.

Hating others, no matter how much they've wronged us, only poisons our own hearts. It keeps us bound in bitterness and robs us of peace. But forgiveness frees us. It doesn't mean we excuse the wrong or forget the pain. It means we release that person from the prison of our hatred, and in doing so, we release ourselves.

Jesus modeled this perfectly. As He hung on the cross, betrayed, beaten, and mocked, He didn't lash out in hate. Instead, He prayed, "Father, forgive them; for they know not what they do ." (Luke 23:34 KJV)

If Jesus could forgive those who crucified Him, surely, He can give us the strength to forgive those who have wronged us. It won't always be easy, but it is always best. Forgiveness isn't for them, it's for you. It allows God's healing to begin in your heart and keeps you aligned with His love.

"Be ye kind one to another, tenderhearted, forgiving one another, even as God for Christ's sake hath forgiven you." Ephesians 4:32 (KJV)

Heavenly Father, I come to You with the pain of being wronged. You see the hurt, the betrayal, and the anger. But Lord, I do not want hatred to live in my heart. I choose to forgive, not because it's easy, but because You have forgiven me. Give me the strength to release every offense and to walk in love. Heal my heart and help me see others through Your eyes. I trust that You are my defender and my healer. In Jesus' name I pray.

Amen and To God Be The Glory!

MARCH 7. - "TIME DECIDES WHO YOU MEET ~ BEHAVIOR DECIDES WHO STAYS"

There is a powerful truth tucked into the quote: "Time decides who you meet in life, but behavior decides who stays." Every encounter, every friendship, and every relationship are part of God's divine timing. But sustaining those relationships, especially meaningful ones, requires the fruit of the Spirit actively working in us.

It's easy to cross paths with others. God orchestrates these meetings for purpose and growth. But for someone to remain in your life, your character matters. Kindness, humility, forgiveness, patience, and love are qualities that build trust and encourage lasting connection.

Relationships aren't just about chemistry or timing; they thrive through mutual respect, godly behavior, and intentional care. As believers, we are called to be peacemakers, to bear with one another in love, and to treat others as Christ has treated us.

"Be completely humble and gentle; be patient, bearing with one another in love." Ephesians 4:2 (NIV)

Heavenly Father, I thank You for the people You've brought into my life. I know that each connection is no accident but a part of Your divine plan. Help me to be a reflection of Your love and character in every relationship. Teach me to be patient, gentle, and forgiving. Let my behavior honor You and build trust with others. Strengthen the relationships that are meant to stay and give me peace in the ones that are only for a season. Above all, I pray all my actions glorify You. In Jesus' name, Amen and To God Be The Glory!

MARCH 8. - "HIS NAME IS JESUS"

Life brings moments when we feel broken, heavy-hearted, and unsure of how to keep going. In those moments, we often search for comfort, for safety, for a steady hand to hold us up. The answer to that longing is not found in this world, it is found in the One who gave His life for us. His name is Jesus.

He doesn't stand far off. He kneels beside us when we've fallen. He wraps us in His peace when sorrow overwhelms us. He gently wipes every tear, understanding each one. Jesus is not only our Savior, but He is also our Shepherd, Comforter, and Friend.

When no one else understands your pain, Jesus does. When the weight feels too much to carry, He lifts it. His love never runs dry, and His arms are always open.

ASK YOURSELF:

Who catches me when I fall?

Who holds me when I'm sad?

Who wipes away my tears?

"His name is Jesus."

"He heals the brokenhearted and binds up their wounds." Psalm 147:3 (KJV)

Lord Jesus, I Thank You for being the One who never leaves my side. When I fall, You catch me. When sadness covers me, You hold me. When tears fall, You gently wipe them away. Help me to remember that I am never alone, no matter how heavy life becomes. Let Your presence be my peace and Your love be my strength. I trust You with my heart, my pain, and my healing. In Your precious name, Amen and To God Be The Glory!

MARCH 9. - "STANDING WITH GOD"

There comes a moment in every believer's life when a decision must be made: Will I stand with God even when it costs me the approval of the world? Or will I conform to the world's standards and risk the eternal weight of God's judgment?

The phrase, "I would rather stand with God and be judged by the world, than to stand with the world and be judged by God," echoes a timeless truth. God never promised us popularity, but He did promise His presence. Choosing His way may separate us from the crowd, but it aligns us with His will, and that is a far greater reward than human applause.

When Noah built the ark, he was mocked. When Daniel prayed, he was thrown into a lion's den. When Jesus preached truth, He was crucified. Yet all stood firmly with God and God stood with them.

Standing with God may mean losing some relationships, facing rejection, or enduring criticism. But remember: God sees. God knows. God rewards. Eternity outweighs every opinion.

Do not conform to the pattern of this world, but be transformed by the renewing of your mind. Then you will be able to test and approve what God's will is--his good, pleasing and perfect will." Romans 12:2 (NIV)

Heavenly Father, please give me the courage to stand with You, even when the world stands against me. Strengthen my heart to endure the judgment of others and remain rooted in truth. Help me to walk boldly in faith, choosing righteousness over acceptance, and truth over popularity. May my life reflect my loyalty to You above all else. In Jesus' name, I pray.

Amen and To God Be The Glory!

MARCH 10. - "LIFTING THE VEIL"

"But their minds were blinded. For until this day the same veil remains unlifted in the reading of the Old Testament, because the veil is taken away in Christ. But even to this day, when Moses is read, a veil lies on their heart. Nevertheless, when one turns to the Lord, the veil is taken away." 2 Corinthians 3:14-16 (NKJV)

In this powerful passage, Paul speaks of a spiritual veil. A barrier that keeps people from fully understanding the truth and glory of God's Word. This veil is not physical; it is a blindness of the heart and mind. Even though the Scriptures were being read, many still could not see the fullness of God's plan because their hearts had not turned toward Christ.

But here is the hope: "Nevertheless, when one turns to the Lord, the veil is taken away." What a beautiful promise! Turning to Jesus removes that barrier. He opens our eyes to His grace, His purpose, and His truth. In Him, we are no longer bound by confusion, legalism, or spiritual blindness. The more we draw near to Him, the clearer our vision becomes.

If you've been walking through a season of confusion, doubt, or struggle to connect with God's Word, remember this promise. It's not about intellectual understanding—it's about the condition of the heart. When you sincerely seek the Lord, He promises to meet you there, to lift the veil, and to reveal Himself to you.

"Open my eyes, that I may see wondrous things from Your law."
Psalm 119:18 (NKJV)

Heavenly Father, I come before You with a humble heart, asking You to remove any veil that keeps me from fully seeing and knowing You. Help me to turn completely to You, so that I may understand Your Word and experience Your truth. Open my eyes, Lord, to see the wonders of Your love and grace. Fill me with the light of Your Spirit and guide me into deeper fellowship with You. In Jesus' name, I pray, Amen and To God Be The Glory!

MARCH 11. - "GOD PROTECTS ME"

There is great comfort in knowing that the Almighty God watches over us. In a world full of uncertainty, fear, and danger, the truth that "God protects me" is more than a hopeful phrase, it is a divine promise. His protection is not just physical, but emotional, spiritual, and eternal.

Even when we walk through the darkest valleys, God surrounds us with His presence. He places His angels around us, and His Spirit within us. The storms may rage, the enemy may strike, and the night may seem long, but the Lord remains our shield.

This passage reminds us that God's protection is constant and complete. From our first breath to our last, and into eternity, He is faithful to guard what belongs to Him. Rest in the safety of His arms today.

"The Lord will protect you from all evil; He will keep your soul. The Lord will guard your going out and your coming in from this time and forever." Psalm 121:7–8

Heavenly Father, thank You for being my protector. In moments of fear, remind me that You are near. When I face uncertainty, help me trust in Your covering. I know that nothing can reach me unless You allow it, and even then, You walk through it with me. Cover me with Your wings, Lord. Guard my heart, my mind, my loved ones, and every step I take. I place my life in Your strong, loving hands. In Jesus' name, Amen and To God Be The Glory!

MARCH 12. - "GOD HAS IT ALL IN CONTROL"

There are times when life feels like a storm. Chaotic, unpredictable, and overwhelming. In these moments, it's easy to let fear take over and forget that we serve a sovereign God who holds everything in His hands. But the truth is this: God has it all in control. Even when we cannot see the full picture or understand the "why," God is working behind the scenes for our good.

He is not caught off guard by our struggles, our losses, or our questions. His plan is perfect, and His timing is always right. When we feel weak, He is our strength. When we're uncertain, He is our guide. Our responsibility is to trust Him. Not just when things are going smoothly, but especially when they are not.

This verse reminds us that God is personally involved in our lives. He is not distant. He will finish the work He started in you. Whatever concerns you today, place it in His hands, He can handle it.

"The Lord will perfect that which concerneth me: thy mercy, O Lord, endureth forever: forsake not the works of thine own hands." Psalm 138:8 (KJV)

Father God, thank You for being in control, even when my world feels out of control. I surrender my worries, my plans, and my fears to You. Remind me daily that Your hands are steady and Your heart is kind. Help me to trust in Your purpose, even when I don't understand the process. Give me peace in the waiting, and strength in the walking. In Jesus' name I pray.

Amen and To God Be The Glory!

MARCH 13. - "LIVE BY WHAT YOU GET ~ MAKE LIFE BY WHAT YOU GIVE"

Life offers many blessings. Material things, time, talents, and relationships. We live day-to-day by what we receive: a paycheck, food, support, opportunities. But true life, the kind that touches eternity, is built by what we give. When we give our time to help others, our love to heal wounds, our resources to meet needs, this reflects the generous heart of Christ.

Jesus didn't come to be served, but to serve and to give. And in giving Himself fully, He gave us life. As His followers, we are called to do the same. Each act of kindness, each sacrifice made in love, builds a life of meaning, legacy, and eternal impact.

It's not about how much we have. It's about how willing we are to share what we've been given. Giving transforms our hearts and lives, and the lives of those around us.

"It is more blessed to give than to receive." Acts 20:35 (NKJV)

Heavenly Father, thank You for all that You've given me. I thank you for every blessing, every gift, every moment. Help me not to hold tightly to what I have, but to live with open hands and an open heart. Teach me to give generously, just as You gave Your Son for me. May my life reflect Your love through my giving. Use what I give, Lord, to bring life, hope, and healing to others. In Jesus' name, Amen and To God Be The Glory!

MARCH 14. - "THE FULL ARMOR OF GOD"

In a world filled with spiritual battles, God does not leave us defenseless. He calls us to stand strong, not in our own strength, but in His. The Apostle Paul reminds us in Ephesians that we are not wrestling against flesh and blood, but against spiritual forces that seek to destroy our faith, peace, and purpose.

To stand firm, we must put on the full armor of God. This armor equips us with truth, righteousness, peace, faith, salvation, and the Word of God. These are not physical weapons, but spiritual ones, designed to protect our hearts and minds and to keep us grounded in Christ.

When life gets hard, when the enemy attacks, when doubt creeps in—remember, you are armed by God. You are not alone. The Lord fights for you, and with His armor, you will be able to stand. Ephesians 6:10-12 (KJV):

"Finally, my brethren, be strong in the Lord, and in the power of his might.

Put on the whole armor of God, that ye may be able to stand against the wiles of the devil.

For we wrestle not against flesh and blood, but against principalities, against powers, against the rulers of the darkness of this world, against spiritual wickedness in high places."

Dear Heavenly Father, thank You for being my strength and shield. Help me to remember that my battle is not against people, but against the spiritual forces of darkness. Clothe me each day in Your holy armor. Wrap me in truth, protect me with righteousness, steady my feet with peace, strengthen my faith, and guard my mind with salvation. Teach me to wield Your Word with wisdom and courage. Help me to stand firm, knowing that victory belongs to You. In Jesus' name, Amen and To God Be The Glory!

MARCH 15. - "FORGIVE AND MOVE ON"

There is great power in forgiveness. Not just for the person being forgiven, but for the one who chooses to release the hurt. When we forgive, we are not saying what was done is okay; we are saying we will no longer let it have control over our hearts. Unforgiveness is a burden, a weight we were never meant to carry. God calls us to lay it down and walk in the freedom of His grace.

Forgiveness doesn't mean restoring trust overnight or returning to unhealthy relationships. It means giving up the right to harbor resentment. When we choose to forgive, we choose healing. And when we move on, we make space for God to fill us with peace.

"And be ye kind one to another, tenderhearted, forgiving one another, even as God for Christ's sake hath forgiven you." Ephesians 4:32 (KJV)

Heavenly Father, thank You for forgiving me, over and over again, even when I fall short. Help me to walk in that same spirit of forgiveness. When I'm tempted to hold on to bitterness or pain, remind me that Your grace is sufficient. I release every hurt into Your hands. Give me the strength to forgive others as You have forgiven me, and the courage to move forward in peace. In Jesus' name I pray.

Amen and To God Be The Glory!

MARCH 16. - "KEEP YOUR MIND ON WHAT IS TRUE ~ PURE ~ RIGHT"
Philippians 4:8 (KJV)

"Finally, brethren, whatsoever things are true, whatsoever things are honest, whatsoever things are just, whatsoever things are pure, whatsoever things are lovely, whatsoever things are of good report; if there be any virtue, and if there be any praise, think on these things."

Our minds are powerful. What we choose to dwell on will shape our attitudes, our emotions, and ultimately, our lives. In Philippians 4:8, Paul gives us a blueprint for holy thinking. Directing our attention away from fear, doubt, and negativity, and focusing it on truth, purity, and righteousness.

In a world full of distractions, temptations, and untruths, keeping our thoughts aligned with God's Word is not just beneficial, it's essential. When we meditate on what is true (God's promises), pure (His love), and right (His ways), we anchor our hearts in peace and grow in spiritual strength.

Let us be intentional. Let us guard our minds as we guard our hearts. Filtering out what doesn't glorify God and holding fast to what uplifts, edifies, and honors Him.

Heavenly Father, thank You for giving me Your Word as a guide for my thoughts and life. Help me to focus on what is true, pure, and right. Let my mind be fixed on Your promises and not the distractions of this world. Cleanse my thoughts and fill me with Your peace. When negativity or doubt creeps in, remind me to meditate on Your goodness and truth. Strengthen me daily to walk in the light of Your Word and reflect Your love. In Jesus' name I pray, Amen and To God Be The Glory!

MARCH 17. - "FASTING FROM PEOPLE IS ALSO IMPORTANT"

There are seasons when God calls us not just to fast from food or worldly pleasures, but from people. While fellowship and community are essential parts of the Christian Walk, there are times when solitude with God becomes necessary for spiritual growth, healing, or clarity. Jesus Himself often withdrew from the crowds, even from His closest disciples to spend time alone with the Father.

When we intentionally step away from others, we make room to hear God more clearly. Our minds are less distracted, our hearts are less entangled, and our spirits are more open. This kind of fast isn't about cutting people off in anger or pride but about pulling back in peace to reconnect with our Creator. It's a sacred pause, a time to reset our priorities and strengthen our identity in Christ apart from the influence of others.

If Jesus needed space to recharge spiritually, so do we. Let your time of fasting from people be a holy appointment with God, not a sign of disconnection, but of divine alignment.

"But Jesus often withdrew to lonely places and prayed." Luke 5:16 (KJV)

Heavenly Father, thank You for the gift of relationships and community, but thank You also for the wisdom to know when to step away and be alone with You. Help me not to feel guilty when You call me to be still and separate for a time. Speak to me in silence. Refresh my soul, reset my mind, and restore my spirit. Let this time apart be a time of drawing nearer to You. I trust that in the quiet, You will reveal what I need for the journey ahead. In Jesus' name I pray.

Amen and To God Be The Glory!

MARCH 18. - "FAMILY IS NOT ALWAYS ABOUT BLOOD"

Family goes far beyond DNA. While blood relatives are a blessing, God often brings people into our lives who become just as close, sometimes even closer than biological family. In Christ, we are united by something far stronger than genetics. We are bonded by the Spirit, by love, and by a shared faith.

Jesus Himself redefined family. When He was told that His mother and brothers were waiting for Him, He responded in a way that pointed to a greater truth when He said: those who do the will of God are His family. This shows us that spiritual connection can be just as sacred as natural ties.

Sometimes, God places people in your life who walk with you, pray for you, lift you up, and love you deeply, even when they don't share your last name. Cherish those relationships. They are divine gifts.

"And he stretched forth his hand toward his disciples, and said, Behold my mother and my brethren! For whosoever shall do the will of my Father which is in heaven, the same is my brother, and sister, and mother." Matthew 12:49–50 (KJV)

Dear God in Heaven, I thank You for the gift of family. Both the ones I was born into and the ones You've brought into my life by grace. Help me to recognize and cherish those who love me, support me, and walk beside me in faith. Let me never take for granted the spiritual family You've given me. Teach me to be that kind of family to others who are loving, loyal, and rooted in You. In Jesus' name, Amen and To God Be The Glory!

MARCH 19. - "JESUS ~ THE ONLY ONE WHO QUALIFIES"

In the story of the woman caught in adultery, the religious leaders dragged her before Jesus, demanding justice. According to the law, she deserved death by stoning. But Jesus, full of wisdom and mercy, responded not with condemnation but with conviction. He reminded them that only the sinless could rightfully pass judgment. And one by one, they dropped their stones and walked away.

This powerful moment reveals a deep truth: Jesus is the only one qualified to throw a stone, yet He chooses grace over judgment. He didn't excuse the woman's sin, but neither did He shame her. Instead, He offered her a second chance: "Go, and sin no more."

We live in a world quick to point fingers, quick to cancel, and slow to forgive. But we are all in need of grace. Before we judge others, we must remember our own brokenness and the mercy that has been shown to us. Only Jesus, who lived without sin, has the authority to judge, and yet, He chooses love, redemption, and restoration.

If the only one qualified to throw a stone chose not to, how much more should we choose grace?

"He that is without sin among you, let him first cast a stone at her." John 8:7 (KJV)

Father God, Thank You for Your mercy that meets me even in my failures. Help me to resist the urge to judge others, remembering that I, too, am a recipient of grace. Teach me to see people through Your eyes: compassionate, patient, and loving. Remind me daily that the only one qualified to condemn me is the one who chose to save me. May I extend that same mercy to others today. In Jesus' name I pray.

Amen and To God Be The Glory!

MARCH 20. - "DON'T BE DISCOURAGED"

There are moments when the weight of life feels overwhelming. Whether it's personal struggles, disappointments, or spiritual weariness, discouragement tries to creep in and take root. But God's Word gently reminds us not to give up. When God says, "Be not dismayed," it's not a mere suggestion, it's a promise wrapped in His presence.

Joshua faced uncertainty and great responsibility, yet God told him to be strong and courageous. Why? Because God was with him. That same promise is for you. Even in silence, confusion, or sorrow, God is still near. He has not abandoned you, and He never will.

Don't be discouraged, lift your eyes. The One who walks with you is greater than anything that stands against you.

"Have not I commanded thee? Be strong and of a good courage; be not afraid, neither be thou dismayed: for the Lord thy God is with thee whithersoever thou goest." Joshua 1:9 (KJV)

Father God, I thank You for being my strength when I feel weak and my peace when I feel overwhelmed. Help me to trust Your presence even when I can't trace Your hand. Replace my discouragement with hope, and my fear with faith. Remind me that You are with me wherever I go and that nothing can separate me from Your love. I choose today to stand in courage, knowing You Walk beside me. In Jesus' name I pray.

Amen and To God Be The Glory!

MARCH 21. - "HOW MANY SCARS ARE JUSTIFIED OUT OF LOVE"

There are moments in life when love blinds us to the harm being done. Whether it's a relationship, friendship, or even family, we sometimes excuse the wounds we receive because we care deeply for the one wounding us. We justify their actions, downplay the pain, and convince ourselves that love must endure suffering, even when it becomes destructive.

But love, in its truest and most godly form, does not inflict wounds. It heals. It protects. It builds up rather than tears down. God's Word reminds us of what love is supposed to look like:

Charity suffereth long, and is kind; charity envieth not; **charity** vaunteth not itself, is not puffed up, doth not behave itself unseemly, seeketh not her own, is not easily provoked, thinketh no evil; rejoiceth not in iniquity, but rejoiceth in the truth; beareth all things, believeth all things, hopeth all things, endureth all things. 1 Corinthians 13:4-8 KJV

When the love we receive contradicts the nature of godly love, it is not from God. The people we allow close to our hearts should not be the ones who leave lasting scars. Healing begins when we recognize our worth in Christ and stop justifying pain as proof of love. Jesus bore scars on the cross, so we wouldn't have to carry the ones made by others.

Dear Father in Heaven, I thank You for revealing the truth about love through Your Word. Forgive me for the times I allowed pain to stay in my life simply because I loved the one who caused it. Help me to discern between love and harm, and to walk in the freedom and healing that comes from You. Teach me to guard my heart, to love wisely, and to know when to let go of relationships that wound instead of heals. Remind me daily that I am worthy of a love that reflects You. In Jesus' name, Amen and To God Be The Glory!

MARCH 22. - "LOYALTY vs COMMON SENSE"

There are times in life when our hearts override our heads. We stay loyal to people, places, or patterns not because it's wise, but because we hope. Hope they'll change. Hope it gets better. Hope love is enough.

But sometimes, loyalty can become a trap. The Bible warns us not to lean on our own understanding but to seek God in all things. When we confuse loyalty with obligation or fear, we can stay in harmful situations far longer than God intended.

God calls us to walk in wisdom and truth. Loyalty, when rooted in love and guided by God, is beautiful. But when it binds us to pain and prevents us from living freely in God's will, it becomes a chain.

Let God lead. Not your guilt, not your history, and not your misplaced loyalty. Trust that He can give you discernment to know when to stay, and the courage to leave when He says go.

"Trust in the Lord with all thine heart; and lean not unto thine own understanding. In all thy ways acknowledge him, and he shall direct thy paths." Proverbs 3:5–6 (KJV)

Father, help me to discern the difference between loyalty and bondage. Give me wisdom to know when You are calling me to remain, and strength to walk away when You are calling me out. Forgive me for the times I stayed longer than I should have out of fear, pride, or guilt. Teach me to trust Your voice more than my emotions. Thank You for always leading me into truth. In Jesus' name I pray.

Amen and To God Be The Glory!

MARCH 23. - "THE CHOICE IS YOURS"

Life constantly presents us with choices. Not just in what we say or do, but in how we respond to the pain, offenses, and disappointments of others. One of the most powerful and life-shaping choices we make is whether to love or withhold love, to forgive or hold on to bitterness.

Jesus taught that love and forgiveness are not just commands, but keys to our peace and joy. When we choose not to forgive, we imprison ourselves, not the person who hurt us. When we choose not to love, we close our hearts to the healing presence of God. True happiness isn't found in controlling others or replaying the offense. It's found in surrender, grace, and freedom.

The truth is: you have a choice. God gives us free will, but He also makes clear the fruit of our decisions. When we love and forgive, we reflect Him. When we don't, we forfeit peace that could have been ours. Don't let your happiness be held hostage by someone else's actions. Choose to be free.

"And be ye kind one to another, tenderhearted, forgiving one another, even as God for Christ's sake hath forgiven you." Ephesians 4:32, KJV

Heavenly Father, thank You for the freedom You give me to choose. Help me to choose love, even when I feel justified in shutting people out. Help me to choose forgiveness, even when the pain is real and deep. Teach me how to release bitterness and walk in the joy and peace that only You can provide. I don't want to be bound by what others have done to me. I want to live in the fullness of Your grace. Today, I choose love. I choose forgiveness. I choose happiness in You. In Jesus' name I pray.

Amen and To God Be The Glory!

MARCH 24. - "CHANGE STARTS WITH YOU"

Too often, we wait for our circumstances to shift or for people to change before we take a step toward growth. But true transformation always begins with one person, you. God is not looking for perfect people; He's looking for a willing heart. He desires to hear your voice, your cries, your praise, your repentance, your truth. Change isn't something that happens around you, it starts within you when you turn your heart toward God.

God is always listening. He's not far off or silent. He's near, waiting for you to invite Him into the process. He wants a relationship, not religion, honest conversation, not perfection. You don't have to wait until you have it all figured out. Start where you are, with what you have. Talk to Him. He is ready to meet you.

When you take one step toward God, He moves toward you with grace, mercy, and the power to change what you can't on your own. The first step is yours. Open your heart. Open your mouth. Change starts with you, and you can believe that God is listening.

"Draw nigh to God, and he will draw nigh to you." James 4:8 (KJV)

Heavenly Father, thank You for never turning away from me. I confess that sometimes I wait too long, hoping something around me will shift when You're calling me to look within. Help me to be honest with You, to bring my heart to You just as it is. Remind me that change doesn't have to be overwhelming when I walk with You daily. Teach me to seek You first, to talk to You freely, and to trust that You hear me every time. Today, I take that first step. Start the change in me. In Jesus' name, Amen and To God Be The Glory!

MARCH 25. - "STOP PLAYING CHURCH"

Our Church Doesn't Need More Glamour ~ It Needs More Jesus

In today's world, it's easy to get caught up in appearances. Flashy lights, impressive buildings, polished performances, and perfect presentations. But the church was never meant to be about entertainment or image. It was meant to be a place where the presence of Jesus is real, where hearts are healed, souls are saved, and lives are transformed.

Glamour fades, but Jesus remains. When we chase after style instead of Spirit, we may impress people but miss the power of God. What our churches truly need isn't more production, it's more presence. More prayer. More truth. More of Jesus at the center of everything we do. He alone brings the hope, peace, and revival our hearts long for.

"That your faith should not stand in the wisdom of men, but in the power of God." 1 Corinthians 2:5 (KJV)

Lord Jesus, please forgive us for the times we've been distracted by outward appearances and forgotten Your presence. Strip away anything in our churches that doesn't glorify You. Help us to hunger not for glamour, but for Your glory. Let Your Spirit move freely among us, stirring revival, healing brokenness, and drawing us closer to You. May our churches reflect more of You and not the world. We want more of You and less of everything else. In Jesus' name I pray.

Amen and To God Be The Glory!

MARCH 26. - "GOD DON'T CONDEMN"

In a world quick to point fingers and slow to extend grace, Jesus calls us to a higher standard: Don't condemn. This is more than a suggestion, it's a command that reflects the heart of God. When we choose to withhold judgment, we leave room for God's mercy to work not only in others, but also in ourselves.

Condemnation is often rooted in pride or pain. We condemn what we don't understand or what reminds us of our own brokenness. But God sees every heart clearly and still offers forgiveness. If He, who is perfect, refuses to condemn those who repent, who are we to cast stones?

Instead of condemnation, let's choose compassion. Instead of harsh words, let's offer understanding. You never know what silent battles someone is fighting. And in showing mercy, we reflect the mercy that God has so freely shown to us.

"Judge not, and ye shall not be judged: condemn not, and ye shall not be condemned: forgive, and ye shall be forgiven." Luke 6:37 (KJV)

Heavenly Father, please help me to walk in the spirit of grace, not judgment. Teach me to see others through Your eyes, with compassion and love. Remind me that I, too, have been forgiven much. Keep my heart humble, my tongue kind, and my hands ready to lift others up instead of tearing them down. In a world full of condemnation, let me be a vessel of Your mercy. In Jesus' name, Amen and To God Be The Glory!

MARCH 27. - "LOVE THEM ENOUGH TO TELL THEM THE WHOLE TRUTH"

Truth and love are not enemies. In fact, true love demands truth. Telling someone what they want to hear may keep the peace for a moment but telling them what they need to hear gently, prayerfully, and with love, can change the course of their life.

God never called us to sugarcoat the gospel or to enable someone's self-destruction with silence. Instead, He calls us to be messengers of truth, seasoned with grace. When we love someone deeply, we become willing to risk their temporary discomfort for their eternal well-being.

However, once we've shared the truth in love, our job is done. We are not responsible for how others receive it, we are responsible for obeying God and delivering it with humility and compassion. Their response is between them and the Lord. Our faithfulness is between us and Him.

"That we henceforth be no more children, tossed to and fro, and carried about with every wind of doctrine, by the sleight of men, but speaking the truth in love, may grow up into him in all things, which is the head, even Christ." Ephesians 4:14–15 (KJV)

Heavenly Father, give me the courage to speak truth in love. Let my words be guided by Your Spirit and not by pride or fear. Help me to love others deeply, so much so, that I'm willing to tell them what they may not want to hear but what they truly need. And once I've spoken, please remind me that their response is not mine to control. Let me trust You with the outcome. In Jesus' name I pray.

Amen and To God Be The Glory!

MARCH 28. - "HOW TO PLAY THE LONG GAME"

The world often chases instant results, quick success, immediate rewards, and fast answers. But God calls His children to a different path: the long game of faithfulness. Doing what's right in God's eyes isn't always easy, and it doesn't always bring immediate recognition or reward. But it builds something stronger, character, trust, and an eternal reward that no one can take away.

Playing the long game means trusting God's timing and doing what pleases Him, even when no one else is watching. It means making decisions not based on what feels good now, but what honors God forever.

It may cost you popularity. It may require sacrifice. But when you align your life with God's will, you're investing in something that lasts beyond this world. God sees every act of obedience, and He promises that in due time, your faithfulness will bear fruit.

"And let us not be weary in well doing: for in due season we shall reap, if we faint not." Galatians 6:9 (KJV)

Precious Lord, please help me to be faithful in the long game. Strengthen me when the path gets lonely or discouraging. Teach me to do what's right in Your eyes, even when no one else understands. I trust that Your timing is perfect and that You honor those who walk in obedience. Give me endurance, patience, and a heart fixed on You. In Jesus' name I pray.

Amen and To God Be The Glory!

MARCH 29. - "WHEN YOU ARE MADE TO FEEL UNWANTED ~ LEAVE or STAY"

There will be moments in life when the atmosphere around you whispers, or even shouts, that you are not wanted. Whether it's in relationships, friendships, a job, or even a ministry, that sting of rejection can crush the spirit. In those moments, the question arises: Do I leave, or do I stay?

Jesus faced rejection too. In His hometown, the people He grew up with refused to believe in Him. Scripture tells us:

"And he did not many mighty works there because of their unbelief." Matthew 13:58 (KJV)

Jesus didn't argue, force Himself into acceptance, or beg for a place. He simply moved on. He understood His value wasn't diminished by their inability to see it. Likewise, your worth isn't determined by someone else's welcome or lack thereof.

So, what should you do? You ask God. You listen. You pray. You discern. Sometimes, God calls us to stay and be a light in dark places. Other times, He releases us so we can grow and thrive elsewhere. Either way, the decision shouldn't be rooted in emotion, but in faith and obedience.

Father God, help me to see myself the way You see me. When I feel unwanted or rejected, remind me that I am chosen, loved, and called by You. Teach me to seek Your will above all else, whether it means staying or walking away. Give me peace in the decision, and strength to follow where You lead me. In Jesus' name I pray.

Amen and To God Be The Glory!

MARCH 30. - "HUMBLE ENOUGH ~ WHEN YOU SERVE SOMEONE WHOSE HURT YOU"

It takes a special kind of humility to serve someone who's caused you pain. The world says walk away, hold a grudge, or get even. But Jesus shows us a different way. The way of grace, humility, and love.

On the night He was betrayed, Jesus knelt to wash the feet of His disciples, including Judas. He knew Judas would betray Him, yet He still served him.

Jesus didn't serve out of weakness but out of strength. He was secure in who He was and obedient to the Father's will. Serving someone who has hurt you isn't about excusing their behavior; it's about honoring God above your feelings.

When you choose to serve in humility, you reflect the heart of Christ. It may not change the other person, but it will change you, and that's often the miracle.

"If I then, your Lord and Master, have washed your feet; ye also ought to wash one another's feet." John 13:14 (KJV)

Dear Lord, give me the strength to walk in humility, even when my heart has been wounded. Teach me to serve not from pride or bitterness, but from the love and grace You've shown me. Help me to reflect You in how I treat others, especially those who have hurt me. Let my actions honor You above all. In Jesus' name, Amen and To God Be The Glory!

MARCH 31. - "A TOUGH LESSON ~ LOVE YOUR ENEMIES"

Loving our enemies is one of the hardest commands Jesus gave us. It goes against every instinct we have. When someone lies about us, hurts us, or treats us unfairly, our natural response is to protect ourselves or retaliate. But Jesus calls us to something higher.

Loving your enemies doesn't mean agreeing with them or excusing their actions. It means choosing to respond with grace instead of bitterness. It's praying for them when you'd rather avoid them. It's showing mercy because you remember how much mercy God has shown you.

It's a tough lesson—but it's one that shapes your heart to be more like Christ's.

"But I say unto you, Love your enemies, bless them that curse you, do good to them that hate you, and pray for them which despitefully use you, and persecute you." Matthew 5:44 (KJV)

Dear Lord, this is not easy. Help me love like You love, even when it hurts. Soften my heart where it's grown hard. Teach me to forgive, to bless, and to pray for those who have wronged me. I want to follow Your example, even when it's hard. In Jesus' name I pray, Amen and To God Be The Glory!

APRIL INTRODUCTION

Life doesn't pause when we're confused, overwhelmed, or hurting. The questions come hard and fast: Why am I going through this? How do I forgive them? What should I do when I feel alone, angry, or afraid? In a world full of opinions and noise, it's easy to get lost searching for clarity. But the Word of God offers more than comfort, it offers truth.

This April, as we journey through Biblical Answers to Life's Pressing Problems, we turn our hearts toward the One who never changes. Each day's devotion is rooted in Scripture, offering not just encouragement, but direction. God's wisdom for real struggles. Whether you're wrestling with relationships, purpose, pain, or personal growth, this month is designed to remind you that God is not silent about your situation.

Jesus said in John 16:33 (KJV):

"These things I have spoken unto you, that in me ye might have peace. In the world ye shall have tribulation: but be of good cheer; I have overcome the world."

You don't have to figure life out on your own. God's Word is full of clarity, hope, and power for whatever you're facing. Let April be the month you lean in, ask hard questions, and listen to God's answers.

Heavenly Father, thank You for being a God who sees us, hears us, and speaks truth into every situation. As I begin this month of devotion, open my heart to receive Your Word. Give me wisdom for every decision, healing for every wound, and strength for every battle. Remind me that no problem is too great when I bring it to You. Help me trust that Your answers are always right and always good. In Jesus' name I pray.

Amen and To God Be The Glory!

APRIL 1. - "A TIME FOR CHANGE"

Sometimes we find ourselves surrounded by wisdom, guidance, and spiritual leadership. We attend the right church, sit under powerful teaching, receive sound advice, and have access to people who genuinely care for our soul. Yet, somehow, we still fall short. We make decisions that sabotage our progress. We slip into patterns where we promised God, and ourselves, we'd never return to. Why?

Because access to truth is not the same as obedience to truth.

Judah had it all: covenant, history, leaders, and God's promises. But Judah still failed. The question isn't whether we have the right voices in our lives. The real question is, are we listening? Are we obeying?

Change doesn't happen simply by having good surroundings. Real change begins when we decide to apply what we've been taught, submit to God's will, and walk in the Spirit even when it's hard.

You've had access to the best. Isn't it time you became your best, for God?

"But be ye doers of the word, and not hearers only, deceiving your own selves."
James 1:22 (KJV)

Heavenly Father, I thank You for placing wise voices and godly leaders in my life. Forgive me for the times I've heard Your truth but chose my own way. I no longer want to live in the cycle of failure and regret. Give me the courage to change. Help me not just to hear, but to do. Teach me to walk in obedience and renew my heart and mind daily. Let this be the moment I truly surrender and move forward in You. In Jesus' name I pray Father God.

Amen and To God Be The Glory!

APRIL 2. - "GUARDING YOUR CIRCLE"

There comes a time in every believer's journey when we must prayerfully evaluate the people we allow close to us. Not everyone is meant to walk with us in every season. Some relationships drain rather than pour into us. Others may look good on the surface but carry hidden motives, distractions, or even harm.

God, in His wisdom and love, wants to protect us. Not just from physical danger but also from emotional, spiritual, and relational harm. He calls us to walk wisely and discern the fruit in others' lives (Matthew 7:16). That doesn't mean we live suspiciously, but it does mean we invite Him to help us see clearly.

If you're praying for God to remove the wrong people and send the right ones, trust that He hears you. Sometimes He ends relationships before we understand why. Sometimes He exposes truths that hurt but heal. God is not just the God of addition; He's also the God of subtraction when it's for your protection.

"Do not be misled: 'Bad company corrupts good character.'" 1 Corinthians 15:33 (NIV)

Heavenly Father, I come to You with a sincere heart, asking for Your divine protection over my relationships. Lord, remove anyone in my life who is not for me, who may secretly harm me, distract me, or keep me from Your will. Help me to see people as You see them, through eyes of wisdom and discernment. Encourage me when I feel lonely or when You remove people I thought I needed. Surround me with those who love You and will love me in truth. Teach me to walk wisely and not emotionally. I trust You to guide my heart and guard my life. In Jesus' name, Amen and To God Be The Glory!

APRIL 3. - "GOD CAME DOWN TO US ~ GOOD FRIDAY"

The phrase "The gospel isn't that you climbed to God, but that God climbed down, bled, rose and now holds you" captures the very heart of Christianity. It reminds us that salvation is not about our effort, our striving, or our ability to "climb up" to God. Instead, it is about God's unimaginable love, where He stepped down into our broken world to redeem us.

From the very beginning, humanity has tried to build ladders to heaven, whether through works, rituals, or self-righteousness. But every attempt fell short because sin created a separation that no human effort could bridge. Then came Jesus, who did not wait for us to find Him, but who left the throne of heaven, clothed Himself in flesh, walked among us, and took on the very sins that weighed us down.

The cross is proof of His descent into our suffering. The resurrection is proof of His victory over what held us captive. And now, He doesn't just leave us to stumble in life on our own, He holds us. The gospel is not only about forgiveness but also about security. When Jesus said, "No one will snatch them out of my hand" (John 10:28 NIV), He was assuring us that His grip is stronger than our weaknesses, our failures, and our doubts.

Think about it: if the gospel depended on us climbing to God, it would fail every time. But because God descended to us, we have a living hope that never fades. This truth should stir humility in us, because we did nothing to earn it, and it should stir joy in us, because we can rest in what Jesus has already accomplished.

"But God commendeth his love toward us, in that, while we were yet sinners, Christ died for us." Romans 5:8 (KJV)

Heavenly Father, I thank You that I don't have to climb up to reach You, because You came down to reach me. Thank You for sending Jesus to bleed, die, and rise again so that I may have life and be held securely in Your hands. Help me to rest in this truth, to live with gratitude, and to share this gospel with others who are still trying to climb ladders that cannot reach You. Keep me in Your grace and remind me daily that I am held by You. In Jesus' name I pray, Amen and To God Be The Glory!

APRIL 4. - "A HOUSE IS NOT A HOME WITHOUT GOD IN IT"
Inspired by Joshua 24:15 (KJV)

A structure can be built with wood, bricks, and nails, but only God's presence can turn that structure into a true home. A house may offer shelter, but it is God who fills it with peace, love, and purpose. Without Him, even the most beautiful home can feel empty.

Joshua boldly declared, "As for me and my house, we will serve the Lord" (Joshua 24:15 KJV). He made it clear that a home aligned with God's will is one built on a firm foundation. Inviting God into your home means surrendering your family, your routines, and your relationships to His lordship. It means praying together, worshiping together, and seeking Him together.

When God is at the center, the atmosphere shifts. There's more forgiveness, more grace, and more direction. A God-filled home doesn't mean perfection, but it does mean His presence. His holy, guiding presence dwelling with you.

"And if it seem evil unto you to serve the Lord, choose you this day whom ye will serve; but as for me and my house, we will serve the Lord." Joshua 24:15 (KJV)

Lord Jesus, I invite You into every room of my home and every corner of my heart. Help me lead my household in serving You with humility and truth. May Your presence dwell here so deeply that all who enter can feel Your peace. Be the foundation of our family, the center of our love, and the guide for all we do. In Jesus' name I pray.

Amen and To God Be The Glory!

APRIL 5. - "THREE MEN, THREE CROSSES, ONE HILL

THINK ON THIS: On Calvary's hill, three crosses stood side by side. Though all three bore men condemned to die, the destiny of each man revealed the eternal truth of God's plan.

One man cursed. His heart hardened, his lips still spoke rebellion even in his final breaths. He mocked Jesus, blind to the grace extended to him. This man died in sin, choosing separation from the only One who could save him.

One man prayed. In humility, he acknowledged his guilt and turned his heart toward the Savior. His plea was simple: "Lord, remember me when You come into Your kingdom" (Luke 23:42 NKJV). In that moment of repentance, Jesus gave him the promise of life: "Today you will be with Me in paradise." This man died to sin, freed from its grip by faith.

One man promised. The sinless Son of God hung on the middle cross. Innocent yet condemned, blameless yet bearing the sins of the world, Jesus fulfilled the Father's plan of redemption. He died for sin ~ not His own, but ours.

Three crosses. Three men. Three eternal outcomes.

- One died condemned. Refusing Christ, his death sealed his separation.
- One died forgiven. Accepting Christ, his death opened the gates of paradise.
- One died innocent. Christ Himself, the spotless Lamb, who laid down His life willingly.

And in that moment of history, the power of death was displayed and defeated:

- One was held by death. Sin bound him forever.

- One was released by death. Death became his doorway to eternal life.

- One conquered death. Jesus rose victorious, crushing the sting of the grave.

Three men on three crosses tell the story of eternity. One lost life, one gained life, and One was life. Jesus declared, "I am the way, the truth, and the life: no man comes unto the Father, but by me" (John 14:6).

Calvary reminds us that the cross demands a response. We are all represented there by the scoffer who rejected, or by the sinner who believed. But only through the Savior in the middle, do we find redemption, hope, and eternal life.

"For He hath made Him to be sin for us, who knew no sin; that we might be made the righteousness of God in Him." 2 Corinthians 5:21 (KJV)

Heavenly Father, we thank You for the sacrifice of Jesus Christ, who bore our sins on the cross so that we could be free. We see ourselves in those three men, but we choose today to stand with the one who prayed, trusting in the One who promised. Lord, help us to live in the power of the cross, remembering that Christ not only died for us but rose again to give us eternal life. May our hearts never forget the price He paid and the victory He secured. Thank You, Jesus, for being our Savior, our Redeemer, and our Life. In Your holy name we pray, Amen and To God Be The Glory!

APRIL 6. - "WHEREVER I AM GOD IS"

Storms in life are inevitable. Unexpected loss, deep disappointments, or seasons of uncertainty. They often come without warning and shake everything we thought was stable. But here's the unshakable truth: no matter where you are or what you're going through, God is right there with you. He is not absent in the storm; He is present in it.

Sometimes we look for God in the calm but forget that He also speaks in the wind and walks on the waves. The disciples saw this firsthand when Jesus met them in the middle of a raging sea. Not from the shore, but by walking through the storm to reach them. He didn't remove the storm first; He showed them He was greater than the storm.

Wherever you are emotionally, physically, or spiritually remember that God is near. The storm may still be raging, but you're not alone. He is your anchor, your peace, and your strength.

"When thou passest through the waters, I will be with thee; and through the rivers, they shall not overflow thee: when thou walkest through the fire, thou shalt not be burned; neither shall the flame kindle upon thee." Isaiah 43:2 (KJV)

Father, thank You for being with me in every storm. When the winds of life are strong and fear rises, help me to remember that You are near. Strengthen my heart and calm my spirit. Remind me that no storm is stronger than You. I trust You to guide me through it and carry me safely to the other side. In Jesus' name I pray.

Amen and To God Be The Glory!

APRIL 7. - "CHOOSE ~ FAITH OR FEAR"

Every day we are faced with a choice: to walk by faith or be paralyzed by fear. Faith and fear both ask us to believe in something we cannot see. Faith believes in God's promises, while fear believes in the worst possible outcome.

Fear whispers, "What if it all goes wrong?" Faith declares, "Even if it does, God is still in control." Fear causes hesitation, but faith moves forward, trusting that God will make a way even when the path isn't clear.

Choosing faith doesn't mean you'll never feel fear. It means you won't let fear have the final say. It means fixing your eyes on Jesus, even when the wind and waves try to distract you. The same God who calmed the storm still walks with you today.

So ~ what do you choose?

"For God hath not given us the spirit of fear; but of power, and of love, and of a sound mind." 2 Timothy 1:7 (KJV)

Lord, help me to choose faith over fear. When doubt rises, remind me of Your power and Your promises. Give me the courage to walk forward, even when I can't see the whole picture. Let my trust in You be stronger than my fear of the unknown. I choose to believe that You are with me, for me, and guiding me. In Jesus' name, amen.

And To God Be The Glory!

APRIL 8. - "YOU'RE ALWAYS SAFE WITH GOD"
When You Journey with God, You Reach Your Destination

Life is a journey filled with detours, delays, and unexpected turns. On our own, we can easily lose direction. But when we walk with God, we're not just wandering, we're being led. Every step taken with Him has purpose, and every road, even the rough ones, moves us closer to the place He's prepared for us.

To journey with God means trusting Him when the path is unclear, obeying Him when it's inconvenient, and depending on Him when we feel weak. It means letting His Word guide us and His Spirit strengthen us. The destination may not always look like what we expected, but when God is with us, we always arrive right where we're meant to be.

Wherever you are today, if you're just starting, waiting, or wondering, please remember this: You'll get there, because you're not alone. When you journey with God, you reach your destination.

"The steps of a good man are ordered by the Lord: and he delighteth in his way."
Psalm 37:23 (KJV)

Heavenly Father, I thank You for walking with me through every season of life. Help me to trust Your direction, even when I don't understand it. Lead me step by step and keep me close to You. Strengthen my faith to keep going, knowing that with You, I will reach the place You've prepared for me. In Jesus' name I pray.

Amen and To God Be The Glory!

APRIL 9. - "SOMETHING BEST REMEMBERED"

Life doesn't always make sense, and challenges can leave us feeling weary, confused, or even forgotten. But in those moments, hold on to these four truths, and remember that they are anchors for your soul:

1. God will make a way.
   Even when there seems to be no way forward, God specializes in doing the impossible. He opens doors that no man can shut.

2. God will fight your battles.
   You don't have to handle everything on your own. The Lord is your defender. Rest in the truth that He sees what you can't and is working on your behalf.

3. Prayer is the best medicine.
   When your heart is heavy, your mind overwhelmed, or your body weak, prayer connects you to the One who gives peace, healing, and strength.

4. Trust God's timing.
   Waiting isn't easy, but God's timing is always perfect. What He promises, He will fulfill—in His way and His time.

When life shakes you, return to these truths. Let them steady your faith and renew your hope.

"Trust in the Lord with all thine heart; and lean not unto thine own understanding. In all thy ways acknowledge him, and he shall direct thy paths." Proverbs 3:5–6 (KJV)

Father, thank You for reminding me that I'm not alone. Help me to remember that You will make a way, fight for me, and bring healing through prayer. Teach me to trust Your timing even when I can't see the full picture. Let these truths settle deep in my heart and guide me through every season. In Jesus' name.

Amen and To God Be The Glory!

APRIL 10. - "WHAT MUST WE DO ~ TO DO THE WORK GOD REQUIRES"
Inspired by John 6:28–29, 40 (KJV)

After witnessing the miracles of Jesus, the people asked a profound question:

"What shall we do, that we might work the works of God?" (John 6:28 KJV).

It's a question many still ask today. How do we please God? What does He require of us? Is it endless good deeds, religious rituals, or personal perfection?

Jesus gave a simple but powerful answer:

"This is the work of God, that ye believe on him whom he hath sent." (John 6:29 KJV).

God's greatest desire isn't that we try to earn His love through performance, but that we trust completely in His Son. Belief in Jesus is not just the beginning of faith—it is the foundation of all that God requires.

And Jesus continued in verse 40:

"And this is the will of him that sent me, that every one which seeth the Son, and believeth on him, may have everlasting life..."

Faith is the key. It opens the door to forgiveness, transformation, and eternal life. God isn't asking for perfect actions—He's asking for a surrendered heart that believes in the One He sent.

"Jesus answered and said unto them, This is the work of God, that ye believe on him whom he hath sent." John 6:29 (KJV)

Lord, help me to rest in the truth that believing in You is the foundation of all that You require. Strengthen my faith and remind me that it's not about doing more but about trusting more. Teach me to walk in simple, daily belief—knowing that through Christ, I have all I need. In Jesus' name, Amen and To God Be The Glory!

APRIL 11. - "I AM NOT ASHAMED TO SAY I STAND WITH THE LORD"

There is a boldness that comes when your heart is fully surrendered to God. In a world that often celebrates compromise, silence, or the rejection of truth, it takes courage to say, "I stand with the Lord." This isn't just a casual declaration, it's a lifestyle. To stand with God means you choose His will over your own, His truth over popular opinion, and His presence over the approval of people.

The Apostle Paul knew this well. Even while imprisoned and persecuted, he declared:

[16] For I am not ashamed of the gospel of Christ: for it is the power of God unto salvation to every one that believeth; to the Jew first, and also to the Greek. Romans 1:16 KJV

Paul's confidence didn't come from his own strength but from the transforming power of the gospel. The same power that saved him is the same power that holds you steady when you stand for Jesus, even when it costs you something.

Being unashamed doesn't mean you're loud or confrontational. It means you live unshaken, convinced that your identity in Christ is worth more than the temporary opinions of others. It's in those moments when standing alone feels hard, that Heaven reminds you: That you are never alone.

Lord, I boldly declare today that I am not ashamed to stand with You. Give me strength to remain faithful, even when the crowd goes the other way. Help me to live with conviction, courage, and compassion reflecting Your truth in all that I say and do. Let my life be a testimony that brings glory to Your name. In Jesus' name I pray.

Amen and To God Be The Glory!

APRIL 12. - "WHEN YOU RECOGINZE YOUR WORTH"

As you begin to understand how God sees you, something powerful happens, your spirit awakens to your true value. You are not defined by people's opinions, past mistakes, or temporary circumstances. You are defined by the One who created you in His image and called you His own.

When you recognize your worth in Christ, it becomes difficult to remain in environments or around people who diminish your value, speak down to your dreams, or treat you like you are less than what God says you are. That's not pride, it's discernment. God never intended for His children to live in places where their light is constantly dimmed, or their heart consistently dishonored.

Jesus knew His worth. He walked with humility, yet He never allowed the opinions of others to derail His mission or identity. Likewise, knowing your worth will help you walk away from relationships that drain you, and walk into places that honor your calling.

"I will praise You, for I am fearfully and wonderfully made; marvelous are Your works, and that my soul knows very well." Psalm 139:14 (NKJV)

Heavenly Father, thank You for creating me with purpose, beauty, and worth. Help me to see myself the way You see me. Please remove any relationship, habit, or thought that makes me question my value. Give me the strength to walk away from people or environments that do not honor who I am in You. Surround me with those who uplift, encourage, and reflect Your love. Let my confidence always rest in Christ alone. In Jesus' name I humbly pray.

Amen and To God Be The Glory!

APRIL 13. - "MARRIAGE IS NOT ONLY ABOUT LOVE ~ IT TAKES COMMITMENT"

Love is a beautiful foundation, but feelings alone are not enough to sustain a marriage. Emotions can rise and fall, but commitment is the decision to stay, to work, to forgive, and to build, especially when things are hard. Real love shows up through dedication, through choosing your spouse daily, and through honoring your vows even when it's not easy.

Marriage is a covenant, not a contract. It's not based on performance, but on promise. God designed marriage as a reflection of His unwavering commitment to us. Just as Christ is faithful to the Church, we are called to be faithful to one another—through joy and pain, in strength and in weakness.

Commitment doesn't mean perfection, but it does mean perseverance. It means praying when you feel like walking away. It means choosing grace when offense tries to divide. When love is paired with unwavering commitment, marriages not only survive—they thrive.

"Above all, love each other deeply, because love covers over a multitude of sins."
1 Peter 4:8 (NIV)

Lord, thank You for the gift of marriage and for showing us what true commitment looks like. Help us not to rely on feelings alone, but to be rooted in faithful love that reflects You. Teach us how to stay, to serve, and to grow together even in difficult seasons. Strengthen every marriage that is struggling and restore hearts that have grown weary. Let our love be more than words, let it be a daily choice. In Jesus' name, Amen and To God Be The Glory!

APRIL 14. - "LEAVE SOMETHING THAT'S LASTING"

We all know that life on earth is temporary. Our days are numbered, but our impact doesn't have to be. The goal is not to live forever in the flesh, but to create a legacy of faith, love, and purpose that continues to echo long after we're gone.

Jesus lived only 33 years on this earth, yet His impact is eternal. His love, His teachings, and His sacrifice reshaped the world forever. In the same way, we're called to live intentionally, to sow seeds of kindness, truth, and godliness that will bear fruit for generations.

Ask yourself: What will remain when I'm gone? Will your children remember your prayers? Will your community remember your service? Will heaven be fuller because you lived on mission?

God doesn't ask us to be eternal on earth. He asks us to be faithful. And when we live a life of purpose, we build something that time can't erase. Something that points others back to Him.

"Let your light shine before others, that they may see your good deeds and glorify your Father in heaven." Matthew 5:16 (NIV)

Father, thank You for reminding me that my time here is short, but my impact can be eternal. Help me to use each day wisely, to speak words that uplift, and to do good that glorifies You. Teach me to build a legacy of faith and love that lives far beyond me. May my life shine with Your light and lead others to know You. In Jesus' name, Amen and To God Be The Glory!

APRIL 15. - "HE HEARD WHAT YOU DIDN'T"

Sometimes people walk out of our lives, or God removes them in ways we don't expect or understand. It can hurt, feel like rejection, or leave us wondering what we did wrong. But here's the truth: God hears what we don't. He sees what's said in silence, discerns hidden motives, and knows what's coming around the corner.

That person who left your life: God heard the conversation you never did. He saw the intentions you couldn't, and He removed them not to punish you, but to protect you. Sometimes God answers prayers by subtracting, not adding. He's not just editing your life, He's guarding your purpose.

Trust His hand even when you don't see His plan. If God removed them, then you didn't need them for where He's taking you. His moves are always strategic, loving, and purposeful. Let go in peace, knowing He's making room for what's better.

"The Lord will fight for you; you need only to be still." Exodus 14:14 (NIV)

God, thank You for seeing what I can't and hearing what I don't. Even when I feel the pain of loss, help me trust that Your protection is in every removal. Give me peace in Your decisions and the courage to keep moving forward without regret. Remind me that Your plan is always for my good. In Jesus' name I pray.

Amen and To God Be The Glory!

APRIL 16. - "THE LORD WON'T HOLD IT AGAINST YOU ~ FINDING GRACE IN YOUR MESS"

We all have moments when we make choices that lead us down the wrong path. Whether out of weakness, ignorance, or pride. And yet, one of the most beautiful truths about God is that His grace reaches even into our self-made messes. He doesn't wait for us to fix it all before coming to our aid. He steps into our chaos, rescues us with love, and restores us without shame.

God isn't in the business of reminding you of your failures. He's in the business of redeeming your story. His mercy rewrites what guilt tries to erase. And His love is deeper than your worst mistake. He knows every wrong turn, every misstep, and still chooses to be your Deliverer.

"The Lord is gracious and full of compassion, slow to anger and great in mercy. The Lord is good to all, and His tender mercies are over all His works." Psalm 145:8-9 (NKJV)

Father, thank You for being so patient with me. There are times I've made choices that led me into situations I shouldn't have been in. But You never turned Your back on me. You lifted me out with grace, not condemnation. Help me to never take Your mercy for granted and give me the wisdom to walk in Your ways moving forward. In Jesus' name, Amen and To God Be The Glory!

APRIL 17. - "WORRY ~ SOLVES NOTHING"

Worry has a sneaky way of creeping into our thoughts. It convinces us that by obsessing over the problem, somehow, we'll gain control. But the truth is, worry never solves anything. It doesn't change the situation. It only drains our energy, clouds our judgment, and robs us of peace.

God never intended for us to carry the weight of the world on our shoulders. He invites us to trust Him with every burden, every unknown, and every fear. When we trade worry for faith, we make room for God to move. Worry may be natural, but peace is supernatural and that's what He offers freely to His children.

"Can any one of you by worrying add a single hour to your life?" Matthew 6:27 (NIV)

Father, I confess that I often worry about things I cannot control. Help me to remember that worry is fruitless, but faith in You is powerful. Teach me to bring every concern to You in prayer and to trust that You are already working on my behalf. Replace my anxiety with Your perfect peace. In Jesus' name, Amen and To God Be The Glory!

APRIL 18. - "BLOOM IN GRACE"

Just as flowers bloom in the right season and under the right conditions, so does grace flourish in a heart that's alive in Christ. Where there is spiritual life, where hearts are open to God, grace begins to grow. It shows up in forgiveness extended, in love shown when it's undeserved, and in peace that surpasses understanding.

God's grace is not only sufficient it's fruitful. It multiplies in us and through us when we surrender to His care. Even in broken soil and beneath cloudy skies, grace has a way of pushing through. You may not always see it at first, but where there is spiritual life, grace will bloom, quietly, beautifully, and in perfect time.

"But he said to me, 'My grace is sufficient for you, for my power is made perfect in weakness.' Therefore I will boast all the more gladly about my weaknesses, so that Christ's power may rest on me." 2 Corinthians 12:9 (NIV)

Lord, thank You for the grace that grows in the soil of my life. Even when I feel weak or unworthy, Your grace continues to bloom. Teach me to recognize Your hand in every season and help me to be a reflection of Your grace to others. Let my life be a garden where Your mercy and love take root and flourish. In Jesus' name, Amen and The Glory!

APRIL 19. - "DON'T LET REGRET HOLD YOU BACK"

Regret is a powerful emotion. It reminds us of the things we wish we had done differently, such as the words we didn't say, the choices we wish we could change, and the opportunities we let pass by. But if we're not careful, regret can become a chain that keeps us locked in the past and unable to move forward into the future God has for us.

God never intended for us to live in shame or regret. Through Christ, we are forgiven, redeemed, and made new. What once held us back can now become a testimony of God's grace and transformation. Don't let regret stop you from becoming who God created you to be. Let it drive you closer to Him, not further away.

"Forget the former things; do not dwell on the past. See, I am doing a new thing! Now it springs up; do you not perceive it?" Isaiah 43:18–19 (NIV)

Lord, I thank You for being the God of new beginnings. Help me not to live in regret, but to trust in Your grace and forgiveness. Teach me to learn from my past but not be defined by it. Fill me with hope for the future and the courage to move forward in faith. In Jesus' name, Amen and To God Be The Glory!

APRIL 20. - "THREE TRUTHS OF LIFE"

God calls us to be people of faith, not fear. So often, the breakthrough we're waiting for requires our obedience, courage, and willingness to move. These three truths remind us that while God provides, He also expects us to take action.

1. If you don't go after it – God places dreams, opportunities, and purpose before us, but we must pursue them with faith.

2. If you don't ask – Scripture says we have not because we ask not. God invites us to come boldly and ask Him for what we need.

3. If you don't step forward – Growth comes through motion. Even a small step in the right direction can lead to a life-changing path.

Faith is more than believing, it's moving. Don't let fear, doubt, or comfort keep you stuck. Go after what God has placed in your heart. Ask boldly. Step forward. He's already gone ahead of you.

"Ask, and it will be given to you; seek, and you will find; knock, and it will be opened to you."
Matthew 7:7 (NKJV)

Lord, give me the courage to go after what You've called me to. Help me to ask boldly, seek diligently, and step forward in faith, even when I don't see the whole picture. I trust that as I move, You will guide every step. Strengthen my heart to live with purpose, not passivity. In Jesus' name, Amen and To God Be The Glory!

APRIL 21. - "LIVING IN THE LIGHT OF GLORY"

Life often hands us challenges, and if we're not careful, we'll find ourselves constantly searching for what's wrong, what's missing, what's broken, what hurts. But that's not the life God intended for us. We weren't created to live in a perpetual state of discontentment. We were created to live abundantly, joyfully, and with deep gratitude, even in the midst of imperfection.

Sometimes, it's easier to count our disappointments than our blessings. We focus on what didn't work out, who left, what failed, or how much more we think we need to be happy. But this perspective steals our joy, dulls our faith, and blinds us to the beauty right in front of us.

Joy is not found in the absence of trouble; it is found in the presence of God. When we start to live for reasons that we do have to be joyful, our breath, our salvation, our family, the lessons learned from pain, the doors God opened and the ones He closed, we begin to realize that our life is already filled with divine evidence of His goodness.

Gratitude doesn't ignore pain, it repositions it. It lifts our eyes from what's going wrong to what's still right. It doesn't wait for everything to be perfect; it rejoices in the truth that God's love is perfect, His grace is sufficient, and His plan is always good, even when we don't understand it fully.

"This is the day the Lord has made; we will rejoice and be glad in it." Psalm 118:24 (NKJV)

God made this day, right here, right now. That means it is infused with purpose, possibility, and a reason to rejoice. You don't have to wait until everything is "fixed" to start living. Choose joy now. Rejoice now. Live in your reasons to be grateful, not your reasons to be bitter.

Father God, forgive me for the times I've allowed negativity, disappointment, or fear to cloud my vision. Teach me to stop searching for reasons to be unhappy and instead open my heart to the countless blessings You've already given me. Help me to see Your goodness in the ordinary moments, to hear Your voice above the noise, and to rest in the joy that comes from knowing You are with me. Shift my perspective, Lord. Help me to live in the light of thankfulness, not the shadows of discontentment. Let my life reflect joy, peace, and unwavering faith in Your plan. Today, I choose to rejoice—not because life is perfect, but because You are present. Amen and To God Be The Glory!

APRIL 22. - "LOVE WITHOUT CONDITIONS"

Love is one of the most powerful gifts God has given us, and how we choose to give and receive it shapes the direction of our lives. In a world filled with conditional relationships. Where love is often based on status, convenience, or mutual benefits, we must learn to discern the difference between people who genuinely love us and those who only show up when it serves their needs.

Unconditional love mirrors the heart of God. It stays steady in the storm, shows up when it's inconvenient, and gives without expecting something in return. These are the people God places in our lives to reflect His love: they encourage us, correct us in love, support us in our weakness, and remain loyal even when we're not at our best.

In contrast, conditional love is often self-serving. It disappears when challenges arise or when we no longer meet someone else's expectations. These relationships leave us feeling drained, used, or abandoned. The reason is because they were never rooted in genuine care, but in convenience.

God never intended for us to chase people who constantly question our worth or only "love" us when it's easy. He calls us into relationships where mutual love, respect, and faith are present. Christ Himself modeled this when He chose to love and lay down His life for us, even when we were still sinners (Romans 5:8). That's the kind of love worth investing in.

Spending time with those who love you unconditionally is not selfish, it's wise. It is a way of protecting your spirit, stewarding your emotional energy, and honoring the kind of love that reflects our Father's heart.

"Do not be misled: 'Bad company corrupts good character.'" 1 Corinthians 15:33 (NIV)

Not everyone deserves access to your heart. Some people are meant to be loved from a distance. God wants you to be surrounded by those who help you grow in faith, speak life into you, and love you not just for what you do—but for who you are.

Father God,

Thank You for the people in my life who love me with Your kind of love: unconditionally, sincerely, and without selfish motives. Help me to see clearly and walk wisely in my relationships. Give me the strength to let go of those who only come around when it benefits them, and the peace to stop seeking approval where it will never be given. Lord, teach me to invest my time, my heart, and my energy into the people You've placed in my life to uplift, encourage, and walk with me in truth. Let me also be someone who loves others unconditionally, and without expecting anything in return. Purify my relationships and help me honor You in how I love and who I let close to me. In Jesus' Name I pray, Amen and To God Be The Glory!

APRIL 23. - "GOD IS GOOD ALL THE TIME"

It's a phrase we often say: God is good all the time. But do we truly grasp its depth? When life is going well, it's easy to declare His goodness. But what about when we're in the middle of grief, confusion, or pain? Is God still good then?

Yes. Absolutely. Unchangingly.

God's goodness is not based on our circumstances; it's rooted in His nature. He is always good, because He is good. From the beginning of time, His goodness has flowed through His actions: in how He forgave Adam and Eve, how He delivered the Israelites, how He sent His only Son to save us, and how He walks with us daily through grace, mercy, and blessings.

His grace gives us what we don't deserve ~ salvation, favor, strength.

His mercy withholds what we do deserve ~ punishment, condemnation, separation.

And His blessings ~ They're His constant reminders that He sees us, provides for us, and delights in us.

Even in our lowest moments, His grace covers us. In our rebellion, His mercy chases us. And in our waiting, His blessings still find us. The truth is that God's goodness isn't seasonal it's eternal. We just have to learn to see it, even in unexpected ways.

When we live with the assurance that God is always good, our faith is no longer swayed by what we see but grounded in who He is.

David didn't say God's goodness and mercy might follow us, he said they will. That's the confidence we have as children of God. His goodness is not limited to Sundays, mountain-top experiences, or when we feel worthy. It's daily. It's faithful. And it never runs out.

"Surely goodness and mercy shall follow me all the days of my life: and I will dwell in the house of the Lord forever." Psalm 23:6 (KJV)

Heavenly Father, thank You for being good, not just sometimes, but all the time. Thank You for Your unending grace that lifts me up, Your tender mercy that forgives me, and Your blessings that remind me of Your love. Teach me to trust in Your goodness even when I can't see the full picture. Help me to live in a posture of praise, knowing that Your character never changes. Let my life be a testimony that You are good in the morning, in the waiting, and in the midnight hour. Remind me that Your grace is enough, Your mercy is new every morning, and Your blessings are beyond what I could earn. I give You all glory and honor. In Jesus' name I pray, Amen and To God Be The Glory!

APRIL 24. - "A PRAYER FOR THE STRUGGLING"

Some days are heavy. Some battles aren't visible. And some people are walking through storms they never speak of. It's in these quiet, often unseen moments of struggle that our hearts are called to intercede for others. To carry their names before God when they may not have the strength to pray for themselves.

Whether it's a friend battling anxiety, a loved one dealing with loss, or someone just trying to make it through the day without breaking, the Lord sees every burden. He hears every unspoken cry. And He responds not always by removing the storm, but by giving grace to endure it, strength to rise, and hope to believe that better is still coming.

As believers, we are called to stand in the gap. Our prayers can go where our hands cannot. When we lift our loved ones to God, we place them in the care of the One who knows them completely and loves them unconditionally. He is the healer of hearts, the lifter of heads, and the anchor in every storm.

So today, let this be your sacred act of love: to pray for those still struggling. Whether they're facing financial hardship, emotional turmoil, spiritual battles, or physical illness, remember God is able. He is faithful. And He is near to all who call on Him.

There is power in compassion, and healing in prayer. When we carry others to the Lord in love, we become part of their healing story.

"Carry each other's burdens, and in this way you will fulfill the law of Christ." Galatians 6:2 (NIV)

Heavenly Father, today I come before You with a heavy heart for my friends and loved ones who are still struggling. You know every challenge they face. Every silent tear, every anxious thought, every weight that presses on their soul. Lord, meet them where they are. Wrap them in Your peace that surpasses understanding. Strengthen them for the tests of today and give them courage for tomorrow. Help them feel Your presence in the middle of their storm. Restore what has been broken. Renew what has been drained. Remind them they are not forgotten and that You are fighting their battles even now. Let them see glimpses of Your goodness in small ways and know that better days are ahead. Use me, Lord, as a vessel of encouragement, compassion, and support. Let my words uplift and my prayers cover. For every struggling heart, I speak peace, provision, healing, and hope in the name of Jesus. Amen and To God Be The Glory!

APRIL 25. - "THE WISDOM OF SILENCE"

In a world driven by opinions, arguments, and noise, silence is often misunderstood as weakness. Yet, in God's Word, silence is frequently a mark of wisdom, restraint, and spiritual maturity. There is a time to speak, but there is also a time to be still, especially when dealing with foolishness.

A fool, according to Scripture, is someone who rejects wisdom, despises correction, and acts in arrogance. Engaging in endless debates or trying to prove your point to someone unwilling to hear the truth is not only exhausting, but it can also pull you out of character and away from peace. That's why silence, in certain moments, is not avoidance, it is strength under control.

When Jesus stood before Pilate and His accusers, He didn't argue or defend Himself with long speeches. He remained silent not because He lacked authority, but because He possessed it. His silence revealed a deep trust in the Father's will and a refusal to be drawn into fruitless conflict.

Choosing silence doesn't mean you're surrendering to the foolish, it means you're refusing to lower your standard to meet their chaos. You're protecting your peace and honoring God's wisdom. It takes more strength to hold your tongue than to win an argument.

"Do not answer a fool according to his folly, or you yourself will be just like him."
Proverbs 26:4 (NIV)

This scripture reminds us that responding to foolishness on the fool's level only makes us look like them. Instead, we are called to be slow to speak, quick to listen, and always guided by the Holy Spirit in how and when we respond.

Father God, thank You for the wisdom found in Your Word. In a world full of noise and conflict, it teaches me the strength of silence. Help me to discern when to speak and when to hold my peace. Give me self-control to walk away from foolish arguments that waste my energy and disturb my spirit. Help me to imitate Jesus in His confidence, grace, and wisdom knowing that I don't have to prove anything to anyone when I am secure in You. May my silence speak louder than any words when it comes to protecting my peace and living out Your truth. Lord, help me to remain humble, calm, and full of grace—even in the face of provocation. Let my response, or lack of it, reflect Your heart and not my emotions. In Jesus' name I pray, Amen and To God Be The Glory!

APRIL 26. - "FAITH BEYOND LOGIC"

This phrase, often attributed to Albert Einstein, speaks to the power of thinking beyond limits. Logic has its place, it helps us make sound decisions, understand processes, and navigate the natural world. But there is a realm where logic ends, and faith begins. And for believers, that's where God often does His greatest work.

God is not confined to human logic. His ways are higher, His plans greater, and His timing perfect, though often beyond our understanding. Many of the most miraculous moments in Scripture defied logic:

- Moses parting the Red Sea,
- A virgin giving birth to the Savior,
- Jesus walking on water,
- The dead being raised to life.

None of these things make sense through human reasoning. But they became reality through divine power and faith.

Imagination, when surrendered to God, becomes a vision of what can be through Him. Faith-filled imagination helps us dream bigger, pray bolder, and walk confidently toward a future that doesn't yet exist. It's not about fantasy, it's about believing that with God, all things are possible (Matthew 19:26).

If we only operate by what is logical, we will limit ourselves to what we can control. But when we lean into God's vision for our lives through faith, creativity, and trust, we open ourselves to everywhere He wants to take us. God wants to take you beyond the predictable and into the extraordinary. Trust Him with your dreams. Surrender your logic when He calls you to step into faith. Because when imagination is combined with trust in God, the possibilities are limitless.

"Now to Him who is able to do immeasurably more than all we ask or imagine, according to His power that is at work within us." Ephesians 3:20 (NIV)

Heavenly Father, Thank You for giving me a mind to reason and a heart to dream. Teach me to trust You beyond what makes sense. Help me to lean not on my own understanding, but to acknowledge You in all my ways. Fill my heart with holy imagination that comes from Your Spirit, not my fear. Let me dream boldly, pray courageously, and follow faithfully even when I don't have all the answers. I believe You are able to do far more than I could ever ask or imagine. Use my life for something greater than logic could ever explain. Lead me, guide me, stretch me. Take me not just from A to B, but everywhere You've purposed for me to go.

In Jesus' name I pray, Amen and To God Be The Glory!

APRIL 27. - "TEN SIMPLE BLESSINGS ~ ONE FAITHFUL GOD"

Sometimes we overlook the everyday blessings because we're waiting for the big breakthrough. But if we slow down and take inventory, we'll find that God has already filled our lives with more than enough.

1. Home – A place of shelter and belonging, whether grand or humble, is a refuge from the world.

2. Food – Daily provision is a reminder of God's faithfulness to care for our physical needs.

3. Kindness – Even one act of compassion is evidence that God's love still flows through people.

4. A heart with good wishes – A tender, hopeful heart reflects God's own nature in us.

5. Water – Clean water is a gift many don't have, yet it sustains life every single day.

6. Contentment – The peace of being grateful for what is, even as we pray for more.

7. Trying to be better – The desire to grow is proof that God is working within us.

8. A dream – Hope for the future keeps us moving forward with purpose.

9. Clean clothes – A simple reminder of dignity, self-respect, and provision.

10. Breath – The ultimate sign that God has given us another chance to live, love, and serve.

These blessings may not always seem miraculous, but they are the very threadwork of grace. God doesn't just show up in burning bushes or parted seas. He shows up in meals on the table, kind words from a friend, and the quiet moments when you remember, "I'm still here."

Everything we have—great or small—flows from His hand. Gratitude opens our eyes to see it. When we pause to count the blessings that we often ignore, we find ourselves overwhelmed not by what we lack, but by how much we already have.

"Every good gift and every perfect gift is from above, coming down from the Father of lights, with whom there is no variation or shadow due to change." James 1:17 (ESV)

Gracious Father, thank You for the simple blessings that fill my life each day. Thank You for a home to rest in, food to nourish my body, and water that gives life. Thank You for kindness from others, a heart that still hopes, and dreams that remind me You're not finished with me yet. Even when life is hard, I can still find You in these daily gifts. Lord, help me to never take them for granted. Help me to live with a heart of thankfulness and contentment. Continue shaping me into who You've called me to be. Thank You for breath in my lungs and strength for another day. May I use every blessing not just for my comfort, but to bring You glory and to bless others. In Jesus' name I pray, Amen and To God Be The Glory!

APRIL 28. - "ONLY ASK OF THE FATHER"

In our human understanding, we often pray with limits. We ask God for what we think is possible or necessary. But God doesn't respond based on the size of our prayers, He responds according to the greatness of His power, love, and purpose.

When Solomon stepped into leadership, he didn't ask God for riches, influence, or victory over enemies. He asked for wisdom to govern the people well. His heart pleased the Lord so deeply that God not only gave him unmatched wisdom but added wealth, honor, and peace beyond measure (1 Kings 3:10–14). His request was kingdom-minded, and God answered in overflow.

Abraham longed for one thing, a son. In his old age, he simply wanted to see God's promise come to life through Isaac. But God's vision went far beyond one child. He promised Abraham that his descendants would outnumber the stars and that through him, all the nations of the earth would be blessed (Genesis 22:17–18). Abraham asked for a son; God gave him a legacy.

These stories show us that when our hearts are aligned with God's will, when we ask from a place of trust, faith, and surrender, God often responds with more than we imagined. Not because we deserve it, but because He delights in blessing His children.

You may be asking for healing, peace, direction, provision, or restoration. You might be hoping for just enough to get by. But remember, we serve a God who specializes in abundance, not just meeting needs, but exceeding them.

Let this be your hope today: God hears you, and He is working on more than what you've requested. Sometimes the answer comes in unexpected ways, but His heart is always to bless, to multiply, and to show Himself faithful.

"Now to Him who is able to do exceedingly abundantly above all that we ask or think, according to the power that works in us." Ephesians 3:20 (NKJV)

Gracious Father, thank You for being a God of abundance. Thank You for reminding me through the lives of Solomon and Abraham that You not only hear my prayers, but You respond in ways that go beyond what I can ask or imagine. Strengthen my faith as I wait, and help me to ask with boldness, trust, and humility. Lord, align my heart with Your will so that my desires reflect Your purpose. Where I ask for little, surprise me with much. Where I ask for survival, bring me into overflow. Where I ask for one breakthrough, release generations of blessing. I believe You are not only able, but willing to give more than I ask for, according to Your glory and grace. In Jesus' name I pray, Amen and To God Be The Glory!

APRIL 29. - "THE PURPOSE GOD CALLED YOU ~ TO WIN SOULS NOT ARGUMENTS"

In a world where debates rage on every platform, from dinner tables to social media feeds, it's easy to get drawn into the noise. Everyone wants to be right. Everyone wants to be heard. But as believers, our calling isn't to prove a point. it's to point people to Jesus.

God never instructed us to argue people into the kingdom. Instead, He called us to love, serve, and speak truth with grace. Arguments may win applause, but love wins hearts. Logic may challenge the mind, but only the Holy Spirit transforms the soul.

When Jesus encountered the woman at the well, He didn't shame her or argue theology, He offered her living water (John 4). When He saw Zacchaeus in a tree, He didn't call out his sins, He invited Himself to dinner (Luke 19). In both cases, transformation came through connection, not confrontation.

Too often, we confuse being "bold in faith" with being combative. But Paul reminds us in 2 Timothy 2:24–25 that "the Lord's servant must not be quarrelsome but must be kind to everyone, able to teach, and not resentful." Correction, when needed, should come with gentleness, because our goal isn't to win an argument, but to reflect the love of Christ.

Yes, truth matters. But truth without love becomes noise. Arguments may silence someone for a moment, but love opens their heart for eternity.

Wisdom is not proven by how loudly we speak, but by the fruit our lives produce. When we walk in love, peace, and patience, we become a tree of life, drawing people not to our opinions, but to the Savior.

"The fruit of the righteous is a tree of life, and the one who is wise saves lives." Proverbs 11:30 (NIV)

Father God, Thank You for calling me to be a vessel of Your love and truth. Forgive me for the times I've been more concerned with being right than being righteous. Teach me to reflect Your heart, to love first, listen well, and speak truth in grace. Lord, help me to resist the temptation to argue and instead focus on winning souls for Your kingdom. Let my life be a living testimony that draws others to You, not through debate, but through compassion, kindness, and Christlike humility. Fill my words with wisdom and my actions with love. Give me discernment to know when to speak and when to stay silent. Above all, may everything I do lead others closer to You. In Jesus' name I pray, Amen and To God Be The Glory!

APRIL 30. - "SNATCHED BY GRACE ~ WHEN JESUS GRABBED ME"

There are moments in our lives when it seems like the enemy has won. When sin has entangled us, when shame has silenced us, when darkness has surrounded us so tightly that escape feels impossible. We've all been there: stuck in patterns we couldn't break, places we never thought we'd go, or battles we thought we'd never survive. In those moments, the devil celebrates too soon. He thinks he's secured the victory over your life.

But then Jesus steps in.

Not because we were strong enough to climb out. Not because we were perfect enough to be worthy. But because grace grabbed us. Jesus reached into our pit, our pain, our brokenness and pulled us out. He didn't wait until we got it all together. He came while we were still trapped, still hurting, and still falling.

That's the power of the gospel. When the devil thought he had the final say, Jesus declared, "It is finished." When Satan rejoiced over your defeat, Jesus redeemed your story. He didn't just rescue you, He claimed you. He made you His. He turned your shame into testimony and your scars into strength.

Now you walk, not as one barely escaping the fire, but as one sealed by grace, covered in mercy, and walking in the power of a Savior who never let you go.

God is not just a lifter ~ He is a rescuer. When others gave up on you, when even you gave up on yourself, Jesus stepped in and said, "You are mine."

"He lifted me out of the slimy pit, out of the mud and mire; he set my feet on a rock and gave me a firm place to stand." Psalm 40:2 (NIV)

Lord Jesus, thank You for grabbing me when I was too weak to grab hold of You. Thank You for reaching into the mess of my life and pulling me out with mercy in Your hands. The devil thought he had me, but You had a greater plan. You never let me go, even when I let go of hope. Lord, help me never forget the power of Your rescue. Let my life be a living testimony of how You save, redeem, and restore. Strengthen me to walk in freedom and use my story to reach others who feel trapped by the lies of the enemy. Thank You for the cross. Thank You for grace. Thank You for grabbing me ~ You saved me. In Jesus' name I pray, Amen and To God Be The Glory!

MAY INTRODUCTION

As we turn the pages into the month of May, we find ourselves deep within the heart of spring. A season of growth, renewal, and reflection. Just as nature flourishes around us, this is a time for us to allow God's Word to blossom within our lives, especially as we confront the challenges that weigh heavily on our hearts.

Life's pressing problems do not wait for a convenient time to arise. They come in waves, unexpected illnesses, financial strain, broken relationships, overwhelming anxiety, and uncertain futures. But we do not face these trials alone, nor are we left without direction. God has already spoken. His Word is a lamp to our feet and a light to our path (Psalm 119:105), and it holds the answers we need. It's not always what we want, but it's always what is right, healing, and true.

This month's devotional journey is designed to bring biblical clarity to the complex issues we face daily. Each devotion aims to highlight a specific problem and pair it with God's timeless wisdom and hope. Whether you are seeking peace in your mind, direction in your decisions, or healing in your relationships, the answers can be found in the truth of Scripture.

Let May be a month of alignment where your soul syncs with God's voice. May every burden you carry be met with a promise. May every question you ask be met with His truth. And may every devotional remind you that God's Word is not just ancient text, but a living answer.

"Come to me, all you who are weary and burdened, and I will give you rest."
Matthew 11:28 (NIV)

Heavenly Father,

As we enter this new month, we open our hearts to Your wisdom. Help us not to lean on our own understanding but to seek Your answers in all things. As we face life's pressing problems, remind us that You are our ever-present help in times of trouble. Guide us through every devotional moment this month and let Your truth settle deep in our spirits. Let Your Word bring light to our darkness, peace to our storms, and direction to our confusion. In Jesus' name we pray, Amen and To God Be The Glory!

MAY 1. - "BOUNDARIES AND PEACE ~ CHOOSING TO LET GO"

There comes a time in our walk with God when we must make peace with the fact that not every broken relationship is meant to be mended, especially when we are not the ones who caused the damage. It's painful. It can feel unchristian. But it's also freeing.

The phrase "Unfortunately, I don't want to rebuild bonds I didn't break. You crossed the line, and I didn't, so I'm good," may sound harsh at first glance. But upon deeper reflection, it is a declaration of clarity, boundaries, and emotional responsibility. There is wisdom in knowing when to stop extending yourself for people who continuously mishandle your heart. Forgiveness is always necessary, but reconciliation is optional and sometimes, it's unwise.

Jesus Himself had boundaries. He didn't entrust Himself to everyone (John 2:24-25). He knew when to walk away from toxic environments, when to confront, and when to remain silent. As believers, we're often taught to keep the peace at all costs, but the Bible never instructs us to be doormats. Rather, we're called to be peacemakers, not peacekeepers. There is a difference. One avoids conflict to maintain false harmony. The other pursues truth and justice, even if it leads to separation.

"If it is possible, as far as it depends on you, live at peace with everyone."
Romans 12:18 (NIV)

This verse doesn't place all responsibility on your shoulders it says, "as far as it depends on you." If you've done your part and someone continues to betray your trust, cross your boundaries, or treat you with dishonor, you are not obligated to restore a relationship that has been repeatedly broken by someone else's actions.

Rebuilding a bond takes two people willing to own their faults and commit to change. If one party refuses, peace is still possible, it just may not include proximity. And that's okay. Releasing someone doesn't mean you don't love them. It means you love God, yourself, and your peace enough not to stay entangled in what He has released you from.

Father God, I thank You for the wisdom to know when to hold on and when to let go. I release the pressure to fix what I didn't break. Help me walk in truth and peace without guilt or bitterness. Teach me to forgive, but also to guard my heart. If reconciliation is Your will, prepare both hearts. But if the season has ended, help me to move forward with grace. Let my boundaries honor You, and may peace rule in my life. In Jesus' name, Amen and To God Be The Glory!

MAY 2. - "UNBREAKABLE STRENGTH"

"You can't break a person who gets their strength from God." This statement isn't pride, it's divine confidence. It is the quiet, unshakable assurance that no matter what life throws at you, the God within you is greater than the storm around you.

There are moments in life when people expect you to fall apart. After the betrayal, after the loss, after the diagnosis, after all the disappointment. But when your strength is rooted in God, your foundation is immovable. You may bend, but you won't break. You may cry, but you won't crumble. Why? Because your strength doesn't come from your circumstances, your own willpower, or the approval of others. It comes from the One who never changes.

God's strength is not just given in abundance, it's perfected in our weakness. That means even when you feel like you have nothing left, He steps in with more than enough. People may look at you and wonder how you're still standing, how you're still smiling, how you're still pushing forward. They won't understand it, and honestly, they don't have to. Because what's holding you together is invisible to the human eye but undeniable in its power. The presence of God.

When the enemy's plan was to break you, God's plan was to build you. When others left you, He stayed. When you felt forgotten, He remembered. When you were weak, He became your strength. That kind of divine reinforcement makes you unbreakable. Not because of who you are, but because of who He is in you.

"God is our refuge and strength, an ever-present help in trouble." Psalm 46:1 (NIV)

This verse is a powerful reminder that God isn't just strong, He is our strength. He's not far away or unavailable; He is ever-present ~ right in the thick of the struggle, the trial, the pressure. You're never alone, and because He is with you, you cannot be defeated.

Heavenly Father, thank You for being the source of my strength. When life gets heavy and the battle grows fierce, please remind me that I am not alone. Strengthen my heart, renew my mind, and keep my spirit anchored in You. Teach me to draw daily from Your well that never runs dry. Even when I feel weak, help me trust that Your power is working within me. Let the world see not my strength, but Yours shining through my life. I declare that because of You, I am unbreakable. In Jesus' name, Amen and To God Be The Glory!

MAY 3. - "STANDING IN THE GAP ~ MY PRAYER FOR FAMILY"

When those closest to us, our family, are going through difficult seasons, it affects our hearts deeply. Whether it's illness, financial hardship, emotional struggles, or spiritual battles, watching someone you love suffering, can leave you feeling helpless. But as believers, we are never without power, we have the gift of prayer.

Prayer is not our last resort; it is our first line of defense. It is how we partner with God to bring heaven's help into the lives of those we care about. When you pray for a family member in distress, you're not just speaking words into the air. You're calling on the God of comfort, provision, healing, and restoration to step into their situation with His mighty hand.

Sometimes your loved ones may be too weary or broken to pray for themselves. That's when your intercession becomes their covering. Like the friends who lowered the paralyzed man through the roof to get to Jesus (Mark 2:1–12), your prayers can carry them closer to the One who can do what no one else can. Your faith, standing in the gap, can move mountains on their behalf.

In times of crisis, your job is not to fix everything, it's to be faithful in prayer. Even if you can't be physically present, your prayers travel where your feet cannot. God sees. God hears. God moves.

We were never meant to walk alone. God created families not just by blood, but by spiritual bond. When one of us is hurting, all of us feel it. And when we lift one another up, we become the hands and heart of Christ in motion.

"Carry each other's burdens, and in this way you will fulfill the law of Christ."
Galatians 6:2 (NIV)

Heavenly Father, today I lift up to you every family member who is walking through a hard time. Lord, You know the burdens they carry, the silent tears, the heavy hearts, the unanswered questions. I ask You to meet them right where they are. Be their healer, their provider, their peace, and their strength. Surround them with Your presence and remind them they are not alone. Help them feel Your love in tangible ways. Open doors no man can shut, and give them clarity, wisdom, and endurance to make it through. If they are weak, be their strength. If they are discouraged, be their hope. Let Your grace cover every situation and bring beauty out of their pain. I trust You, Lord, to do what only You can do. Thank You for being faithful to my family, even in the fire. In Jesus' name, Amen and To God Be The Glory!

MAY 4. - "LETTING GO AND LETTING GOD"

There's a quiet strength in surrender. Not the kind of surrender that signals defeat, but the kind that declares: "God, I trust You more than I trust myself." When you've carried burdens that were never meant to be yours. Problems you couldn't solve, hurts you couldn't heal, and worries that drained your peace. There comes a moment when the only wise thing left to do is to let go.

"Today I'm letting go of problems, hurt, and worries, and putting it all in Your hands. I'm letting go." That is not just a statement, it's a decision. A holy release. It is an act of faith that acknowledges you were never created to carry everything alone.

We often try to manage our own chaos, fix our own pain, and control our outcomes, only to end up frustrated, anxious, and exhausted. But God invites us to bring it all to Him, not partially, not gradually, but fully. There is healing in the release. There is peace in the surrender. And there is power in handing it over to the One who holds the universe together and still knows every detail of your life.

Letting go doesn't mean you don't care. It means you care enough to give it to the One who can truly handle it. It's trusting God with your now, your next, and everything in between. He sees the wounds no one else sees, hears the cries no one else hears, and holds the answers no one else can offer.

Jesus doesn't offer more advice or more pressure, He offers rest. He invites you to come close, drop the heavy baggage at His feet, and receive what you've been missing: peace, strength, and reassurance that you are not alone.

"Come to Me, all you who are weary and burdened, and I will give you rest." Matthew 11:28 (NIV)

Father God, today I'm letting go. I release the weight of problems I cannot fix, the wounds that still hurt, and the worries that have kept me up at night. I lay them all at Your feet, trusting that You are more than able to carry what's too heavy for me. I surrender the need to control and the fear of what's next. Fill me with Your peace and remind me that You are working even when I can't see it. Heal what is broken, restore what is lost, and guide me forward in faith. I don't need all the answers, I just need to know You're with me. And You are. Thank You for being the safe place where I can let go. In Jesus' name, Amen and To God Be The Glory!

MAY 5. - "MY GOD IS GOOD ALL THE TIME"

Life is full of seasons. Some marked by joy and abundance, and others by sorrow and struggle. But through it all, one truth remains unshaken: God is good. His goodness is not a fleeting emotion or a circumstantial favor. His goodness is an unchanging part of His nature.

When life is going well, doors are opening, prayers are being answered, and peace fills your soul, it's easy to say, "God is good." But what about when life turns in the other direction? When prayers seem unanswered, grief enters, and nothing makes sense? Is God still good?

The answer is a resounding yes. God's faithfulness does not depend on how we feel. It is anchored in who He is. His love is constant, His presence unceasing, and His promises unfailing. Whether you are standing on the mountaintop or walking through the valley, the same God is with you. The same goodness follows you. The same mercy sustains you.

When we understand that God's faithfulness isn't based on our circumstances but on His character, we learn to trust Him more deeply. We worship in the storm, not because we like the storm, but because we know who is in control of it. We lift our hands in brokenness, not because we aren't hurting, but because we know healing is coming.

God's goodness isn't seasonal, it's eternal. And His faithfulness stretches from generation to generation. When we can say, "God is good," in both the highs and the lows, we're not ignoring reality, we're declaring a greater one: God is who He says He is, and that's always.

"The Lord is good, a stronghold in the day of trouble; and He knows those who trust in Him."

Nahum 1:7 (NKJV)

This verse reminds us that God's goodness isn't just for the good days. He is our refuge in the day of trouble. He doesn't abandon us when things get tough. He stands with us, walks beside us, and carries us when we're too weak to walk.

Faithful Father, thank You for being the same yesterday, today, and forever. In every season of life, whether full of joy or full of tears You are good. Help me to trust Your heart even when I don't understand Your hand. Let me rest in the truth that Your faithfulness never changes, no matter what my situation looks like. When I'm standing on the mountaintop, may I praise You. When I'm walking through the valley, may I cling to You. Teach me to see Your goodness not just in what You do, but in who You are. Thank You for being my anchor, my refuge, and my forever faithful God. In Jesus' name, Amen and To God Be The Glory!

MAY 6. - "LOVE YOURSELF A LITTLE EXTRA ~ GIVE YOURSELF GRACE"

There are seasons in life when the weight of responsibility seems too heavy to bear. You're juggling commitments, silently carrying emotional burdens, and showing up for others even when your own heart is weary. It's in these moments that God gently whispers: "Love yourself a little extra right now." Not out of selfishness but out of wisdom, restoration, and alignment with His grace.

We often extend compassion freely to others but struggle to give it to ourselves. We hold ourselves to impossible standards, expecting perfection while ignoring our humanity. But God doesn't demand perfection, He desires surrender. He invites us into a rhythm of grace, where we rest in His sufficiency rather than strive in our own strength.

Consider this: if God, who is perfect, shows you mercy, who are you to withhold it from yourself?

Jesus sees what others overlook. He knows the thoughts you hide behind your smile, the pain you press down just to get through the day, and the fears that sneak into your mind at night. And still, He offers you rest and not just physical, but soul deep rest.

You don't have to carry it alone. You don't have to have all the answers. You don't have to be everything for everyone. What you do have to do is show yourself grace, lean into God's presence, and trust that He is working through your effort even when you can't see it.

Loving yourself a little extra means pausing for breath. It means giving yourself permission to be human. It means acknowledging that doing your best is enough. Most importantly, it means remembering that God is proud of you. Not only for what you've accomplished, but because you are His.

"Come to me, all you who are weary and burdened, and I will give you rest. Take my yoke upon you and learn from me, for I am gentle and humble in heart, and you will find rest for your souls. For my yoke is easy and my burden is light." Matthew 11:28-30 (NIV)

Heavenly Father, I thank You for seeing me when I feel invisible and for knowing the burdens I carry in silence. Lord, I'm balancing more than I can manage alone, and yet You promise rest, peace, and grace. Teach me to love myself with the same compassion You give me. Help me to be gentle with my heart, patient with my progress, and faithful to come to You when I feel overwhelmed. Let me find rest in Your presence and strength in Your promises. Thank You for walking with me, holding me up, and reminding me that I don't have to do this life alone. In Jesus' name I pray, Amen and To God Be The Glory!

MAY 7. - "SOME BATTLES ARE BETTER LEFT TO THE LORD"

There's a natural urge in all of us to defend ourselves. To speak up when we've been misunderstood, to clap back when we've been disrespected, and to correct when we've been falsely accused. The desire to make things right on our own is strong, especially when our name, integrity, or heart is on the line.

But wisdom reminds us that not every situation demands our response. Sometimes, silence is strength, humility is louder than words, and the greatest show of faith is standing still and letting God take control.

When emotions are high and justice feels far away, it takes spiritual maturity to pause and say, "Lord, this battle is Yours." It's not a sign of weakness to walk away, it's wisdom. It's not cowardice to remain quiet, it's courage that trusts God more than self.

"The Lord will fight for you; you need only to be still." Exodus 14:14 (NIV)

This verse was spoken to the Israelites as Pharaoh's army pursued them. They were trapped between a vast sea and a powerful enemy. Panic and fear rose, but God gave them a divine strategy: be still. In the natural, it made no sense. But spiritually, it was the path to miraculous deliverance.

And so it is with us.

Sometimes, the most powerful thing we can do is stand back. Instead of explaining ourselves to people committed to misunderstanding us, we rest in the confidence that God knows the full story. Instead of retaliating in anger, we walk in grace and allow God to defend us. We stop trying to "win" and choose instead to trust that God will vindicate in His time and His way. This is not about silence rooted in fear, it's about peace rooted in faith.

Father God, I come to You with a heart that longs for justice, understanding, and peace. There are situations where I want to speak out, defend myself, or take matters into my own hands. But today, I choose to trust You. Teach me when to speak and when to be silent. Give me the strength to walk in humility and the faith to let You fight on my behalf. Help me release the desire for control, and rest in the assurance that You are working all things together for my good. Thank You for being my Defender, my Shield, and my Peace. In Jesus' name I pray, Amen and To God Be The Glory!

MAY 8. - "THE CALLING ATTRACTS THE ATTACK ~ BUT YOU HAVE AUTHORITY"

When God places a calling and anointing on your life, you become a threat to the enemy's agenda. You may wonder why certain battles have intensified, why opposition rises every time you take a step forward, or why discouragement hits just when you begin to walk in obedience. It's not a coincidence, it's spiritual warfare.

The truth is, the more anointed you are, the more the enemy tries to distract, delay, or destroy you. But here's the good news: he may try, but he cannot win.

The Word does not say that weapons won't form, it says that they won't prosper. That means the enemy may launch attacks, but God has already declared the outcome. Victory is yours. The enemy is already defeated because of the finished work of Jesus Christ.

You are not fighting for victory, but you are fighting for victory. As a child of God, you carry divine authority. When the enemy whispers lies, you respond with truth. When fear creeps in, you answer with faith. When setbacks come, you press forward with confidence, not in yourself, but in the God who called and anointed you.

The same Spirit that raised Christ from the dead lives in you (Romans 8:11). That power isn't passive. It speaks, it moves, it wars, and it wins. So don't let the attack make you retreat. Let it confirm you're headed in the right direction. Keep moving. Keep praying. Keep proclaiming the victory.

"No weapon formed against you shall prosper, and every tongue which rises against you in judgment You shall condemn. This is the heritage of the servants of the Lord, and their righteousness is from Me," says the Lord. Isaiah 54:17 (NKJV)

Father God, I Thank You for the calling and anointing on my life. I understand that it brings attacks, but I also understand that You've given me victory and authority over the enemy. Help me to stand firm in faith, even when the battle is fierce. Remind me that no weapon formed against me will prosper, and that every lie of the enemy must fall. Strengthen my spirit, renew my mind, and keep my heart anchored in truth. I will not stop. I will keep moving forward, fully armored, fully empowered, and fully convinced that You are fighting for me. In Jesus' victorious name I pray, Amen and To God Be The Glory!

MAY 9. - "MAKING THE NAME OF JESUS KNOWN"

In a world where personal branding, recognition, and influence often dominate the conversation, it's easy to fall into the trap of seeking the spotlight for ourselves, even while doing the work of the Lord. But as followers of Christ, our true purpose is not self-promotion; it is Christ-exaltation. Everything we do should point back to Jesus. Not to our talents, our platforms, or our achievements, but to the One who saved us, called us, and empowers us.

The heart of true ministry is humility. It's saying, "Not to us, Lord, but to Your name be the glory." Our gifts, our calling, and our opportunities are not meant to build monuments to ourselves but altars to Him.

When we make our lives about Christ and not ourselves, we shift the focus from ego to eternity. Our aim is not applause, but impact. Not fame, but faithfulness. Not legacy, but Lordship ~ His Lordship.

Let us continually examine our motives: Are we seeking to be seen, or are we seeking to make Jesus seen? Are we living to make our name known, or are we living to make His name great?

When the spotlight finds you, reflect it upward. When opportunities come, use them as platforms to proclaim Him. And when recognition fades, rest knowing that your reward is eternal.

"He must increase, but I must decrease." John 3:30 (ESV)

These were the words of John the Baptist, a man who had his own followers, his own voice, and his own ministry. Yet, when Jesus appeared, John joyfully stepped back so that Christ could step forward. That's the posture of a true servant of God: the willingness to fade into the background so that Jesus can shine in the foreground.

Heavenly Father, thank You for choosing me to be a vessel for Your glory. Forgive me for the times when I've made it more about myself than about You. Lord, help me to decrease so that You may increase in every area of my life. Let my words, my work, and my witness point others to Jesus. Keep my heart humble and my spirit aligned with Your will. I pray everything I do brings honor to Your name alone. Use me not to build my own name, but to magnify Yours because it is only the name of Jesus that saves, heals, and transforms. In Jesus' name I pray, Amen and To God Be The Glory!

MAY 10. - "A MOTHER'S DAY PRAYER"

Motherhood is a divine calling, a sacred responsibility, and a reflection of God's nurturing heart. Whether you are a biological mother, spiritual mother, or a woman who has mentored and nurtured others, your role carries eternal significance. On Mother's Day, we pause to honor the love, sacrifice, and faithfulness that mothers embody.

A mother's love is unique. It mirrors God's unconditional love, steadfast, patient, and unwavering. Proverbs 31:28–29 (KJV) reminds us: "Her children arise up and call her blessed; her husband also, and he praiseth her. Many daughters have done virtuously, but thou excellest them all."

This scripture highlights the impact of a mother's life. The seeds of faith, character, and love sown by a mother influence generations. Even in times of fatigue, uncertainty, or challenge, a mother's prayers, encouragement, and guidance echo long after her words are spoken.

A Mother's Day prayer is not only for children to honor mothers, it is a time for mothers to commit their families, their lives, and their hearts to God. It is a moment to seek wisdom, patience, and strength from Him, recognizing that apart from His guidance, the weight of motherhood can be overwhelming. It is a prayer that acknowledges both the blessings and the challenges of this holy role.

Today, whether you are receiving honor as a mother or praying for the mothers in your life, let this be a moment of spiritual reflection and thanksgiving. Let it be a reminder that every act of love, no matter how small, is seen by God and treasured in heaven.

Heavenly Father, I lift up all mothers today. I thank You for the gift of their love, strength, and guidance. Bless them with wisdom to lead with grace, patience to nurture in every season, and strength to persevere through challenges. Surround them with Your peace, protection, and joy. May their hearts be encouraged, their efforts honored, and their lives continue to reflect Your goodness. Lord, let Your favor rest upon them, and let their children rise to call them blessed. We thank You for the gift of motherhood and for the ways mothers reflect Your love to the world.

Amen and To God Be The Glory!

MAY 11. - "SITTING WITH THE BROKEN"

In a world obsessed with status, recognition, and influence, we often measure greatness by who we stand with, celebrities, leaders, or people with power. But the heart of Christ doesn't celebrate proximity to greatness; it honors compassion toward the hurting. True spiritual maturity isn't proven by how high we climb, but by how low we're willing to go to lift others up.

The phrase, "I'm not interested in whether you stood with the great. I'm interested in whether you sat with the broken," reflects the very nature of Jesus Himself. He consistently chose the company of the brokenhearted, the outcast, the sinner, and the forgotten. He didn't avoid their pain, He entered it.

When others crossed the street to avoid the leper, Jesus reached out and touched him. When religious leaders avoided the sinful woman, Jesus allowed her tears to fall at His feet. He sat with the Samaritan woman at the well, dined with tax collectors, and wept at Lazarus' tomb. Jesus didn't seek a throne among the powerful; He knelt beside the crushed in spirit.

To follow Him is to do the same.

Sitting with the broken isn't glamorous. It often goes unnoticed. But it reflects a Christlike heart. When we sit with someone in their grief, listen without judging, pray for someone others have abandoned, or show kindness to the outcast, we are doing holy work. We are becoming the hands and heart of Jesus in a hurting world.

This kind of love requires humility, patience, and a willingness to be uncomfortable. But this is the Gospel in action. We were once the broken ones Jesus sat with. He picked us up with grace and healed us with truth. Now He calls us to do likewise.

"The Lord is near to the brokenhearted and saves the crushed in spirit." Psalm 34:18 (ESV)

Lord Jesus, Teach us to value what You value. Let us not be impressed by power or distracted by fame but drawn to the places where Your heart dwells among the hurting, the forgotten, and the broken. Give us eyes to see the wounded around us and hearts willing to respond. Break down our pride and comfort so that we may sit with others in their pain, offering Your love, Your hope, and Your peace. Remind us daily that You sat with us in our brokenness and still do. Help us carry that same compassion to others. In Your name we pray, Amen and To God Be The Glory!

MAY 12. - "HOW TO SURRENDER TO GOD'S WILL"

Surrendering to God's will is not a passive act. It is an intentional daily choice to trust in the sovereignty and goodness of the One who sees all, knows all, and works all things for our good. Yet, for many of us, surrendering is one of the hardest things to do. Why? Because it requires us to give up control, lay down our pride, and place our trust in a plan we cannot fully see.

Let's walk through some key steps to truly surrendering to God's will:

1. Trust God's Plan

When life doesn't go the way we envisioned, it's tempting to doubt whether God is truly working on our behalf. But faith reminds us that His ways are higher and better than ours. Trusting God's plan means believing He is working, even when we don't understand the "why" or "how."

"'For I know the plans I have for you,' declares the Lord, 'plans to prosper you and not to harm you, plans to give you hope and a future.'" Jeremiah 29:11 (NIV)

2. Release the Need for Control

Control is often rooted in fear, the fear of failure, pain, or uncertainty. But surrender means opening our clenched fists and allowing God to take the lead. What we try to control, we often idolize. Letting go is not weakness; it's obedience.

3. Seek God's Guidance

Surrender does not mean becoming passive. It means actively seeking God's direction through prayer, Scripture, and wise counsel. When we acknowledge Him in all our ways, He promises to direct our paths.

"Trust in the Lord with all your heart and lean not on your own understanding; in all your ways submit to him, and he will make your paths straight." Proverbs 3:5–6 (NIV)

4. Accept God's Correction

Sometimes surrender comes through correction. When God reveals areas where we are off course. He's not punishing us; He's guiding us back to His will. A surrendered heart accepts correction and grows from it.

"Those whom I love I rebuke and discipline. So be earnest and repent."

Revelation 3:19 (NIV)

5. Cast Your Anxieties on Him

Anxiety often signals that we are carrying burdens never meant for us. Surrender means casting those anxieties onto the Lord and trusting Him to sustain us.

"Cast all your anxiety on him because he cares for you." 1 Peter 5:7 (NIV)

6. Acknowledge God's Sovereignty

At the core of surrender is the belief that God is sovereign—completely in control, perfectly wise, endlessly good. Even when life feels chaotic, God's throne is never shaken.

"The Lord has established his throne in heaven, and his kingdom rules over all."

Psalm 103:19 (NIV)

True surrender is not a one-time event. It is a lifestyle, a constant yielding of our desires, expectations, and plans to the will of a loving and holy God. As we surrender, we make room for peace, direction, and transformation. It's in letting go that we find freedom.

Heavenly Father, I come before You today with open hands and a willing heart. Teach me how to surrender fully to Your will. Help me to trust Your plan even when it doesn't make sense. Free me from the illusion of control and guide me in Your truth. Give me the courage to accept Your correction, the faith to cast my anxieties on You, and the humility to acknowledge Your sovereignty over every part of my life. Let Your will be done, not mine. Mold me, lead me, and use me for Your glory. In Jesus' name, Amen and To God Be The Glory!

MAY 13. - "GOD STILL USES THE BROKEN"

The woman at the well is one of the most powerful testimonies of grace, restoration, and purpose in Scripture. Her story reminds us that no matter how complicated our past may be, Jesus is still willing and more than able to use us for His glory.

This woman had been married five times and was living with a man who was not her husband. She was rejected by society, judged by others, and likely carried shame that felt impossible to shake. She went to draw water at the well in the heat of the day avoiding others, hiding in plain sight. Yet, it was at that exact moment that Jesus met her.

He didn't avoid her. He didn't condemn her. He engaged her in conversation, revealed His identity as the Messiah, and offered her "living water", eternal life and complete restoration. What happened next was astounding: she left her water jar, ran into the town, and became one of the first evangelists. This once-rejected woman led others to Jesus!

The world may count you out, label you by your mistakes, or reduce you to your past. But Jesus looks at you and sees purpose. He sees your potential, not your failures. He offers restoration, not rejection. The woman at the well was not disqualified by her brokenness, she was positioned by it to display God's grace.

If you've been told you're too messed up, too far gone, or too broken to be used by God, remember this: Jesus doesn't consult your past to determine your future. His mercy rewrites your story. He doesn't just tolerate you; He chooses you.

Your history does not cancel your destiny.

"Many of the Samaritans from that town believed in him because of the woman's testimony, 'He told me everything I ever did." John 4:39 (NIV)

Lord Jesus, Thank You for seeing beyond my past and calling me into purpose. Help me to release the shame, the labels, and the lies I've believed about myself. Remind me daily that You are the God who redeems, restores, and repurposes broken lives. Use my story to bring others to You, just like the woman at the well. Help me to walk boldly in the truth that I am loved, forgiven, and chosen by You. Let nothing from my past hinder what You desire to do through me. In Jesus' name I pray, Amen and To God Be The Glory!

MAY 14. - "LOVING ~ FORGIVING ~ LETTING GO"

One of the most difficult truths in the journey of faith is learning that you can love someone, forgive them, even wish them well and still move on without them. As believers, we are called to love and extend grace, but that does not always mean we must stay in relationships or environments that hinder our growth, rob us of peace, or keep us bound to cycles God is calling us out of.

Letting go is not the same as giving up. It's not bitterness, resentment, or hate, its wisdom, obedience, and healing. When Jesus taught us to forgive, He never said we must remain entangled with those who consistently harm us, dishonor us, or refuse to change. Sometimes, moving forward without someone is a holy act of surrender that protects your peace and makes room for God's best.

You can forgive from a distance. You can love without reconnecting. You can want what's best for them while recognizing that staying may no longer be what's best for you. Forgiveness is a command; reconciliation is a process and sometimes, it's not meant to happen in full, especially when boundaries are repeatedly violated or trust is broken beyond repair.

Jesus Himself walked away from certain people. He loved perfectly, forgave completely, but still chose distance when necessary because His mission could not be compromised. There's a time to stay and a time to step away, and both can honor God when done with prayer, humility, and grace.

Don't let guilt keep you tied to what God is freeing you from. You can move forward, healed and whole, and still walk in love.

"If it is possible, as far as it depends on you, live at peace with everyone."
Romans 12:18 (NIV)

This scripture recognizes that peace isn't always about staying. Sometimes peace requires distance. And that's okay.

Father God, I thank You for teaching me that love and forgiveness don't always mean holding on. Help me to release relationships that are no longer aligned with Your will. Give me the strength to set boundaries in love, and the grace to forgive fully without carrying bitterness. Teach me how to move forward with peace in my heart and compassion in my spirit. Heal me in the places where letting go has been painful and remind me that You are leading me into greater freedom, deeper healing, and closer intimacy with You. In Jesus' name I pray, Amen and To God Be The Glory!

MAY 15. - "CONFORMED TO HIS IMAGE"

"For whom he did foreknow, he also did predestinate to be conformed to the image of his Son, that he might be the firstborn among many brethren." Romans 8:29 (KJV)

Romans 8:29 is a powerful reminder that God's purpose for our lives goes far beyond momentary comfort or earthly success. His ultimate desire is that we be conformed to the image of His Son, Jesus Christ. This process known as sanctification is not always easy, but it is divine, intentional, and full of eternal significance.

When Paul writes that God "foreknew" us, he is pointing to the intimate knowledge and sovereign love God had for us even before the foundation of the world. And in that divine foreknowledge, He "predestinated" us, not to destruction, but to transformation. God's goal is not just to save us from sin, but to shape us into the likeness of Jesus. Every trial we endure, every victory we celebrate, every lesson we learn is part of the refining process to make us more like Him.

To be conformed to Christ's image means we begin to reflect His character, His humility, His obedience, His love, His purity, His patience, and His faithfulness. It's a lifelong journey. Some days we may feel like we're far from that image, but God is patient. He is the Master Potter, shaping us with wisdom and love, using every circumstance good or bad for our growth and His glory (Romans 8:28).

This verse also reminds us that Jesus is "the firstborn among many brethren." He paved the way. We are not walking a path unknown to Him, He has gone before us. And because of Him, we are now part of the family of God. What an honor to be counted among His brethren and called to look more like Him with each passing day!

So, take heart if you feel stretched, tested, or refined, know that you are being formed. Not forgotten, not abandoned, but shaped into something holy.

Father God, I thank You for Your perfect plan for my life. Thank You for loving me enough not just to save me, but to transform me. Shape me into the image of Jesus, even when the process is uncomfortable. Teach me to reflect His love, His humility, and His obedience in all I do. Help me not to resist Your refining hand but to yield to it, knowing You are doing a greater work in me. Let my life be a reflection of Christ so that others may see Him through me. In Jesus' name I pray, Amen and To God Be The Glory!

MAY 16. - "YOU CAN'T BE BOTH THE BRIDE AND THE SIDE CHICK"

In our modern culture, relationships are often defined by divided loyalties and hidden compromises. But when it comes to our spiritual lives, God demands undivided devotion. The phrase "You can't be the bride of Christ and the side chick of Satan at the same time" is a bold but necessary reminder that spiritual adultery is real, and God will not share His people with the enemy.

The Bible often compares our relationship with God to a marriage. As believers, we are called the bride of Christ, a people set apart, chosen, and adorned with righteousness to be presented without blemish to our Bridegroom. This is not a casual relationship; it is a covenant sealed with the blood of Jesus. Just as no spouse would accept half-hearted love, neither will God.

You can't profess to love Jesus and still flirt with sin. You can't lift holy hands in worship on Sunday and live in compromise Monday through Saturday. Christ died not only to save us from the penalty of sin but also to free us from the power of it. Being the bride of Christ means walking in purity, loyalty, and commitment. It means refusing to entertain the enemy's advances, no matter how subtle or appealing they may appear.

Ask yourself honestly: Are there areas in your life where you're trying to keep one foot in the world and one foot in the Kingdom? God sees the heart and He desires all of it.

Let's recommit today. Let's be fully His. The world may offer temporary pleasure, but Christ offers eternal joy, peace, and love that never fails.

"Ye adulterers and adulteresses, know ye not that the friendship of the world is enmity with God? whosoever therefore will be a friend of the world is the enemy of God."

James 4:4 (KJV)

James uses strong language to confront believers who try to walk with God while holding hands with the world. The term "adulterers and adulteresses" isn't about physical unfaithfulness, but spiritual infidelity when we give our hearts to things or people that oppose the will of God.

Heavenly Father, please forgive me for the times I have compromised my walk with You. Cleanse me from divided affections and teach me to love You with all my heart, soul, mind, and strength. I no longer want to live with one foot in the world and one in Your Kingdom. I choose You fully, completely, and unashamedly. Help me walk as Your faithful bride, dressed in righteousness, waiting eagerly for Your return. Thank You for Your grace and patience, and for never giving up on me. In Jesus' name I pray, Amen and To God Be The Glory!

MAY 17. - "YOU CAN'T HAVE IT BOTH WAYS"

Worship is more than a song, a raised hand, or a church attendance record. True worship flows from a heart aligned with the heart of God, and the very essence of God is love. To say we love God but mistreat people is to contradict the foundation of the faith we claim to follow. The phrase "You can't treat people like garbage and worship at the same time because God is love" confronts a dangerous disconnect that too often creeps into our spiritual lives.

It's impossible to worship in spirit and in truth while harboring hatred, unforgiveness, or cruelty. Jesus Himself said in Matthew 5:23–24 that if you're offering a gift at the altar and remember someone has something against you, you must first go and be reconciled before presenting your worship. God does not separate how we treat people from how we treat Him.

We can sing beautifully, serve faithfully, and pray eloquently. But if our hearts are cold, harsh, or indifferent toward others, our worship becomes hollow. People are made in the image of God. When we dishonor them, we dishonor Him.

This isn't a call to perfection, it's a call to sincerity. A heart of true worship is a heart that loves deeply, forgives quickly, and treats others with compassion and dignity, even when it's hard. Love doesn't mean enabling sin or avoiding truth, but it always means approaching others with the heart of Christ.

So today, let this phrase serve as a heart-check. Do your worship and your relationships align? Do your songs to God echo in the way you speak to others? May we not just sing about love but live it.

"He that loveth not knoweth not God; for God is love." 1 John 4:8 (KJV)

This verse doesn't say that God is loving sometimes or that He acts lovingly, it says God is love. It's His very nature. So, when we, as children of God, fail to reflect love in how we treat others, we are misrepresenting Him. We are claiming intimacy with a God we do not resemble.

Heavenly Father, please search my heart and reveal any place where I've failed to love others as You have loved me. Forgive me for the times I've worshipped You with my lips while mistreating others with my actions. Help me to reflect Your love in every relationship, every word, and every decision. May my worship not just be in songs and prayers, but in how I treat the people You've placed in my life. Make me a vessel of Your love so that others may see You through me. In Jesus' name I pray, Amen and To God Be The Glory!

MAY 18. - WHEN EVERYTHING FALLS APART ~ TRUST GOD"

There are seasons in life when everything seems to unravel. Relationships break, health declines, finances dry up, or grief strikes without warning. In those moments, nothing makes sense. You pray, you cry, you question, and sometimes you wonder if God is even there. But in the stillness of your pain, when you have no answers and your strength is gone, there is power in simply whispering, "God, I know it's Your plan, just help me through it."

This is not a sign of weakness. It is the greatest display of faith.

When life crumbles, you don't need to have the answers. You just need to know the One who does. Trust doesn't erase the pain, but it anchors your soul to hope. Saying, "Lord, I don't get it, but I know You're in it," is not resignation it's worship. It's an offering of brokenness, laid at the feet of a faithful God who specializes in restoring what's been shattered.

Throughout Scripture, we see faithful men and women walk through darkness before stepping into purpose. Joseph was betrayed and imprisoned before becoming a ruler. Job lost everything before receiving double restoration. Even Jesus had to endure the cross before the resurrection.

So, when your heart is heavy and your path unclear, just close your eyes and say, "God, I trust Your plan. Please help me through it." He hears you. He sees you. And He will bring you through.

"Trust in the Lord with all thine heart; and lean not unto thine own understanding. In all thy ways acknowledge him, and he shall direct thy paths." Proverbs 3:5–6 (KJV)

These verses remind us that faith doesn't require full understanding; it requires full surrender. God's plan is often hidden behind seasons of confusion and chaos, yet His hand never leaves us. His promises still stand when our world is falling apart.

Father God, I don't always understand what's happening in my life. Sometimes it feels like everything is falling apart and I'm barely holding on. But today, I choose to trust You. I believe that even when I can't see the way, You are guiding me. Give me strength to keep going and faith to believe in Your purpose. Help me to rest in Your promises and surrender my fears. Carry me through every storm and let my heart remain anchored in You. In Jesus' name, Amen and To God Be The Glory!

MAY 19. - "WHEN GOD RELOCATES YOU FOR GROWTH"

There are times in life when God disrupts our plans, moves us out of comfort zones, and places us in unfamiliar territory. It can be unsettling and even painful. But what if that shift is not a punishment, but divine protection? What if it's not rejection, but redirection?

The truth is, sometimes God chooses to move you, relocate you, or reposition you simply because the seed He put inside of you will not thrive in the wrong environment.

God is not only the Giver of purpose, but He is also the Master Gardener. And like any good gardener, He knows the soil that is best for what He's planted in you.

"And the Lord said unto Abram, Get thee out of thy country, and from thy kindred, and from thy father's house, unto a land that I will shew thee." Genesis 12:1 (KJV)

When God called Abraham, He didn't give him all the details. He simply said, "Go." Why? Because Abraham's destiny couldn't grow where he was. The people, the mindset, and the atmosphere around him couldn't support the seed God had placed within him. So, God moved him not to destroy him, but to develop him.

The same is true for us. God knows when we're in toxic environments, stagnant situations, or surrounded by voices that drown out His call. And because He loves us and is committed to His purpose in us, He will shake things up. That job, relationship, city, or community may have been good for a season, but when God sees that it can no longer sustain your growth, He will move you.

Being relocated spiritually, emotionally, or physically isn't always comfortable. It might feel like loss or abandonment. But often, it's God making room for your expansion. The seed inside you, your calling, your gifts, your dreams, were never meant to stay buried. They were meant to grow, flourish, and bear fruit.

So, if you find yourself in transition, don't panic. Don't resist. Ask God to help you recognize the new ground He's preparing. Trust His timing. Trust His hand. And trust that the same God who planted the seed will bring it to harvest in His perfect place, at His perfect time.

Father God, thank You for caring enough about me to move me when I don't even know I need to be moved. Help me to trust You when You shake up my comfort and relocate me to unfamiliar places. Teach me to see change as a sign of Your love and protection, not punishment. Remind me that the seed You planted in me is valuable and needs the right soil to thrive. Give me courage to follow You wherever You lead, and faith to believe that my growth is part of Your greater plan. In Jesus' name, Amen and To God Be The Glory!

MAY 20. - "DON'T BE IMPRESSED BY STATUS ~ BE MOVED BY CHARACTER"

In today's culture, it's easy to be drawn to the surface. Money, degrees, titles, and social media followers are often seen as symbols of success and importance. But as believers, we are called to see beyond what the world praises and to value what heaven esteems.

"Don't be impressed by money, degrees, followers, or titles. Be impressed by kindness, integrity, humility, and generosity."

This phrase isn't just a wise statement it's a spiritual truth rooted in the character of Christ. God doesn't measure greatness the way the world does. In fact, many of the people we might overlook are the very ones God exalts.

"But the Lord said unto Samuel, Look not on his countenance, or on the height of his stature; because I have refused him: for the Lord seeth not as man seeth; for man looketh on the outward appearance, but the Lord looketh on the heart." 1 Samuel 16:7 (KJV)

When Samuel went to anoint the next king of Israel, he almost chose someone based on outward appearance. But God reminded him and us, that true worth is measured by what lies within. A kind heart, a humble spirit, and a generous soul carry more eternal value than any title or accolade ever could.

Jesus, the King of Kings, was born in a manger not a palace. He rode a donkey not a chariot. He washed feet, not to impress, but to serve. His life redefined greatness, not through status, but through sacrifice.

As followers of Christ, our admiration should align with His values. Be impressed by the person who listens more than they speak. Be inspired by the one who gives without expecting anything in return. Be drawn to those who choose honesty over popularity and humility over applause.

The world is filled with people chasing attention. But God is looking for hearts that reflect His own. If we're going to be impressed by anything, let it be the quiet strength of godly character.

Heavenly Father, please teach me to see people the way You see them. Help me not to be swayed by outward success, but to admire the qualities that reflect Your heart, kindness, integrity, humility, and generosity. Keep me grounded in truth and focused on character over clout. Shape my life to be a reflection of who You are and let others see Your love in how I live. May my values honor You in every way. In Jesus' name I pray, Amen and To God Be The Glory!

MAY 21. - "THE STRENGTH BEHIND THE SMILE"

Life has a way of wounding us deeply. Betrayals, disappointments, losses, and repeated heartbreaks can carve valleys into the soul. Some hurts are so intense they leave no visible scars, yet they echo through our thoughts, emotions, and even how we see ourselves and others. But then there's you ~ the one who still smiles.

That smile isn't denial. It's not pretense. It's resilience. Its strength born from brokenness, hope that survived the storm, and faith that refused to die. Every smile after a season of pain is a silent testimony: "I've been through fire, and I'm still standing."

God never promised a life without pain, but He did promise His presence in it. And He treasures those who choose to keep going, to keep loving, and yes, to keep smiling, even when it hurts. Your ability to smile after being wounded shows that God's healing hand is on you, even when you don't fully feel it. You are not weak for feeling pain, you are strong because you continue to show up, even with a tender heart.

"We are hard pressed on every side yet not crushed; we are perplexed, but not in despair; persecuted but not forsaken; struck down, but not destroyed." 2 Corinthians 4:8-9 (KJV)

This passage reminds us that though the world tries to break us, it cannot overcome us. Not because of our own power, but because of God's sustaining grace within us. When your heart has every reason to shut down, but you keep showing up with joy and compassion, that's a reflection of Christ's victory at work in you.

Father God, thank You for the strength You've given me, even when I felt weak. Thank You for every moment You held me when I thought I would break. Lord, help me to keep smiling, not out of denial, but from a place of deep trust in You. Heal every unseen wound. Renew my joy daily. Let my smile be a light to others, a testimony of Your grace, and a sign that You are my strength even when I am weary. Help me continue to love and to live from a whole heart, anchored in You. In Jesus' name I pray, Amen and To God Be The Glory!

MAY 22. - "SUBMITTING TO THE FULL CONUSEL OF GOD"

In a world where personal preference is often elevated above truth, it's easy to approach the Bible like a buffet. Picking and choosing the parts that are comforting and rejecting the parts that are challenging. But the Word of God is not subject to our preferences. It is truth eternal, unchanging, and authoritative.

When we treat Scripture as optional or negotiable, we're not submitting to God, we're setting ourselves up as our own god. This is dangerous, because partial obedience is still disobedience. A faith built on convenience will collapse when tested, but a faith built on the whole Word of God will endure every storm.

There are parts of the Bible that confront our attitudes, expose our sin, and challenge our comfort zones. But that is precisely what the Word is meant to do. It is not just a source of encouragement. It is a tool for correction, transformation, and alignment with the heart of God.

God's Word is not a collection of suggestions; it is His divine revelation to humanity. The Bible wasn't written to be edited by human opinion but to shape the hearts and lives of those who seek Him. Our posture must be one of surrender, not selective agreement.

"All scripture is given by inspiration of God, and is profitable for doctrine, for reproof, for correction, for instruction in righteousness:

That the man of God may be perfect, thoroughly furnished unto all good works."

2 Timothy 3:16–17 (KJV)

Lord God, forgive me for the times I've treated Your Word casually or selectively. Help me to receive all of Your truth, even when it challenges me. Soften my heart where it has grown hard and open my eyes to see what You are really saying. Teach me to walk in obedience, not comfort. I want to follow You fully, not just when it's easy. Let Your Word correct me, shape me, and lead me into righteousness. I submit every part of my life to Your authority.

In Jesus' name, Amen and To God Be The Glory!

MAY 23. - "WILLING TO DINE ~ BUT NOT SERVE"

There's a growing trend in modern Christianity where many want the blessings of God without the burden of responsibility. We want the feast, the peace, provision, healing, and favor, but we don't always want the work, sacrifice, service, obedience, or outreach. We long to sit at God's table and receive, but few are willing to roll up their sleeves and labor in His fields.

Jesus spoke directly to this in Matthew 9:37:

"Then saith he unto his disciples, The harvest truly is plenteous, but the labourers are few;"

Matthew 9:37 (KJV)

The Lord's words were not about agriculture but about souls. People in need of salvation, healing, and truth. He saw crowds of hurting, wandering, spiritually starved people and was moved with compassion. Yet instead of pointing to a lack of resources, He pointed to a shortage of workers. The problem wasn't the harvest; it was the absence of willing laborers.

Being a laborer in God's field means to always be available. Whether it's sharing your testimony, serving your church, praying for others, or simply living a life that reflects Christ in the ordinary. The harvest is ready, but the question is: are we ready to do the work?

It's easy to enjoy the blessings of salvation, but God calls us to more than just receiving. He calls us to participate in His mission to serve, to go, to sow, to disciple. If we all want to eat at the table but no one wants to plant, water, or reap, then who will bring in the harvest?

Heavenly Father, I thank You for inviting me to Your table of grace. But Lord, I don't want to be someone who only receives and never serves. Stir my heart to labor in Your fields. Open my eyes to the hurting, the lost, and the overlooked. Give me a servant's heart and a willing spirit. Help me to be faithful not just in prayer, but in action. Let me be counted among those who work for Your kingdom, knowing that the harvest is too valuable to leave untouched. In Jesus' name, I pray.

Amen and To God Be The Glory!

MAY 24. - "BREAKING WHAT RUNS IN THE FAMILY"

So often, we hear people say, "It runs in my family". Referring to cycles of addiction, anger, poverty, broken marriages, depression, or sickness. These declarations are made casually, even jokingly, but they carry the weight of agreement. When we accept bondage as our inheritance, we unknowingly give it permission to continue.

But if you are in Christ, your bloodline has changed. You are no longer bound to the curses of your earthly family; you have been adopted into the family of God, redeemed by the blood of Jesus. The cross didn't just secure your personal salvation; it shattered every generational curse that once claimed dominion over your lineage.

Jesus did not leave us defenseless. He gave us authority, not just over individual attacks but over patterns and principalities. The cycles that bind your parents, grandparents, and great-grandparents do not have to bind you. In His name, you can declare freedom for yourself, your children, and generations yet unborn.

You must stop speaking defeat and start declaring the Word. Stop normalizing dysfunction just because it's familiar. What "runs in your family" must bow to what flows from the throne of Heaven. And what flows from Heaven is grace, healing, restoration, and generational blessing.

"Behold, I give unto you power to tread on serpents and scorpions, and over all the power of the enemy: and nothing shall by any means hurt you." Luke 10:19 (KJV)

Father God, thank You for the authority You've given me through Jesus Christ. Today, I renounce every generational curse spoken or unspoken, seen or unseen, that has tried to rule over my family. I declare in the name of Jesus that every cycle of bondage is broken, every stronghold is torn down. I choose to walk in the freedom, righteousness, and new identity You have given me. I speak blessings over my household and future generations. Let Your victory define my bloodline from this day forward.

In Jesus' powerful name I pray, Amen and To God Be The Glory!

MAY 25. - "WHEN THE BACKSLIDER RETURNS ~ CHECK YOUR HEART"

One of the most powerful moments in the life of a church is when someone who has fallen away returns. Whether they were gone for months or years, the decision to come back to the house of God is not made lightly. It takes humility, courage, and the prompting of the Holy Spirit.

Yet sadly, instead of being met with open arms, returning believers are sometimes met with cold stares and whispered reminders of their past. But Scripture challenges this spirit of pride and judgment, because when a sinner returns, heaven rejoices. If heaven is celebrating and we are criticizing, something is deeply wrong with our hearts.

"I say unto you, that likewise joy shall be in heaven over one sinner that repenteth, more than over ninety and nine just persons, which need no repentance." Luke 15:7 (KJV)

This verse follows Jesus' parable of the lost sheep. Where the shepherd leaves the ninety-nine to go after the one. The story is not just about salvation; it's about restoration. It's about a heart that mirrors the Father's, a heart that values redemption over reputation.

If our first instinct is to recall someone's failures instead of honoring their return, then it's not the backslider who's out of step with God, it's us. Judgment blocks the flow of grace. Pride positions us as spiritual gatekeepers, when God has called us to be spiritual welcomers.

God doesn't need our memory of someone's sin, He's already cast it into the sea of forgetfulness. What He needs is our compassion, our humility, and our willingness to celebrate when one of His children finds their way home.

Father God, please forgive me for every time I've judged someone based on their past instead of celebrating their return to You. Cleanse my heart of spiritual pride and fill me with Your love and grace. Help me to see people the way You see them, as redeemed, restored, and worthy of a new beginning. When the backslider returns, let my heart rejoice, not accuse. Remind me daily that I, too, have fallen short, and it's only by Your mercy that I stand. Make me an agent of welcome, healing, and grace.

In Jesus' name I pray, Amen and To God Be The Glory!

MAY 26. - "LET THE LION ROAR ~ IT WILL DEFEND ITSELF"

In a world overflowing with opinions, false narratives, and shifting values, it is tempting to feel like we must argue, explain, or defend every piece of truth we believe. We think if we don't shout loud enough, the truth will be buried under lies. But the truth ~ God's truth ~ is not fragile. It doesn't tremble in the face of opposition. It is living, powerful, and fierce. Like a lion, it does not need protection; it needs release.

The enemy tries to intimidate us into silence, suggesting that truth is offensive, outdated, or unloving. But truth is not a weapon for hate, it is a key to freedom. Jesus said plainly, "And ye shall know the truth, and the truth shall make you free." (John 8:32, KJV). This truth is not just information; it is revelation. It is Christ Himself that said, "I am the way, the truth, and the life." (John 14:6 KJV).

When you walk in truth, you walk in alignment with God's character. And when you speak truth, even when it's unpopular, you are not standing alone, you are releasing something eternal. Truth may be resisted for a moment, but over time, it will rise, roar, and rule. You don't have to manipulate outcomes or engage in every argument. Let truth stand. Let it breathe. Let it fight. It always wins.

We must also remember that our posture matters. We speak the truth in love (Ephesians 4:15), not with arrogance or pride. We don't use truth to crush people, but to call them into the light. We don't fight for victory, we stand from victory, knowing the Lion of Judah has already triumphed.

"For we can do nothing against the truth, but for the truth." 2 Corinthians 13:8 (KJV)

Heavenly Father, I thank You for being the God of truth. In a world full of noise and deception, remind me that Your truth is unshakable. Teach me to speak it boldly, live it consistently, and trust it fully. Help me to resist the urge to over-defend what You have already declared. Let me be a vessel through which Your truth is made known, not by force, but by faith. Strengthen my heart when I face resistance and give me peace in knowing that the truth will always outlast the lie. In Jesus' name I pray, Amen and To God Be The Glory!

MAY 27. - "FAITHFULNESS OVER POPULARITY"

There's no question about it, we are living in days where darkness is often called light, and light is dismissed as outdated or intolerant. What God has called sin is now being normalized, justified, and even applauded. The lines between holy and profane are being blurred in culture, media, and sometimes even in the church. But as believers, we are not called to adjust our convictions to fit in. We are called to stand firm, loving, and unshakable on the unchanging truth of God's Word.

Being faithful means refusing to compromise even when compromise makes it feel more comfortable. It means choosing obedience over acceptance and truth over trend. When we stand for what God has said, we stand with Him. And when we stand with Him, we are never alone, even if the world turns its back.

Remember, Jesus Himself was rejected, ridiculed, and ultimately crucified not because He was unkind or unjust, but because He spoke truth in love. The same will happen to His followers. But He also said: "Blessed are ye, when men shall revile you, and persecute you for my sake. Rejoice, and be exceeding glad: for great is your reward in heaven." (Matthew 5:11–12 KJV).

You may be called old-fashioned. You may be mocked. You may be left out. But none of that compares to hearing Him say, "Well done, good and faithful servant."

This stand won't always be easy. In fact, it may cost you friends, followers, and favor in the world's eyes. But the applause of men cannot compare to the approval of God. Jesus warned us about this:

"Woe unto you, when all men shall speak well of you! for so did their fathers to the false prophets." (Luke 6:26, KJV).

Truth is not a popularity contest. It is a divine standard.

"Be not conformed to this world: but be ye transformed by the renewing of your mind, that ye may prove what is that good, and acceptable, and perfect, will of God."

Romans 12:2 (KJV)

Father, give me the courage to stand for Your truth in a world that often celebrates compromise. Help me to walk in love without wavering in conviction. Strengthen my heart when I feel the weight of rejection or misunderstanding. Remind me daily that my calling is to be faithful, not popular. Let my life reflect the light of Christ in both word and action. Keep me rooted in Your Word and remind me that You are with me, even when the world is against me. In Jesus' name I pray, Amen and To God Be The Glory!

May 28. - "LET THEM THINK YOU DON'T KNOW"

One of the most powerful displays of restraint and wisdom in Scripture is found in the way Jesus handled Judas. Jesus, in His divinity, knew from the very beginning that Judas would betray Him. He knew Judas's heart, his secret intentions, and his ultimate role in the plan of redemption. Yet, Jesus never publicly exposed him. He didn't shame him. He didn't call him out in front of the others. He allowed Judas to walk beside Him, to eat with Him, and even to serve Him, all while knowing exactly who he was and what he would do.

This teaches us something deeply profound: not every snake needs to be stomped in public. Some betrayals, some disloyalties, some hidden agendas are best handled in silence and surrendered to God. There is wisdom in knowing and yet saying nothing. There is strength in discernment that doesn't demand display.

Often, we want to confront, to expose, to defend ourselves. But sometimes, God calls us to do what Jesus did, let them think you don't know. Why? Because exposing them prematurely can interrupt God's greater plan. Jesus understood that Judas's betrayal would lead to the cross, and the cross would lead to our salvation. Even betrayal, in the hands of God, becomes part of the victory.

You don't have to address every whisper, respond to every false friend, or prove you're right. When you know who you are and whose you are, you can walk in peace even in the presence of betrayal. Let them think you're unaware. Stay close to the Father. Keep walking in integrity. And trust that nothing escapes the eyes of God.

"The LORD shall fight for you, and ye shall hold your peace." Exodus 14:14 (KJV)

Heavenly Father, help me walk in wisdom and restraint. Teach me to hold my peace when my flesh wants to confront. Give me the grace to love even those I know are not genuine. Thank You for being my defender and for seeing what others don't. Strengthen me to trust Your timing and Your justice. May I always choose discernment over drama, and purpose over pride. I surrender every Judas in my life to You, knowing that Your plan is greater than my need to respond. In Jesus' name I pray, Amen and To God Be The Glory!

MAY 29. - "NOTHING IS OUT OF HIS CONTROL"

When we read the Bible, we're not just reading stories, we're reading evidence. Page after page, God proves that what seems impossible to man is completely possible with Him. Time and time again, He moves in ways that defy nature, logic, and human limitation. Why? Because He is sovereign, all-powerful, and always in control.

Daniel stood surrounded by hungry lions, yet not one tooth touched him, because God sent an angel and shut their mouths (Daniel 6:22). Moses faced the Red Sea in front of him and an angry army behind him and God split the waters so His people could walk through on dry ground (Exodus 14:21-22). Sarah, far beyond childbearing years, laughed at the thought of having a child, yet God turned her laughter of disbelief into a laughter of joy as she held Isaac in her arms (Genesis 21:6). And Lazarus, four days dead, heard the voice of Jesus call him out of the grave and he came walking out, alive and whole (John 11:43-44).

These miracles are not just stories of what God has done, they are reminders of what He can still do. You may be facing a closed door, deep grief, a frightening diagnosis, a financial crisis, or a spiritual battle that feels unbearable. But nothing you are going through today is beyond God's reach. The same God who worked wonders for Daniel, Moses, Sarah, and Lazarus is the same God working behind the scenes of your life right now.

You don't have to understand how He'll do it. You just need to believe that He will. Trust His timing. Trust His methods. Trust His heart. When the situation looks dead, delayed, or dangerous, remember who your God is. He is still shutting mouths, parting seas, fulfilling promises, and raising the dead.

"Behold, I am the LORD, the God of all flesh: is there any thing too hard for me?"

Jeremiah 32:27 (KJV)

Father God, I thank You that nothing I face is out of Your control. You are the same yesterday, today, and forever. Remind me in moments of fear or doubt that You still perform miracles. Strengthen my faith like Daniel, my obedience like Moses, my patience like Sarah, and my hope like Lazarus. Help me to trust You even when I don't see the way. I surrender every worry, every obstacle, and every burden to You. Work in my life according to Your perfect will. In Jesus' name I pray, Amen and To God Be The Glory!

MAY 30. - "GOD IS NOT THROUGH WITH ME YET"

In life, there are always people who secretly, or openly, hope that we stumble and fall. Some may even set traps, spread lies, or sit on the sidelines just waiting for our downfall. But what they fail to realize is that when God has spoken a word over your life, no enemy, no hater, and no scheme can stop His plans from coming to pass.

The Word tells us in Isaiah 54:17 (KJV): "No weapon that is formed against thee shall prosper; and every tongue that shall rise against thee in judgment thou shalt condemn. This is the heritage of the servants of the Lord, and their righteousness is of me, saith the Lord."

This scripture reminds us that while weapons may be formed, while opposition may rise, and while people may expect you to fail, the outcome is not in their hands, it is in God's hands. Their disappointment will be proof of God's appointment over your life.

Think of Joseph. His brothers plotted against him, sold him into slavery, and expected him to be forgotten and destroyed. But God elevated him from the pit to the palace. Or consider Daniel, his enemies threw him into the lion's den, fully expecting his demise. Yet God shut the mouths of the lions, and the very ones who plotted against him were put to shame.

Your story is no different. The same God who defended Joseph, Daniel, and countless others is the God who fights for you. He is not just preparing to bless you, He is preparing to bless you in the sight of those who doubted you. Their expectations will be disappointed because God's promises will not fail.

When God raises you up, it will serve as a testimony that no human opinion, no evil agenda, and no expectation of failure can override the favor and covering of the Lord. Walk boldly, because your success is already sealed in Heaven.

Father, I thank You for being my shield and my defender. Thank You that every plot, plan, and scheme against my life will fail. I declare that no weapon formed against me shall prosper, and that every tongue that rises in judgment shall be condemned. Lord, turn the expectations of my enemies into disappointment and let Your glory be revealed through my victory. Position me in the place You have ordained and let my life be a living testimony of Your power and faithfulness. I trust that You are fighting for me, lifting me, and establishing me in the presence of those who expected me to fall. In Jesus' mighty name I pray.

Amen and To God Be The Glory!

MAY 31. - "KNOW YOUR WORTH ~ WALK IN GOD'S VALUE"

Devotional: "Know Your Worth—Walk in God's Value"

One of the most exhausting roads you can walk is the path of trying to prove your worth to people who've already made up their minds about you. The truth is, no matter how kind, talented, generous, or faithful you are, some people will overlook you, underestimate you, or reject you. But that doesn't define you. God does.

God's love is not based on public opinion or personal preference. You were created in His image, fearfully and wonderfully made (Psalm 139:14). Before you ever performed, pleased, or proved yourself, God already called you valuable. That is your identity, not in the eyes of others, but in the eyes of your Creator.

Jesus Himself was not accepted by everyone. He was rejected in His hometown. Betrayed by someone close. Mocked by the very ones He came to save. If the Son of God was not always appreciated, you will not be either. And that's okay. Because your calling isn't to be liked ~ your calling is to be faithful.

When someone doesn't see your worth, it says more about them than it does about you. Love them, pray for them, but don't lose yourself trying to win them. Honor who you are in Christ. Surround yourself with people who see you through God's lens. Those who build, encourage, and challenge you in truth and love.

Don't settle in places where your presence is tolerated but not valued. Don't stay where you're constantly questioned, doubted, or overlooked. God's people walk with dignity. And those who are meant to walk with you will recognize the God-given value in you, not just when you're at your best, but even in your struggles.

"Cast not away therefore your confidence, which hath great recompence of reward."

Hebrews 10:35 (KJV)

Heavenly Father, I truly thank You for creating me with value, purpose, and beauty that cannot be diminished by rejection or mistreatment. Please remind me daily that I am enough because I am Yours. Teach me to stop seeking validation from others and to rest in the truth of who You say I am. Give me wisdom to walk away from relationships that devalue me, and courage to walk toward those who uplift and honor the calling on my life. Help me to never forget that my worth is not in who accepts me, but in who created me. In Jesus' name I pray, Amen and To God Be The Glory!

JUNE INTRODUCTION

Life doesn't wait for us to be ready. Its demands come quickly, its trials come unexpectedly, and its pain often without explanation. In a world full of noise, opinions, and confusion, what we truly need isn't another theory or trend, but truth. For the month of June, Biblical Answers to Life's Pressing Problems is designed to walk with you, day by day, into the wisdom of God's Word, offering hope, clarity, and divine solutions to the challenges we all face.

This month, we will confront issues of fear, disappointment, rejection, loneliness, temptation, waiting, grief, and spiritual dryness. These are not abstract theological concepts, they are real struggles faced by real people. But the beauty of the Bible is that it does not shy away from human pain. Instead, it speaks directly into it, offering not only comfort but transformation.

The goal of this devotional is not just to provide answers, but to guide you back to the "Answer That's Found in Jesus Christ". Every devotional you read will be grounded in Scripture, rooted in truth, and centered on the redeeming love of God. Whether you're in a storm or coming out of one, whether you're at the edge of breakthrough or in the midst of a battle, these pages are for you.

Let June be a month of pressing in when life presses hard. Let it be a time of surrender, restoration, and revelation. God's Word still speaks and when it does, it brings peace, power, and perspective.

"This poor man cried, and the Lord heard him, and saved him out of all his troubles."

Psalm 34:6 (KJV)

Heavenly Father, we enter this month with open hearts and expectant spirits. Life may bring questions, but we know You hold every answer. Teach us through Your Word. Heal us through Your Spirit. Strengthen us in our struggles. As we read, reflect, and pray, let Your truth take root in our hearts and produce the fruit of faith, peace, and purpose. Lord, we don't just want to read about You—we want to walk with You. Speak clearly, move deeply, and be glorified daily. In Jesus' name we pray, Amen and To God Be The Glory!

JUNE 1. - "YES, I'M CHANGED ~ THE OLD ME WAS TOO WEAK"

Change isn't always visible to everyone, but it is deeply personal and powerfully spiritual. When God begins to transform your life, He doesn't just upgrade your habits, He rebuilds your foundation. And that means the version of you that once gave in, broke down, gave up, or tried to fit in, had to go.

The old version of you may have smiled on the outside but was drowning on the inside. The old you might have tolerated mistreatment, lived for approval, feared rejection, or stayed silent when you should have spoken truth. But then something happened, and grace stepped in and gave you the strength to be changed.

The change didn't come because you got stronger on your own. It came because you met the One who is strong in your weakness.

As 2 Corinthians 12:9 (KJV) reminds us: "And he said unto me, My grace is sufficient for thee: for my strength is made perfect in weakness"

God doesn't discard you for being weak. He builds something new in the place of your brokenness. He gives you the courage to walk away from what drained you, the discernment to avoid what trapped you, and the strength to become who He destined you to be.

So yes, you're changed. Not because you're pretending to be better, but because you refused to remain bound. You allowed God to strip away the fragile, people-pleasing, sin-tolerating version of yourself. And now, you're rooted in truth, clothed in strength, and carried by grace.

You don't owe anyone an explanation for your growth. Keep becoming. Keep healing. Keep walking. Your transformation is your testimony.

Therefore, if any man be in Christ, he is a new creature: old things are passed away; behold, all things are become new." 2 Corinthians 5:17 (KJV)

Lord, thank You for changing me. Thank You for not leaving me in the weakness of who I used to be. I praise You for the strength You've placed inside me, not because of who I am, but because of who You are in me. Help me to never long for the version of myself that You've delivered me from. Keep shaping me into who You've called me to be. May I continue to walk in boldness, truth, and freedom. In Jesus' name I pray, Amen and To God Be The Glory!

JUNE 2. - "TRUST THE TRANSITION"

There are moments in life when everything seems to be falling apart. Doors that were once open slam shut. Opportunities dry up. Relationships end. Plans fail. And in those moments, it can feel like you've been abandoned, rejected, or forgotten. But what if the closed door wasn't punishment, it was divine protection? What if it was God's gentle nudge or forceful that pushed you into something greater?

You see, God often sees what we cannot. He knows what lies ahead and what is no longer serving your destiny. But the truth is, we are creatures of comfort. We settle into routines, environments, and relationships even if they're not good for us because they're familiar. And sometimes, the only way God can get us to move forward is by unsettling our comfort and disrupting our plans.

Think about the children of Israel. They cried out for deliverance in Egypt, but once they were freed and faced the unfamiliar wilderness, they longed to go back to slavery. Why? Because the unknown is often scarier than the known, even when the known is toxic. But God had no intention of letting them go back. The Red Sea didn't just part for them to walk through, it closed behind them to ensure they couldn't return.

When a door closes in your life, it may be God's way of saying, "I have something better. You've stayed here long enough." Don't waste time trying to pry open what God has shut. Instead, trust the transition. God is not just removing you from something, He's preparing you for something.

The discomfort of your current circumstances may be the very soil God is using to birth your next season. Trust that even in the pain, the confusion, and the uncertainty, remember God is still in control. He's not just the God of open doors; He's also the God of closed ones.

"Forget the former things; do not dwell on the past. See, I am doing a new thing! Now it springs up; do you not perceive it? I am making a way in the wilderness and streams in the wasteland." Isaiah 43:18–19 (NIV)

Father God, thank You for being a loving and wise Father who knows what's best for me, even when I don't understand. Help me to trust You in seasons of transition. When You close doors, remind me that it's not rejection, it's redirection. Give me the strength to let go of what's behind and the courage to step into what's ahead. Teach me to discern Your movement and follow You with confidence, knowing that Your plans for me are good. I surrender my fear, my doubt, and my need for control. Heavenly Father, I trust You with the unknown. In Jesus' name, Amen and To God Be The Glory!

JUNE 3. - "WHAT TRIED TO BREAK ME ~ BUILT ME"

There's something powerful about surviving what was meant to destroy you. Every attack, every betrayal, every lie, every attempt to tear you down, God has a way of using it all to strengthen and shape you. What the enemy meant for evil, God will always use for good.

People may have tried to break your spirit. They may have laughed when you fell, spoken ill of your name, or counted you out. But here you are still standing. Wiser. Stronger. Closer to God. The very battles that were meant to bury you became the training ground for your endurance, your faith, and your authority.

Joseph in the Bible knew this well. His own brothers betrayed him. He was thrown into a pit, sold into slavery, wrongfully imprisoned, and forgotten. But despite it all, God elevated him to a position of power in Egypt. And when he finally faced the very people who tried to destroy him, he didn't seek revenge. Instead, he declared, "You intended to harm me, but God intended it for good." (Genesis 50:20 NIV)

It takes a mature heart and a healed spirit to look back at what you went through and say, "Thank you. You didn't break me you built me." Your enemies unknowingly helped you grow. They revealed who you were not, so you could discover who you really are. They tried to clip your wings, but they only taught you how to fly higher.

So don't carry bitterness, carry testimony. Don't stay wounded, walk in your healing. And don't give your enemies credit for your strength, give God the glory. Because He is the One who turned your pain into power, your scars into wisdom, and your past into purpose.

But those who hope in the Lord will renew their strength. They will soar on wings like eagles; they will run and not grow weary, they will walk and not be faint." Isaiah 40:31 (NIV)

Father, thank You for being my strength when I was weak and my protector when I was under attack. Thank You for turning what was meant to break me into something that built me. I release every person who tried to harm me and declare that I am stronger, wiser, and more grounded in You because of what I've endured. Use every trial to mold me into who You've called me to be. Help me to walk in forgiveness, rooted in grace, and focused on my purpose. I will not be bitter ~ I will be better. And I will give You all the glory for my growth.

In Jesus' name, Amen and To God Be The Glory!

JUNE 4. - "YOU ARE THE ANSWER

God is sovereign, yet He chooses to partner with us to carry out His will on earth. One of the most powerful ways He moves is through people, ordinary people with willing hearts and open hands. When you find yourself in a position to help someone, that moment is sacred. It's not random. It's no coincidence. It's divine alignment. God is using you to answer a cry that reached His throne.

Imagine someone on their knees crying out for relief, direction, or a breakthrough. They feel forgotten or unseen. But then, God places them on your heart. Or you cross paths with them at the exact moment they need help. That's not by chance; it's a divine assignment. You are standing in the gap as God's representative, delivering His love in a tangible form.

Too often, we think miracles come in thunder and lightning, but many of God's greatest miracles show up quietly. Sometimes through a kind word, a financial blessing, a meal shared, a door opened. When you respond with compassion, generosity, or presence, you are fulfilling a holy purpose. You're not just doing a good deed, you're participating in the miraculous.

Helping others is not only a privilege; it's a form of worship. It honors the heart of God. It reflects the life of Jesus, who constantly poured Himself out for others. He saw people not as interruptions, but as opportunities to love.

And let us not forget: the way we treat others is a reflection of our faith. When we help, encourage, and lift up those around us, we reflect the very character of Christ. So, whenever you have the ability to help someone, don't hesitate. Don't overthink it. Rejoice and move in love because in that moment, you are the answer to a prayer.

"Carry each other's burdens, and in this way you will fulfill the law of Christ."

Galatians 6:2 (NIV)

Heavenly Father, thank You for choosing to use me as a vessel of Your love and provision. Help me to never overlook the moments where I can be the answer to someone else's prayer. Keep my heart sensitive and my spirit obedient. Remind me that every opportunity to help is an opportunity to glorify You. Let my life reflect Your compassion and may every act of kindness point others back to You. I am honored to serve, and I trust You to work through me. In Jesus' name, Amen and To God Be The Glory!

JUNE 5. - "WHAT TRULY MATTERS"

Life has a way of pulling us in many directions. From the demands of work to the pressures of success, to the constant comparison that comes with the world around us. We can easily lose sight of what's truly important. But when the noise settles, and the day winds down, we're reminded that peace doesn't come from perfection, performance, or possessions. It comes from presence, purpose, and perspective.

At the end of the day, it's not the unchecked boxes or the unfinished to-do list that define your worth. What really matters is that your loved ones are safe, you gave the day your honest effort, and you carry a heart full of gratitude for what God has already provided.

God never asked you to be perfect, He simply calls you to be faithful. He doesn't judge your life by the size of your house, your bank account, or your status. He looks at your love, your obedience, your humility, and your gratitude.

When your loved ones are well, that's a gift, cherish it. When you've done your best, that's enough, rest in it. And when you take a moment to pause and thank God for what you do have instead of worrying about what you don't, that's worship, live in it.

Gratitude is not just a feeling; it's a perspective that shifts everything. It realigns your heart with heaven. It reminds you that God's blessings often come in the form of the simple, the quiet, and the steady. The breath in your lungs. The roof over your head. The laugh of a child. A moment of peace.

Let today end with thanksgiving. Let your heart be still and your spirit be reminded: God is with you, you are loved, and what truly matters is already in your hands.

"Give thanks in all circumstances; for this is God's will for you in Christ Jesus."

1 Thessalonians 5:18 (NIV)

Heavenly Father, I thank You for the precious gift of life. Thank You for my loved ones, for the strength to do my best each day, and for all that You have provided. Help me not to chase what the world says matters but to find peace in what You value most, faithfulness, love, and gratitude. Teach me to rest in the assurance that I am enough when I give You my best. May my heart remain thankful, even in the ordinary moments. In Jesus' name, Amen and To God Be The Glory!

JUNE 6. - "UNSHAKABLE PEACE"

There is a deep freedom that comes when you learn to guard your peace. As long as your emotions are tethered to the behavior of others, you will live on a roller coaster of reactions, up one minute, down the next. But God never called you to live at the mercy of someone else's attitude, approval, or inconsistency. He called you to live anchored in Him.

We must come to understand that not every comment, every look, or every act of neglect deserves a response. People are human flawed, moody, wounded, and imperfect. Their actions can sometimes stem from their own issues and have nothing to do with you. Yet how often do we allow those moments to rob us of our joy, derail our day, or shift our perspective?

Emotional maturity in Christ looks like learning how to respond with wisdom instead of reacting with offense. It's recognizing that your value is not determined by someone's mood, and your peace is not negotiable. It's remembering that peace is a fruit of the Spirit, not a gift from people.

Even Jesus was misunderstood, betrayed, mocked, and rejected. Yet, He never allowed the actions of others to pull Him out of purpose. He remained rooted in the Father's will and never allowed the noise of people to override the voice of God.

When you find your identity and stability in Christ, your mood becomes steady because your soul is settled. You stop internalizing the temporary behaviors of others and start living with eternal perspective. Don't let insignificant actions cause significant damage. Protect your peace. Guard your spirit. Choose joy on purpose.

"You will keep in perfect peace those whose minds are steadfast, because they trust in you." Isaiah 26:3 (NIV)

Father, I thank You for the peace that surpasses all understanding. Help me to be rooted in You so deeply that I am not easily shaken by the actions or attitudes of others. Teach me to respond with grace and not react in emotion. Strengthen my heart so that I do not seek validation from people but remain grounded in Your truth. Let Your Spirit guide my mood, my words, and my reactions. I surrender the need to control what others do and ask for the discipline to control how I respond. In Jesus' name, Amen and To God Be The Glory!

JUNE 7. - "GRASPING AIR ~ THE FUTILITY OF RESISTING GODS PLAN

There are seasons in life where we find ourselves fighting battles that were never meant for us. We resist, we push, we strive, and sometimes we even rebel, because what God is doing doesn't align with what we had envisioned. But fighting against God's plan is like grasping air: it leads nowhere. You may clench your fists, wave your arms, and exhaust yourself trying to control the outcome, but in the end, you're left with nothing to hold onto. No peace, no progress, no power. Just empty hands and a weary heart.

Jonah is a perfect example of this truth. Called by God to go to Nineveh, Jonah fled in the opposite direction, boarding a ship to Tarshish. His resistance didn't cancel God's call; it only delayed the inevitable and brought him unnecessary hardship. He found himself in a storm, then in the belly of a great fish. Why? Because no matter how far we run or how hard we fight, we cannot outmaneuver the sovereign will of God.

We must come to understand that God's plan is not just unstoppable, it's always better. What He orchestrates is filled with purpose, timing, and grace. What He allows, He uses. When we surrender to His will, even when we don't fully understand it, we make space for His peace to flood our lives. Resistance leads to exhaustion, but surrender leads to rest.

It's not weakness to submit to God's plan; it's wisdom. The Creator of the universe does not make mistakes. His vision stretches beyond our short-sighted view. So instead of grasping at air, open your hands. Release your will. Embrace His. That's where breakthrough lives—in the center of God's will, not in the corner of your comfort zone.

"Woe to those who quarrel with their Maker, those who are nothing but potsherds among the potsherds on the ground. Does the clay say to the potter, 'What are you making?'"

Isaiah 45:9 (NIV)

Heavenly Father, forgive me for the times I've fought against Your plan, thinking my way was better or easier. Help me to recognize that Your ways are higher than mine and that Your purpose for my life is filled with grace and goodness. Teach me to trust You even when the path is unclear. Give me the strength to surrender and the humility to follow. May I stop grasping at what cannot be held and instead take hold of the peace that comes from obedience. Let my heart be aligned with Yours, and let my life be a reflection of Your divine plan. In Jesus' name I pray, Amen and To God Be The Glory!

JUNE 8. - "WHO TO STAY CLOSE TO"

Relationships are powerful. They either build you up or break you down. They push you toward your purpose or pull you away from it. That's why it's essential to be intentional about who you allow close to your heart. There is a clear difference between people who genuinely want more for you and those who only want more from you. The former are blessings ~ God-sent encouragers who pray for you, challenge you, and celebrate your progress. The latter are often draining, manipulative, or self-serving ~ taking from your cup without ever helping to fill it.

Jesus modeled this truth perfectly. While He loved everyone, He did not entrust Himself to everyone (John 2:24). He surrounded Himself with disciples who, despite their flaws, wanted to walk with Him, learn from Him, and support the mission He was sent to fulfill. Even within the twelve, He had an inner circle, Peter, James, and John ~ those He allowed into His most intimate moments. Not because they were perfect, but because they were positioned to receive and respond, not just consume and withdraw.

Discernment is a spiritual tool that protects your purpose. Not everyone who walks with you is meant to speak to you. Some people are drawn to your light, not to help it shine brighter, but to use it for their own gain. But those who want more for you pray for your peace, cheer for your growth, and correct you in love, those are divine connections. Stay close to them. They are God's way of watering your spirit and sharpening your walk.

Your circle should be filled with people who honor your calling, not just your capacity. People who push you toward healing, not keep you stuck in cycles. People who invest in your becoming, not just benefit from your being. Ask yourself today: Do the people around me feed my faith or drain my strength?

"As iron sharpens iron, so one person sharpens another." Proverbs 27:17 (NIV)

Father God, Thank You for the gift of godly relationships. Help me to discern who truly wants more for me and to release those who only want more from me. Give me wisdom to walk in love, but not in naivety. Surround me with people who encourage, sharpen, and support the purpose You've placed in me. Father, help me be the kind of person to others who gives without draining and uplifts without demanding. Align my relationships with Your will and let every connection lead me closer to You. In Jesus' name I pray, Amen and To God Be The Glory!

JUNE 9. - "THE POWER OF STEPPING AWAY"

In a world that glorifies hustle, performance, and constant engagement, stepping away can feel like weakness. But in the Kingdom of God, stepping away, when led by the Spirit, is often one of the most powerful things you can do.

There is power in stepping away from confusion so that you can find clarity.

Power in stepping away from toxic relationships so that you can preserve your peace.

Power in stepping away from things that once fit but no longer align with your purpose.

Power in stepping away not out of defeat, but out of discernment.

Jesus, our perfect example, often stepped away. He withdrew from the crowds, from the noise, even from His closest friends, not because He was running from responsibility, but because He was reconnecting with His Father. Luke 5:16 says, "But Jesus often withdrew to lonely places and prayed." His stepping away wasn't avoidance; it was alignment. It was how He recharged, refocused, and prepared to fulfill His mission.

Sometimes the greatest act of strength is to know when to let go, when to pause, when to be still, and when to walk away, not in fear, but in faith. Stepping away allows God to step in. It creates room for healing, reflection, and divine redirection. It is a declaration that your worth is not found in your activity but in your identity as a child of God.

So, whether you're stepping away from drama, expectations, distractions, or even from something good that has simply run its course, do it boldly, prayerfully, and with peace. There is power in your pause. There is strength in your stillness. And there is favor in your faith to walk away when God says, "It's time."

"Come to me, all you who are weary and burdened, and I will give you rest." Matthew 11:28 (NIV)

Gracious Father, thank You for reminding me that stepping away is not always a sign of weakness, but often a demonstration of wisdom. Teach me to recognize when You are calling me to release, to pause, or to walk away. Help me not to cling to things that are draining me or distracting me from Your voice. Give me the courage to trust that my value is not in what I do, but in who I am in You. Let every step I take forward or as I step away be led by Your Spirit. In Jesus' name, Amen and To God Be The Glory!

JUNE 10. - "GRATEFUL FOR EVERYTHING ~ ENTITLED TO NOTHING"

In a culture that often whispers (and sometimes shouts), "You deserve it," it's easy to drift into a mindset of entitlement. Believing that good things are owed to us simply because we want them or work hard enough. But the truth is, the very breath in our lungs is a gift. Nothing we have is guaranteed, but everything we receive is a reflection of God's grace.

When we realize, we aren't entitled to anything, we become deeply grateful for everything.

Gratitude grows in the soil of humility. When we understand that we're not promised tomorrow, we begin to cherish today. When we know that salvation is not earned but freely given, we worship more passionately. When we recognize that even the smallest blessings, such as food, shelter, and peace of mind, are not entitlements but divine mercies ~ we shift from complaining to praising.

This mindset not only pleases God but transforms us. It strips away pride, entitlement, and comparison. It turns moments into miracles and routines into worship. The more we focus on what we don't deserve, the more we are awed by what we do have.

Jesus illustrated this in Luke 17, when He healed ten lepers. Only one returned to say thank you. The others received the same miracle but failed to express gratitude. Why? Perhaps entitlement dulled their awareness of the gift. But the one who came back understood: he wasn't owed healing. He was given mercy. And that understanding led him to fall at Jesus' feet in thanks.

Gratitude is powerful. It opens your eyes, softens your heart, and lifts your spirit. The next time you're tempted to say, "I deserve better," pause and ask, "What has God already given me that I never deserved at all?" That's where joy begins—at the intersection of humility and gratitude.

"Every good gift and every perfect gift is from above, and cometh down from the Father of lights, with whom is no variableness, neither shadow of turning." James 1:17 (KJV)

Heavenly Father, I thank You for every blessing, both great and small. Forgive me for the times I've approached life with a sense of entitlement. Help me to recognize that all I have is because of Your mercy and grace. Create in me a heart that is deeply grateful, humble, and content. Teach me to appreciate the ordinary and to worship You for the extraordinary. Let thankfulness be my lifestyle, not just a momentary feeling. In Jesus' name I pray, Amen and To God Be The Glory!

JUNE 11. - "NEVER STOP DOING GOOD"

In a world that can feel cold, unfair, and unkind, it's easy to become hard-hearted. Life will tempt you to hate, to retaliate, to isolate, or to close yourself off. But the Spirit of God calls us higher. He calls us to live with compassion, humility, gratitude, and grace no matter what we face. And it is through this kind of living that we most clearly reflect the character of Christ.

The phrase, "Hate no one no matter how much they've wronged you," challenges us to release bitterness and embrace forgiveness. Hate is a heavy burden that chains us to the offense. But forgiveness, though not always easy, is liberating. Jesus taught us to love our enemies and pray for those who persecute us, not because they deserve it, but because He loved us when we were undeserving too (Romans 5:8).

"Live humbly no matter how wealthy you become." True wealth is not measured in material possessions but in the richness of a surrendered heart. Humility is not thinking less of yourself; it is thinking of yourself less. No matter how much God blesses us, we are to walk humbly, remembering that every good thing comes from Him, not ourselves (Deuteronomy 8:18).

"Think positively no matter how hard life is." This is not about blind optimism, but about faith-filled perspective. When life gets difficult, God doesn't call us to ignore reality, but to cling to hope. Philippians 4:8 reminds us to fix our thoughts on what is true, noble, right, and pure. It is in choosing gratitude over grumbling that we find strength to endure.

"Give much even when you've been given little." Generosity is not about abundance; it's about attitude. The widow with two small coins gave more than all the wealthy because she gave with a pure heart (Mark 12:41–44). When we give, even in lack, we declare that God is our source.

"Forgive all, especially yourself." Forgiving others is difficult, but forgiving ourselves can be even harder. Yet holding on to guilt and shame only delays our healing. Jesus died not only to forgive us, but to free us. Let it go. Accept His grace. Move forward.

And finally, "Never stop praying for the best for everyone." Prayer is not only powerful, it's transformational. Praying for others, even those who've hurt us, keeps our hearts soft and aligned with God's will. It shifts our focus from pain to purpose, from offense to intercession.

In all things, we are called to reflect the relentless love of Jesus. These principles aren't just good advice, they are the fruit of a life surrendered to the Holy Spirit. And when we live this way, we become light in dark places, peace in the midst of storms, and hope in a hurting world.

"Let love be without dissimulation. Abhor that which is evil; cleave to that which is good. Be kindly affectioned one to another with brotherly love; in honour preferring one another. Rejoicing in hope; patient in tribulation; continuing instant in prayer."
Romans 12:9–10, 12 (KJV)

Father God, I thank You for being my constant example of love, grace, and mercy. Help me to live in a way that honors You, not returning evil for evil, but doing good even when it's hard. Give me the strength to forgive, the courage to give, the humility to stay grounded, and the wisdom to see life through Your eyes. Let my heart be soft, my words be kind, and my spirit be generous. And above all, teach me to never stop praying for others, for myself, and for this world. In Jesus' name I pray, Amen and To God Be The Glory!

JUNE 12. - "GOD CALLS THE UNLIKELY"

All throughout the Bible, God seems to have a pattern: He rarely chooses the most qualified, the most celebrated, or the most obvious candidate for His work. Instead, He calls on the unlikely, the ones the world overlooks, dismisses, or even doubts. Why? So that when the task is accomplished, there is no question that it was His power at work and not human ability.

Moses was a fugitive who claimed he couldn't speak well, yet God chose him to stand before Pharaoh and lead an entire nation out of Egypt. Gideon was hiding in fear when God called him to lead Israel's army to victory. David was a shepherd boy, forgotten even by his own family, until God anointed him king. The disciples were fishermen, tax collectors, and zealots, ordinary men who turned the world upside down through the power of the Holy Spirit.

When God chooses the unlikely, He strips away the notion that success is based on status, skill, or strength. Instead, the spotlight shifts to Him. It's in our weakness that His strength is perfected (2 Corinthians 12:9). Being "unlikely" in the world's eyes simply means you are the perfect candidate in God's. He delights in using the underestimated to accomplish the unimaginable.

So, if you feel overlooked, underqualified, or unworthy, take heart, you are exactly the kind of person God loves to call. When He works through you, people will have no choice but to see His glory, because they will know it wasn't you ~ it was Him.

"But God chose the foolish things of the world to shame the wise; God chose the weak things of the world to shame the strong." 1 Corinthians 1:27 (NIV)

Heavenly Father, I thank You for reminding me that You do not call the qualified, but You qualify the called. Help me to embrace the truth that my weaknesses are opportunities for Your strength to shine. Remove any fear, doubt, or insecurity that holds me back from stepping into the purpose You have placed on my life. I pray that everything I do points others to You, so that Your power and glory are undeniable. In Jesus' name I pray.

Amen and To God Be The Glory!

JUNE 13. - "YES, I'M THAT KIND OF FRIEND

True friendship is not built on flattery or sugar-coated words. It's built on love, honesty, and a commitment to help one another grow in Christ. The Bible teaches us that "Faithful are the wounds of a friend, but the kisses of an enemy are deceitful" (Proverbs 27:6 KJV). This means a real friend cares more about your spiritual health than your temporary comfort.

Sometimes, the truth stings. It's easier to nod along, stay silent, or say what someone wants to hear so we avoid conflict. But a godly friend understands that silence in the face of sin, destructive choices, or spiritual drifting is not kindness, it's neglect. Love compels us to speak truth, even when it risks misunderstanding or offense.

Jesus Himself modeled this with His disciples. He rebuked Peter when he spoke out of step with God's will. He corrected James and John when their ambitions got in the way of the Kingdom's purpose. In each case, His words were firm, but His heart was full of love.

When we choose to be the kind of friend who speaks truth in love, we give our friends the gift of accountability. We remind them of God's Word, God's will, and their God-given identity. And while they may not thank us in the moment, those words have the power to protect, correct, and restore them for years to come.

Being this kind of friend takes courage, humility, and prayer. It means we must also be willing to receive truth from others with the same grace we extend. Friendship rooted in honesty is not just about keeping each other happy, it's about keeping each other holy.

"Faithful are the wounds of a friend; but the kisses of an enemy are deceitful."

Proverbs 27:6 (KJV)

Lord, thank You for the gift of true friendship that is grounded in love and truth. Help me to be the kind of friend who speaks with grace, even when my words are hard to hear. Give me the courage to love enough to confront and the humility to listen when I need correction. Let my friendships be marked by honesty, faithfulness, and a shared desire to grow closer to You. In Jesus' name I pray, Amen and To God Be The Glory!

JUNE 14. - "THE STATE OF CONTENTMENT"

Contentment is not about having everything we want, it's about trusting that what God has provided is enough for today. In a world that constantly tells us we need more and more. More money, more recognition, more possessions, more status, it's easy to slip into the trap of dissatisfaction. The danger is that if we do not learn to be content with what we have, we will always be chasing something else, and nothing will ever feel like enough.

The Apostle Paul understood this deeply. In Philippians 4:11–12, he wrote that he had learned to be content in any circumstance, whether in plenty or in want. That "learning" didn't happen overnight; it was the fruit of walking with God, trusting His plan, and finding joy in His presence rather than in earthly gain.

Discontentment robs us of gratitude and blinds us to the blessings we already have. It creates a restless heart, one that is always reaching but never resting. True satisfaction is not found in things, people, or achievements, it is found in Christ alone. When our hearts are anchored in Him, we can face every season whether in abundance or lack, in peace.

Choosing contentment doesn't mean you stop dreaming or striving for better; it means your joy is no longer dependent on what you achieve or acquire. It means you can praise God for where you are, while trusting Him for where He's taking you.

"But godliness with contentment is great gain." 1 Timothy 6:6 (KJV)

Lord, thank You for all You have given me. Teach me to find joy in the blessings I already have, and to trust Your timing for what is to come. Help me to resist the pull of comparison and the lie that I need more to be fulfilled. Let my heart be anchored in You so that I can live with peace, gratitude, and contentment in every season. In Jesus' name I pray, Amen and To God Be The Glory!

JUNE 15. - "REMEMBER Ephesians 4:26–27 ~ DON'T GIVE THE DEVIL OPPORTUNITY"

Anger is a natural human emotion, but when left unchecked, it can quickly become a foothold for the enemy. The Bible warns us in Ephesians 4:26–27: "Be angry and do not sin; do not let the sun go down on your anger and give no opportunity to the devil." This means that while feeling anger isn't necessarily a sin, holding on to it, feeding it, and letting it grow into resentment can open the door for the enemy to sow division, bitterness, and destruction in our hearts and relationships.

When we refuse to address anger, it festers. It changes the way we think, speak, and treat others. The longer it sits in our hearts, the more room it gives the devil to whisper lies — lies about ourselves, about others, and even about God. What starts as a small hurt can grow into a barrier that blocks love, joy, and peace from flowing in our lives.

That's why God calls us to deal with anger quickly. To have hard conversations, extend forgiveness, and release offenses before the day ends. This isn't just for the benefit of the person who wronged us; it's for the health of our own souls. Forgiveness breaks the enemy's grip and frees us to live in the light of God's grace.

Tonight, before the sun sets, ask yourself: Is there someone I need to forgive? Is there an offense I've been holding on to? Hand it over to God and let Him bring peace to your heart. Closing the door to anger is how we keep the enemy from ever getting a foothold in the first place.

"Be angry, and do not sin: do not let the sun go down on your wrath, nor give place to the devil." Ephesians 4:26–27 (NKJV)

Lord, I thank You for the reminder that unresolved anger can give the enemy a foothold in my life. Help me to address offenses quickly, to speak the truth in love, and to extend forgiveness as You have forgiven me. Remove bitterness from my heart, and replace it with peace that surpasses all understanding. Let my actions, even in moments of frustration, reflect Your love and bring glory to Your name. In Jesus' name I pray, Amen and To God Be The Glory!

JUNE 16. - "REMEMBER PROVERBS 29:16 ~ THE DOWNFALL OF EVIL"

This proverb contrasts two realities:

The rise of wickedness brings more sin. When evil people flourish, especially in positions of influence their behavior sets lower standards and emboldens others to follow suit. Sin becomes normalized and even celebrated in such environments.

Hope remains for the righteous. Despite appearances of progress and dominance of wrongdoing, the righteous are assured of seeing the downfall of the wicked. God's justice will prevail, and ultimately His righteousness will triumph.

In today's world where corruption, immorality, and injustice often seem to go unchecked, this verse serves as a powerful reassurance. We are called to walk in integrity amidst chaos, anchored by the faith that fleeting evil will not prevail. Every act of righteousness and every step taken in faithfulness honors God, and in due time, God's justice will be seen clearly.

"When the wicked thrive, so does sin, but the righteous will see their downfall."

(Proverbs 29:16)

Heavenly Father, thank You for the wisdom of Your Word and the assurance that, though wickedness may flourish for a time, You are sovereign and righteous justice will prevail. Help me to remain steadfast in integrity and faith even when evil appears to be rising around me. Strengthen my heart with patience, trusting that in Your time, the proud will fall and Your faithful children will witness Your judgment. Let my life reflect Your truth and bring glory to Your name. In Jesus' name I pray, Amen and To God Be The Glory!

JUNE 17. - "GUARDING A GOOD HEART WITHOUT HARDENING IT"

When you have a good heart, you tend to give more than you keep for yourself. You trust beyond reason, you love without limits, and you help without hesitation. But often, the very people you bless will be the ones who betray you. It's one of the hardest lessons to learn, and that is goodness doesn't always produce gratitude in others.

Even Jesus experienced this. He healed the sick, fed the hungry, and forgave sinners, yet He was betrayed with a kiss by someone in His inner circle. Having a good heart will sometimes attract people who take advantage, manipulate, or deceive. That doesn't mean you should stop being good; it means you must learn to guard your heart without building walls that keep love out.

Guarding your heart doesn't mean becoming cold, bitter, or suspicious. It means having wisdom to discern who can be trusted with the treasures of your time, love, and energy. It means setting boundaries, so your compassion is not exploited, while still allowing God's love to flow through you.

If you've been backstabbed, remember, God sees every injustice. He will repay, restore, and redeem what was taken. Your good heart is not the problem; it's your crown. Keep it pure but let God teach you how to wear it with wisdom.

"Above all else, guard your heart, for everything you do flows from it." Proverbs 4:23 (NIV)

Heavenly Father, I thank You for giving me a heart that loves deeply. Help me not to grow bitter when others betray or misuse my kindness. Teach me to guard my heart with Your wisdom, to love without being naive, and to forgive without enabling harm. Heal the wounds caused by betrayal and restore my trust in Your goodness. May my love always reflect Yours, pure yet wise. In Jesus' name, Amen and To God Be The Glory!

JUNE 18. - "FROM A TRAP HOUSE TO THE CHURCH HOUSE"

One of the most beautiful truths of the Gospel is that God specializes in transformation. He takes what the world deems hopeless and breathes new life into it. He can turn an alcoholic into an apostolic preacher, a quiet and timid soul into a bold, Spirit-filled tongue talker, a joint roller into a holy roller, a so-called zero into a hero, a "nobody" into a "somebody," and a sinner bound by chains into a saint washed by the blood. Only God can take someone from the trap house to the church house and give them a testimony that shakes the gates of hell.

The enemy loves to convince people that their past disqualifies them from God's future. But God's Word tells a different story. Your past is simply the canvas on which He paints His masterpiece of grace. Every broken place becomes a platform for His power. Every mess becomes a message. Every setback becomes a setup for a comeback.

The Apostle Paul knew this firsthand. Once a persecutor of Christians, he became one of the greatest apostles of all time, not because of his own merit, but because of God's mercy.

It doesn't matter how far you've fallen or how long you've been bound, God's arm is never too short to save. The same God who raised Jesus from the dead is the same God who can raise you from the ashes of addiction, sin, and shame.

"Therefore if any man be in Christ, he is a new creature: old things are passed away; behold, all things are become new." 2 Corinthians 5:17 (KJV)

Heavenly Father, I thank You that no one is beyond Your reach. Thank You for the transforming power of the blood of Jesus. Take every broken piece of my life and use it for Your glory. Help me to see others through eyes of grace, believing that if You can change me, You can change anyone. From the trap house to the church house, let my testimony be living proof that You still save, deliver, and set free. In Jesus' name, Amen and To God Be The Glory!

JUNE 19. - "LET GOD LEAD ~ NOT YOUR EMOTIONS"

Our emotions are powerful. They can inspire us, warn us, or even protect us. But if left unchecked, they can also mislead us, causing us to react impulsively, speak recklessly, or make choices we later regret. Many times, the most damaging decisions are not made after careful thought but in the heat of the moment when emotions run high.

That's why we must be intentional about pausing before we act. One moment in God's presence can shift everything. Anger can turn into peace, confusion into clarity, and fear into faith. When we take time to stop and pray, we invite the Holy Spirit to steady our hearts and guide our steps.

Jesus Himself modeled this. Before choosing His twelve disciples, He spent the night in prayer (Luke 6:12-13). Before facing the cross, He went to the Garden of Gethsemane to seek His Father's will. If the Son of God stopped to pray before major decisions, how much more should we?

When you pause to pray, you're not wasting time, you're gaining wisdom. You're allowing the voice of God to quiet the noise of your feelings. And in that stillness, His peace will become the anchor for your choices.

"Be anxious for nothing, but in everything by prayer and supplication with thanksgiving let your requests be made known unto God. And the peace of God, which passeth all understanding, shall keep your hearts and minds through Christ Jesus."

Philippians 4:6-7 (KJV)

Heavenly Father, please help me not to be ruled by my emotions. Teach me to stop, pray, and seek Your guidance before I decide or act. Remind me that one moment in Your presence can change everything. Fill me with Your peace and give me wisdom to make decisions that honor You. In Jesus' name, Amen and To God Be The Glory!

JUNE 20. - "WHEN THE BATTLE BEGINS"

There's a common misconception that following Jesus means life will suddenly be free of trials and struggles. But the truth is, becoming a Christian doesn't end the battle, it begins a greater one. Before Christ, we often went along with the ways of the world and the schemes of the enemy. But once we belong to Him, we become a direct target for spiritual opposition.

When we choose to follow Jesus, we are declaring war on the kingdom of darkness. Temptations may intensify. Old habits may try to pull us back. The enemy will look for ways to discourage, distract, and destroy our faith. But the good news is we don't fight alone. God equips us with spiritual armor, surrounds us with His presence, and gives us His Word as our weapon.

Paul reminds us in Ephesians 6:12: "For we wrestle not against flesh and blood, but against principalities, against powers, against the rulers of the darkness of this world, against spiritual wickedness in high places." (KJV)

Yes, the war is real, but so is our victory in Christ. Every battle we face is an opportunity to see God's power at work. Our strength is not in ourselves but in the One who has already overcome the world (John 16:33).

If you're feeling the weight of the fight, remember, it's a sign you're on the right side. The enemy doesn't waste energy on those who aren't a threat to his plans. Stand firm. Suit up in God's armor. And know that the One who called you is faithful to see you through.

Heavenly Father, I truly thank You for calling me into Your kingdom, even knowing the battles that would come. Strengthen me for the fight and help me to stand firm in Your truth. Remind me that the war I face is spiritual, and that in Christ, I already have the victory. Clothe me in Your armor daily and keep my eyes fixed on You. In Jesus' name I pray, Amen and To God Be The Glory!

JUNE 21. - "IN RECOGNITION TO OUR FATHERS ~ ON FATHERS DAY"

Father's Day is more than a holiday, it is an opportunity to honor and reflect upon the gift of fatherhood, both in earthly terms and through our Heavenly Father. Earthly fathers carry the weight of responsibility to guide, protect, provide, and nurture their children, but their greatest calling is to model the love and character of God in the home.

When we think about fatherhood in the light of Scripture, we are reminded that true fatherhood begins with God Himself. He is the ultimate example of patience, provision, and love. Even when earthly fathers fall short, God remains steadfast, proving Himself to be the perfect Father who never fails us.

"As a father has compassion on his children, so the Lord has compassion on those who fear him." Psalm 103:13 (NIV)

This verse captures the essence of a father's role. Compassion is not weakness it is strength clothed in love. A father is not only a provider of material needs but also a spiritual covering. He is called to reflect God's heart by showing mercy, grace, and care, guiding his children toward righteousness.

Fathers may often feel the weight of inadequacy or pressure, but the reminder of Psalm 103:13 is that God equips those He calls. Fatherhood is not walked alone, God partners with fathers, giving wisdom, strength, and courage to raise children in the fear of the Lord.

As we celebrate this Father's Day, let us:

Honor fathers for the sacrifices they make, both seen and unseen.

Encourage fathers to continue leaning on God as their source of wisdom.

Remember that whether our earthly fathers are present, absent, or have passed on, we all share in the eternal security of having a Heavenly Father who never leaves nor forsakes us.

Heavenly Father, we thank You for the gift of fathers and the role they play in our lives. Bless every father with strength, wisdom, and compassion to lead their families in Your ways. For those who may feel the weight of inadequacy, remind them that You are their guide and source of help. For fathers who are weary, refresh their spirit. For those who have gone before us, we give thanks for the legacy they left behind. And Lord, for those who never knew their earthly fathers or experienced brokenness in that relationship, we thank You that You are the perfect Father, faithful, loving, and everlasting. We honor You above all today, our ultimate Father, and give You all the glory. In Jesus' mighty name we pray, Amen and To God Be The Glory!

JUNE 22. - "LOOKING BACK TO MOVE FORWARD"

There are moments in life when the road ahead seems impossibly long. The dreams we hold, the healing we seek, or the growth we desire can make us feel like we're barely making progress. But sometimes, God invites us to pause, not to give up, but to look back. Not with regret, but with gratitude.

You may think you still have a long way to go, but when you glance over your shoulder, you'll see the miles of battles fought, lessons learned, and victories big and small that God has already carried you through. That's not by your strength alone. Every step has been under His watchful eye, every tear collected by His hand, and every stumbling moment turned into a steppingstone by His grace.

Israel experienced this same truth. Over and over, God reminded His people to remember where they had been and how far He had brought them out of slavery, through the wilderness, and into promise. Sometimes the greatest fuel for moving forward is remembering that if He brought you this far, He will not leave you now.

"Being confident of this very thing, that he which hath begun a good work in you will perform it until the day of Jesus Christ." Philippians 1:6 (KJV)

Heavenly Father, thank You for the journey so far. When I get discouraged by how far I still have to go, please remind me of the mountains You've already moved and the valleys You've already carried me through. Fill my heart with gratitude for the progress You have made in me and give me the strength to keep walking in faith toward the future You have prepared. I trust that the work You started in me will be completed in Your perfect timing. In Jesus' name I pray, Amen and To God Be The Glory!

JUNE 23. - "FAITH THAT BUILDS"

Faith is powerful, but faith that is alive always produces action. Noah didn't just believe God's warning about the coming flood; he put his belief into motion. God told him to build an ark, and Noah obeyed. Not for a week, not for a month, but for years, enduring ridicule, doubt, and the weariness of long, hard labor.

Faith alone didn't save Noah. His trust in God moved him to build the ark, plank by plank, according to God's instructions. If Noah had only believed but never acted, the floodwaters would have swept him away like everyone else. His faith was made complete by his obedience.

In our own lives, it's easy to say we trust God. But real trust shows up in the choices we make, the sacrifices we endure, and the discipline we keep, even when others don't understand. Sometimes building your "ark" looks like daily prayer, consistent worship, studying His Word, forgiving when it's hard, or standing firm in holiness while the world mocks you.

Faith is the foundation, but obedience builds the shelter. God's promises are always sure, but He often calls us to partner with Him through action. Just as the ark became Noah's place of salvation, your obedience today is preparing a place for your deliverance tomorrow.

"By faith Noah, being warned of God of things not seen as yet, moved with fear, prepared an ark to the saving of his house; by the which he condemned the world, and became heir of the righteousness which is by faith." Hebrews 11:7 (KJV)

Dear Lord, I thank You for the reminder that faith and obedience go hand in hand. Help me to move beyond words and into action, building according to Your instructions. When work feels hard, long or lonely, strengthen my hands and steady my heart. May my obedience be a testimony of my trust in You and may the "ark" You call me to build be a vessel for Your glory. In Jesus' name I pray, Amen and To God Be The Glory!

JUNE 24. - "REMEMBERING YOUR WORTH IN CHRIST"

One of the deepest pains in life isn't just losing someone you value, it's losing yourself in the process of valuing them too much. When our hearts are bound so tightly to another person that we forget our own worth, we begin to live in imbalance. We pour out everything for them yet leave nothing for ourselves. In doing so, we unintentionally place them in a position that only God should hold in our hearts.

This isn't about becoming selfish; it's about remembering that you, too, are God's creation, fearfully and wonderfully made. Your value isn't determined by how much someone else loves, appreciates, or accepts you. It's defined by the One who designed you with purpose and calls you His own.

When you lose sight of your identity in Christ, you risk shaping your worth around people who may never see you the way God does. Relationships, no matter how beautiful, are healthiest when both people remember their individual value in the Lord. Loving someone should never cost you the love and respect you owe yourself as God's child.

God never asks you to diminish your light so someone else can shine. He calls you to walk confidently in your identity, so your love for others flows from a place of wholeness—not emptiness. When you value yourself as God values you, you can love others without losing yourself.

"I will praise thee; for I am fearfully and wonderfully made: marvelous are thy works; and that my soul knoweth right well." Psalm 139:14 (KJV)

Heavenly Father, thank You for reminding me of my worth in You. Forgive me for the times I've lost sight of who I am by focusing too much on pleasing others. Teach me to value myself the way You value me and help me to love others from a place of strength, not depletion. Restore my confidence in Your design for my life and keep me grounded in my identity as Your beloved child. In Jesus' name, Amen and To God Be The Glory!

JUNE 25. - "LET THEM TALK ~ STAY TRUE TO GOD'S PATH"

Life will always have an audience. Some cheering you on, others criticizing your every move. The truth is, whether you do good or do bad, someone will always have something to say. Jesus Himself was perfect, yet He was still accused, mocked, and misunderstood. If even the Son of God could not escape the judgment of others, why should we expect any different?

When we allow the opinions of people to guide our steps, we give them control over our peace. But when we anchor ourselves in God's truth, we realize that our worth and direction come from Him alone. Your calling is too important to be derailed by gossip, criticism, or misunderstanding.

If you live to please people, you will always feel the pressure to change who you are. But if you live to please God, you will find the freedom to be exactly who He created you to be. So, keep doing what God has placed in your heart. Walk in integrity. Love without condition. Serve with humility. And when the chatter comes, and it will, let it be background noise to the sound of your obedience.

Remember, at the end of your life, you will stand before God, not a crowd of critics. Live for the "Well done" from Him, not the applause or approval of people.

"Whatever you do, work heartily, as for the Lord and not for men." Colossians 3:23 (ESV)

Lord, help me to keep my eyes fixed on You, not on the opinions of others. Teach me to walk in obedience to Your will, even when others misunderstand or criticize me. Give me strength to stay faithful, courage to be who You've called me to be, and grace to love those who speak against me. My life belongs to You, and I will live for Your approval alone. In Jesus' name I pray, Amen and To God Be The Glory!

JUNE 26. - "LETTING GO OF WHAT YOU CAN'T CONTROL"

Worry is a silent thief. It creeps in quietly, often starting with a small thought, then growing until it steals your joy, your peace, and your focus. We convince ourselves that worrying will somehow prepare us for what's coming, but the truth is it changes nothing about the outcome and everything about our spirit.

Some situations in life simply have no clear answers right now. We face trials, delays, and uncertainties that we cannot fully explain. But God never asked us to understand everything. He asked us to trust Him in everything. When we release the weight of "needing to know," we make room for His peace to guard our hearts.

Jesus addressed this very struggle in Matthew 6, reminding us that worry does not add a single hour to our lives. Instead, He points us to the birds of the air and the lilies of the field, for God cares for them without their striving, and He will surely care for us.

We must learn to hand over the questions we can't answer and the problems we can't solve to the One who holds all wisdom and power. When we stop trying to carry it all, we discover the freedom to live in the present, to enjoy God's blessings today, and to rest in the truth that He's already working on tomorrow.

"Casting all your care upon him; for he careth for you." 1 Peter 5:7 (KJV)

Lord, I confess that I often allow worry to rob me of joy and peace. Help me to trust You fully, even when I don't have all the answers. Teach me to release every burden into Your hands and to rest in the assurance that You are in control. Fill my heart with peace that surpasses all understanding and keep me rooted in the truth of Your care for me. In Jesus' name, Amen and To God Be The Glory!

JUNE 27. - "THE WHOLE TRUTH OF THE GOSPEL"

One of the most dangerous lies circulating in our world today is the belief that everyone will automatically go to heaven simply because Christ died for all. While it is true that His death was sufficient for every person, the gift of salvation is not applied to every life without faith and obedience to the Gospel. Telling people otherwise may seem comforting, but it is spiritually cruel. It gives false assurance where repentance, belief, and transformation are required.

The Apostle Paul gives us the foundation of the Gospel in 1 Corinthians 15:1–4. He reminds us that Christ died for our sins according to the Scriptures, that He was buried, and that He rose again on the third day. But Paul also warns that we must receive this Gospel and stand in it, holding fast to the truth, lest we believe in vain. The Gospel is not just a story, it is a call to respond.

When we share a watered-down version of salvation, we remove the urgency for repentance, the need for faith, and the call to follow Christ daily. We must speak the truth in love: Yes, Jesus died for all, but the way to eternal life is through Him alone, and we must believe, repent, and walk in obedience to His Word. Anything less is not the Gospel, it's a counterfeit comfort that leads people further from God's truth.

We are called to be messengers, not editors, of God's message. The loving thing to do is to share the Gospel in its fullness, even when it's uncomfortable, because the truth is the only thing that truly saves.

"Moreover, brethren, I declare unto you the gospel which I preached unto you, which also ye have received, and wherein ye stand; By which also ye are saved, if ye keep in memory what I preached unto you, unless ye have believed in vain. For I delivered unto you first of all that which I also received, how that Christ died for our sins according to the scriptures; And that he was buried, and that he rose again the third day according to the scriptures." — 1 Corinthians 15:1–4 (KJV)

Lord, give me the courage to share Your Gospel in its fullness and truth. Help me to love people enough to tell them what they need to hear, not just what they want to hear. Guard my heart from compromising Your Word for the sake of acceptance and fill me with boldness to speak of Christ's death, burial, and resurrection as the only way to eternal life. May I always be faithful to the message You entrusted to us. In Jesus' name I pray, Amen and To God Be The Glory!

JUNE 28. - "SURROUNDED AND COVERED"

As believers, we are not promised a life free from the enemy's attacks. In fact, Scripture makes it clear that the devil prowls like a roaring lion, seeking someone to devour (1 Peter 5:8). But we are not left defenseless. We have the mighty protection of God's Spirit and the cleansing, covering power of the blood of Jesus.

No matter what the devil and his agents are plotting against you, they will not succeed. Why? Because the fire of the Holy Spirit surrounds you like a wall that no demonic force can penetrate. Just as God placed a hedge of protection around Job, He places His divine shield over you and your household.

The blood of Jesus is not just a symbol it is a spiritual weapon. It declares that you belong to God, that your sins are forgiven, and that Satan has no legal right over your life. Every scheme, trap, or curse formed against you is already defeated in Jesus' name. When the enemy comes in like a flood, the Spirit of the Lord lifts up a standard against him (Isaiah 59:19).

So, walk in confidence today. You are not unprotected. You are not alone. Heaven's armies stand guard over you, the Holy Spirit's fire surrounds you, and the blood of Jesus speaks a better word over your life. The devil may try ~ but he will never win.

"No weapon that is formed against thee shall prosper; and every tongue that shall rise against thee in judgment thou shalt condemn. This is the heritage of the servants of the LORD, and their righteousness is of me, saith the LORD." Isaiah 54:17 (KJV)

Heavenly Father, I thank You for the covering of the blood of Jesus over my life and my household. I stand in faith, knowing that no weapon formed against me will prosper. Surround me with the fire of Your Holy Spirit and let every plan of the enemy be destroyed. Fill me with peace and confidence that I am safe in Your hands. In Jesus' name, Amen and To God Be The Glory!

JUNE 29. - "TUSTING THE UNSEEN PLAN"

Life has a way of throwing moments at us that shake our foundation. Some seasons bring joy and clarity, while others seem clouded with pain, confusion, and uncertainty. The phrase "Everything happens for a reason" is easy to say when life feels good, but it becomes a test of faith when we face heartbreak, betrayal, loss, or unexpected change.

The truth is, the "reason" isn't always visible in the moment. Sometimes it hurts so much that we can't see past the tears. Sometimes it's so hard that the weight on our chest makes it difficult to breathe. Yet, in the midst of it all, God's hand is still at work.

God's divine plan doesn't promise us a pain-free journey, but it does promise that every single detail, even the most difficult ones, are working together for a greater purpose. Just like a tapestry woven from threads of many colors, our lives are made up of bright and dark moments that God uses to create a masterpiece. The dark threads are just as important as the light ones, because without them, the full picture wouldn't be complete.

The enemy wants us to believe that pain is pointless. He wants us to think God has abandoned us in our trial. But the truth is that your trial is part of your testimony. Your pain is part of your preparation. Your tears water the seeds of growth you can't yet see.

Romans 8:28 reminds us: "And we know that all things work together for good to those who love God, to those who are the called according to His purpose."

This doesn't mean all things are good in themselves. Such as loss, illness, disappointment, and betrayal are real and hurt deeply. But God takes even those things and bends them toward our ultimate good. Sometimes, what we thought was the end of our story was simply God turning the page to something better.

So even when you don't understand, never stop trusting God. His timing is perfect. His plan is flawless. And one day, when you look back, you'll see that every valley, every storm, and every unanswered question was leading you to exactly where you were meant to be.

Heavenly Father, I thank You that even when I cannot understand, I can trust You. When life hurts and feels unfair, remind me that Your ways are higher than my ways and Your thoughts are higher than my thoughts. Help me to rest in Your promises and believe that You are working all things together for my good. Give me peace in the waiting, strength in the trial, and unwavering faith in Your plan. I surrender my life to You, knowing that You see the full picture when I can only see a piece. In Jesus' name I pray, Amen and To God Be The Glory!

JUNE 30. - "WHEN DISRESPECT BECOMES YOUR ANSWER"

There are moments in life when we pray for clarity, when we plead with God to show us if we should hold on or let go, trust or walk away. Sometimes, we expect a gentle sign or a peaceful nudge. But often, the answer comes in a form we didn't want to see, and that's through someone's actions, words, or behavior. The disrespect is the closure.

When someone consistently dishonors you by ignoring your worth, mistreating your heart, or dismissing your boundaries, that is God showing you the truth. You don't need a second opinion when the evidence is already in front of you. Disrespect, no matter what the excuse, reveals a person's heart posture toward you.

This doesn't mean we stop loving people in the way Christ commands. It means we love them from a safe distance when necessary. Jesus Himself walked away from towns that rejected Him (Matthew 10:14). He knew that staying in a place where He was not valued would only hinder the mission the Father had given Him.

When the disrespect comes, it is not a call for revenge, it's an invitation to release. God is protecting you, redirecting you, and freeing you from what could damage your purpose. Sometimes the closure isn't a long conversation or an official goodbye; it's simply accepting the truth that their behavior has already spoken.

Ephesians 4:31–32 (NIV) reminds us: "Get rid of all bitterness, rage and anger, brawling and slander, along with every form of malice. Be kind and compassionate to one another, forgiving each other, just as in Christ God forgave you."

This means we can acknowledge the disrespect, learn from it, and still choose to walk in forgiveness. Not because they deserve it, but because we deserve peace. Disrespect doesn't define you, it frees you. Closure isn't always given with a bow; sometimes, it's wrapped in a lesson. And once you see it, you don't have to keep reopening the door that God has already shut.

Heavenly Father, thank You for the times when You make the truth clear, even when it comes in ways that hurt. Help me to recognize when someone's actions are revealing their heart and giving me the courage to let go without bitterness. Teach me to forgive, not for their sake alone, but so I can walk in freedom and peace. Guard my heart from offense and lead me toward the people and places that honor the calling You've placed on my life. In Jesus' name I pray, Amen and To God Be The Glory!

JULY INTRODUCTION

The month of July marks the heart of the year. A season when many of us pause to reflect on where we've been and where we're going. For some, the first half of the year has been full of blessings. For others, it's been marked by trials, disappointments, or questions that seem to have no easy answers. Whether you are celebrating victories or wrestling with challenges, God's Word remains an unshakable source of wisdom, comfort, and guidance.

This month, our devotionals are built around the reality that life often presents us with pressing problems. Such issues that demand attention, strain our faith, and sometimes leave us feeling unsure of what to do next. The world offers countless opinions, but as believers, we must turn to the unchanging truth of Scripture. The Bible does not just speak to our eternal salvation, it also speaks to our daily struggles. It addresses worry, fear, relationships, finances, temptation, grief, and the storms that life throws our way.

God's Word doesn't just tell us what is right, it shows us how to live it out. It doesn't just give us answers, it offers hope, peace, and strength to endure while we wait for those answers to unfold. This is why the July devotionals will focus on connecting specific life challenges with direct biblical solutions. Each reading will be a reminder that the same God who parted the Red Sea, raised the dead, and calmed the storm still moves on behalf of His children today.

Proverbs 3:5–6 (KJV) captures the heart of this month's theme: "Trust in the Lord with all your heart and lean not on your own understanding; in all your ways acknowledge Him, and He shall direct your paths."

In July, we invite you to open your heart, quiet your mind, and let God's truth be the lens through which you view your challenges. Every pressing problem you face is an opportunity for God to reveal His power, His wisdom, and His faithfulness in your life.

Heavenly Father, as we step into this month of July, we thank You for the gift of Your Word. Which is a lamp to our feet and a light to our path. Help us to come before You with open hearts, ready to receive Your truth for every challenge we face. Teach us to trust Your timing, to lean on Your wisdom, and to find peace in Your promises. May each devotional draw us closer to You and equip us to face life's pressing problems with faith and courage. In Jesus' name I pray, Amen and To God Be The Glory!

JULY 1. - "A WOMAN WHO SHAKES THE KINGDOM OF DARKNESS"

Be the kind of woman who, when your feet hit the floor in the morning, the devil says, "Oh no, she's up."

When a godly woman rises each morning with her heart fixed on Christ, she becomes more than just another believer starting her day, she becomes a force that unsettles the kingdom of darkness. Such a woman is not easily moved by trials, nor intimidated by the enemy's schemes, because she knows who she belongs to and where her strength comes from.

The devil fears the praying woman, the worshiping woman, the woman who knows her authority in Christ. He knows that when she gets up, her words carry weight, her prayers shift atmospheres, and her presence pushes back darkness. This kind of woman is not defined by her circumstances but by her covenant with God. She understands that each morning is not just another day, but another opportunity to walk in victory, to shine the light of Christ, and to remind the enemy of his defeat at Calvary.

This doesn't mean life is free from battles. It means she has chosen to stand firm, clothed in the armor of God, and refuses to be silent or passive in her faith. She's the kind of woman who prays over her family, intercedes for her community, stands on the promises of God, and refuses to bow to fear. She knows that greater is He who is in her than he who is in the world.

"Submit yourselves therefore to God. Resist the devil, and he will flee from you." James 4:7 (KJV)

This scripture reminds us that the power of a godly woman is not in her own strength, but in her submission to God. Her strength comes from obedience, her boldness from faith, and her victory from the Spirit of the Lord living inside her.

Heavenly Father, I thank You for the gift of this new day. I rise with a heart of gratitude, ready to walk in Your strength and not my own. Lord, clothe me with Your armor and cover me with Your blood. Let my life reflect Your power, so that when the enemy sees me rise, he trembles at the authority of Christ within me. Use my words, my prayers, and my actions to push back darkness and advance Your Kingdom. Keep me steadfast, unmovable, and always abounding in Your work. In Jesus' name I pray. Amen and To God Be The Glory!

JULY 2. - "THE GIFT OF GODLY FRIENDSHIP AND BROTHERHOOD"

Life has a way of revealing who truly stands with you. When the sun is shining, the road is smooth, and the victories are many, friends are plentiful. But when the clouds gather, the winds howl, and you find yourself walking through the valley of trials, the crowd often thins out, and it is in those moments that the truth of Proverbs 17:17 comes alive.

"A friend loveth at all times, and a brother is born for adversity." Proverbs 17:17 (KJV)

This verse draws a powerful distinction between two types of relationships ~ friendship and brotherhood.

1. A Friend Who Loves at All Times

A godly friend is not swayed by circumstances. Their love is constant, not just in seasons of joy, but also in times of hardship, failure, and weakness. This love reflects the nature of Christ, who is the ultimate Friend that "sticks closer than a brother" (Proverbs 18:24). A friend who loves at all times offers encouragement, correction, and compassion. They see your worth even when you're too weary to see it yourself.

2. A Brother Born for Adversity

The second part of the verse speaks to a bond forged for the storms. A brother, whether by blood or by spiritual kinship, is often revealed and refined in the fires of adversity. While a friend may choose to stay, a brother feels compelled to stand. They shoulder the burden with you, fight alongside you, and refuse to let you battle alone.

3. God's Design for Community

God never intended for His children to walk through life isolated. Ecclesiastes 4:9-10 reminds us, "Two are better than one ~ For if they fall, the one will lift up his fellow." True friends and brothers are God's provision for your journey, divinely placed to lift you, shield you, and remind you that you are never abandoned.

As believers, we are called to be that friend who loves at all times and that brother who stands firm in adversity. This means showing up when it's inconvenient, loving when it's costly, and holding on when others let go.

Heavenly Father, I thank You for the gift of true friendship and brotherhood. Teach me to love as You love, steadfast, sacrificial, and without condition. Help me to be the kind of friend who reflects Christ's heart and the kind of brother or sister who stands firm in times of trouble. Surround me with people who will walk with me in both sunshine and storm and give me the grace to be that same source of strength to others. May my life honor You in every relationship You entrust to me. In Jesus' name I pray, Amen and To God Be The Glory!

JULY 3. - "VICTORY ON MY KNEES IN PRAYER"

The world teaches us to fight with force, strategy, and visible power. But in the Kingdom of God, the greatest victories are won in the most unexpected place, and that's on our knees in prayer.

When life's battles rise against us, we often feel the urge to respond in our own strength with arguing, controlling, or worrying. But the believer knows that the real battlefield is spiritual. Ephesians 6:12 reminds us, "For we wrestle not against flesh and blood, but against principalities, against powers, against the rulers of the darkness of this world." If the battle is spiritual, then the weapons must be spiritual.

1. Prayer as a Weapon

Prayer is not a last resort; it is our first and most powerful weapon. It invites God's presence into our situation, shifts the atmosphere, and unleashes His authority over the enemy's plans. Every time we kneel in surrender, heaven moves on our behalf.

2. Kneeling as Surrender and Power

Being on your knees is a physical sign of spiritual submission. It says to God, "I can't win this without You." In that posture, weakness is transformed into strength, because we are relying not on our ability, but on the Almighty's power.

3. The Assurance of Victory

When you fight on your knees, you fight from a position of victory, not defeat. Jesus has already overcome the world (John 16:33). Your prayer aligns you with His victory and places every problem under His authority.

When we pray, we are not just speaking words—we are declaring war against the enemy's attacks, taking ground in the Spirit, and partnering with God's will. That is why battles are truly won in the secret place, where no one sees but God, yet results are witnessed by all.

IF ONLY YOU WOULD JUST REMEMBER:

"This is how I fight my battles ~ on my knees in prayer. Prayer is not my last resort; it is my first weapon. When I kneel before God, I stand in victory over the enemy, because I'm fighting from a place of surrender and divine strength. The battle may be invisible, but the results are undeniable, for the effectual fervent prayer of the righteous truly avails much (James 5:16). In prayer, I am never alone, never powerless, and never defeated because God Himself fights for me."

"The effectual fervent prayer of a righteous man availeth much." James 5:16 (KJV)

Lord Almighty, please teach me to fight my battles on my knees, in full surrender to You. Remind me that my strength is in You alone and that prayer is my greatest weapon. When the storms rage and the enemy attacks, please help me to resist fear and choose faith. Fill my words with power and my heart with trust, knowing that You go before me and fight for me. I declare that victory belongs to You, and I will stand firm in that truth. In the mighty name of Jesus, Amen and To God Be The Glory!

JULY 4. - "LETTING GO TO WALK THROUGH"

Sometimes God is ready to usher us into new seasons, greater blessings, and wider opportunities. But we can't enter because our hands are still clinging to the old. The "door knob" in your life may represent a past relationship, a familiar comfort zone, an old mindset, or even a place where God's grace has already moved on. You want the "clothes" (symbolizing provision, covering, and readiness) and the "open doors" (symbolizing opportunity and breakthrough), but you can't receive them if your grip is still on what God has told you to release.

1. Letting Go Requires Trust

When we hold on to what's behind us, we are in essence saying we trust it more than the unknown God is leading us into. True faith is often tested at the threshold when you can't see the whole path ahead, but you know God is calling you forward.

2. Your Hands Must Be Free to Receive

A closed hand cannot receive anything new. God sometimes requires us to release old things so that our hands are free to embrace His promises. Isaiah 43:18-19 reminds us, "Remember ye not the former things. Behold, I will do a new thing." Letting go is an act of faith that clears the way for what's next.

3. Walking Through the Door

An open door is meaningless if you never step through it. Some people miss their divine season because they stay at the threshold, hesitant and half-committed. Letting go of the "door knob" means you're ready to fully enter, without looking back.

The truth is, God never closes one chapter without preparing the next. But the transition requires movement—you can't live in two rooms at once. Today, God may be calling you to release what feels comfortable so you can step into what is miraculous.

"Brethren, I count not myself to have apprehended: but this one thing I do, forgetting those things which are behind, and reaching forth unto those things which are before." Philippians 3:13 (KJV)

Heavenly Father, I thank You for every open door You have prepared for me. Help me to release the things, places, and mindsets that keep me stuck in the past. Give me the courage to trust You fully, even when I can't see the whole plan. I choose to loosen my grip on what was so that I can take hold of what is to come. I declare that I will walk through every door You open, clothed in Your righteousness and covered by Your favor. In Jesus' name, Amen and To God Be The Glory!

JULY 5. - "FORGIVENESS ~ THE KEY TO FREEDOM"

Forgiveness is one of the hardest acts of obedience God calls us to—yet it is one of the most liberating. Many people misunderstand forgiveness as condoning hurtful actions or restoring broken trust. But true, biblical forgiveness is not about approving of someone's behavior; it is about releasing them from the debt they owe you so that you can walk free from the chains of bitterness.

1. Forgiveness Is for You

Holding on to unforgiveness is like drinking poison and expecting the other person to suffer. It slowly eats away at your peace, joy, and spiritual growth. When you forgive, you are not saying, "What they did was okay." You are saying, "I will not let what they did keep me bound."

2. Forgiveness and Trust Are Not the Same

Forgiving someone does not automatically mean restoring full trust or returning to the same level of closeness. Trust is rebuilt through consistent actions over time, while forgiveness is a decision of the heart to release resentment. Jesus calls us to forgive, but He also teaches us to be wise (Matthew 10:16). Sometimes, wisdom means loving someone from a distance.

3. Forgiveness Allows You to Move On

When you forgive, you unclog the spiritual pipeline that allows God's blessings to flow into your life. Unforgiveness keeps you tethered to the moment of pain; forgiveness sets you free to move forward into God's plans for you. Philippians 3:13 reminds us to forget what is behind and press toward what is ahead.

Forgiving may not change the past, but it changes your future. It heals your heart, strengthens your spirit, and opens the door for God to restore and elevate you beyond what you lost.

"And be ye kind one to another, tenderhearted, forgiving one another, even as God for Christ's sake hath forgiven you." Ephesians 4:32 (KJV)

Heavenly Father, I thank You for the mercy and forgiveness You have shown me. Help me to extend that same forgiveness to others. Not because they deserve it, but because You command it and because I want to walk free. Give me the strength to release every offense and the wisdom to guard my heart where trust has been broken. Heal the wounds in my spirit, restore my peace, and lead me forward into the life You have prepared for me. In Jesus' name, Amen and To God Be The Glory!

JULY 6. - "DON'T YOU DARE GIVE UP"

If you are reading this, it means the enemy's worst attacks have already failed. He tried to destroy you, but God's hand protected you. Now, unable to take you out, the devil often shifts his tactics, he tries to wear you down. He comes at times, but not always with sudden storms, but with a steady drip of discouragement, frustration, and fatigue. His hope is that you'll become so weary that you'll surrender your faith, your joy, and your purpose.

But here is the truth: seasons change, but God doesn't. Your situation may shift, your emotions may rise and fall, people may come and go, but the God who brought you through your last trial is the same God who will bring you through this one. "Jesus Christ is the same yesterday and today and forever" (Hebrews 13:8). The devil wants you to focus on what's changing; God wants you to anchor your hope in what never changes and that's His faithfulness.

The enemy's strategy is to drain you so much that you start believing lies: "It's not worth it. I can't keep going. I must not be making a difference." But that's when you must remember that your endurance is not built on your strength alone. Isaiah 40:31 promises that those who wait on the Lord will renew their strength, mount up with wings like eagles, run and not grow weary, walk and not faint.

You may feel tired right now, but this is not the end of your story. Don't give up — not on God, not on the calling He placed on your life, not on the promises He has spoken over you. The season you're in will change, but His love, His power, and His presence will remain constant.

Let us not be weary in well doing: for in due season we shall reap, if we faint not."

Galatians 6:9 (KJV)

Heavenly Father, I thank You that the enemy's attacks have not prevailed because Your hand has been upon me. When I feel worn down and weary, remind me that my strength comes from You alone. Help me to stand firm in faith, to trust that this season will change, and to rest in the truth that You never change. Give me the courage to keep going, the perseverance to keep believing, and the hope to keep expecting Your goodness. In Jesus' name I pray, Amen and To God Be The Glory!

JULY 7. - "THE STRENGTH OF SILENCE"

This verse paints a contrast between two kinds of hearts. The one lacking wisdom and the one filled with understanding. A person who is "void of wisdom" speaks with carelessness, allowing criticism, gossip, and judgment to flow freely from their lips. Their attitude toward others is marked by contempt rather than compassion. Such behavior is not only unkind, but it also reveals an absence of spiritual insight.

In contrast, the "man of understanding" recognizes the power and consequences of words. He knows that once spoken, they cannot be taken back. This kind of person chooses silence, not because they have nothing to say, but because they have learned that wisdom sometimes speaks loudest through restraint.

Holding your peace takes discipline. It requires humility to admit that not every offense needs a response and not every situation calls for your opinion. The man or woman of understanding values harmony and chooses love over pride and trusts God to handle matters beyond their control.

Jesus Himself demonstrated this during His trial. Though falsely accused, mocked, and ridiculed, He did not retaliate. His silence was not weakness, it was strength under control and anchored in the will of His Father.

THINK ON THIS:

Before you speak, ask: Will this help or harm? Will it heal or hurt?

Pray for self-control to stay silent when silence is wiser than speech.

Remember: what you do not say can be just as important as what you say.

"He that is void of wisdom despiseth his neighbour: but a man of understanding holdeth his peace." Proverbs 11:12 (KJV)

Heavenly Father, please teach me the wisdom of holding my peace. Help me to speak only what is true, kind, and necessary. Remove from my heart the tendency to judge, despise, or speak ill of others. Fill me with the understanding that my words carry power and that sometimes the greatest power is found in silence. May my responses reflect the love and patience of Christ. In moments of provocation, let Your Spirit guide my tongue and guard my heart. In Jesus' name I pray, Amen and To God Be The Glory!

JULY 8. - "TRUE RICHES ~ TRUE WISDOM ~ TRUE KINDNESS

The world often measures worth by possessions, titles, or social standing. Yet, God's standard for greatness is very different. The phrase, "Some of the most generous people have no money. Some of the wisest people have no education. Some of the kindest people hurt the most," reminds us that human value is not bound by what we have but by who we are in God's eyes.

Generosity is not limited to the wealthy. In fact, some of the most generous souls are those who know what it means to lack. They may not be able to give money, but they give time, compassion, encouragement, and services that often matter more than currency. In Luke 21:1–4, Jesus praised the poor widow who gave two small coins, saying she gave more than all the wealthy contributors, because she gave from her heart.

Wisdom is not always learned in classrooms or earned with degrees. Some of the wisest people have never sat in a lecture hall, but life has been their teacher and God their instructor. James 1:5 tells us, "If any of you lack wisdom, let him ask of God, that giveth to all men liberally." Godly wisdom is a gift, not a diploma.

Kindness, too, is often born from pain. Those who have been deeply hurt often understand the importance of gentleness and empathy. They know what it feels like to be on the receiving end of cruelty, and they choose instead to extend mercy. Their scars become a ministry, proving that God can turn brokenness into beauty.

We must remember that God doesn't see as the world sees. The richest man in heaven's eyes may have empty pockets. The wisest may have never worn a cap and gown. The kindest may have been forged in the fires of suffering. What truly counts is the condition of the heart and the willingness to love, serve, and forgive as Christ did.

"Man looketh on the outward appearance, but the LORD looketh on the heart."

1 Samuel 16:7 (KJV)

Heavenly Father, I thank You for reminding us that true value is not found in wealth, degrees, or a pain-free life, but in a heart surrendered to You. Teach us to see people as You see them. To honor the generous who give from little, to respect the wise who have learned from life, and to cherish the kind who love despite their own pain. Help us to walk in humility, compassion, and faith, knowing that these are the true treasures of Your Kingdom. In Jesus' name, Amen and To God Be The Glory!

JULY 9. - "SEEING GODS LOVE IN EVERYTHING"

Those who are truly great in God's Kingdom are not necessarily the ones the world applauds, but those who have learned to recognize His love in everything. The great are not blind to life's struggles, but they have trained their eyes and hearts to see God's fingerprints in both the blessings and the burdens.

Recognizing God's love in everything is a matter of perspective. In the morning sunlight, we see His warmth. In the trials, we see His refining hand. In the laughter of loved ones, we see His joy. Even in our tears, we can feel His comfort. This kind of vision doesn't come naturally, it grows from a relationship with Him, from knowing His character and trusting His heart.

David understood this when he wrote in Psalm 136, a psalm repeating the refrain, "for His mercy endureth forever." No matter what event he recounted, be it in creation, deliverance from enemies, daily provision, David recognized it all as an act of God's enduring love.

When we learn to recognize God's love in everything, our gratitude becomes deeper, our faith becomes stronger, and our peace becomes unshakable. This doesn't mean we deny pain; it means we trust that God's love is still present in it. Romans 8:28 reminds us, "And we know that all things work together for good to them that love God, to them who are the called according to His purpose."

The truly great are those who know that nothing is wasted in God's plan. They see His love in the sunrise and in the storm, in the answered prayer and in the patient waiting.

"O give thanks unto the LORD; for he is good: for his mercy endureth for ever."

Psalm 136:1 (KJV)

Heavenly Father, I truly thank You for Your love that never fails and never fades. Help us to recognize Your hand in every moment of our lives, even the joyful and the challenging. Teach us to see beyond the surface, to notice the ways You protect, provide, guide, and comfort us daily. May our hearts overflow with gratitude, and may we live in a way that reflects our deep trust in Your goodness. In every circumstance, let us proclaim that Your love endures forever. In Jesus' name, Amen and To God Be The Glory!

JULY 10. - "BLESSED BEYOND WHAT WE DESERVE"

When we say, "Thank You God for blessing me so much more than I deserve," we are expressing a deep truth about the nature of God's grace. None of us can ever earn the love, mercy, and blessings He pours into our lives. We fall short daily, yet His faithfulness never fails.

The reality is, if God only gave us what we truly deserved, none of us would have hope. Our sins, mistakes, and weaknesses leave us unworthy of His favor. But that is where His grace steps in, grace that is unearned, unmerited, and undeserved. Ephesians 2:8–9 reminds us, "For by grace are ye saved through faith; and that not of yourselves: it is the gift of God: Not of works, lest any man should boast."

Think about your life for a moment. The breath in your lungs. The roof over your head. The meals on your table. The people you love. The times God protected you from dangers you didn't even see. The prayers He answered and even the ones He didn't, because He knew better. All of these are blessings far beyond what we could ever earn.

Gratitude shifts our hearts. It takes our eyes off what we think we lack and places them on the abundance God has already given. When we acknowledge that we are blessed beyond measure, our pride melts away, and humility grows. We stop demanding and start praising. We stop complaining and start worshiping.

The truth is, God blesses us not because we are good, but because He is good. And the more we recognize that, the more we will walk in joy, peace, and awe of His love.

"Bless the LORD, O my soul, and forget not all his benefits: Who forgiveth all thine iniquities; who healeth all thy diseases; Who redeemeth thy life from destruction; who crowneth thee with lovingkindness and tender mercies." Psalm 103:2–4 (KJV)

Heavenly Father, I come before You with a heart full of gratitude. Thank You for blessing me far beyond what I could ever deserve. Thank You for salvation, for life, for protection, and for the countless mercies You give each day. Help me to never take Your blessings for granted, but to live with a spirit of thankfulness in all circumstances. May my life be a reflection of Your goodness, and may I always remember that every good thing comes from You. In Jesus' name, Amen and To God Be The Glory!

JULY 11. - "CHASING GOD ABOVE ALL ELSE"

The phrase, "If you chase after God as much as you chase after your desires, your life will be transformed," speaks to one of the greatest spiritual truths: whatever we pursue most passionately becomes the center of our lives. Far too often, people spend their best energy chasing after wealth, recognition, relationships, or personal dreams only to find that even if they achieve them, the satisfaction is temporary.

The truth is, nothing this world offers can compare to knowing God. Earthly possessions fade, popularity shifts, and achievements lose their shine. But a deep relationship with the Lord brings joy, peace, and purpose that can never be taken away. Jesus Himself gave us the key in Matthew 6:33 (KJV): "But seek ye first the kingdom of God, and his righteousness; and all these things shall be added unto you."

Chasing after God means making Him your highest priority and not just fitting Him into your schedule when it's convenient. It means starting your day in His presence, consulting Him before making decisions, and longing for His approval more than the world's applause. When you pursue Him above all else, He aligns your heart with His will, reshapes your desires, and orchestrates your life in ways you could never plan on your own.

And here's the beauty of when you seek Him first, everything else finds its proper place. You may still have dreams and goals, but they will no longer control you. Your identity won't be tied to what you have, but to Who you belong to. You will discover that in chasing God, you actually receive more than you ever could by chasing your own desires.

"Delight thyself also in the LORD: and he shall give thee the desires of thine heart."

Psalm 37:4 (KJV)

Heavenly Father, I thank You for the reminder that nothing compares to knowing You. Forgive me for the times I have chased after things that could never satisfy. Help me to seek You first, above every other pursuit. Align my desires with Your will and teach me to find joy and fulfillment in Your presence. I trust that as I make You my priority, You will provide everything I need in Your perfect timing. In Jesus' name, Amen and To God Be The Glory!

JULY 12. - "STRENGTH FORGED THROUGH GOD"

The phrase, "I am a strong woman. Everything that hits me in life I've dealt with. I've cried myself to sleep, picked myself back up, and wiped my tears. I've grown from things that were meant to break me. I get stronger by the day and have God to thank for that," is a testimony of resilience, but more importantly, it is a testimony of God's sustaining power.

True strength is not the absence of pain or difficulty. It's the ability to endure, adapt, and rise again after the storms of life have knocked you down. The world often thinks strength comes from self-reliance, but the believer knows that real strength comes from leaning on the Lord. Every tear you've cried, every sleepless night you've endured, and every setback you've overcome is evidence that God has been holding you together when you felt you were falling apart.

Isaiah 40:29–31 (KJV) says, "He giveth power to the faint; and to them that have no might he increaseth strength. Even the youths shall faint and be weary, and the young men shall utterly fall: But they that wait upon the LORD shall renew their strength; they shall mount up with wings as eagles; they shall run and not be weary; and they shall walk and not faint."

The enemy may have intended certain challenges to break you, but God used them to build you. He took the moments you thought were your end and turned them into the foundation for a stronger future. With every battle, you learned more about His faithfulness. With every heartbreak, you discovered His comfort. With every loss, you experienced His ability to restore.

So, when you stand tall today, it's not just because you are strong, it's because God has been your strength. You are not a survivor by accident; you are a testimony of His grace.

"God is our refuge and strength, a very present help in trouble." Psalm 46:1 (KJV)

Heavenly Father, I thank You for being my strength in every season of my life. Thank You for holding me together when I felt like breaking and for giving me the courage to rise again. Help me never forget that my resilience comes from You, not from myself. Continue to guide me, sustain me, and strengthen me so that I may face every challenge with faith. May my life be a living testimony of Your power and grace. In Jesus' name, Amen and To God Be The Glory!

JULY 13. - "ONCE YOU GET A TASTE OF PEACE"

There comes a moment in life when you experience a level of peace so deep, so freeing, and so soul-refreshing that you realize nothing is worth losing it again. For years, you may have tolerated chaos, drama, manipulation, or even subtle toxicity because you thought that was "just life" or you didn't want to hurt anyone's feelings. But once God grants you a true taste of His peace, you begin to recognize the priceless value of it.

Peace is not passive, it's powerful. It's not merely the absence of conflict, but the presence of God's order in your mind, spirit, and environment. When you encounter it, you begin to guard it like a treasure. Suddenly, certain conversations, relationships, and situations that used to drain you now feel like a threat to the serenity God gave you. You're no longer afraid to say "no," to set boundaries, or even to let go of what you once clung to, because nothing compares to the stillness of your soul when it rests in God's presence.

Jesus Himself modeled this. He would often walk away from crowds, separate Himself from noise, and spend time alone with the Father (Luke 5:16). Why? Because peace is sustained through intentional connection with God. And to protect that peace, you sometimes have to cut off some things, and yes, even people who disturb it.

Scripture says in Philippians 4:7 (KJV): "And the peace of God, which passeth all understanding, shall keep your hearts and minds through Christ Jesus."

This peace doesn't come from the world, so it can't be taken away unless we allow it. God's peace is both a shield and a guard for our hearts and minds. But it's up to us to decide to protect it, even if it means making hard choices.

Once you've tasted that level of wholeness, you realize that protecting your peace is not selfish, it's stewardship. You are honoring the gift God gave you.

Heavenly Father, I thank You for the gift of Your perfect peace that surpasses all understanding. Teach me to recognize it, cherish it, and protect it. Give me the courage to set boundaries, to walk away from situations that disrupt my spirit, and to stand firm in the stillness You have given me. Remind me that in keeping my peace, I am keeping my focus on You. Let nothing and no one steal what You have poured into me. In Jesus' name, Amen and To God Be The Glory!

JULY 14. - "SMILE AND REJOICE"

There are moments in life when it feels like the odds are stacked against you. The challenges are many, the support seems small, and the voices of opposition seem louder than the voices of encouragement. But in these moments, God calls you not to fear, not to panic, but to smile and rejoice. Why? Because what you see with your natural eyes is not the full picture.

In 2 Kings 6:15–17, Elisha's servant woke up to see a vast enemy army surrounding the city. Terrified, he cried out to the prophet, "Alas, my master! How shall we do?" But Elisha, calm and confident, replied, "Fear not: for they that be with us are more than they that be with them." Then he prayed for his servant's eyes to be opened and suddenly, the servant saw the hills filled with horses and chariots of fire all around them.

The truth is, you may feel outnumbered in the physical, but in the spiritual, Heaven's armies are surrounding you. You may feel like you have little earthly backup, but God's presence, His angels, and His power far outweigh any opposition. You don't have to see every detail to trust the outcome. You just have to believe that the God who is for you is greater than anything against you.

Smiling and rejoicing is not denial; it's faith. It's declaring, "I trust God's protection, even when I can't see it yet." It's resting in the fact that no weapon formed against you shall prosper (Isaiah 54:17) and that God's plans for you cannot be overturned.

When you remember who stands with you, and that's the Creator of heaven and earth, you realize you were never truly in the minority. His presence tilts the balance in your favor every time.

"Fear not: for they that be with us are more than they that be with them." 2 Kings 6:16 (KJV)

Heavenly Father, I thank You that I am never truly outnumbered when You are by my side. Open my spiritual eyes to see the depth of Your protection and the strength of Your presence. Teach me to smile in the face of opposition and to rejoice even in the midst of battle, knowing victory belongs to You. Let my confidence rest not in what I see, but in who You are. In Jesus' name, Amen and To God Be The Glory!

JULY 15. - "I WILL NOT TOLERATE WHAT I DID IN THE PAST"

There comes a point in your walk with God when your spirit matures, your discernment sharpens, and your standards rise. The things you once tolerated, whether out of fear, insecurity, a desire to please others, or simply not knowing your worth, no longer have a place in your life. This isn't pride; it's growth. It's a sign that God has healed, strengthened, and elevated you to a place where compromise is no longer an option.

When we come to Christ, we are called to transformation. 2 Corinthians 5:17 (KJV) reminds us: "Therefore if any man be in Christ, he is a new creature: old things are passed away; behold, all things are become new." Old mindsets, old tolerances, and old patterns must die so that the new life God has for us can fully flourish.

In the past, you might have allowed disrespect, mistreatment, or spiritual attacks to go unchecked because you didn't fully realize your authority in Christ. But now you understand you are a child of the King, and your peace, dignity, and spiritual well-being are worth protecting. You are no longer afraid to set boundaries, to speak truth, and to stand firm on the Word of God.

Even Jesus demonstrated this principle. There were times He was silent and times He walked away from situations, refusing to tolerate anything that was not in alignment with His Father's will. Your refusal to tolerate certain things now is not a sign of weakness or bitterness. It is evidence that you've learned your value in God and will no longer settle for less than what He intends for your life.

This stand is not about revenge, but about reverence. Reverence for the God who created you, redeemed you, and calls you His own. By standing firm, you protect not just yourself, but the purpose God placed in you.

Heavenly Father, I thank You for the growth You have brought into my life. Thank You for opening my eyes to see my worth in You and for giving me the courage to stand firm in my convictions. Help me to never return to the things that once drained me or diminished me. Strengthen my resolve to walk in Your truth, set godly boundaries, and honor the work You've done in me. Let my stance be a testimony of Your transforming power. In Jesus' name, Amen and To God Be The Glory!

JULY 16. - WHEN THE STORM CLEARS THE WAY"

Storms have a way of shaking everything in our lives. The wind howls, the rain beats down, and visibility is reduced to almost nothing. In those moments, fear can creep in and whisper that the end is near. But as children of God, we must remember that storms are not always meant to destroy us. Some are designed by the hand of God to move things out of our way, to redirect our steps, and to prepare the ground for something new.

When the disciples were caught in the storm on the Sea of Galilee (Mark 4:35–41), they thought they were going to perish. Yet, Jesus was in the boat with them. The storm didn't sink them, it revealed His authority over wind and waves. Likewise, the storm you're facing today may be the very thing God is using to remove hindrances you didn't even realize were there.

Sometimes, God sends a storm to remove toxic relationships, close unfruitful doors, or disrupt comfort zones that are keeping us from our calling. Other times, He allows a storm to strip away distractions so we can clearly see the next step He has for us. What looks like chaos is often divine construction.

If you feel like the winds are strong and the rain is heavy, remember this—when the storm passes, you will look back and realize the path ahead is clearer, straighter, and more purposeful than before. Trust the One who commands the seas; His plans are always for your good.

"And we know that all things work together for good to them that love God, to them who are the called according to his purpose." Romans 8:28 (KJV)

Heavenly Father, thank You for reminding me that not every storm is my enemy. Help me to see Your purpose even in life's fiercest winds. Remove whatever is not of You, and clear the path You want me to walk. Give me the faith to stand still and trust that You are working all things together for my good. I surrender my fears, my doubts, and my plans to You. In Jesus' name, Amen and To God Be The Glory!

JULY 17. - "WITHOUT LOVE ~ WITHOUT DREAMS ~ WITHOUT GOD

Life is full of pursuits, career goals, relationships, and personal ambitions. But if we strip away the core essentials of our existence, everything else collapses. The phrase "Without love we feel nothing, without dreams we accomplish nothing, without God we are nothing" is a sobering reminder of how fragile life becomes when the foundation is missing.

Without Love, We Feel Nothing

Love is not just an emotion ~ it's the very essence of God's nature. Scripture tells us plainly in 1 John 4:8 (KJV), "He that loveth not knoweth not God; for God is love." Love softens hearts, breaks down walls, heals wounds, and fuels compassion. Without love, our hearts grow cold, our connections become transactional, and our lives lose warmth. Even acts of service, if done without love, become hollow gestures (1 Corinthians 13:2). Love is what keeps our humanity intact.

Without Dreams, We Accomplish Nothing

Dreams are more than wishful thinking ~ they are the visions and goals God plants in our spirit to inspire forward motion. Joseph dreamed, and that dream carried him through betrayal, slavery, and prison until he stood in the palace (Genesis 37–41). Dreams birth purpose, give meaning to our work, and motivate us to endure hardship. Without dreams, we wander aimlessly, accomplishing little because we lack a destination to press toward. God Himself says in Jeremiah 29:11, "For I know the thoughts that I think toward you~ to give you an expected end." That expected end is the God-given dream He desires us to pursue.

Without God, We Are Nothing

This truth is the cornerstone. You can have love for people and big dreams, but without God, they have no eternal value. Jesus declared in John 15:5 (KJV), "For without me ye can do nothing." God is the giver of life, the sustainer of breath, the source of wisdom, and the anchor of our souls. Without Him, all our efforts are temporary, and our joy fades quickly. With Him, even the smallest act and the simplest dream become meaningful and lasting.

If we want a fulfilled life, we must hold these three together: Love as the heartbeat, dreams as the vision, and God as the source. Lose one, and life begins to unravel. Lose God, and everything else collapses completely.

"I am the vine, ye are the branches: He that abideth in me, and I in him, the same bringeth forth much fruit: for without me ye can do nothing." John 15:5 (KJV)

Heavenly Father, thank You for reminding me of the essentials that truly matter. Fill my heart with Your love so I may feel deeply and give freely. Rekindle the dreams You have planted within me and give me the courage and discipline to pursue them. Above all, keep me anchored in You, for I know that without You, my life has no true meaning. Help me to live every day with love, vision, and faith in Your presence. In Jesus' name I pray. Amen and To God Be The Glory!

JULY 18. - "ITS NOT HOW MUCH SCRIPTURE YOU KNOW ~ IT'S HOW MUCH SCRIPTURE YOU LIVE"

We live in a time where access to the Bible has never been easier. There are printed Bibles in countless translations, Bible apps, audio recordings, and daily devotionals at our fingertips. Yet, the true test of our relationship with God is not how many verses we can recite from memory, but how deeply His Word has taken root in our lives.

Knowing Scripture is important. Jesus Himself quoted it to defeat the enemy in the wilderness. But knowledge without application is like having a pantry full of food and never eating; it won't nourish or sustain you. The Pharisees in Jesus' day knew the Scriptures inside and out, yet their lives often failed to reflect God's heart. Jesus rebuked them because they had head knowledge but not heart transformation (Matthew 23:27-28).

When the Word becomes alive in you, it changes how you think, speak, and act. James 1:22 warns us, "But be ye doers of the word, and not hearers only, deceiving your own selves." This means the power of God's Word is revealed when it is put into action, when it shapes your choices, governs your attitudes, and directs your steps.

You may not remember the exact chapter and verse for every truth, but if you live out forgiveness, mercy, integrity, humility, and love, you are demonstrating the Word in its purest form. People may not remember the verses you can quote, but they will remember how you made them feel, how you treated them, and how your life reflected the character of Christ.

So don't be discouraged if you aren't a Bible scholar. God is not impressed by how much we can say from His Word, He is moved when we live His Word. Let every verse you know be a seed that grows into fruit others can see and taste.

But be ye doers of the word, and not hearers only, deceiving your own selves. James 1:22

Heavenly Father, thank You for the gift of Your Word that guides, corrects, and comforts me. Teach me not only to know Your Scriptures but to live them daily. Help my life to be a testimony that reflects Your truth in my speech, my actions, and my decisions. Let others see Christ in me not just by what I say but by how I live. May every word I read be applied in my heart so I can be a light in a dark world. In Jesus' name, Amen and To God Be The Glory!

JULY 19. - "FROM MY LIPS TO GODS EAR ~ FAMILY"

There is a sacred intimacy in prayer. The moment when the thoughts in our hearts become words on our lips, and those words rise before the throne of God. When we say, "From my lips to God's ear," it is a declaration of trust, a confidence that the One who created the universe is also deeply attentive to the quiet whispers of our souls.

As we step into a new week, the world around us may feel uncertain. Worries about our families, our needs, our safety, and our future can easily cloud our peace. But Scripture reminds us that God is not a distant ruler; He is a loving Father who hears, cares, and responds. In 1 Peter 5:7 (KJV) we are told:

"Casting all your care upon him; for he careth for you."

This verse is not an empty sentiment; it is an instruction and a promise. God does not want us to carry the weight of worry. He wants us to bring every concern, the big and the small, directly to Him. When we release our anxieties into His capable hands, we make room in our hearts for His peace.

Our prayer this week is not just for protection and provision, but also for the right people and the right opportunities to cross our paths. We ask for strength to endure, wisdom to choose well, and the assurance that even if we stumble, God's hand will lift us up. And when our emotions overwhelm us, His Spirit will comfort us.

Faith means believing that once we've spoken to God, He has heard us. His answer, whether immediate or unfolding over time, will always be for our good. This week, let us walk forward with the confidence that the One who hears us will guide us safely through.

Dear God, from my lips to Your ear, I give You this week ahead. Remove my worries and replace them with peace. Watch over my family and me. Provide for our needs and bless us beyond measure. Grant us strength to stand, wisdom to decide, and discernment to know Your will. Place in our paths people who are helpful, loving, and kind. If we weep, comfort us. If we fall, lift us up. Keep our hearts steady and our steps secure. Bring us safely through, covered in Your mercy and guided by Your light. In Jesus name I pray.

Amen and To God Be The Glory!

JULY 20. - "MORE THAN PAPER ~ BUILDING A MARRIAGE THAT LASTS"

Many people view marriage as the ultimate guarantee, a legal binding that ensures two people will stay together forever. But the truth is, a marriage license is only paper. That paper can mark the start of something beautiful, but it cannot sustain a relationship on its own. What truly keeps a marriage strong is the unseen, daily investment of the heart, respect, trust, understanding, friendship, and faith.

A relationship built solely on the document will crumble under the weight of life's storms. But a marriage grounded in mutual respect means you honor each other's dignity even when you disagree. Trust means you feel safe in each other's presence and words, knowing there's honesty behind every conversation. Understanding means you listen with empathy instead of judgment. Friendship keeps the joy alive, reminding you that you are not only lovers, but also companions who laugh, dream, and grow together. And above all, faith in God is the anchor that keeps your marriage steady when everything else is shifting.

Scripture reminds us of this truth: "Though one may be overpowered, two can defend themselves. A cord of three strands is not quickly broken." – Ecclesiastes 4:12 (NIV)

The "three strands" are you, your spouse, and God. Without that third strand, marriage becomes fragile. But when God is woven into your relationship, He provides the strength to forgive when it's hard, to love when feelings fade, and to endure when circumstances challenge your bond.

The reality is marriage is not simply staying together. It's choosing each other every single day, even when emotions change and life gets hard. The paper may be the record of your vows, but your daily actions are the true proof of your commitment.

Heavenly Father, Thank You for the gift of marriage and the joy of companionship. Help us remember that a wedding day is only the beginning, and that the real work of love is built in the days, months, and years that follow. Teach us to honor each other with respect, to guard our trust, to deepen our understanding, and to cherish the friendship we share. Above all, may our marriage be bound together by faith in You, the One who holds us both. Let our union be a reflection of Your steadfast love. In Jesus' name. Amen and To God Be The Glory!

JULY 21. - "THE PAIN OF GRIEF ~ IT'S LIKE HAVING BROKEN RIBS"

Grief is a strange companion. It walks with you in silence, sits with you in the quiet moments, and makes itself known when you least expect it. It's like having broken ribs. From the outside, you may look completely fine. People might even think you've "moved on" or "healed." But on the inside, with every breath, there is a deep aching pain that reminds you something is not as it once was.

Broken ribs don't heal overnight. You can't put a cast on them; you just have to endure the process of recovery. Similarly, grief doesn't follow a schedule. It cannot be rushed. And no matter how strong your faith is, there are moments when the pain catches you unexpectedly. Such as when a song, a smell, or a memory makes you feel like you're gasping for breath again.

David understood this when he wrote, "The Lord is close to the brokenhearted and saves those who are crushed in spirit" (Psalm 34:18, NIV). God doesn't minimize your pain or hurry you along. He draws near it. Like a gentle healer, He supports you in the unseen places where no one else can reach.

When we are grieving, there is a temptation to hide it, to put on a brave face so the world doesn't see the cracks. But the truth is God sees. He knows that with every breath, you are carrying both the weight of loss and the effort of living. And He promises not just to comfort you but to strengthen you so that eventually, the breaths hurt less, and joy finds its way back in.

Grief may never leave you entirely, just as some wounds always leave a scar. But in the presence of the Lord, the pain becomes lighter, the breath becomes deeper, and the hope of eternity reminds you that brokenness here will one day be fully mended there.

"The Lord is close to the brokenhearted and saves those who are crushed in spirit."

Psalm 34:18 (NIV)

Heavenly Father, You see the pain that others cannot. You know the weight I carry with each breath. Thank You for drawing near to my broken heart and for holding me when I feel like I can't hold myself together. Teach me to breathe in Your comfort and exhale my grief into Your hands. Help me to trust that healing, even if slow, is happening under Your care. Give me strength for the moments when the ache feels fresh and let my heart rest in the hope that one day, there will be no more sorrow, no more pain, and no more tears. In Jesus' name, Amen and To God Be The Glory!

JULY 22. - "THE LORD WILL FIGHT FOR YOU"

"The Lord shall fight for you, and ye shall hold your peace." Exodus 14:14 (KJV)

There are moments in life when the battles we face feel overwhelming. When the weight of opposition, hardship, or uncertainty threatens to crush our spirit. Just like the children of Israel at the Red Sea, we often find ourselves caught between impossible circumstances: behind us, the pursuing enemy; before us, the raging waters. Fear rises, faith wavers, and it seems as though there is no way forward.

But in this powerful verse, God gives a divine promise through Moses: "The Lord shall fight for you." Notice it does not say, "The Lord might fight for you," but rather He shall. It is certain. The God who brought Israel out of Egypt was not about to abandon them at the sea's edge. In the same way, the God who has carried you this far will not leave you in the middle of your struggle.

This verse teaches us two key truths:

The battle belongs to the Lord. Too often we wear ourselves out trying to fight spiritual battles in our own strength. But there are some battles we cannot win by human wisdom, effort, or strategy. These are the moments when we must trust God to step in and do what only He can do. He is the mighty warrior, the defender of His people, and the One who never loses.

Peace is your posture of faith. "And ye shall hold your peace." This means staying calm, resisting panic, and keeping your heart steady. Holding your peace doesn't mean ignoring the problem; it means choosing to rest in the confidence that God is working on your behalf. Your peace is a sign of your trust in Him. When others expect you to fall apart, you stand still in quiet assurance, knowing the Lord has already gone before you.

When you release the battle into God's hands, you will see Him part the seas in your life, making a way where there was no way. Just as the Israelites walked through on dry ground, you too will come out on the other side victorious—not because of your power, but because of His.

"Be still and know that I am God: I will be exalted among the heathen, I will be exalted in the earth." Psalm 46:10 (KJV)

Heavenly Father, I thank You for being my defender, my warrior, and my deliverer. Lord, You see the battles I am facing, both seen and unseen. Teach me to rest in Your promise and to trust in Your power. Help me to hold my peace and keep my faith strong, even when fear and doubt try to overwhelm me. I surrender every battle into Your hands today, knowing that You will fight for me and bring me through in victory. I give You all the glory, honor, and praise for what You have done, what You are doing, and what You will do. In Jesus' mighty name I pray. Amen and To God Be The Glory!

JULY 23. - "IF NOT NOW WHEN ~ THE TIME IS NOW"

Many of us live as if life is always somewhere else, waiting to begin. We say, "One day, when I have more money, when I'm married, when my children are grown, when I'm healed, when I finally get that job or opportunity then my life will begin." But God whispers to us that life is not "out there" in some distant future. It is right here, right now.

When you say, "I'm looking forward to my next life. Oh, here it comes. It's called now," you're declaring a powerful truth: each new moment God gives you is your next life. Every sunrise is a fresh chance to walk in His purpose. Every breath is a gift of renewal. Every "now" moment is infused with God's presence.

The enemy would love to keep us chained to the regrets of yesterday or the anxieties of tomorrow. But Scripture tells us that God is the God of the present tense. "This is the day which the Lord hath made; we will rejoice and be glad in it" (Psalm 118:24 KJV). Notice, it does not say yesterday was the day or tomorrow will be the day, it says this is the day.

When you embrace the now, you stop waiting for permission to live and start walking in the fullness of who God created you to be. You realize that your healing, your breakthrough, your joy, and your peace do not begin "someday." They begin the moment you decide to live in God's presence, in the now.

So, instead of waiting for life to change, declare: "My new life is here. My next life is now. God has given me this very moment, and I will live it with faith, gratitude, and purpose."

"Therefore, do not worry about tomorrow, for tomorrow will worry about itself. Each day has enough trouble of its own." Matthew 6:34 (NIV)

Heavenly Father, thank You for reminding me that my life is not hidden in the past or postponed to the future. You have given me this very moment as a gift, and I choose to embrace it fully. Help me to walk in gratitude, faith, and purpose today. Teach me to see Your hand at work in my now and to trust that You are making all things new, even in this very moment. I will not miss what You are doing by looking too far ahead or too far behind. My next life is here, and it is called now. In Jesus' name I pray. Amen and To God Be The Glory!

JULY 24. - "TRUST ~ LOVE ~ AND TRUTH IN A BROKEN WORLD"

The phrase "Some say trust gets you killed, love gets you hurt, and being real gets you hated" echoes the painful reality of living in a fallen world. People are often betrayed when they put their trust in the wrong hands, wounded when they love deeply, and rejected when they choose honesty over hypocrisy. These experiences can leave scars, and sometimes they tempt us to shut down our hearts altogether to stop trusting, stop loving, and stop being real.

But God calls us to live differently.

Trust in people may fail, but trust in God never fails. Human love may wound, but God's love heals and restores. Being real may bring rejection, but God honors truth and integrity. The enemy wants us to believe that protecting ourselves through walls of mistrust, bitterness, and silence is the safest way to live. But the Word of God tells us that freedom, strength, and eternal security are found when we live according to His Spirit, not our fears.

Jesus Himself lived this out. He trusted His Father even unto death on the cross. He loved humanity so deeply that He bore betrayal, denial, and unimaginable pain. He was real and spoke the truth without compromise, even when it caused Him to be hated and crucified. And yet, through that trust, love, and truth, salvation was birthed for all of us.

When you feel that trusting others might destroy you, remember that God is your ultimate refuge. When love leaves you hurting, let it point you to the everlasting love of Christ that never fails. And when your authenticity brings hatred, rejoice, for Jesus said: "Blessed are ye, when men shall revile you, and persecute you for great is your reward in heaven" (Matthew 5:11–12 KJV).

The reality is this: living God's way will cost you something in this world, but it will secure for you everything in eternity. Do not allow betrayal, heartbreak, or rejection to harden you. Instead, let them press you closer to the God who sees, heals, and vindicates.

"The LORD is my strength and my shield; my heart trusted in him, and I am helped: therefore my heart greatly rejoiceth; and with my song will I praise him." Psalm 28:7 (KJV)

Heavenly Father, I come before You with an open heart. I confess that sometimes trust feels dangerous, love feels painful, and honesty feels costly. But Lord, I choose to keep my heart soft before You. Teach me to trust in You above all else. Heal me where love has left scars and remind me of Your unfailing love that never abandons me. Give me courage to remain real and truthful, even if it means being misunderstood or rejected. Let my life be a reflection of Jesus, who trusted, loved, and walked in truth until the very end. Keep me rooted in Your Word and covered by Your Spirit. In Jesus' mighty name I pray.

Amen and To God Be The Glory!

JULY 25. - "LIFE HAS TWO RULES ~ ALL INVOLVING NEVER QUIT"

Life is often compared to a race, a journey filled with unexpected turns, steep hills, and valleys of discouragement. Along the way, we encounter obstacles that tempt us to stop, give in, or settle for less than God's best. Yet there are two simple but powerful rules that serve as a compass for pressing forward:

1. Never quit.

2. Always remember rule number one.

These rules aren't about stubborn pride or blind persistence, they are about spiritual endurance. The enemy's greatest weapon is discouragement, and if he can convince us to give up, he doesn't need to fight us anymore. But when we refuse to quit, we align ourselves with God's promises, knowing that our victory is not in our own strength but in His.

The apostle Paul encourages us in Galatians 6:9 (KJV): "And let us not be weary in well doing: for in due season we shall reap, if we faint not."

Notice the condition in this scripture: if we faint not. The harvest, the breakthrough, the answer to our prayers ~ these blessings are promised if we simply keep going. God's timing is perfect, and though it may seem delayed, it is never denied. Quitting forfeits the blessing, but endurance secures it.

Think of Joseph, who endured betrayal, false accusation, and years in prison. He could have given up at any point, but he held on to the dream God gave him. In the end, he was elevated to second-in-command in Egypt, saving nations from famine. His life demonstrates that those who refuse to quit walk straight into God's purpose.

The rules are simple, but living them out requires faith. When you are tired, pray. When you feel defeated, remember the promises of God. When you don't understand why things are happening, trust His plan. Keep moving forward, because quitting is not an option in the Kingdom of God.

Heavenly Father, I thank You for the reminder that life is not about perfection, but persistence. Strengthen my faith when I feel weak, and renew my spirit when discouragement tries to overtake me. Help me to hold tightly to Your promises and never give up, no matter the battles I face. Teach me to endure with patience, to walk by faith, and to trust that in due season I will reap a harvest if I do not faint. I choose today to never quit, and to always remember that You are my strength and my victory. In Jesus' name I pray.

Amen and To God Be The Glory!

JULY 26. - "LIVING WITH OLD AGE ~ A BLESSING TO BE HERE"

As the years go by, many of us smile when we think back to a time when "old age" was just a number in our imagination. We thought it was something far away, only in our heads. But then, reality starts to settle in. The gray hairs, the aches, the creaking joints, and the slower pace remind us that time has marched on. What once was "mental" has now become "physical."

Yet, the beauty of aging in Christ is that while the body may grow weaker, the spirit can grow stronger. Scripture reminds us: "Therefore we do not lose heart. Though outwardly we are wasting away, yet inwardly we are being renewed day by day." 2 Corinthians 4:16 (NIV)

Our joints may ache, and our bodies may tire more quickly, but God is still renewing us from the inside out. Old age is not just a sign of decline, it is also a crown of wisdom, testimony, and faithfulness. The years etched in our bodies are evidence of the journey we have traveled and the grace that has sustained us.

Think of the patriarchs of the Bible, from Abraham, Sarah, Moses, Anna, Simeon, and many of whom God used mightily in their advanced years. Though their bodies bore the marks of time, their spirits were alive with faith and hope. Old age, with all its challenges, is still a gift because it reflects God's sustaining power over our lives.

So, when your joints ache or your body feels heavy, don't be discouraged. Instead, see it as a reminder that this earthly vessel is temporary, but your inner man is being strengthened daily by the Spirit of God. Each wrinkle tells a story of survival. Each ache is a reminder of endurance. And each day is another opportunity to glorify God with the wisdom that only time and His grace can teach.

Heavenly Father, thank You for the gift of life and the years You have allowed me to see. Though my body feels the weight of time and my joints sometimes ache, I rejoice that my spirit is still being renewed by Your presence. Help me to embrace each season of life with gratitude, patience, and faith. May my latter days be filled with wisdom, peace, and joy, knowing that You are my strength even when my body grows weary. I place my hope not in the strength of my flesh but in the eternal renewal that comes through You. In Jesus' name I pray, Amen and To God Be The Glory!

JULY 27. - "SATURATED IN HIS WORD"

When you place a teabag in hot water, the longer it stays, the deeper and richer the flavor becomes. At first, the water may look light and weak, but given time, the teabag transforms into the cup until it's fully infused. Our spiritual life works in much the same way. The more we allow God's Word to saturate our hearts and minds, the stronger our faith, our understanding, and our prayers become.

Many people want instant strength in prayer, quick clarity in decisions, or immediate transformation in their walk with Christ. But just as tea needs time to steep, so do we. The Spirit of God works within us gradually, filling us with truth, wisdom, and power as we consistently sit in His presence. A rushed prayer here or a quick verse there may refresh us for a moment, but deep transformation comes through dwelling through and abiding in Him.

Jesus Himself said in John 15:7 (KJV): "If ye abide in me, and my words abide in you, ye shall ask what ye will, and it shall be done unto you." Notice the condition: His words must remain in us. That "remaining" is like the teabag in the water, it's not a quick dip; it's a steady soaking. The longer His words abide in us, the more our desires align with His will, and the more powerful and effective our prayers become.

A life steeped in the Word produces clarity in what truly matters to God. It teaches us patience when trials weigh heavy, joy when burdens are overwhelming, and confidence when the enemy attacks. Just as a strong cup of tea refreshes and strengthens the body, God's Word fortifies the spirit.

Let this be a reminder: do not rush away from His presence. Linger in His Word. Meditate on His promises. Saturate your mind with His truth. The more you do, the stronger your prayers will be. Not because of many words, but because of the depth of connection with the Father.

Heavenly Father, I truly thank You for the power of Your Word that transforms and strengthens us. Teach us to linger in Your presence and to meditate on Your truth until it fully saturates our hearts. Help us to align our desires with Yours so that our prayers carry the weight of Your will. Make us strong in faith, steadfast in prayer, and clear in understanding of what truly matters to You. Lord, may our lives reflect the richness of time spent with You. In Jesus' name, we pray.

Amen and To God Be The Glory!

JULY 28. - "STAND FIRM ON GODS TRUTH ~ NOT CULTURE"

In every generation, the church is confronted with cultural pressures. Societies evolve, values shift, and moral boundaries are often redrawn by human standards. But God's Word stands unchanging. The moment a church begins to adjust its message, values, or doctrine to align with cultural trends rather than the eternal truth of Scripture, it forfeits its loyalty to Christ and bows to the god of this world.

Paul warned us of this very danger: "Do not be conformed to this world, but be transformed by the renewing of your mind, that you may prove what is that good, and acceptable, and perfect, will of God." Romans 12:2 (KJV)

When a church becomes more concerned with being accepted by culture than being faithful to Christ, it ceases to be a light in darkness. Jesus called His followers to be salt and light, distinct, preserving truth, and exposing deception. If the salt loses its savor, it becomes worthless (Matthew 5:13).

The god of this world, Satan, thrives when truth is watered down and when people embrace compromise. He disguises lies as "progress" and deception as "inclusion," luring churches into replacing biblical conviction with cultural accommodation. But true love and true freedom are only found in Christ and His Word.

The church must not bend truth to culture; instead, it must call culture to repentance and reconciliation with God. A church that stands on the unshakable Word of God may be unpopular, criticized, or even persecuted, but it will remain faithful to the Lord of glory.

Let us remember that we are not called to follow the god of this world; we are called to follow Jesus Christ, who is the same yesterday, today, and forever (Hebrews 13:8).

Heavenly Father, we come before You with humbled hearts, asking for the strength to remain faithful in a world that constantly shifts its values. Lord, protect Your church from compromise and deception. Keep us rooted in Your Word, unafraid to speak truth even when it is unpopular. Let us be bold witnesses of Christ, shining as lights in the midst of darkness. May our lives and our churches glorify You and not conform to the fleeting values of this age. Strengthen us, Lord, to stand firm until the end. In Jesus' mighty name we pray, Amen and To God Be The Glory!

JULY 29. - "IMAGINE THIS..."

So many people live their lives building on foundations that are not solid, philosophies of men, traditions passed down, popular opinions, or even personal feelings. We often lean on what "sounds right" or what society pushes, forgetting that truth is not found in shifting ideas but in the eternal Word of God.

The Bible is not just an old book collecting dust on a shelf, it is living, breathing, and powerful. It is God's voice preserved for us, a manual of life, correction, and salvation. To ignore it is to starve your soul, but to open it is to be fed, healed, and transformed.

The sobering reality is that lies always sound convincing until the truth is revealed. Imagine reaching the end of your life only to realize that the answers were within your reach all along, sitting in the very pages you never opened. That's why Jesus said, "And ye shall know the truth, and the truth shall make you free." (John 8:32 KJV).

When you read the Word, you discover God's heart, His promises, His warnings, and His plan of salvation through Jesus Christ. The truth of Scripture cuts through every deception, every false belief, every worldly philosophy, and it gives you an unshakable foundation to stand on.

Today, don't wait until it's too late. Dust off that Bible. Open it. Read it. Let God's truth set you free from every lie that has chained your mind and heart. For in those pages is life eternal, hope unshakable, and peace unexplainable.

Heavenly Father, please forgive me for the times I have ignored Your Word and sought answers elsewhere. Lord, open my eyes to see truth, open my ears to hear Your voice, and soften my heart to receive Your wisdom. Break every lie I have believed and replace it with Your everlasting truth. Let me never take Your Word for granted but let me hunger and thirst after righteousness daily. Thank You for preserving the truth for me in Scripture. In Jesus' name, I pray.

Amen and To God Be The Glory!

JULY 30. - "ARE YOU UNKNOWINGLY DRIFTING AWAY FROM GOD"

Drifting rarely happens suddenly, it is almost always a slow and quiet process. A boat tied loosely to the dock does not break away in one dramatic moment; rather, it slips little by little until it is far out into the waters. In the same way, many of us can unknowingly drift away from God without realizing it.

Pride, bitterness, unforgiveness, hatred, neglect of prayer, and the busyness of life can all serve as silent currents that pull us further away from His presence. Pride whispers, "You can do this on your own." Bitterness says, "Don't forgive they don't deserve it." Hate builds walls instead of bridges. Neglect says, "I'll pray tomorrow, I'll read later." And before we know it, our hearts are no longer tender toward God.

The danger of drifting is not always obvious in the beginning. You can still be going to church, still be singing songs, and still be saying prayers, but your heart can be slowly sliding away from intimacy with Him.

Hebrews 2:1 (KJV) warns us: "Therefore we ought to give the more earnest heed to the things which we have heard, lest at any time we should let them slip."

God calls us to vigilance. Staying close to Him requires intentional effort with daily prayer, repentance, forgiveness, humility, and worship. Just as a boat must be firmly anchored to remain safe at the dock, our souls must be anchored in Christ to avoid drifting into spiritual danger.

Take a moment today to ask yourself: Am I closer to God now than I was a year ago? Or am I slowly, unknowingly drifting? If you recognize signs of drifting, don't despair. God's grace is greater than our failures. He is always ready to restore, forgive, and draw us back into His loving presence.

Heavenly Father, I come before You humbly today, asking You to search my heart. If there are hidden areas of pride, bitterness, hatred, or neglect, reveal them to me. Lord, forgive me for the times I have drifted from You without realizing it. Anchor me again in Your Word and in Your love. Give me a heart that longs for Your presence daily and the discipline to walk closely with You. Keep me from spiritual drift and draw me nearer to You every day. In Jesus' name, I pray.

Amen and To God Be The Glory!

JULY 31. - "WHERE DID THE TIME GO"

There's a moment in life when the years catch up to us. One day, we are full of youthful energy, chasing dreams, making plans, and moving as though life will never slow us down. Then, suddenly, we find ourselves sitting on the edge of the bed, asking, "Where did the time go?"

Time is one of the greatest gifts God has given us, yet it is also one of the most fleeting. Scripture reminds us in James 4:14 (KJV): "Whereas ye know not what shall be on the morrow. For what is your life? It is even a vapour, that appeareth for a little time, and then vanisheth away."

Life is fragile and short, and the years seem to pass more quickly with each season. That realization can bring sorrow if we dwell only on what is lost. But as believers, it should stir us to live with greater purpose, gratitude, and urgency for the things of God.

When we look back and wonder, "Where did the time go?" the answer is simple, time has gone exactly where we allowed it to. That is why Scripture calls us to redeem the time. Ephesians 5:16 (KJV) says, "Redeeming the time, because the days are evil." Every day we are given is another opportunity to love better, forgive freely, worship deeply, and serve faithfully.

Though youth fades, strength weakens, and life shifts, our hope in Christ remains unshakable. God promises that while our outward bodies may grow older, our inner spirit is being renewed day by day (2 Corinthians 4:16). That means no matter what the mirror or the calendar says, God is still working in us, and His purpose for our lives continues until our final breath.

So instead of dwelling in regret, let's sit on the edge of the bed with gratitude. Let's thank God for the years behind us and ask Him for wisdom to live the days ahead with intentional faith. Time is passing, yes, but it's not gone. Every sunrise is another gift, and every moment is another chance to glorify the Lord.

Heavenly Father, I truly thank You for the gift of time and the years You have carried me through. Forgive me for the moments I have wasted and help me to redeem the days I still have left. Teach me to number my days, that I may apply my heart unto wisdom. When I feel the weight of passing years, remind me that my life is in Your hands, and my purpose is not over. Strengthen me daily, renew my spirit, and let my remaining time be a testimony of Your grace. In Jesus' name I pray.

Amen and To God Be The Glory!

AUGUST INTRODUCTION

Life does not come without struggles. Each new day brings with it new responsibilities, unexpected challenges, and questions that sometimes seem to have no answer. In a world filled with confusion, pain, and uncertainty, we often find ourselves asking: Where do I turn? How do I handle this problem? What is the right decision?

The truth is the answers we seek are not found in worldly wisdom, temporary pleasures, or fleeting opinions. The Word of God is our eternal guide. It is living and powerful (Hebrews 4:12), able to provide direction, comfort, correction, and encouragement for every circumstance we face. As Paul reminded Timothy, "All Scripture is given by inspiration of God, and is profitable for doctrine, for reproof, for correction, for instruction in righteousness: That the man of God may be perfect, thoroughly furnished unto all good works" (2 Timothy 3:16–17 KJV).

This month's devotional Biblical Answers to Life's Pressing Problems is designed to help you lean on Scripture when life feels overwhelming. August is often a month of transition: the heat of summer begins to shift, school years restart, and seasons of life bring new beginnings and new pressures. It is a reminder that while seasons change, God does not. He remains our constant anchor, offering wisdom for today and hope for tomorrow.

Every pressing problem whether it's fear, loneliness, broken relationships, financial struggles, or uncertainty about the future has an answer in God's Word. Through prayer and reflection, you will find that the Bible is not only a spiritual book, but also a practical guide for everyday living.

As you walk through these daily devotionals, allow the Holy Spirit to open your heart and renew your mind. Receive the peace that comes from knowing that God has not left you without answers. He has given you His Word as a lamp unto your feet and a light unto your path (Psalm 119:105).

"Trust in the Lord with all thine heart; and lean not unto thine own understanding. In all thy ways acknowledge him, and he shall direct thy paths." Proverbs 3:5–6 (KJV)

Heavenly Father, we come to You at the beginning of this new month with grateful hearts. Thank You for Your Word that provides guidance, strength, and wisdom for every problem we face. Lord, we confess that too often we lean on our own understanding instead of fully trusting in You. As we enter into this month of devotionals, open our eyes to see Your truth, soften our hearts to receive Your correction, and strengthen our faith to walk in obedience. Teach us to depend on You for answers to life's pressing problems and remind us that You are always near. May Your Spirit guide us day by day, and may Your peace rest upon us as we seek You first in all things. In Jesus' name we pray.

Amen and To God Be The Glory!

AUGUST 1. - "BULLYING IS NOT OK ~ ESPECIALLY IN SCHOOLS"

Bullying is one of the most painful and destructive behaviors we see in schools today. It is not simply "kids being kids." It wounds hearts, shatters confidence, and in some cases, leaves lifelong scars. God did not create us to tear one another down, but to build one another up in love. The Bible makes it clear that cruelty, mocking, and oppression are not pleasing to Him.

In Ephesians 4:29 (KJV), the Word says: "Let no corrupt communication proceed out of your mouth, but that which is good to the use of edifying, that it may minister grace unto the hearers." This scripture reminds us that our words and actions should be tools of encouragement, not weapons of destruction. When students bully others through words, gestures, exclusion, or physical harm, they are choosing to act outside of God's will.

School is meant to be a safe place of learning and growth, but bullying makes it a battlefield of fear and insecurity. God calls us to be different. Instead of standing by silently or joining in with cruel laughter, He urges us to show compassion and courage. To the one being bullied: you are not worthless, you are precious. To the one who bullies: God sees beyond your anger or insecurity and calls you to repentance and change. To the one who witnesses bullying: you are given the opportunity to stand for what is right.

Jesus taught in Matthew 7:12 (NIV): "So in everything, do to others what you would have them do to you, for this sums up the Law and the Prophets." This "Golden Rule" is a direct weapon against bullying. Imagine if every student treated others with the same respect and kindness they desired, schools would be transformed into places of joy, safety, and hope.

So today, let us make a personal commitment: bullying is not OK. We will not tolerate it ourselves. We will not encourage it in others. We will seek to stand up for those who are hurting and live out the love of Christ in every classroom, hallway, and playground.

Heavenly Father, we come before You with humble hearts, asking for Your protection over every child and teenager who faces the pain of bullying. Surround them with Your love and remind them of their worth in Christ. Give strength to those who are afraid to stand up for themselves, and courage to those who witness bullying to speak out and defend what is right. Lord, soften the hearts of those who bully, and replace their anger or insecurity with love and compassion. Let our schools be filled with peace, kindness, and respect. Help us to remember always that words can either destroy or heal, and may we choose healing. In Jesus' name we pray.

Amen and To God Be The Glory!

AUGUST 2. - "JESUS ~ THE SOURCE OF TRUE LIFE"

Science teaches us that the human body requires four basic elements to survive: water, air, food, and light. Without them, life cannot continue. Yet, the Word of God reveals a deeper truth. Our spiritual lives are sustained by the same essentials, but in their truest and eternal form, they are all found in Jesus Christ.

Water: Jesus declared, "Whoever drinks the water I give them will never thirst. Indeed, the water I give them will become in them a spring of water welling up to eternal life" (John 4:14, NIV). Just as our bodies wither without physical water, our souls dry up without His living water. Only Jesus can quench the deep thirst within our hearts.

Food: He also said, "I am the bread of life. Whoever comes to me will never go hungry" (John 6:35, NIV). Food nourishes and strengthens the body, but Jesus nourishes the soul. When we partake of Him—through His Word, His Spirit, and His presence—we are strengthened to walk in victory and sustained in times of weakness.

Air: Scripture reminds us that God breathed into Adam the "breath of life" (Genesis 2:7). Later, Jesus breathed on His disciples and said, "Receive the Holy Spirit" (John 20:22). Just as we cannot go a moment without air, we cannot survive spiritually without the breath of Christ filling us through the Holy Spirit.

Light: Jesus boldly proclaimed, "I am the light of the world. Whoever follows me will never walk in darkness but will have the light of life" (John 8:12, NIV). Light exposes truth, guides our path, and gives us vision. Without the light of Christ, we stumble in darkness. But in Him, our steps are ordered, our way is made clear, and our lives shine with purpose.

When we see it this way, it becomes crystal clear: we don't just need Jesus occasionally; we need Him for life itself. Without Him, we are spiritually dehydrated, starved, breathless, and lost in the dark. But with Him, we are nourished, refreshed, filled, and guided into eternal life.

So, while science explains the physical, Scripture reveals the spiritual—true life is found in Jesus Christ.

"For in Him we live and move and have our being." Acts 17:28 (NIV)

Heavenly Father, I thank You for sending Jesus, the source of everything I need to truly live. He is my living water, my bread of life, the breath that sustains me, and the light that guides me. Lord, help me to never seek life apart from Him but to remain rooted in His presence daily. Teach me to drink deeply, eat fully, breathe freely, and walk boldly in the life that only Jesus provides. Keep me aware that without Him I am nothing, but with Him I have everything. In Jesus' mighty name I pray.

Amen and To God Be The Glory!

AUGUST 3. - "FEAR NOT ~ FOR GOD IS WITH YOU"

"Be strong and of a good courage, fear not, nor be afraid of them: for the Lord thy God, he it is that doth go with thee; he will not fail thee, nor forsake thee." Deuteronomy 31:6 (KJV)

Life often places us in situations that test our strength, courage, and trust in God. Whether it's stepping into the unknown, facing opposition, or battling trials that feel bigger than us, the temptation to give in to fear is very real. Fear whispers that we are alone, outnumbered, and destined to fail. But the Word of God in Deuteronomy 31:6 speaks louder than fear and reassures us with a timeless truth: God Himself goes with us, and He will never fail us nor forsake us.

Moses spoke these words to the Israelites as they prepared to cross into the Promised Land under Joshua's leadership. They were about to face fortified cities, giants, and nations stronger than themselves. Yet, the battle was never theirs alone, it was the Lord's. What made their courage possible was not their own strength, but the presence of God walking with them every step of the way.

This same promise extends to us today. God has not changed. His character is the same yesterday, today, and forever. If He was faithful to His people then, He will be faithful now. Courage is not the absence of fear but the confidence that God is greater than whatever we face. He has already gone before us, He stands beside us, and He upholds us with His mighty hand.

When you feel like the odds are stacked against you, remember that the God who created the heavens and the earth is fighting for you. When fear tells you to quit, let faith remind you of His promise: "I will never leave thee, nor forsake thee" (Hebrews 13:5 KJV). You are not abandoned. You are not forsaken. You are never walking into any battle alone.

So, rise up today with courage. Lift your head, square your shoulders, and walk forward in faith knowing that the King of Glory goes before you. The enemies you see are no match for the God who surrounds you.

Heavenly Father, I thank You for the powerful promise that You will never leave me nor forsake me. Strengthen me to walk in courage and faith, even when fear tries to overtake me. Help me to trust that You are always with me, before me, behind me, and beside me. Remind me daily that I do not fight battles alone, for the Lord my God is my strength, my shield, and my refuge. May I always rest in Your presence and walk boldly into the destiny You have prepared for me. In Jesus' name, I pray.

Amen and To God Be The Glory!

AUGUST 4. - "SOMETHINGS ARE NOT ACCEPTABLE ~ ESPECIALLY FOR LOVE"

Love is a powerful and sacred gift from God, but love was never meant to be twisted into permission for mistreatment. Too often, people confuse love with tolerance of harmful behavior. They believe that to prove their love, they must endure words or actions that break them down. But this is not the kind of love God designed for His children.

True love never requires you to lose your worth. God calls us to love one another, but He never commands us to stay in a place where our spirit is being crushed. In fact, the Word says, "Above all else, guard your heart, for everything you do flows from it" (Proverbs 4:23, NIV). Guarding your heart means protecting the precious value God placed in you. Allowing someone to mistreat you while excusing it under the name of "love" is not guarding your heart, it is neglecting it.

Jesus Himself set boundaries. Though He loved deeply, He did not allow people's rejection, insults, or manipulation to define His identity or diminish His mission. In John 2:24-25, it says, "But Jesus did not commit Himself unto them, because He knew all men, and needed not that any should testify of man: for He knew what was in man." Even Christ, full of love and compassion, understood that not every person had His best interest at heart.

Love must be rooted in truth, respect, and mutual honor. Real love does not destroy, diminish, or degrade. The Apostle Paul describes love as patient, kind, not self-seeking, and never delighting in evil (1 Corinthians 13). That definition shows us what love should look like and what it should not.

If you are allowing someone to treat you poorly because you love them, remember this: your value is not negotiable. You are God's creation, His masterpiece, and His child. To honor Him is to honor yourself, refusing to allow mistreatment to masquerade as love. Sometimes the most loving thing you can do for yourself and even for the other person is to set boundaries or walk away from relationships that do not align with God's standard of love.

Heavenly Father, thank You for reminding me that Your love sets the standard for how I should be treated and how I should treat others. Give me the wisdom to recognize when love is pure and when it has been distorted by selfishness or mistreatment. Strengthen me to set godly boundaries that protect my heart and honor the worth You have placed in me. Help me to walk in love without compromising my dignity as Your child. I choose to guard my heart and trust You to guide me in every relationship. In Jesus' mighty name, Amen and To God Be The Glory!

AUGUST 5. - "WHEN YOU HAVE GOD ~ YOU HAVE EVERYTHING"

The phrase "Where there is love there is life. Where there is life there is hope. Where there is hope there is faith. Where there is faith, miracles happen. Where there is peace there is God, and when you have God, you have everything" speaks to the beautiful progression of God's presence working in every part of our lives. It is a reminder that everything begins and ends with Him.

1. Where there is love, there is life.

Love is the foundation of all things because God is love (1 John 4:8). Without love, we are empty, but with it, we find true life. Love breathes meaning into existence, bringing light where there was once darkness. Love revives broken hearts and restores relationships.

2. Where there is life, there is hope.

As long as there is breath in your body, there is hope. No matter how difficult your situation may seem, life itself is evidence that God is not finished with you yet. Hope is the anchor that keeps us steady in storms and reminds us that tomorrow holds the promise of change.

3. Where there is hope, there is faith.

Hope gives birth to faith, for faith is the substance of things hoped for (Hebrews 11:1). Hope looks ahead with expectation, but faith acts boldly in the present, trusting that God is able to do the impossible.

4. Where there is faith, miracles happen.

Jesus said, "If you have faith as small as a mustard seed nothing will be impossible for you" (Matthew 17:20 NIV)). Faith moves the hand of God. It opens the door for healing, breakthrough, and transformation. What seems humanly impossible becomes possible through the power of God.

5. Where there is peace, there is God.

Peace is the evidence of God's presence. It is not the absence of trouble but the calm assurance that He is in control. When God's peace rules our hearts, fear and confusion are silenced. "The peace of God, which transcends all understanding, will guard your hearts and your minds in Christ Jesus" (Philippians 4:7).

6. When you have God, you have everything.

At the end of it all, everything flows back to God. With Him, you lack nothing. He is your provider, protector, and sustainer. He is your healer, redeemer, and friend. With God, you are never alone, and His presence guarantees victory.

"And now these three remain: faith, hope and love. But the greatest of these is love."

1 Corinthians 13:13 (KJV)

Heavenly Father, I truly thank You for being the source of love, life, hope, faith, peace, and miracles. Remind us daily that when we walk with You, we truly have everything we need. Help us to love others as You love us, to live with hope even in dark seasons, to strengthen our faith in times of trial, and to rest in the peace that only You can give. We declare that with You by our side, we are complete and victorious. In Jesus' mighty name, Amen and "To God Be The Glory"!

AUGUST 6. - "DON'T IGNORE THE SIGNS OF DISCERNMENT"

Before God elevates you, He often pulls back the veil to reveal the true intentions of those around you. When God is preparing to take you higher, He also begins to separate you from people who cannot go where He is taking you. This process may feel painful because it exposes hidden motives, jealousy, and dishonor from those you may have once trusted. But in His wisdom, God is protecting your destiny.

Discernment is a gift from God, and ignoring the signs He reveals can cost you peace, progress, and even your spiritual protection. Joseph, for example, shared his dream with his brothers only to discover their hearts were filled with envy and hatred (Genesis 37). Yet that rejection and betrayal positioned him for the very place of elevation God intended.

When God reveals the intentions of others, He is not doing it to harden your heart but to guide your steps. Some people are meant to walk beside you and strengthen you on the journey. Others are only meant to be loved from a distance so that their influence does not contaminate the assignment God has placed on your life.

Elevation requires purification of motives, relationships, and environments. God removes the unnecessary so you can carry the weight of His calling without distraction. The key is not to resist His revealing work. Trust Him, embrace discernment, and allow Him to do the pruning so you can flourish in the new season.

"For there is nothing covered, that shall not be revealed; neither hid, that shall not be known." Luke 12:2 (KJV)

Heavenly Father, I thank You for being a God who reveals hidden things. Thank You for protecting me from those whose intentions are not pure. Give me the courage to accept the truth You show me and the strength to walk away from what no longer serves Your purpose in my life. Teach me to love people as You love them, even when I must love them from afar. Lord, prepare my heart for elevation, and surround me with people who will walk with me in truth, integrity, and unity. May I never ignore the signs of Your discernment. In Jesus' name I pray, Amen and To God Be The Glory!

AUGUST 7. - "A GOAL WITHOUT A PLAN IS JUST A WISH"

The phrase "a goal without a plan is just a wish" reminds us of the importance of both vision and discipline in the life of a believer. It is easy to have dreams, desires, or intentions, but unless those desires are backed by action, strategy, and prayerful guidance, they remain unfulfilled hopes.

God Himself is a planner. From the creation of the world, He did not act randomly. The book of Genesis shows order and structure: first light, then land, then plants, animals, and finally humanity. Even salvation came through a divine plan foretold through prophecy, fulfilled in Christ, and applied through the Holy Spirit. God demonstrates to us that purposeful planning aligned with His will brings results.

The Bible teaches in Proverbs 21:5 (KJV): "The thoughts of the diligent tend only to plenteousness; but of every one that is hasty only to want."

This verse reveals that careful, diligent planning leads to abundance, while careless living leads to lack. A Christian's goals should not just be casual wishes. They should be Spirit-led, written down, prayed over, and pursued with consistent action.

When we set goals without plans, we set ourselves up for frustration. For example, saying "I want to grow closer to God this year" is a noble goal. But unless it is followed by a plan such as committing to daily prayer, consistent Bible study, fasting, or joining a fellowship, that goal remains an empty desire. Similarly, saying "I want financial freedom" without budgeting, saving, and tithing makes it nothing more than a wish.

God honors faith, but He also honors order and action. Faith without works is dead (James 2:26). Prayers set the foundation, but planning and disciplined execution builds the structure. When our goals are placed in God's hands, and we walk in diligence, He blesses the work of our hands.

ASK YOURSELF:

Are there areas in my life where I've been wishing instead of planning?

Have I invited God into my planning process, or am I relying on my own strength?

What small, practical steps can I take today to turn my goal into a reality with God's guidance?

Heavenly Father, thank You for being the God of order, wisdom, and divine strategy. Forgive me for the times I've had dreams and desires but failed to bring them before You with a clear plan. Lord, align my goals with Your will, and give me the diligence to act faithfully on the vision You've placed in my heart. Teach me to be disciplined, prayerful, and intentional, so that my goals are not just wishes but testimonies of Your faithfulness. Bless the work of my hands and let my plans prosper as they are established in You. In Jesus' name I pray.

Amen and To God Be The Glory!

AUGUST 8. - "THE GIFT OF A TRUE FRIEND"

Making a hundred friends is not a miracle. The miracle is to make a single friend who will stand by your side, even when hundreds are against you.

Friendship is one of God's most beautiful gifts, yet not all friendships are created equal. Many can smile with you in times of plenty, but very few will stand firm with you in seasons of hardship, betrayal, or isolation. In a world where loyalty often wavers, finding one true friend who loves you, prays for you, and supports you when the world seems against you is a miracle worth cherishing.

The Bible speaks to this profound truth: "A friend loveth at all times, and a brother is born for adversity." Proverbs 17:17 (KJV)

Always notice the phrase: True friendship is not seasonal. It is not dependent on your wealth, your status, or your influence. A true friend reflects the heart of Christ. One who loves sacrificially, forgives readily, and walks with you in valleys as well as on mountaintops.

Jesus Himself modeled this perfect friendship. In John 15:13, He said, "Greater love hath no man than this, that a man lay down his life for his friends." He laid His life down not just for His disciples, but for us, making Himself the truest and most faithful friend we could ever have. Even when the crowd turned against Him, He stood firm in love. That is the miracle of friendship ~ loyalty in adversity.

In your journey, you may meet hundreds of acquaintances, but only a handful will prove to be genuine. Do not be discouraged if the numbers seem few, because one true friend in Christ is more valuable than a multitude who disappear when the storm rages. And remember while God may bless you with an earthly friend who remains by your side, He Himself is the Friend who will never leave nor forsake you (Hebrews 13:5).

So, treasure those rare souls who stand with you in the fire. Thank God for them. But also lean into the eternal friendship of Jesus Christ ~ the One who will never abandon you, even if the world turns its back.

Heavenly Father, I thank You for the gift of friendship. Lord, teach me to value the rare and precious friends who stand with me in times of joy and in times of hardship. Help me also to be that kind of friend to others, reflecting Your love and loyalty. Most of all, thank You for being my truest Friend, the One who never leaves me and always walks beside me. Strengthen my heart to trust You when others fall away and let me find comfort in knowing You are always near. In Jesus' name, I pray.

Amen and To God Be The Glory!

AUGUST 9. - "JOY KEEPS YOU YOUNG"

The phrase "You don't stop having fun when you get old, you get old when you stop having fun" reminds us that aging is not just a number it is also a mindset. God created us to live in joy, laughter, and peace. Life will bring trials, but it was never God's intention for His children to carry the weight of the world on their shoulders without joy.

Scripture reminds us in Proverbs 17:22 (KJV): "A merry heart doeth good like a medicine: but a broken spirit drieth the bones."

This verse reveals a divine secret: joy and laughter are God's medicine for the soul, the mind, and even the body. A heart filled with joy has a healing effect. It strengthens our spirit, improves our outlook, and gives us renewed strength to face each day. When we stop finding joy in life, when we stop laughing, smiling, and enjoying the blessings God has given to us, we grow weary, discouraged, and "old" in spirit, no matter our actual age.

Think about children: their energy and laughter are not tied to their years, but to their hearts. In the same way, God calls us to carry a childlike spirit of joy into adulthood and even into old age. Jesus Himself said in Matthew 18:3 that unless we become like little children, we cannot enter the Kingdom of Heaven. That does not mean being childish, it means keeping a heart that trusts, rejoices, and delights in the Father.

Even in seasons of hardship, we are not called to be heavy-hearted. Paul, who endured many trials, could still declare, "Rejoice in the Lord always: and again I say, Rejoice" (Philippians 4:4). Joy is not tied to circumstances, it is tied to the unchanging presence of God.

So today, I choose joy. Sing. Laugh. Dance. Enjoy the blessings God has placed around you. Do not let the burdens of life rob you of the youthful spirit God designed you to carry. A joyful heart keeps you spiritually strong, physically renewed, and alive with purpose. Remember: you don't grow old when the years add up, you grow old when you let joy fade away.

Heavenly Father, I thank You for the gift of joy. Thank You for reminding me that true youth is found in a heart that rejoices in You. Help me to carry a merry spirit, no matter what my age or circumstances. Teach me to laugh, to celebrate, and to enjoy the blessings You have placed in my life. Lord, let Your joy be my strength and keep me renewed each day in Your presence. In Jesus' name I pray. Amen and To God Be The Glory!

AUGUST 10. - "YOU CAN NOT PICK UP WHILE YOU'RE STILL HOLDING"

Life in Christ is often about letting go in order to take hold. Many of us pray for peace, joy, and confidence, yet wonder why those things seem out of reach. The truth is, you cannot pick up self-esteem if you are still clinging to self-loathing. You cannot carry confidence if fear still has a grip on your heart. You cannot embrace love while your hands are closed tightly around hate.

The Word of God makes it clear: transformation comes when we release the old and make room for the new. Paul writes, "Therefore, if anyone is in Christ, he is a new creation; the old has passed away, behold, the new has come." (2 Corinthians 5:17, ESV).

Notice how the order goes: "the old has passed away" before "the new has come." That means there must be a release. Many of us try to live in both worlds. Wanting to hold onto bitterness but also wanting the healing of love, or desiring boldness while still nurturing fear. But God's kingdom doesn't work that way. He invites us to lay burdens down before He places blessings into our lives.

Think of it like holding onto heavy bags. If your hands are full of things weighing you down, such as resentment, shame, and guilt, you will not have the strength or space to pick up what God has for you. Jesus Himself said, "Come to me, all who labor and are heavy laden, and I will give you rest." (Matthew 11:28, ESV). Rest only comes when we release the load into His hands.

So, if you want confidence, drop fear. If you want joy, release sorrow. If you want love, let go of hate. If you want peace, surrender anxiety. God cannot fill hands that are already clenched shut. But when you open them, when you let go, you'll find that He is faithful to replace what you release with something far greater.

Heavenly Father, I come before You today with honesty. I confess that too often I hold onto things that keep me from experiencing Your fullness, such as fear, self-doubt, anger, and bitterness. Lord, I release them into Your hands right now. Teach me to let go so that I may take hold of what You have promised me confidence, peace, love, and joy. Fill the empty places in my heart with Your Spirit, and remind me that in Christ, I am a new creation. Thank You for making me whole again. In Jesus' name I pray.

Amen and To God Be The Glory!

AUGUST 11. - "ACCOUNTABILITY AS A MIRROR OF THE HEART"

Accountability can often feel uncomfortable. It can sting, leaving you defensive or even resentful toward the one holding you accountable. But more often than not, the discomfort arises not from the words themselves, but from the truth they reveal. When we are unwilling to recognize our own shortcomings or the ways our actions affect others, feedback can feel like an attack.

The heart of accountability is reflection. It is a mirror designed by God to show us where we may have strayed, hurt others, or neglected our responsibilities. When we read difficult words about our behavior, pause for a moment, and let them sink in, we allow the Holy Spirit to work within us.

It's not a punishment; it's an invitation to grow. Accountability helps us see blind spots in our character, to repent where necessary, and to adjust our behavior in ways that glorify God. The key is humility. A humble heart receives correction not with anger or denial but with openness and prayerful reflection.

Sometimes, the message may need to be read multiple times before it fully resonates. God's truth often works progressively, guiding us gently yet firmly toward transformation. Remember, accountability is not meant to shame us but to align us with righteousness and to protect our relationships from harm.

When we embrace accountability with a teachable heart, we experience growth, restoration, and mercy. And as we do so, we become the kind of people who inspire trust, strengthen communities, and walk faithfully in God's plan.

"Whoever conceals their sins does not prosper, but the one who confesses and renounces them finds mercy." Proverbs 28:13 (NIV)

Heavenly Father, Thank You for Your Word that teaches us the value of truth and accountability. Forgive me for the times I have become defensive or ignore the correction of others. Help me to see accountability as a gift rather than an attack. Give me a humble heart that is willing to reflect, repent, and grow. Teach me to respond with grace when confronted with my faults and to walk in integrity in all I do. May my actions honor You and uplift those around me. In Jesus' name, I pray.

Amen and To God Be The Glory!

AUGUST 12. - "YOU CANNOT BREAK A PERSON WHO GETS THEIR STRENGTH FROM GOD"

Life has a way of testing us in ways we could never prepare for. Trials, disappointments, and battles come unexpectedly, and sometimes it feels as though the weight of the world is on our shoulders. But here is the truth: you cannot break a person who draws their strength from God. The reason is simple, their foundation is not rooted in themselves, in people, or in circumstances, but in the Almighty, who never fails.

The psalmist declares in Psalm 28:7 (KJV): "The Lord is my strength and my shield; my heart trusted in him, and I am helped: therefore my heart greatly rejoiceth; and with my song will I praise him."

When you anchor your life in God, you become unshakable. Problems may bend you, but they cannot break you. Enemies may rise against you, but they cannot overcome you. Storms may rage, but they cannot sink you, because your strength is not natural, it is supernatural.

Think of a tree planted by the rivers of water. The wind may blow and the seasons may change, but because its roots are nourished from a constant, unending source, it stands firm. That's the life of a believer who trusts in God. No matter how fierce the battle, God's strength becomes their shield.

Paul testified in 2 Corinthians 12:9–10 that God's strength is made perfect in weakness. This means even when you feel tired, broken, or at your lowest, God steps in with a power that cannot be destroyed. The enemy may try to break you, but what he does not understand is that every attempt only drives you deeper into the arms of your Heavenly Father.

So, the next time life throws its hardest punches, remind yourself: I am not standing in my strength. I am standing in God's strength, and His strength cannot be broken.

Heavenly Father, I thank You for being my source of strength, my refuge, and my shield. I acknowledge that without You, I am weak, but with You, I am unshakable. Lord, remind me daily to lean on You and not on my own understanding. Help me to trust in Your power when life tries to break me. Let my heart rest in the assurance that You are my strength and that no weapon formed against me shall prosper. Thank You for being my unbreakable foundation. In Jesus' name, I pray.

Amen and To God Be The Glory!

AUGUST 13. - "CURSES TURNED INTO BLESSINGS"

There are moments in life when it feels like the odds are stacked against us. Enemies rise, words are spoken against us, traps are set, and storms seem tailor-made to destroy us. But the truth of God's Word is that no curse, no plot, and no scheme can override the power of God's love for His children.

In Deuteronomy 23:5, Israel faced a hired prophet, Balaam who was commanded to speak a curse over them. Yet God Himself intervened. Instead of allowing the curse to settle, He transformed it into a blessing. Why? Because He loved His people. The same truth holds for you today: what the enemy intended for harm, God is using to shape, elevate, and bless you.

This principle is echoed throughout Scripture. Joseph, betrayed by his brothers, falsely accused, and thrown into prison, looked back and declared, "You meant evil against me, but God meant it for good" (Genesis 50:20). The cross itself is the greatest testimony of this truth. What was meant to shame and destroy Jesus became the pathway to salvation for the entire world.

Child of God, the curses spoken over your life cannot stick. The weapons formed against you cannot prosper (Isaiah 54:17). Every trap the enemy sets will only position you closer to God's purpose. Sometimes, what looks like a curse in the moment, or a betrayal, a delay, or a disappointment, becomes the very doorway through which God ushers in His blessing.

Hold fast to this truth: because God loves you, He will not allow the curses of your enemies, the weight of your past, or the darkness of your trials to define you. He is the God who turns curses into blessings, sorrow into joy, and ashes into beauty.

"Nevertheless the Lord your God would not hearken unto Balaam; but the Lord your God turned the curse into a blessing unto you, because the Lord your God loved you."

Deuteronomy 23:5 (KJV)

Heavenly Father, I thank You that no weapon formed against me shall prosper. Thank You for turning every curse, every negative word, and every scheme of the enemy into a blessing for my life. Remind me daily of Your unfailing love, that I may walk in confidence and not fear. Strengthen my faith to trust that even in the hardest moments, You are working all things together for my good. I give You the glory for victories I cannot yet see, knowing that what was meant to curse me is being transformed into a testimony of Your power and grace. In Jesus' mighty name I pray, Amen and To God Be The Glory!

AUGUST 14. - "DO UNTO OTHERS AS YOU WOULD HAVE THEM TO DO UNTO YOU"

The phrase "Do unto others as you would have them do unto you" is one of the most powerful guiding principles Jesus gave us. It is not just a moral saying; it is a divine instruction that challenges us to live out the heart of God in our daily interactions.

This teaching, often called the Golden Rule, is found in Matthew 7:12 (KJV): "Therefore all things whatsoever ye would that men should do to you, do ye even so to them: for this is the law and the prophets."

Here, Jesus summarized the essence of the law and the prophets love, respect, fairness, and compassion. It is easy to demand kindness, honesty, and patience from others, but this scripture calls us to first extend those same virtues ourselves.

When we practice this principle, we reflect the character of Christ. To treat others as we desire to be treated requires humility, empathy, and selflessness. If we want mercy, we must show mercy. If we want forgiveness, we must be quick to forgive. If we want love, we must love first.

This teaching also reminds us that relationships, whether in family, friendship, work, or community, are built on reciprocity. Our actions have a ripple effect. When we sow goodness into the lives of others, we reap goodness in return. Conversely, if we sow bitterness and cruelty, that harvest eventually finds its way back to us.

Living this way doesn't mean allowing ourselves to be mistreated, but rather that we make intentional choices to respond in a way that honors God. Even when others fall short, our call remains the same, to reflect Christ's love through our actions.

"Therefore all things whatsoever ye would that men should do to you, do ye even so to them: for this is the law and the prophets."
– Matthew 7:12 (KJV)

Heavenly Father, Thank You for the reminder that my life is meant to reflect Your love. Help me to treat others the way I desire to be treated. With kindness, respect, patience, and compassion. Teach me to look beyond myself and consider the feelings and needs of those around me. Where I have fallen short, forgive me and guide me to do better. Lord, let my words and actions be a light that points others back to You. May I sow goodness, so that Your name may be glorified through my life. In Jesus' name, I pray.

Amen and To God Be The Glory!

AUGUST 15. - "GOD NEVER SENDS YOU OUT ALONE"

Life has a way of confronting us with situations that seem overwhelming. Whether it's a financial hardship, a health crisis, a broken relationship, or the silent battles of the heart, the weight of life can often feel too heavy to bear. In those moments, the enemy whispers lies that you are alone, that no one understands, and that God has forgotten you. But the truth of God's Word reminds us of something far greater: God never sends you into situations alone.

The Lord not only goes before you to prepare the way, but He also stands beside you to strengthen you and walks behind you to cover and protect you. His presence surrounds you on every side. This truth brings peace and confidence, because no matter the storm, the Shepherd does not abandon His sheep.

In Deuteronomy 31:8 (KJV) it says: "And the Lord, he it is that doth go before thee; he will be with thee, he will not fail thee, neither forsake thee: fear not, neither be dismayed."

This verse reveals the full extent of God's care. He is ahead of you making the crooked places straight, He is beside you offering comfort and strength, and He is behind you shielding you from dangers you cannot see.

So, whatever situation you are facing right now, whether known or unknown, rest in the assurance that God's presence is your constant companion. He is not a distant God who watches from afar; He is Emmanuel, "God with us." The same God who parted the Red Sea, walked with the three Hebrew boys in the fiery furnace, and shut the lions' mouths for Daniel is walking with you today.

Therefore, you can face the unknown with confidence. You are never outnumbered, never abandoned, and never uncovered. You are fully surrounded by the presence of the Almighty.

Heavenly Father, I truly Thank You for the reminder that I am never alone. Thank You for going before me to prepare the way, for standing beside me as my strength, and for walking behind me as my shield. Lord, calm every fear and silence every doubt within me. Help me to trust Your presence in every situation I face. May I walk in confidence knowing that You will never leave me nor forsake me. Surround me and my loved ones with Your divine protection and peace. In Jesus' mighty name, I pray.

Amen and To God Be The Glory!

AUGUST 16. - "ANXIETY AND CONFUSSION IS NOT JESUS WAY"

Life often presents us with moments that bring overwhelming anxiety and deep confusion. Our thoughts can race in different directions, our hearts grow restless, and peace seems far out of reach. But as children of God, we must remember this important truth: anxiety and confusion are not from Jesus.

The Word of God reminds us in 1 Corinthians 14:33 (KJV): "For God is not the author of confusion, but of peace, as in all churches of the saints."

This verse makes it clear that confusion is not birthed from the Spirit of Christ. Jesus does not bring chaos into our hearts; He brings calm. He does not plant worry in our minds; He offers wisdom and clarity. He does not allow fear to rule us; He gives us His perfect peace.

When you find yourself wrestling with anxiety, it is important to pause and recognize the source. The enemy thrives on creating distractions, doubts, and disorientation to pull you away from your trust in God. But Jesus said in John 14:27 (KJV):

"Peace I leave with you, my peace I give unto you: not as the world giveth, give I unto you. Let not your heart be troubled, neither let it be afraid."

This peace is not temporary nor circumstantial, it's an everlasting gift. When our lives feel out of control, we can anchor ourselves in Jesus, who never changes. His peace surpasses understanding, and His Spirit guides us into truth.

To walk in this peace, we must surrender our anxious thoughts to Him daily. Philippians 4:6-7 instructs us to bring everything before God in prayer with thanksgiving, and in return, His peace will guard our hearts and minds. The presence of Jesus replaces anxiety with assurance and confusion with clarity.

So today, remind yourself: if it is confusion, it is not from Jesus. If it is anxiety, it is not from Jesus. Jesus brings peace, light, and direction.

Heavenly Father, I thank You that You are not the author of confusion but the giver of peace. When anxiety tries to grip my heart, remind me that it is not from You. When confusion clouds my mind, help me to lean into Your Word and trust Your Spirit for direction. Lord, I surrender my worries, fears, and uncertainties to You right now. Fill me with Your peace that surpasses all understanding and guide me into clarity and rest. I declare that my mind and heart belong to Jesus, and in Him, I will not be shaken. In Jesus' name I pray, Amen and To God Be The Glory!

AUGUST 17. - "LOVE BEYOND MISTAKES"

At an early age, many of us come face-to-face with a hard truth: people make mistakes. Some mistakes are small, others leave scars, and some shake the foundation of our trust. Life quickly teaches us that even those we love will sometimes fall short of our expectations, disappoint us, or even hurt us. Yet, in those moments, the real question is not only about their failure, but also about our response.

Do we allow their mistake to define the relationship forever? Or do we weigh their failure against the love and bond we share with them? Love does not deny that wrong was done, but it considers whether the relationship is worth restoring and healing.

Scripture reminds us of this powerful truth in 1 Peter 4:8 (KJV): "And above all things have fervent charity among yourselves: for charity shall cover the multitude of sins."

This verse doesn't mean we ignore wrongdoing or excuse destructive behavior. Instead, it points us toward a higher principle: love has the power to forgive, to heal, and to keep relationships alive where bitterness could have destroyed them. When we choose love over anger, we choose freedom over bondage. Forgiveness is not always easy, it stretches us, humbles us, and tests us. But it also draws us closer to the heart of God, who loved us so deeply that He forgave us despite our many mistakes.

To forgive does not mean to tolerate abuse, nor does it mean trust is automatically restored. But it does mean we release ourselves from the chains of unforgiveness and choose to see the person beyond their failure. It is asking: Is this mistake bigger than the love God has placed in my heart for them?

Every relationship, whether family, friendship, or marriage, will face this question. And in each case, we are invited to lean on the wisdom of God. His love for us demonstrates the highest standard: though we fall daily, He remains faithful.

Heavenly Father, thank You for teaching me the power of love and forgiveness. I know that people make mistakes, and at times, I have been hurt by them. Give me the strength to discern when to let go of offense and to cover mistakes with love. Help me to walk in Your grace, to forgive as You have forgiven me, and to value the bonds of love above bitterness and pride. Heal my heart where it has been wounded, and guide me to love others with wisdom, compassion, and truth. In Jesus' name, Amen and To God Be The Glory!

AUGUST 18. - "JESUS TURNS DELAYS INTO PROGRESS"

Life is a journey filled with seasons of growth, advancement, and purpose. However, sometimes it can feel as though invisible barriers are slowing us down. We pray, we work hard, we plan, but something unseen seems to resist progress. The truth is, Scripture teaches us that there are spiritual forces at work that try to hinder the plans of God's children.

Daniel experienced this in Daniel 10:12-13, when an angel of the Lord told him that his prayer had been heard the first day he prayed, but the "prince of the kingdom of Persia" resisted the answer for twenty-one days until angelic reinforcement came. This account reveals that delays are not always denials; sometimes they are battles in the unseen realm.

But the good news is this: every evil power working against your progress has already been defeated at the Cross. Jesus declared in Luke 10:19 (KJV): "Behold, I give unto you power to tread on serpents and scorpions, and over all the power of the enemy: and nothing shall by any means hurt you."

When you stand in the authority of Jesus Christ, you are not begging for victory, you are enforcing the victory that Christ already won. The devil may try to block, delay, or discourage, but he cannot override God's will for your life. By faith, you must rise up and declare: "Every evil power delaying my progress is broken in Jesus' mighty name."

Your breakthrough is not in the hands of man, nor is it dependent on circumstances, it is secured by the blood of Jesus. Delays must bow, chains must break, and closed doors must open when the power of God is declared over your life.

Heavenly Father, I thank You for the authority You have given me through Jesus Christ. I come against every evil power that has been assigned to delay my progress, block my blessings, or hinder my destiny. By the blood of Jesus and the power of His mighty name, I declare that every chain is broken, every obstacle is removed, and every demonic assignment is canceled. I walk forward in faith, victory, and divine acceleration. Lord, let Your will be done in my life, and let Your name be glorified in my testimony. In Jesus' mighty name, I pray.

Amen and To God Be The Glory!

AUGUST 19. - "IT'S BETWEEN YOU AND GOD ~ ANYWAY"

Mother Teresa once said: "People are often unreasonable and self-centered. Forgive them anyway. Give your best anyway. For you see, in the end, it's between you and God; it's never between you and them anyway."

These words remind us of one of the deepest truths in our Christian walk: our lives are not lived for the approval of men, but for the glory of God. The world may not always recognize your sacrifices, your kindness, or your faithfulness. People may take advantage of your love, misunderstand your motives, or even repay your goodness with cruelty. Yet, God calls us to continue to love, forgive, and give our best, not because others deserve it, but because He is worthy.

Jesus Himself is our greatest example. On the cross, as He endured rejection, mockery, and pain, He prayed: "Father, forgive them, for they know not what they do" (Luke 23:34 KJV). His forgiveness was not conditional on the actions of others, because it flowed from His love for the Father and His mission to save the world.

When you forgive anyway, you release yourself from the bondage of bitterness and allow God's peace to reign in your heart. When you give your best anyway, even when unappreciated, you store up treasures in heaven where moth and rust cannot destroy (Matthew 6:20). When you live with eternity in view, you remember that every word, every deed, and every sacrifice is seen by God, even if unseen by man.

The truth is, people will sometimes disappoint you, betray you, or treat you unfairly. But God's Word encourages us in Colossians 3:23-24 (KJV):

"And whatsoever ye do, do it heartily, as to the Lord, and not unto men; knowing that of the Lord ye shall receive the reward of the inheritance: for ye serve the Lord Christ."

This verse reminds us that our service, our love, and our obedience are not ultimately for people, but for God. And when we stand before Him, it will never be about how others treated us, but how we responded to them with faith, with love, with perseverance, and with forgiveness.

Heavenly Father, Thank You for reminding me today that my life is not lived for the approval of men, but for Your glory. Help me, Lord, to forgive even when it's hard, to love even when it's not returned, and to give my best even when it goes unnoticed. Strengthen my heart to remember that my reward is in You, not in the praise of people. May my actions reflect Your love and may I live daily with eternity in mind. Keep me faithful to You, Lord, knowing that in the end, it's always between You and me. In Jesus' name I pray, Amen and To God Be The Glory!

AUGUST 20. - "A TEACHABLE SPIRIT"

This simple yet profound truth applies to every area of our walk with God. A closed heart resists instruction, correction, and wisdom, while an open and determined heart becomes unstoppable because it is fueled by the power of growth and understanding.

The Bible reminds us in Proverbs 1:5 (KJV): "A wise man will hear and will increase learning; and a man of understanding shall attain unto wise counsels." Wisdom is not automatically given, it requires humility, openness, and a desire to grow. God Himself cannot pour new revelation into a vessel that refuses to be filled. The unwilling heart builds walls around itself, cutting off the very help that could have lifted it.

But when you are determined to learn, when you hunger for truth, guidance, and direction, you tap into a divine flow that no opposition can hinder. A teachable spirit attracts mentors, opportunities, and divine instruction. It is determination that keeps you seeking even when you don't fully understand. It is determination that pushes you past failure, past pride, past fear, and straight into God's wisdom and success.

Jesus said in Matthew 5:6 (KJV): "Blessed are they which do hunger and thirst after righteousness: for they shall be filled." Hunger opens the door to filling. Determination guarantees progress. When you posture yourself to keep learning from the Word of God, from the Spirit of God, and even from life experiences, you become unstoppable. Not because of your strength, but because you are walking in the flow of God's wisdom.

So, ask yourself today: Am I resisting learning because of pride, stubbornness, or fear? Or am I positioning myself with a teachable and determined spirit? If you remain unwilling, no one can force you. But if you are determined, nothing and no one, not even the enemy can hold you back.

Heavenly Father, give me a humble and teachable spirit. Remove pride, stubbornness, and fear from my heart so that I may receive Your wisdom. Help me to hunger after truth and thirst for righteousness, knowing that You will fill me. Strengthen my determination to keep learning, keep growing, and keep following Your Word. Let no obstacle stop me from becoming who You have called me to be. In Jesus' name I pray.

Amen and To God Be The Glory!

AUGUST 21. - "BE THANKFUL FOR TODAY"

The phrase "be thankful for today and never take anyone or anything for granted, life is a blessing" is both a reminder and a command for the believer. So often we live as though tomorrow is guaranteed, when in reality, every day we open our eyes is a gift from God. Each sunrise is His whisper: "I have given you another day, another chance, another blessing."

Life itself is a miracle. From the breath in your lungs to the heartbeat in your chest, you are experiencing the sustaining power of God. Yet, in the busyness of life, it is easy to overlook His daily mercies and take both people and blessings for granted. Family, friends, health, opportunities, even small acts of kindness, all of these are gifts entrusted to us. When we neglect gratitude, we dishonor the Giver.

Gratitude is not just a feeling, it is a posture of the heart. It acknowledges that everything we have comes from above. When we practice thankfulness, our perspective shifts from what we lack to what we already possess. It opens the door for joy, peace, hope, and love to overflow in our lives.

Scripture reminds us: "This is the day which the Lord hath made; we will rejoice and be glad in it." Psalm 118:24 (KJV)

Today is not just another day, it is "The Lord's Day". He handcrafted it with purpose. He filled it with opportunities to grow, to love, to forgive, to bless, and to be blessed. When you embrace gratitude, you not only see the beauty of today, but you also begin to see the fingerprints of God in every detail.

So let us live with hearts full of thanksgiving. Let us value the people in our lives while we still have them. Let us see life not as a burden but as a blessing. And may our cups indeed overflow, not with material possessions, but with the eternal treasures of joy, peace, hope, and love that come from God alone.

Heavenly Father, thank You for the precious gift of life today. Forgive me for the times I have taken Your blessings and the people around me for granted. Teach me to live with a heart of gratitude and to recognize that every breath is from You. Fill my cup until it overflows with joy, peace, hope, and love so that I may share these blessings with others. Help me to rejoice in this day You have made and to never miss the beauty in the small things. In Jesus' name I pray.

Amen and To God Be The Glory!

AUGUST 22. - "BE THE RAINBOW INSTEAD OF THE CLOUD"

Life has a way of bringing storms into people's paths. Some storms are loud and violent, leaving devastation in their wake. Others are quiet but heavy, lingering like gray skies that refuse to move on. Many times, we cannot stop someone else's storm, but we can choose to be the rainbow that brings them hope after the rain.

When we think of a rainbow, we think of beauty, brightness, and a promise that the storm will not last forever. In Scripture, the rainbow is a symbol of God's covenant and His faithfulness (Genesis 9:13). It was His way of reminding humanity that even after judgment and floodwaters, mercy and grace would prevail. In the same way, when we choose to "be the rainbow in someone's cloud," we reflect God's love and mercy to those who feel stuck in their storm.

This does not always require big gestures. Sometimes, being the rainbow is as simple as offering a smile, listening without judgment, extending forgiveness, or sending a word of encouragement. To someone drowning in despair, even the smallest act of kindness can feel like a ray of sunshine breaking through the clouds.

Jesus tells us in Matthew 5:14–16 (KJV): "Ye are the light of the world. A city that is set on an hill cannot be hid. Neither do men light a candle, and put it under a bushel, but on a candlestick; and it giveth light unto all that are in the house. Let your light so shine before men, that they may see your good works, and glorify your Father which is in heaven."

Being the rainbow is not about drawing attention to ourselves, but about reflecting God's light and His promises. Every rainbow points back to heaven. In the same way, when we offer hope to others, our lives should point them to the unfailing love of Christ.

Storms are inevitable, but God always provides reminders of His presence, and often, He uses us to do so. Today, ask yourself: Whose cloud can I brighten? Whose storm can I help ease? Even one act of kindness, rooted in love, can be the rainbow someone desperately needs.

Heavenly Father, thank You for being my light and my hope in every storm. Teach me to reflect Your love and kindness in the lives of others. Help me to be the rainbow that reminds someone that their storm will not last forever and that You are faithful to bring them through. Let my words, actions, and presence point others back to You. In Jesus' name, Amen and To God Be The Glory!

AUGUST 23. - "BE THE REASON"

When we think about influence, most often we think of titles, positions, or power. But true influence in the Kingdom of God does not come from status; it comes from the condition of the heart. The phrase "be the reason why people believe in pure hearts, good vibes, and kind souls" points us toward living a life that reflects Christ in such a way that others see His goodness in us.

The world is full of deceit, selfishness, and division, but God calls His children to rise above that and to live as light-bearers. Your words, actions, and even your quiet presence can plant seeds of hope and healing in someone else's heart. It may be a gentle smile, a listening ear, or a simple act of kindness that convinces someone that love still exists, that goodness is not extinct, and that purity of heart is possible.

Jesus Himself said: "Blessed are the pure in heart: for they shall see God."

Matthew 5:8 (KJV)

A pure heart reflects God's character. A kind soul mirrors Christ's compassion. A life lived with genuine love and positivity ("good vibes") carries the fragrance of heaven in a world that so often smells of bitterness and despair. When you choose to embody these qualities, you are not just encouraging others, you are witnessing Christ to them.

Your influence might be the very thing that restores someone's faith in humanity and, more importantly, points them toward God. When people encounter your kindness, they should sense that it flows from something greater, and that's your relationship with Christ. That is how they begin to believe not only in good people but in a good God.

Heavenly Father, thank You for Your perfect love and for the example of Jesus Christ, who walked this earth with a pure heart, a compassionate spirit, and a kind soul. Lord, help me to be a living testimony of Your goodness. Let my actions reflect Your light, my words carry peace, and my presence bring encouragement. May others believe in love, kindness, and hope because they see You working through me. Keep my heart pure, my spirit humble, and my soul anchored in Your truth. In Jesus' name I pray.

Amen and To God Be The Glory!

AUGUST 24. - "BELIEVE IT AND RECEIVE IT"

When God speaks a promise, it is not a suggestion, nor is it wishful thinking. It is a declaration sealed by His character and power. Deuteronomy 28:12 reminds us that the Lord Himself has treasures in heaven reserved for His children. He promises rain in due season, blessings on the work of our hands, and abundance that allows us to lend and not borrow. This is not a man-made dream but a divine covenant.

The key to unlocking these promises lies in two simple actions: believe it and receive it. Believing is not merely acknowledging God's promises in theory but having faith that they are already established in your life. It means standing on His Word even when your circumstances look dry and barren. Receiving, on the other hand, requires aligning your life with that belief. You open your hands, your heart, and your mindset to walk as though it is already done.

God's blessings are not limited by time, economy, or circumstances. The rain of His goodness falls "in His season," not necessarily in ours. That means there may be waiting, there may be sowing, and there may be preparation before the harvest. Yet the faithful believer holds on, declaring, "If God said it, I believe it—and that settles it."

Faith transforms promises into reality. Just as a seed must be planted before it grows, so must belief be planted in your heart before you can receive the harvest. Doubt will always try to whisper, but faith shouts louder: "The Lord is faithful. His Word cannot fail."

So today, whatever you are praying for, whether it be peace in your home, healing in your body, provision in your finances, or restoration in your relationships, stand firm on your belief. Speak life. Expect the rain. Walk as though the windows of heaven are already open over you. Believe it. Receive it. And watch God do what only He can do.

"The Lord shall open unto thee His good treasure, the heaven to give the rain unto thy land in His season, and to bless all the work of thine hand: and thou shalt lend unto many nations, and thou shalt not borrow." Deuteronomy 28:12 (KJV)

Heavenly Father, thank You for being a faithful God who keeps His promises. I believe Your Word in Deuteronomy 28:12, that You will open the heavens and bless the work of my hands. Lord, help me to walk by faith and not by sight. Teach me to trust Your timing, to expect Your rain, and to position myself to receive every blessing You have prepared for me. Remove every trace of doubt and replace it with unwavering faith. I declare today that I believe it and I receive it in Jesus' mighty name.

Amen and To God Be The Glory!

AUGUST 25. - "LIVING UP TO WHAT GOD PUT IN YOU"

There is a beautiful truth hidden in the phrase: "Your friends will believe in your potential; your enemies will make you live up to it."

Friends see your gifts, talents, and calling. They encourage you, cheer you on, and remind you of what you can become. But sometimes, it's the resistance, criticism, and opposition of enemies that force you to step fully into that potential. Without the pressure of adversity, some of us would never discover the depth of strength, wisdom, and perseverance God placed within us.

Joseph's brothers hated him, yet their jealousy pushed him closer to his destiny. David's Goliath wasn't just an enemy, it was an opportunity for him to walk into kingship. Even Jesus had opposition that revealed the fullness of His mission. Enemies are not always setbacks; often, they are setups for God's greater purpose.

The Apostle Paul reminds us in Romans 8:28 (KJV): "And we know that all things work together for good to them that love God, to them who are the called according to his purpose."

"All things" include the love of friends and the pressure from enemies. Your friends believe in your potential, but your enemies force you to rise, fight, and prove what God already placed inside you. Without them, you might remain comfortable. With them, you are sharpened, refined, and elevated into your destiny.

Instead of resenting those who oppose you, begin to see them as unintentional contributors to your growth. They push you to pray harder, work smarter, and depend on God more deeply. Their attempts to break you are the very tools God uses to build you.

Heavenly Father, I thank You for surrounding me with true friends who encourage and uplift me. But I also thank You for my enemies, because they unknowingly push me into the fullness of Your purpose. Teach me not to fear opposition, but to recognize Your hand at work in every situation. Strengthen me so that I may live up to the potential You have placed within me. Use every trial, every critic, and every adversary to shape me into the person You designed me to be. In Jesus' mighty name I pray, Amen and To God Be The Glory!

AUGUST 26. - "HUMILITY IN A WORLD OF ENTITLEMENT"

We live in a world that constantly pushes entitlement, striving, and competition. Society often measures worth by titles, possessions, and achievements. The pressure to always be the best and to get ahead, even if it means stepping over others has caused pride to thrive and humility to diminish. Yet, God's Word reminds us that true greatness is not in exalting ourselves, but in lowering ourselves before Him and serving others.

The spirit of entitlement tells us we deserve recognition, blessings, or positions. But humility recognizes that everything we have and are, comes from God. The world says, "Push harder to get ahead," but humility says, "God will lift me in His time." The world seeks to outshine others, but humility seeks to glorify God.

Scripture tells us: "Do nothing out of selfish ambition or vain conceit. Rather, in humility value others above yourselves, not looking to your own interests but each of you to the interests of others." Philippians 2:3-4 (NIV)

Jesus Himself modeled humility when He washed the feet of His disciples. Though He was the Son of God, He did not cling to His divine status but came to serve, not to be served. This is the standard He set for us. Humility doesn't mean thinking less of ourselves; it means thinking of ourselves less and allowing God to shape our hearts with gratitude, patience, and love.

When we live with humility, we release the burden of striving to prove ourselves. We rest in the confidence that God's favor, not human applause, is what matters. True promotion, peace, and purpose come from God, not from competing with others.

Heavenly Father, thank You for reminding me that humility is the way to Your heart. Forgive me for the times I've been caught up in entitlement, pride, and the endless striving of this world. Help me to walk in humility, serving others with love and honoring You in all I do. Teach me to trust Your timing and Your plan, knowing that You will lift me up when the time is right. May my life reflect Jesus, who humbled Himself for my sake. In His name I pray.

Amen and To God Be The Glory!

AUGUST 27. - "BIBLE EMERGENCY NUMBERS"

Life has a way of presenting us with emergencies. Moments of sudden sorrow, fear, weakness, or confusion. In the natural way, when an emergency happens, we dial 911 and wait for help to arrive. But as children of God, we have a higher hotline, one that is never busy, never out of service, and never requires a phone. It is the Word of God, filled with promises that meet us in every crisis of the heart and soul.

Life is filled with moments where we find ourselves in spiritual emergencies. Some days sorrow overwhelms us, other days worry weighs us down and sometimes fear creeps in to paralyze our hearts. In those moments, many people instinctively reach for a phone to call someone they trust. We have a direct connection to Heaven through His Word and prayer.

Think of the Bible as having "emergency numbers." When sorrow floods in, there is a verse that comforts. When anger rises, there is a scripture that calms. When loneliness creeps in, there is a promise that assures us of God's presence. For every trouble that comes, there is a Word that answers, and it is available 24/7, no signal required, no voicemail waiting, just direct access to the throne of heaven.

That verse to remind you that God is present, listening, and able to deliver. When you are sorrowful, you can "dial" Psalm 34:18: "The Lord is near to the brokenhearted and saves the crushed in spirit." When you are fearful, you can "dial" Isaiah 41:10: "Fear thou not; for I am with thee: be not dismayed; for I am thy God: I will strengthen thee; yea, I will help thee; yea, I will uphold thee with the right hand of my righteousness."

The psalmist reminds us: "The righteous cry, and the LORD heareth, and delivereth them out of all their troubles." Psalm 34:17 (KJV)

Notice it says all their troubles. That means there is not a single situation, whether it be sorrow, fear, betrayal, weakness, or temptation that does not already have an answer waiting in the Scriptures. God has stocked His Word with healing balm, with weapons for warfare, with light for the dark path. Unlike earthly hotlines that may place you on hold or transfer you to another department, the Bible provides immediate access to God's promises. Prayer is your direct petition to Heaven, and no appointment, technology, or phone service is required. The Lord Himself assures us in Jeremiah 33:3: "Call unto me, and I will answer thee, and shew thee great and mighty things, which thou knowest not."

This truth is a powerful reminder that no matter what changes life may bring, be it joy, pain, fear, or uncertainty, the Word of God remains your unshakable guide. Heaven's line is never busy. God's ear is always open. His Word is living and active, available 24/7, and tailored for every season of life.

So, the next time you find yourself in an emergency, don't panic ~ open your Bible, dial the right scripture, and let Heaven's comfort answer your heart.

Heavenly Father, I thank You that Your Word is always near, alive, and powerful. Thank You for making Yourself available to me at all times. When I am sorrowful, fearful, worried, or overwhelmed. Help me to remember that I never need to wait in line for Your presence, for You are always just a prayer away. Teach me to seek Your promises in Your Word as my emergency numbers, my first response in times of need, and not my last resort. Strengthen my faith to trust in Your unfailing help. In Jesus' name, I pray.

Amen and To God Be The Glory!

AUGUST 28. - "IF OPPORTUNITY DOES NOT KNOCK ~ BUILD A DOOR"

There are times in life when we wait for opportunity to knock, but the knock never comes. The world teaches us that doors of success, promotion, and blessing will just appear if we wait long enough. But faith teaches us something different. Sometimes God calls us not to wait for the door, but to build it ourselves through obedience, faith, and perseverance.

Think of Noah. God gave him a command to build an ark when rain had never fallen from the sky. There was no "door of opportunity" for him to walk through, only ridicule, opposition, and uncertainty. Yet by faith, Noah built what God told him to build. That ark became the very door of salvation for him and his family (Genesis 6:13-22).

When opportunity doesn't present itself, don't despair. Instead, seek God's wisdom. Sometimes the missing door is an invitation to create something new, to step out in faith, or to develop gifts God has already placed inside you. Just as David used a simple sling and stone when there was no warrior's armor to fit him, God may ask you to use what you have in your hand to create a way where none seems to exist.

This truth reminds us: when opportunity does not build a door, faith can. God has given us the ability to pray, to believe, to work diligently, and to trust that He orders our steps. The Lord is not limited by man-made doors. He is the Master Architect, able to create openings where walls once stood.

"Behold, I have set before thee an open door, and no man can shut it: for thou hast a little strength, and hast kept my word, and hast not denied my name." Revelation 3:8 (KJV)

Heavenly Father, I thank You for being the God who makes a way when there seems to be no way. Forgive me for the times I have waited passively instead of moving forward in faith. Teach me to build when there is no door, to believe when there is no sign, and to trust You even when the path is unclear. Strengthen my hands to work, my heart to hope, and my spirit to keep pressing forward. Let every step I take be guided by Your Word and anointed by Your Spirit. In Jesus' name I pray. Amen.

To God Be The Glory!

AUGUST 29. - "REST IN GODS ASSURANCE"

There are times when life feels heavy, uncertain, and overwhelming. The struggles of yesterday, the weight of today, and the fear of tomorrow can easily rob us of peace. Yet, in the midst of all this, God speaks a gentle but powerful word: "Rest in Me."

When God says, "I am already at work in your life," it is a reminder that He is not idle. Even when you cannot see it, His hand is moving behind the scenes, orchestrating events for your good. The situations that look impossible to you are not beyond His control. He is a God who turns setbacks into stepping stones, pain into purpose, and trials into testimonies.

The Lord promises to turn around every bad situation. What the enemy meant for harm, God will use for your good (Genesis 50:20). What looked like the end will become a new beginning. No valley is too deep, no storm too strong, and no wound too painful for the healing touch of God. He is both a Restorer and a Healer.

Not only will He bless you, but He will bless your family as well. His covenant love extends beyond you, touching those connected to you. Where there is brokenness, He will bring healing. Where there is lack, He will provide. Where there is fear, He will bring peace.

"Come unto me, all ye that labour and are heavy laden, and I will give you rest. Take my yoke upon you, and learn of me; for I am meek and lowly in heart: and ye shall find rest unto your souls. For my yoke is easy, and my burden is light." Matthew 11:28–30 (KJV)

Heavenly Father, I thank You for reminding me that I can rest in You. Even when my eyes cannot see, I trust that You are already working in my life. Lord, turn around every bad situation and let Your power be made known. Bless my family, provide for our needs, and heal every wound that requires Your touch. Help me to release my worries into Your hands and walk in faith, knowing You are faithful to keep Your promises. In Jesus' name, Amen and To God Be The Glory!

AUGUST 30. - "SOME SITUATIONS GOD WANTS TO CHANGE YOUR HEART"

Life often brings us into circumstances that test our patience, faith, and endurance. We pray for God to move quickly, to shift the situation, to remove the pain, or to bring instant relief. But sometimes, His silence or delay is not neglect, it is intentional. God is more interested in the transformation of your heart than the alteration of your circumstances.

When Paul cried out three times for God to remove his thorn, the Lord did not change Paul's situation. Instead, He gave Paul a deeper revelation: "My grace is sufficient for thee: for my strength is made perfect in weakness" (2 Corinthians 12:9, KJV). God did not take away the thorn, but He changed Paul's perspective, his heart posture, and his reliance on divine strength.

Many times, we think deliverance only looks like God removing the problem. But true deliverance can also be God changing us in the middle of the problem. When our hearts are transformed, we gain spiritual maturity, deeper trust, and unshakable faith. That is why some trials linger, not because God cannot remove them, but because He is using them to prune us, refine us, and mold us into the likeness of Christ.

Ask yourself: What is God trying to teach me in this season? Is He showing me patience? Is He teaching me humility? Is He developing endurance? When we shift our focus from "Lord, change this" to "Lord, change me," we begin to see His hand at work in powerful ways.

Your situation may not change overnight, but your heart can change in an instant if you yield it to Him. And when your heart changes, the situation may not have power over you anymore.

"And I will give you a new heart, and a new spirit I will put within you. And I will remove the heart of stone from your flesh and give you a heart of flesh." Ezekiel 36:26 (ESV)

Heavenly Father, thank You for reminding me that sometimes the purpose of my trial is not to change my situation but to change my heart. Lord, help me not to resist the lessons You are teaching me. Create in me a clean heart and renew a right spirit within me. Give me the strength to endure and the faith to trust Your timing. Even when I don't see the immediate change I desire, let me see the change You are making in me. Thank You for loving me enough to mold me into the person You've called me to be. In Jesus' name, I pray.

Amen and To God Be The Glory!

AUGUST 31. - "TRUE CHARACTER"

When we think about character, we often associate it with reputation, integrity, or how we live our lives in public. Yet, true character is revealed in the hidden moments, the times when no one is watching and when the person we are interacting with has nothing to offer us in return.

The phrase, "Character is how you treat someone who can do nothing for you," cuts straight to the heart of Christlike living. It reminds us that love, kindness, and humility are not measured by what we gain, but by what we give. Our Lord Jesus modeled this perfectly. He served the poor, touched the lepers, fed the hungry, and spoke to those society had cast aside. He did not seek power, fame, or human rewards; instead, He humbled Himself to wash His disciples' feet (John 13:14-15).

Scripture tells us: "Do nothing out of selfish ambition or vain conceit. Rather, in humility value others above yourselves, not looking to your own interests but each of you to the interests of the others." Philippians 2:3-4 (NIV)

The true test of our character is how we treat the powerless, the overlooked, and the forgotten. Do we extend grace to the homeless man on the street? Do we show patience with someone who struggles to understand? Do we honor those who may never have the means to honor us back?

When we choose compassion over pride and selflessness over self-interest, we reflect the heart of God. Every act of kindness toward "the least of these" is service unto Christ Himself (Matthew 25:40).

Heavenly Father, Thank You for teaching us through Your Word that true greatness is found in humility and service. Help us to see people the way You see them, as precious, valued, and worthy of love, regardless of what they can or cannot give in return. Strip away selfish motives from our hearts and replace them with the pure desire to serve. May our character reflect the love of Christ in every interaction, especially with those who cannot repay us. Let our lives be living testimonies of Your grace. In Jesus' name I pray, Amen and To God Be The Glory!

SEPTEMBER INTRODUCTION

As we enter into the month of September, we are reminded that life does not pause in its challenges. Pressing problems, whether in our homes, our health, our finances, or our faith, often rise up like waves, threatening to overwhelm us. Yet, in these very moments, God calls us not to despair, but to lean into His Word. For every question we carry, for every burden we bear, and for every valley we walk through, Scripture holds a timeless answer.

This devotional for September has been prayerfully crafted to lead us back to the source of all wisdom and strength: God's Word. Life may shift with changing seasons, but the truth of Scripture remains steadfast and immovable. Just as summer transitions into autumn, so too do our lives enter different phases and trials. But the Word of God assures us that even in transition, we are never alone, and there is always a divine solution for every earthly problem.

The Apostle Paul wrote in 2 Timothy 3:16-17 (KJV): "All scripture is given by inspiration of God, and is profitable for doctrine, for reproof, for correction, for instruction in righteousness: That the man of God may be perfect, thoroughly furnished unto all good works."

This month, let us allow the Spirit of God to illuminate His Word in a fresh way. These devotionals are not just words on a page, but living truths meant to equip you with hope, direction, and courage for the daily battles you face. September can be the month where you stop wrestling with the weight of unanswered questions and begin resting in the fact that God already holds the answers.

Whether you are seeking peace in a storm, guidance in confusion, or healing for a broken heart, the message of this devotional remains the same: God's Word is sufficient, His promises are sure, and His love is unshakable.

Heavenly Father, we thank You for the gift of a new month and the opportunity to grow in Your Word. As we open this devotional, we invite Your presence into our hearts and minds. Speak to us through Your Scriptures and reveal the answers we need for the challenges we face. Strengthen our faith, renew our hope, and remind us that no problem is greater than Your power. May this month be one of transformation, breakthrough, and peace as we cling to the promises of Your Word. In Jesus' mighty name we pray, Amen and To God Be the Glory!

SEPTEMBER 1. - "PERFECT LOVE CAST OUT FEAR"

Fear is one of the greatest weapons the enemy uses against the people of God. Fear paralyzes faith, clouds judgment, and keeps us from fully trusting in God's promises. But John reminds us, that God's perfect love drives fear away. Where His love reigns, fear loses its grip.

When you truly embrace the love of God, you understand that you are secure in Him. His love is unchanging, unconditional, and unshakable. It covers your past, sustains your present, and secures your future. Fear thrives on uncertainty, but God's love is certainty itself, it reassures you that nothing can separate you from Him (Romans 8:38–39).

This verse also warns that fear has torment. Fear keeps us in cycles of anxiety, dread, and insecurity. But when you abide in God's love, your heart is at peace, because you know that even in trials, His love will not fail you. To be made perfect in love means maturing in faith to the point where you rest in God's goodness, regardless of circumstances.

Ask yourself today: Am I living in fear, or am I resting in God's perfect love? If fear is dominating your thoughts, replace it with the truth of His Word. Speak His promises over your life. Remind yourself daily that His perfect love covers you. As you draw nearer to Him, His love will fill every corner of your heart, leaving no room for fear.

"There is no fear in love; but perfect love casteth out fear: because fear hath torment. He that feareth is not made perfect in love." 1 John 4:18 (KJV)

Heavenly Father, I thank You for the perfect love You have poured out through Jesus Christ. Your love is greater than my fears, my doubts, and my insecurities. Lord, when fear tries to take hold of me, remind me of Your Word and help me to rest in Your unchanging love. Teach me to walk in faith and confidence, knowing that I am covered by Your grace and surrounded by Your peace. Perfect Your love in me, Lord, that I may live boldly, free from fear, and filled with Your Spirit. In Jesus' mighty name I pray.

Amen and To God Be The Glory!

SEPTEMBER 2. - "FEED YOUR MIND HOPE"

Life can pull your thoughts in a thousand different directions. Worries about tomorrow, regrets from yesterday, and the noise of the present moment. But peace begins when you make a conscious choice to anchor your mind, your hope, and your trust in God.

To set your mind on God is to choose His truth over your fears. To place your hope in Him is to believe that His promises are greater than your current problems. And to trust Him means leaning not on your own understanding but resting in the assurance that He is working all things together for your good.

When your mind is fixed on God, you begin to experience His perfect peace. Not because everything around you is perfect, but because you've chosen to look to the One who is.

"Thou wilt keep him in perfect peace, whose mind is stayed on thee: because he trusteth in thee." Isaiah 26:3 (KJV)

Dear Lord, help me to set my mind on You daily. When distractions come, when anxiety rises, and when life feels overwhelming, remind me to turn my focus back to You. Let my hope be rooted in Your promises and my trust grounded in Your unchanging faithfulness. Fill me with Your peace as I keep my thoughts fixed on You. In Jesus' name, amen.

"And To God Be The Glory"

SEPTEMBER 3. - "WE FALL DOWN ~ BUT WE GET BACK UP AGAIN"

Life has a way of humbling us. No matter how strong our faith is, no matter how determined our spirit, we all stumble. We all fall short of the glory of God (Romans 3:23). The difference between defeat and victory is not found in whether we fall ~ but in whether we rise again.

The phrase "we fall down, but we get back up again" carries the truth of God's grace. A saint is not someone who never fails. A saint is someone who refuses to stay down, who allows God's mercy to lift them, cleanse them, and restore them. Falling reminds us of our humanity, but getting up again reminds us of God's divinity working inside us.

Consider Peter, who denied Jesus three times. He fell, and his shame was deep. Yet Christ restored him, reminding him of his purpose: "Feed my sheep" (John 21:17). David also fell into sin, yet he rose again after repentance and became known as a man after God's own heart. These stories remind us that failure is not final when grace is present.

Proverbs 24:16 declares: "For a just man falleth seven times, and riseth up again: but the wicked shall fall into mischief."

The just man is not described as one who never falls, but one who rises again each time, empowered by faith and God's love.

So, if you've stumbled, don't let guilt chain you down. Don't let shame keep you from moving forward. God's forgiveness is greater than your failure, and His mercy is new every morning (Lamentations 3:22–23). Rise up, child of God. Dust yourself off, lift your eyes toward heaven, and take the next step.

Falling does not disqualify you ~ staying down does. But when you rise, you show the world that your hope is not in your own strength, but in the God who raises the fallen and makes the broken whole again.

Heavenly Father, I thank You for Your grace that lifts me when I fall. Lord, I confess that I am weak at times and stumble in my walk, but I thank You that Your mercy restores me. Give me the courage to rise again, the strength to keep walking, and the faith to believe that You are not finished with me yet. Help me to remember that my identity is not in my failures, but in Your love and forgiveness. Strengthen me to keep pressing forward, trusting that every fall is an opportunity for Your glory to shine through my life. In Jesus' name, Amen and To God Be The Glory!

SEPTEMBER 4. - "LOVE IN ACTION"

When Paul describes love in this passage, he isn't talking about a fleeting feeling or an emotional high. He is teaching us about the divine nature of love, God's kind of love, agape love. This love is not self-centered, conditional, or temporary. It is steadfast, enduring, and rooted in God Himself, for "God is love" (1 John 4:8 NIV).

Notice how Paul frames love: he doesn't merely define it in abstract terms, but in action and character. Love suffers long, it has patience with people even when wronged. Love is kind, it actively seeks the good of others. Love does not envy or boast, for it is secure in God and doesn't need to compete. Love refuses to be proud or behave rudely. It doesn't push its own agenda but seeks the well-being of others.

True love doesn't allow anger to control it. It refuses to dwell on wrongs or keep score of offenses. Instead of delighting in gossip, bitterness, or sin, love finds its joy in truth and righteousness. It carries burdens, chooses to believe in the best, keeps its hope alive, and endures through hardships.

In essence, Paul shows us that love is the reflection of Christ Himself. Every quality listed here was lived out by Jesus in His ministry, His relationships, and ultimately at the cross. When we walk in this love, we reflect the heart of Christ to a broken world.

Yet, this love is not easy in our own strength. We may find ourselves impatient, easily provoked, or tempted to keep records of wrongs. That is why we must rely on the Holy Spirit to pour God's love into our hearts (Romans 5:5). Only through Him can we consistently live out this supernatural love.

So today, ask yourself: Am I walking in this love? Do my words and actions align with the patient, kind, and enduring love described here? Let us not just read about love, let us embody it, for love is the greatest testimony of our faith (John 13:35).

4 Charity suffereth long, and is kind; charity envieth not; charity vaunteth not itself, is not puffed up,

5 Doth not behave itself unseemly, seeketh not her own, is not easily provoked, thinketh no evil;

6 Rejoiceth not in iniquity, but rejoiceth in the truth;

7 Beareth all things, believeth all things, hopeth all things, endureth all things.

1 Corinthians 13:4-7 KJV

Thank You for teaching me what true love is through Your Word and through the life of Jesus Christ. Help me to walk in this kind of love daily with patience, kindness, humility, and forgiveness. Remove any bitterness, envy, or pride from my heart, and fill me with the love of Christ that bears, believes, hopes, and endures all things. May my life be a reflection of Your perfect love so others may see You in me. Strengthen me through the power of the Holy Spirit to live in love, even when it's difficult. In Jesus' name I pray, Amen and To God Be The Glory!

SEPTEMBER 5. - "MY STRENGTH IN CHRIST ALONE"

Life is full of moments that test our strength. There are seasons when the burdens feel too heavy, the storms too fierce, and the challenges too overwhelming. Yet, in those very moments, we are reminded of a powerful truth: our strength does not come from ourselves, it comes from Christ.

Paul, when writing to the Philippians, was not living in comfort or abundance. He was in prison, yet he penned these words with assurance and confidence. His declaration was not one of human ability but of divine empowerment. He had learned to be content whether he was abased or abounding, hungry or full, because his reliance was not on circumstances but on the sustaining power of Christ.

When Paul says, "I can do all things," he is not speaking of personal ambition or self-exaltation. Instead, he is testifying that no matter the trial, no matter the season, or whether in lack or in plenty ~ Christ's strength within him was more than enough. This same truth is for us today.

When life feels unbearable, Christ is the One who carries us.

When we feel unworthy or incapable, He reminds us that His grace is sufficient.

When we face obstacles that seem impossible, His power makes a way.

The beauty of this verse is that it shifts our focus away from self-reliance and onto divine reliance. The world teaches us to be self-made, but the Word teaches us to be Christ-sustained. True victory, true peace, and true endurance come when we lean on His strength and not our own.

Whatever mountain stands before you, whatever valley you walk through, you can declare with confidence: "I can do all things through Christ which strengtheneth me." This is not a boast of pride but a confession of faith. Faith in the One who conquered death, defeated sin, and dwells within you to empower your every step.

"I can do all things through Christ which strengtheneth me." Philippians 4:13 (KJV)

Heavenly Father, I thank You for the reminder that my strength comes not from myself but from Christ who lives in me. Lord, when I feel weak, weary, or overwhelmed, help me to lean fully on Your power and not my own. Teach me to walk in faith, content in every circumstance, knowing that You are enough for me. Strengthen my heart, renew my mind, and let my life reflect the victory and power that come through Christ alone. In Jesus' name I pray, Amen and To God Be The Glory!

SEPTEMBER 6. - "GOD IS LOVE"

The apostle John makes one of the most profound declarations in all of Scripture: God is love. This truth is not simply a description of what God does, but a declaration of who God is. His very essence, His nature, and His being is love. Every action He takes, every word He speaks, and every plan He unfolds is rooted in His perfect love.

To know God is to know love. If love is absent in our lives toward others, toward ourselves, and toward God, it is evidence that we have not truly grasped who He is. Love is not a suggestion, nor is it a shallow feeling; it is the very heartbeat of our faith.

When we look at the life of Jesus, we see this truth lived out in full. He loved the outcast, forgave the sinner, healed the broken, and laid down His life for the world. That love was not conditional, it was sacrificial. And it is the same love He calls us to demonstrate to those around us.

Sometimes it is easier to say we know God than it is to show God's love. But John reminds us that love is the proof of our relationship with Him. Without love, our words are empty, our works are hollow, and our faith is incomplete. True love is patient, kind, forgiving, and long suffering. It reflects God's character in us.

Ask yourself today: Am I showing God's love in my words, my actions, and my heart? If we struggle in this, the answer is not to try harder in our own strength but to abide in God, for His love flows through us when we remain in Him.

"He that loveth not knoweth not God; for God is love." John 4:8 (KJV)

Heavenly Father, thank You for reminding me that You are love itself. Forgive me for the times when I have not shown love to others. Teach me to love as You love—to be patient, kind, forgiving, and gracious. Fill my heart with Your Spirit so that my words and actions reflect the truth of who You are. Help me to walk daily in the power of Your love, so others may see Christ in me. In Jesus' name I pray.

Amen and To God Be The Glory!

SEPTEMBER 7. - "DON'T GET YOUR ROLE TWISTED"

So often, as believers, we feel a burden when we share God's Word or testify about His goodness. We want to see instant results such as changed hearts, tears of repentance, and lives transformed right before our eyes. But the truth is, that is not our role. Scripture makes it clear: our responsibility is to plant and water the seed, but only God gives the increase.

Paul said it plainly in 1 Corinthians 3:6-7 (KJV): "I have planted, Apollos watered; but God gave the increase. So then neither is he that planteth any thing, neither he that watereth; but God that giveth the increase."

This truth humbles us and frees us at the same time. It humbles us because it reminds us that salvation and transformation are not about us, our eloquence, or our efforts. It frees us because we don't carry the impossible weight of trying to change someone's heart. Only God can reach into the deepest part of a person's soul and turn stone into flesh (Ezekiel 36:26).

Our job is obedience. When God nudges us to share a word of encouragement, to testify about His goodness, or to offer the gospel to someone, our responsibility is to plant the seed faithfully. The seed may seem small, and at times we may feel it goes unnoticed, but seeds grow underground before anything is ever seen above ground. You may never know how your simple word, act of kindness, or prayer waters the soil of someone's heart.

Don't get your role and God's role mixed up. Your role is obedience; God's role is transformation. You plant, you water, but God alone brings forth life. Trust Him with the process and remember that no seeds sown in His name is ever wasted.

Heavenly Father, thank You for reminding me that my calling is to plant seeds of Your Word and to trust You with the growth. Forgive me for the times I've tried to carry burdens that belong only to You. Teach me to walk in obedience, speak in boldness, and leave the results in Your hands. I believe that every seed I plant will bear fruit in Your perfect timing. Lord, help me to rest in Your power and not in my own. In Jesus' name I pray, Amen and To God Be The Glory!

SEPTEMBER 8. - "BETTER OR BITTER ~ WHAT'S YOUR CHOICE"

Life is full of experiences that shape us. Some bring joy while others bring pain. But the real defining moment is not simply what happens to us, but how we respond. Every trial, disappointment, or betrayal presents us with a choice: we can either grow better or we can become bitter. One will keep us moving forward into God's purpose, and the other will chain us to the past.

Bitterness is a silent thief. It creeps into the heart after hurt and whispers that holding on to anger, resentment, or self-pity will protect us. But in reality, bitterness poisons the soul and keeps us from experiencing the fullness of God's grace. Hebrews 12:15 warns us: "See to it that no one falls short of the grace of God and that no bitter root grows up to cause trouble and defile many." Bitterness doesn't just stop us, it spreads. Contaminating our peace, relationships, and faith.

Choosing to become better, however, is choosing healing. Becoming better does not mean ignoring pain but surrendering it to the Lord and allowing Him to transform it into wisdom, compassion, and strength. Joseph in the Bible could have lived bitter after being betrayed by his brothers and falsely accused, but instead he allowed God to use his suffering to refine him. He declared to his brothers in Genesis 50:20 (NIV), "You intended to harm me, but God intended it for good to accomplish what is now being done, the saving of many lives."

Better comes when we release what hurt us, forgive what tried to break us, and trust God with what we don't understand. Better is looking forward; it keeps us growing, learning, and pressing toward the destiny God has for us. Bitter keeps us trapped but better sets us free.

Today, ask yourself: Will I let this situation make me bitter, or will I let God use it to make me better? Your future depends on the choice.

Looking diligently lest any man fail of the grace of God; lest any root of bitterness springing up trouble you, and thereby many be defiled; Hebrews 12:15 (KJV)

Heavenly Father, I come before You today asking for Your strength to choose better over bitter. Lord, I surrender every wound, disappointment, and betrayal into Your hands. Uproot any root of bitterness that tries to grow in my heart, and replace it with peace, healing, and wisdom. Teach me to forgive as You forgive me, and help me to see trials not as stumbling blocks but as steppingstones toward the purpose You have for my life. May my life be a testimony that through You, pain can produce growth, and trials can birth victory. In Jesus' mighty name, I pray.

Amen and To God Be The Glory!

SEPTEMBER 9. - "THE MIRACLE OF CONTINOUS PRAYER"

Prayer is not just a religious duty; it is the heartbeat of our relationship with God. When we make prayer a habit, it transforms from being a routine into a lifeline. Every time we bow our heads or whisper a word to God, we are acknowledging His sovereignty and inviting His presence into our lives. Over time, prayer ceases to be something we do only in crisis or need; it becomes the rhythm by which we live.

When prayer is consistent, miracles are no longer rare events. They become the evidence of God's constant movement in our lives. The miracle is not always dramatic. It may be the peace that floods your soul in the middle of chaos, the strength to endure what once would have broken you, the healing of a body, or the restoration of a broken relationship. When you walk with God through daily prayer, you live in expectancy, knowing that His hand is always at work.

The Bible reminds us: "Pray without ceasing." 1 Thessalonians 5:17 (KJV)

This scripture shows us that prayer should not be limited to a set time of day but should become woven into every part of our lives. A habit of prayer keeps our hearts aligned with God's will and opens the door for Him to move in miraculous ways. Think of Daniel, who prayed three times a day even when it could cost him his life. His habit of prayer opened the way for God to shut the lions' mouths. Think of Elijah, who prayed fervently, and the heavens responded with both drought and rain. Their lives prove that when prayer is the habit, miracles follow.

Beloved, when you cultivate prayer as a lifestyle, you are not just speaking to God, you are inviting Heaven to intervene on earth. Prayer positions you to see the miraculous, not because of who you are, but because of who God is.

Heavenly Father, I thank You for the privilege of prayer, the gift that connects me to Your power and presence. Teach me to make prayer my daily habit, not only in times of trouble but in every moment of my life. Lord, let my heart be in constant communion with You, so that miracles become the natural fruit of my faith and obedience. Help me to trust You, wait on You, and expect great things from You. May my life testify that You are a God of wonders. In Jesus' mighty name I pray, Amen and To God Be The Glory!

SEPTEMBER 10. - "HONORING GOD WITH SUBSTANCE"

When God calls us to honor Him with our substance and with the firstfruits of all our increase, He is teaching us a kingdom principle of stewardship, trust, and worship. To honor God with our substance means that everything we have, our time, talents, finances, possessions, and even our influence, belongs to Him first. We are simply stewards, entrusted with resources to manage for His glory.

The principle of firstfruits reveals where our priorities truly lie. Giving God the first and best portion is an act of faith that says, "Lord, You are my source. I trust You to provide and sustain me." When we put God first, He promises abundance, not just materially, but spiritually and relationally. Our barns filled with plenty and presses bursting with new wine symbolize overflowing blessings, joy, and provision that only God can bring.

It's not about the size of the gift, but the posture of the heart. The widow who gave two mites (Luke 21:1–4) gave more in God's eyes than the wealthy, because she gave out of her lack with full trust in Him. Honoring God with our substance isn't about loss, it's about opening the door to supernatural gain, peace, and security in Him.

When we withhold from God, we reveal a heart that struggles to trust His faithfulness. But when we release and honor Him with the best of what we have, He multiplies it back in ways we could never imagine.

Today, reflect on whether you are giving God your first and your best, or only what is left over. Remember, God doesn't need our possessions ~ He desires our devotion, expressed through obedience.

"Honour the Lord with thy substance, and with the firstfruits of all thine increase: So shall thy barns be filled with plenty, and thy presses shall burst out with new wine." Proverbs 3:9–10 (KJV)

Heavenly Father, thank You for every blessing and provision You have placed in my hands. I acknowledge that all I have comes from You, and I commit to honor You with my substance and with the firstfruits of my increase. Teach me to be a faithful steward and to put You first in all areas of my life. Let my giving reflect my trust in You, and may my life overflow with Your abundance, peace, and joy. I believe that as I honor You, You will supply all my needs according to Your riches in glory through Christ Jesus. In Jesus' name, I pray.

Amen and To God Be The Glory!

SEPTEMBER 11. - "OVERCOMING THE VOICES OF DOUBT"

"There are two types of people who will tell you that you cannot make a difference in this world: those who are afraid to try, and those who are afraid you will succeed."

When God places a calling, dream, or vision within you, the enemy often uses voices of discouragement to silence you. These voices may come from those who never attempted to walk in their own calling, or from those who fear what your success might reveal about their own lack of faith and effort. Either way, their words are rooted in fear not in truth.

Scripture reminds us: "For God hath not given us the spirit of fear; but of power, and of love, and of a sound mind." 2 Timothy 1:7 (KJV)

Fear causes some people to settle for less than God's best, and it causes others to envy those who dare to rise higher. But as children of God, we are not bound by fear or by the opinions of others. We are equipped with His Spirit, and that means we have power, courage, and divine authority to fulfill our God-given purpose.

Your calling may intimidate others, but it should encourage you because it means you are walking a path ordained by God. Remember, Jesus Himself faced opposition from religious leaders who were afraid of His influence and power. Yet He never allowed their fear or jealousy to stop Him from accomplishing His Father's will. In the same way, you must not allow doubt, criticism, or envy to derail the assignment God has entrusted to you.

The truth is, you were created to make a difference. You carry light in a world full of darkness. Every step of obedience, every act of faith, every word of truth you speak shifts the atmosphere. And whether others are afraid to try or afraid of your success, their words cannot cancel God's plan.

Heavenly Father, I thank You for the purpose You have placed within me. Help me to stand strong when voices of doubt and fear arise around me. Remind me that You have not given me a spirit of fear, but of power, love, and a sound mind. Silence the lies of the enemy and strengthen me to keep moving forward in obedience to Your call. May my life be a light that glorifies You, and may every step I take bring me closer to fulfilling the destiny You have designed for me. In Jesus' mighty name, Amen and To God Be The Glory!

SEPTEMBER 12. - "THE LORD'S STOREHOUSE OF BLESSINGS"

God's Word reminds us that He is the keeper of an inexhaustible storehouse, a treasure chest in heaven that never runs dry. When Moses spoke these blessings to Israel, he declared that obedience would unlock access to God's abundance, not just rain for the fields, but provision for every aspect of life.

"The Lord shall open unto thee his good treasure, the heaven to give the rain unto thy land in his season, and to bless all the work of thine hand: and thou shalt lend unto many nations, and thou shalt not borrow." Deuteronomy 28:12 (KJV)

Notice the promise: "in his season." This means God's blessings are not random. They are timely, perfectly aligned with His divine calendar. Often, we may grow weary because we do not see the fruit of our labor immediately, but the Lord assures us that He has appointed seasons for rain and harvest. What looks like delay is preparation. When the season comes, nothing can stop the outpouring of His blessing.

The verse also says God will "bless all the work of thine hand." This doesn't mean blessings fall without our participation. The work of our hands, whether in business, ministry, family, or service, becomes the channel through which His abundance flows. A field left unplanted cannot receive rain, and a life without action cannot expect fruit. Faith requires obedience, and obedience opens the heavens.

Finally, the promise of becoming a lender and not a borrower speaks of a life of overflow. God's intention is not just to meet our needs, but to make us a blessing to others. When His storehouse is opened over us, we move from survival to generosity, from lack to abundance, from dependency to influence.

This scripture calls us to trust in the God who holds the keys to every resource and to remain faithful in season and out of season. His treasures are already stored up for you, and when the time is right, He will release them ~ not just for your sake, but so that you can be a blessing to many.

Heavenly Father, I thank You for being the keeper of heaven's storehouse. I trust in Your perfect timing and divine provision. Teach me to remain faithful and obedient, even when I cannot yet see the harvest. Bless the work of my hands and make me fruitful in every season. Lord, let my life overflow with Your goodness so that I may be a lender and not a borrower, a giver and not a taker. Open up the treasures of heaven over me, my family, and my household. I receive this word by faith and declare that I walk in Your abundance. In Jesus' mighty name, Amen and to God Be The Glory!

SEPTEMBER 13. - "YOU ARE MY BELOVED"

"And there came a voice from heaven, saying, Thou art my beloved Son, in whom I am well pleased." Mark 1:11 (KJV)

This verse is one of the most powerful affirmations in all of Scripture. At the baptism of Jesus, before He performed any miracles, before He preached to the crowds, before He went to the cross, the Father declared His love and pleasure over His Son. This truth carries a deep message for us today: our worth and identity are not based on what we do, but on who we are in Christ.

Notice the timing. God spoke these words at the very beginning of Jesus' ministry. He had not yet healed the sick, raised the dead, or delivered the oppressed. Still, the Father's voice thundered with affirmation: "Thou art my beloved Son." This shows us that God's love and approval do not depend on performance, but on relationship.

Many of us live in a constant pursuit of validation from people, achievements, or success. But when we understand that God already calls us beloved because we are in Christ, we can rest in His love. Ephesians 1:6 reminds us that we are "accepted in the beloved." Just as the Father delighted in His Son, He now delights in us who belong to Him.

This verse also teaches us that God's love is vocal and personal. He does not hide His affection for His children. He speaks it, He declares it, and He confirms it by the Holy Spirit in our hearts (Romans 8:16). You may feel unseen, unworthy, or forgotten, but heaven has already declared over you: "You are My beloved child."

When you grasp this truth, it gives you strength in trials, confidence in prayer, and peace in your journey. If God is pleased with you in Christ, no voice of the enemy can condemn you, no opinion of man can disqualify you, and no circumstance can strip away your identity.

Heavenly Father, I thank You for the reminder that my worth and identity are found in You. Just as You declared Jesus as Your beloved Son, I stand today in that same love and acceptance through Him. Teach me to rest in Your approval and not seek validation from the world. Strengthen me to walk daily in the assurance of being Your beloved child. Silence every voice of doubt and help me to live boldly in the confidence of Your love. In Jesus' name I pray.

Amen and To God Be The Glory!

SEPTEMBER 14. - "DO GOOD THNGS WHETHER OTHERS NOTICE OR NOT"

It is easy in today's world to feel pressured to be seen, acknowledged, or validated by others. Social media, public recognition, and the applause of people can sometimes become the motivation behind our actions. But the true measure of goodness is not in how many people notice, but in the sincerity of the heart that gives and serves.

When we do good only to be seen, our reward is temporary, it ends with the applause. But when we do good from a place of love, obedience, and humility, our reward is eternal. God sees every act of kindness, every selfless sacrifice, and every moment when you chose to help someone in need without expecting anything in return.

Jesus Himself taught us this principle: "But when thou doest alms, let not thy left hand know what thy right hand doeth: That thine alms may be in secret: and thy Father which seeth in secret himself shall reward thee openly." Matthew 6:3–4 (KJV)

The world measures success by visibility, but God measures it by faithfulness. A small act done with pure intentions can carry more weight in Heaven than the largest deed done for human praise. True goodness flows from a heart aligned with God's will, not from a desire for recognition.

So, whether it is giving quietly to someone in need, encouraging a weary soul, or serving behind the scenes where no one applauds, just know that your Father sees you. Heaven keeps record of every act done in love.

Heavenly Father, thank You for reminding me that my good works are not for the eyes of men but for Your glory. Help me to serve with humility and to give with a pure heart, expecting nothing in return but the joy of pleasing You. Teach me to value obedience over recognition and sincerity over applause. May my life be a reflection of Your love in both small and great ways. In all things, let You be glorified.

Amen and To God Be The Glory!

SEPTEMBER 15. - "DON'T BE BLIND"

There is a saying that people's actions often reveal more than their words. How someone treats you is usually a reflection of what they truly feel in their heart toward you. Jesus Himself taught us that "by their fruits you shall know them" (Matthew 7:16). In other words, the outward behavior of people gives you a glimpse into their inner condition.

Sometimes we desperately want to believe the best in others, even when their actions consistently communicate something else. We excuse disrespect, overlook mistreatment, or minimize betrayal because we don't want to face the truth. Yet God's Word reminds us to walk in discernment, not denial. Proverbs 4:23 (KJV) says, "Keep thy heart with all diligence; for out of it are the issues of life." The way people treat you flows out of their heart, just as the way you treat others flows out of yours.

Being spiritually blind to reality can cause unnecessary pain. When you allow yourself to ignore clear patterns of dishonor, you remain in relationships or situations God never intended for you to endure. This is not about holding bitterness or judging others, but about walking in wisdom. Love does not mean tolerating toxic behavior; love also involves setting godly boundaries.

Even Jesus, full of love and compassion, did not entrust Himself to everyone. John 2:24 tells us, "But Jesus did not commit himself unto them, because he knew all men." He discerned hearts, recognized motives, and acted accordingly. That same Spirit of discernment dwells in us as believers.

So, when people show you through their actions how they truly feel, pay attention. Do not be blind. Ask God for wisdom to know when to draw near, when to set distance, and when to let go. Protect your peace, guard your heart, and remain anchored in Christ, who will never mistreat or abandon you.

"By their fruits ye shall know them." Matthew 7:16 (KJV)

Heavenly Father, I thank You for giving me the gift of discernment. Open my eyes to see people and situations as they truly are, not as I wish them to be. Help me to recognize when someone's actions reveal a heart that is not for me and give me courage to respond with wisdom and love. Guard my heart from deception and blindness and remind me always that my worth and identity come from You alone. Surround me with people who honor, respect, and uplift me according to Your will. In Jesus' name I pray, Amen and To God Be The Glory!

SEPTEMBER 16. - "YOUR FUTURE IN GODS HANDS"

The phrase "Just because your past didn't turn out how you wanted it to, doesn't mean your future can't be better than you imagined" reminds us of one of the greatest truths in Scripture: God is not finished with you. Too often, people let their past mistakes, disappointments, and regrets dictate the direction of their future. But the Lord specializes in turning broken pieces into beautiful testimonies.

The Bible declares in Isaiah 43:18–19 (KJV): "Remember ye not the former things, neither consider the things of old. Behold, I will do a new thing; now it shall spring forth; shall ye not know it? I will even make a way in the wilderness, and rivers in the desert."

Your past may have been filled with pain, failed relationships, missed opportunities, or decisions you wish you could undo. But the Word of God calls us to stop looking back and instead focus on the new thing God is doing. The past is a classroom, not a prison. You learn from it, but you do not live in it.

Think about Joseph in the Bible. His past was filled with betrayal, lies, and prison. Yet God used that very journey to position him for greatness. His future not only redeemed his past but exceeded anything he could have imagined. The same God who turned Joseph's sorrow into joy, and his pain into purpose is still at work in your life today.

When you surrender your future into God's hands, you step into a place where His plans override your past failures. Jeremiah 29:11 (KJV) reminds us: "For I know the thoughts that I think toward you, saith the Lord, thoughts of peace, and not of evil, to give you an expected end."

Your future in Christ is not just brighter, it is better than you can dream of. Where your vision ends, God's purpose begins.

Heavenly Father, I thank You for being the God of second chances, new beginnings, and restored hope. I release my past into Your hands and refuse to let it control my destiny. Teach me to trust that the plans You have for me are greater than my own. Help me to walk in faith, believing that the future You are preparing for me is filled with peace, joy, and purpose. Strengthen me to let go of regrets, embrace Your promises, and step boldly into the new thing You are doing in my life. In Jesus' name, I pray.

Amen and To God Be The Glory!

SEPTEMBER 17. - "DON'T JUDGE BY YOUR PAST"

There is a powerful freedom that comes when we stop defining ourselves by where we have been and start embracing where God is taking us. Many of us carry the weight of old mistakes, regrets, and broken seasons. We replay them in our minds as though they still determine our worth today. But God, in His mercy, reminds us that the past is not our permanent address.

Your past may explain where you came from, but it does not dictate where you are going. When Christ redeemed you, He gave you a new name, a new identity, and a new future. Scripture reminds us in 2 Corinthians 5:17 (KJV): "Therefore if any man be in Christ, he is a new creature: old things are passed away; behold, all things are become new."

That means your old failures, sins, and disappointments are covered under the blood of Jesus. They no longer have the authority to define you. God does not look at you and see your past; He looks at you and sees His child, washed and made whole.

Imagine trying to drive forward while staring only in the rearview mirror, you would eventually crash. In the same way, constantly living in yesterday's guilt or shame will paralyze your progress. The Lord is calling you to keep your eyes forward. He has new blessings, new opportunities, and new growth waiting for you, but you must first release what's behind you.

Don't judge yourself by your past ~ you don't live there anymore. Where you live now is in the grace of God, in the covering of His love, and in the hope of His promises.

Heavenly Father, thank You for reminding me that I am no longer bound by my past. Help me to release every regret, every mistake, and every chain that tries to hold me captive. Teach me to walk boldly in the new life You have given me through Christ Jesus. I will not look back in shame, but I will look forward in faith, trusting that my best days are ahead. Strengthen me daily to live in the freedom of Your grace and the joy of Your salvation. In Jesus' name I pray.

Amen and To God Be The Glory!

SEPTEMBER 18. - "DON'T LET SMALL MINDS DECIEVE YOU"

There will always be voices around us that try to shrink what God has placed within us. People who cannot see the vision God gave you may attempt to belittle it or discourage you. Sometimes their words are rooted in their own fears, insecurities, or lack of faith. But you must remember this: God's plan for your life is not limited by human opinion.

Joseph's brothers thought his dream was too big. They mocked him, hated him, and tried to stop him. Yet the very dream they tried to kill was the one God used to elevate Joseph and save nations (Genesis 37, 41). David was underestimated by his own family, yet he was chosen as king. Nehemiah was mocked when he dared to rebuild the wall, yet God gave him strength to finish it.

When people tell you your dream is too big, it may actually be confirmation that you are walking in divine purpose. What seems impossible to man is possible with God. Don't let the "small man" whether it's someone else's doubt or your own inner critic, convince you to abandon what God has birthed in your spirit.

"Now unto him that is able to do exceeding abundantly above all that we ask or think, according to the power that worketh in us." Ephesians 3:20 (KJV)

Heavenly Father, I thank You for the dreams and visions You have placed within me. Forgive me for the times I have doubted or allowed the opinions of others to make me feel small. Remind me daily that Your plans are higher than man's plans and that You are able to accomplish far beyond what I could imagine. Strengthen my faith, silence the voices of discouragement, and give me the boldness to pursue the calling You have placed upon my life. Let my dreams be aligned with Your will and bring glory to Your name. In Jesus' mighty name I pray.

Amen and To God Be The Glory!

SEPTEMBER 19. - "NOT ON YOUR TERMS"

There is a sobering truth about relationships. Whether with people or with God: love, trust, and presence are not things to be taken for granted. Too often, we push away those who care for us, thinking they will always remain no matter how we treat them. But Scripture reminds us that we should value relationships and handle them with care, for they are a gift from God.

When we push someone away, repeatedly dismissing their love or ignoring their presence, we run the risk of losing them altogether. Even the most patient heart can grow weary when it is continually rejected. This is why Proverbs 27:17 (KJV) says, "Iron sharpeneth iron; so a man sharpeneth the countenance of his friend." True relationships are meant to build us, not be neglected.

This truth also applies to our relationship with God. Many people push Him away in seasons of plenty, only wanting His presence when trouble comes. But the Bible warns in Isaiah 55:6 (KJV): "Seek ye the Lord while he may be found, call ye upon him while he is near." God is merciful and patient, but He desires to be sought with a sincere heart, not treated as an afterthought.

If we treat people or God casually, assuming they will always wait for us, we can find ourselves standing in regret. Value those who stand with you now. Cherish the people God has placed in your life, and above all, never push God away expecting that His Spirit will always strive with man (Genesis 6:3). Relationships must be nurtured in the present, not postponed for a more convenient season.

Heavenly Father, help me to value the relationships You have blessed me with. Teach me not to push away those who genuinely care for me, and most importantly, never to take Your presence for granted. Give me the wisdom to nurture love, the humility to cherish those around me, and the courage to seek You daily. Lord, I repent for any time I have placed You or others aside, expecting them to wait until I was ready. Restore my heart to love faithfully and consistently. In Jesus' name, I pray.

Amen and To God Be The Glory!

SEPTEMBER 20. - "DON'T QUIT ~ GOD IS ON YOUR SIDE"

There are moments in life when the weight of trials seems unbearable, and quitting feels like the only option. Yet, in those very moments, God often sends a quiet reminder: Don't quit, someone is praying for you right now and you will make it through this. God is on your side.

You are not walking this journey alone. God has placed intercessors in your life. People who are lifting your name to Him in prayer, even when you may not know it. Their prayers are like a shield, covering you in the unseen battles of life. Heaven hears the cries of those who intercede for you, and God responds in His power and love.

Scripture reminds us of this truth in Romans 8:31 (KJV): "What shall we then say to these things? If God be for us, who can be against us?"

This verse assures us that no trial, no weapon, no adversary can prevail when the Lord is on our side. Even when the world seems against you, God stands as your defender. And even when you feel weak, remember that others are standing in prayer, asking God to strengthen and uphold you.

Don't give in to despair, and don't let discouragement dictate your destiny. You will make it through this season. God's grace is carrying you, His Spirit is comforting you, and His power is sustaining you. The prayers being prayed over your life are joining with your own faith to push you forward into victory.

Heavenly Father, I thank You for being my strength when I am weak and my refuge in times of trouble. Thank You for the people who are praying for me, lifting me up before Your throne of grace. Help me to remember that I am not alone, for You are always with me and You place others around me to intercede on my behalf. Lord, give me endurance not to quit and faith to believe that I will make it through every trial. I declare that because You are on my side, I cannot be defeated. In Jesus' mighty name, Amen and To God Be The Glory!

SEPTEMBER 21. - "GOD SEES, GOD HEARS, GOD DELIVERS"

There are moments in life when the weight of our struggles feels unbearable. Tears stream down our faces at night when no one else is around. Prayers seem to echo back in silence, and pain becomes an uninvited companion that lingers far too long. It is in these times that the enemy whispers lies. Telling us we are forgotten, abandoned, or unseen. But the truth of God's Word declares something far greater: God is never blind to your tears, never deaf to your prayers, and never silent to your pain.

From Genesis to Revelation, the testimony of Scripture is clear. God is attentive to His children. Hagar, alone in the wilderness, lifted her voice in despair and God heard her cry (Genesis 21:17). Hannah wept bitterly before the Lord, and He answered her plea with the gift of a son (1 Samuel 1:10–20). The Israelites groaned under Egyptian slavery, and God said, "I have indeed seen the misery of my people. I have heard them crying out. I am concerned about their suffering. So, I have come down to rescue them" (Exodus 3:7-8, NIV).

These accounts remind us that our tears are not wasted. Every drop is noticed by the One who numbers the hairs on our head (Luke 12:7). Our prayers are not in vain, for God bends His ear toward us, even when we feel too weak to form words (Romans 8:26). Our pain does not go unnoticed, because Christ Himself carried sorrow and suffering so that we might one day walk in eternal freedom.

Deliverance may not always come the way we expect, but it always comes according to God's perfect timing and will. Sometimes He delivers us from the storm; other times He delivers us through it. Teaching us resilience, faith, and trust. But His promise stands firm: He will never leave you nor forsake you.

So, when the night feels long and your soul feels weary, hold fast to this truth: God sees, God hears, and God delivers. Your story is not over. Your prayers are not forgotten. And your pain is not without purpose.

"The righteous cry out, and the Lord hears them; he delivers them from all their troubles. The Lord is close to the brokenhearted and saves those who are crushed in spirit." Psalm 34:17-18 (NIV)

Heavenly Father, thank You that You are never blind to my tears, never deaf to my prayers, and never silent to my pain. You are the God who sees me, who hears me, and who delivers me in Your perfect time. Help me to rest in the assurance of Your presence when I feel weary. Teach me to trust that my cries do not go unnoticed and that my pain is not wasted in Your hands. Strengthen my heart to hold on to faith, knowing that You are working all things together for my good. I give You my tears, my prayers, and my pain, and I trust You with the outcome. In Jesus' mighty name, Amen and To God Be The Glory!

SEPTEMBER 22. - "EITHER WAY WE WIN WITH JESUS"

The phrase "If I die, I'll be with Jesus; if I live, He'll be with me. So, if I live or die, I am His. Either way, we win" carries a profound truth that every believer should hold close to their heart. Life and death often feel like opposites, yet for the child of God, both leads to victory.

The Apostle Paul expressed this same assurance in Philippians 1:21 (KJV): "For to me to live is Christ, and to die is gain." To live in Christ means that every breath we take is purposeful, guided, and strengthened by His presence. He walks with us in trials, comforts us in sorrow, and fills our lives with hope and meaning. We are never alone, for His Spirit dwells in us.

But if our earthly journey ends, that is not defeat, it's eternal triumph. Death, which the world fears, is simply the doorway into the fullness of Christ's presence. The sting of death is swallowed up in victory (1 Corinthians 15:55). For the believer, closing our eyes on this side of eternity means opening them in the presence of Jesus.

This truth gives us courage. It removes fear of the unknown and anchors our hearts in peace. Whether in health or sickness, in joy or hardship, we belong to the Lord. Nothing can separate us from His love (Romans 8:38–39).

So, we live boldly, knowing that Christ is with us here. And we rest securely, knowing that if death comes, He has prepared a place for us there (John 14:2–3). Either way, we win—because we are His.

Father, I thank You for the assurance that my life is in Your hands. Whether in living or in dying, I am Yours. Teach me to live each day with confidence, knowing You walk with me through every moment. And if my time on this earth should end, I rejoice that I will be forever with You. Remove fear from my heart, and let me live in the peace of Your promises. I declare that in life or in death, I am victorious through Jesus Christ. In Jesus name I pray, Amen and To God Be The Glory!

SEPTEMBER 23. – "THE SPIRIT OF ESTER ~BOLD AND COURAGEOUS"

In the Book of Esther, we encounter a woman who embodies boldness and courage in the face of fear, uncertainty, and danger. Esther, a queen in a foreign land, was placed in a position of influence not merely for her beauty or status but for a divine purpose. When the lives of her people were threatened, she faced a choice: remain silent to protect herself or risk everything to speak truth and act for the good of others.

Being bold and courageous, as Esther was, means listening to the inner voice God places within us. It requires faith to step out, even when circumstances seem impossible or the cost is high. God positions people in strategic places, not by chance, but so they can make an eternal impact. If you feel the tug of responsibility, the whisper of conviction, or the call to act justly, it is God's Spirit urging you to fulfill His purpose through you.

Courage does not mean the absence of fear; it means acting despite fear. Every time you choose integrity over convenience, service over selfishness, and truth over silence, you reflect God's light and love. Like Esther, your boldness can save lives, bring justice, and glorify God in ways you may never fully see on earth.

"For if you remain silent at this time, relief and deliverance for the Jews will arise from another place, but you and your father's family will perish. And who knows but that you have come to your royal position for such a time as this?" Esther 4:14 (NIV)

This verse reminds us that God places us where we are for His divine purpose. Listening and acting according to His guidance can change destinies, save lives, and accomplish His perfect will.

Heavenly Father, thank You for placing me in the positions I am in for a purpose. Give me the courage and boldness of Esther to stand for truth, to speak out for what is right, and to act for the good of others, even when it requires personal sacrifice. Help me hear Your voice clearly and respond with faith and obedience. Strengthen me to act with wisdom, humility, and love, so that through me, Your will is accomplished and Your name glorified. May I never shrink back in fear but rise boldly, trusting You in every step I take. In Jesus name I pray, Amen and To God Be The Glory!

SEPTEMBER 24. - "GRACE FOR OUR HUMAN MISTAKES"

Life is a journey of learning, growing, and sometimes stumbling. Every one of us, regardless of how faithful or disciplined we strive to be, will at times make mistakes. These mistakes do not define our identity or determine the entirety of our life's path. They are sometimes painful moments, sometimes humbling, but they are opportunities for growth and self-reflection.

The truth is, good people do sometimes make bad choices. A kind, generous, and God-fearing person may act out of fear, impatience, or weakness and make decisions they later regret. This does not make them evil or unworthy; it makes them human. God's mercy is vast and His grace unending. He knows our hearts, our intentions, and our struggles, and He calls us to learn from our errors, not to be enslaved by them.

Carrying the weight of past mistakes unnecessarily can become a heavy burden. It can steal peace, joy, and the confidence God wants for us. Yet, when we acknowledge our mistakes, seek His forgiveness, and commit to growth, we experience the freedom that comes from living under His grace. This does not excuse our errors but transforms them into steppingstones toward maturity, wisdom, and compassion for others.

Remember, God does not desire for anyone to be imprisoned by guilt. He desires restoration. As Psalm 103:12 reminds us, "As far as the east is from the west, so far hath he removed our transgressions from us." Mistakes, when met with repentance and humility, can become powerful testimonies of God's mercy and faithfulness.

Everyone makes mistakes, but God's grace ensures that we are not defined by them. Embrace your humanity, learn from your errors, and trust in God's mercy to guide you forward.

"For all have sinned, and come short of the glory of God." Romans 3:23 (KJV)

Heavenly Father, thank You for Your unfailing love and mercy. I acknowledge that I am human and will make mistakes, but I also know that Your grace is greater than my failures. Help me to forgive myself as You forgive me, to learn from my errors, and to walk in the freedom that Christ has purchased for me. Teach me to extend the same grace to others, recognizing that they too are human and capable of growth. Let my life be a reflection of Your mercy, and may I always rely on Your strength to guide my choices. In Jesus name I pray, Amen and To God Be The Glory!

SEPTEMBER 25. - "FEAR NOT ~ FOR GOD IS WITH YOU"

Fear is one of the greatest weapons the enemy uses against us. It whispers lies into our hearts, making us believe we are alone, unprotected, and incapable of moving forward. Yet, the Word of God reminds us repeatedly that fear has no authority over the children of God. The phrase "Fear not, for God is with you" is not just encouragement, it is a command and a promise.

When we face uncertain situations, fear tries to magnify the problem and minimize our faith. But God's presence changes everything. His presence is not distant; it is immediate, constant, and powerful. Wherever you go, He goes. Whatever you face, He faces with you. Even when life feels overwhelming and dark, His light surrounds you.

The prophet Isaiah beautifully captures this truth in Isaiah 41:10 (KJV): "Fear thou not; for I am with thee: be not dismayed; for I am thy God: I will strengthen thee; yea, I will help thee; yea, I will uphold thee with the right hand of my righteousness."

This verse reminds us of three unshakable truths:

God's Presence – "I am with thee." You are never abandoned.

God's Power – "I will strengthen thee." He gives you what you lack.

God's Protection – "I will uphold thee." His righteous hand sustains you when you feel like you are falling.

Instead of allowing fear to paralyze you, let faith propel you. The same God who parted the Red Sea, shut the mouths of lions, and calmed the raging storm is with you today. You don't have to have all the answers; you just have to trust the One who is with you in every circumstance.

Heavenly Father, I thank You for Your constant presence in my life. When fear rises up, remind me that You are near. Strengthen me when I am weak, comfort me when I am troubled, and guide me when I am uncertain. I choose faith over fear because I know You are my God, my strength, and my protector. Help me to walk boldly in the confidence of Your Word. In Jesus' mighty name, Amen and To God Be The Glory!

SEPTEMBER 26. - "FINISH EACH DAY AND BE DONE WITH IT"

Life is a journey marked with victories, struggles, lessons, and yes, mistakes. The phrase "finish each day and be done with it. You have done what you could. Some blunders and absurdities no doubt crept in, forget them as soon as you can. Tomorrow is a new day. You shall begin it serenely and with too high a spirit to be encumbered with your old nonsense" reminds us of a powerful truth: each day is a gift, and each new morning is a fresh opportunity from God.

We often hold on to regrets, replaying our failures in our minds, burdening our souls with "what ifs" and "if onlys." But God never intended for us to carry yesterday's weight into today. His Word assures us that His mercies are new every morning (Lamentations 3:22–23). This means that no matter how many blunders, mistakes, or absurdities found their way into our day, God gives us permission to release them and step into tomorrow with renewed strength.

Jesus Himself said in Matthew 6:34 (KJV), "Take therefore no thought for the morrow: for the morrow shall take thought for the things of itself. Sufficient unto the day is the evil thereof." Christ reminds us that each day has enough of its own challenges. We cannot afford to drag yesterday's baggage into today. If we do, we rob ourselves of the peace and strength He freely offers.

Finishing each day and being done with it is not about ignoring responsibility or denying mistakes. It is about acknowledging, learning, and leaving them in God's hands. It is about trusting His grace to cover our shortcomings and His power to make all things new. When we wake up to a new sunrise, it is heaven's announcement that God is not finished with us yet.

Let us live serenely, with hearts lifted high, refusing to be encumbered with old nonsense. Yesterday's failures do not define us, God's mercy does. Tomorrow's hope is brighter because He goes before us.

"It is of the Lord's mercies that we are not consumed, because his compassions fail not. They are new every morning: great is thy faithfulness." Lamentations 3:22–23 (KJV)

Heavenly Father, I thank You for the gift of today. I thank You that even in my mistakes, Your grace was present, and Your mercy sustained me. Lord, help me to finish each day and be done with it, leaving behind regrets, failures, and shortcomings. Teach me to release what I cannot change, and to step into tomorrow with joy, peace, and renewed strength. Let me begin each day serenely, with a heart full of faith and a spirit lifted above yesterday's burdens. Thank You for Your endless compassion and for the promise that each morning brings a fresh start. In Jesus' name, I pray. Amen and To God Be The Glory!

SEPTEMBER 27. - "FOCUS AND BUILD ON YOUR STRENGTHS"

Life has a way of highlighting our weaknesses, problems, and setbacks more than our strengths. The enemy often whispers reminders of our failures, hoping to distract us from the potential God has placed within us. Yet, Scripture calls us to renew our minds and walk in the fullness of what God has already equipped us with.

When we continually dwell on what went wrong, who hurt us, or where we fell short, we allow those memories to become stumbling blocks. But when we choose to focus on our God-given strengths, our faith, endurance, skills, resilience, and talents, we are building on the very foundation that God Himself established in us.

Paul writes in Philippians 4:13 (KJV): "I can do all things through Christ which strengtheneth me." Notice that it is not our failures that define us, but the strength of Christ working in and through us. Dwelling on problems magnifies them, but focusing on God's strength magnifies Him.

Think about David before Goliath. He could have dwelled on the fact that he was too young, too small, and lacked armor. Instead, he focused on the strength he had proven in the past. By defeating the lion and the bear through God's help. He built on those victories, and they prepared him for an even greater triumph.

Your setbacks are not the end of your story; they are lessons. Your strengths are steppingstones that God wants you to build upon. Each victory, no matter how small, is a testimony of what God can and will continue to do in your life.

So, shift your focus. Instead of replaying your losses, reflect on your wins. Where God came through for you, how you overcame trials, and how you grew stronger in faith. From that foundation, keep building. God did not bring you this far to leave you. He is still working, strengthening, and positioning you for greater.

Heavenly Father, I thank You for the strengths You have given me and for every victory You've brought me through. Help me to shift my focus away from setbacks and failures, and instead look to the gifts, talents, and faith You have placed within me. Remind me daily that I can do all things through Christ who strengthens me. Build me up, Lord, so that I may continue to grow, overcome, and glorify Your name in every area of my life. In Jesus' name, I pray.

Amen and To God Be The Glory!

SEPTEMBER 28. - "HOW CRITICIZING YOUR KIDS AFFECT THEM"

The phrase, "When you keep criticizing your kids, they don't stop loving you, they stop loving themselves. Let that sink in." carries a sobering truth. As parents, mentors, or guardians, the words we speak carry tremendous weight. Children are like fertile soil. Whatever we plant in them, whether words of life or words of destruction, will take root and shape how they view themselves and the world.

Criticism, when constant and harsh, doesn't build up, it tears down. It creates a voice inside of them that echoes long after our words are gone, causing them to question their worth, their abilities, and their identity. Instead of strengthening them, we may unintentionally weaken their confidence and cripple their growth. Children long for affirmation, guidance, and love, not perfection from themselves but direction from those they look up to.

The Bible reminds us in Ephesians 6:4 (KJV): "And, ye fathers, provoke not your children to wrath: but bring them up in the nurture and admonition of the Lord."

This verse warns us not to exasperate or frustrate our children with constant correction or negative words. Instead, we are called to nurture them with love, patience, encouragement, and godly discipline. Correction is necessary, but it should be balanced with compassion and affirmation. We can guide without crushing, discipline without destroying, and correct without condemning.

When we consistently speak life, we help our children see themselves as God sees them, fearfully and wonderfully made. They begin to understand that their worth does not come from what they do wrong or right, but from who they are in Christ. Love builds confidence. Affirmation strengthens identity. Encouragement equips them to grow.

Let us choose our words wisely. Instead of saying, "You'll never get it right," try, "I know you can do better, and I believe in you." Instead of pointing out every mistake, remind them of their progress and potential. In doing so, we help raise children who love God, love themselves, and grow to fulfill their divine purpose.

Heavenly Father, thank You for the gift of children and the responsibility You have entrusted to us as parents and caregivers. Forgive us for the times we have spoken words that wounded instead of healed. Lord, give us wisdom to guide our children with love, patience, and godly correction. Help us to speak life into their hearts, so they may grow in confidence and know who they are in You. Let our words reflect Your love and our actions point them toward their divine purpose. In Jesus' name we pray, Amen and To God Be The Glory!

SEPTEMBER 29. - "FORGIVE AS YOU WOULD LIKE TO BE FORGIVEN"

Forgiveness is one of the deepest and most powerful expressions of the Christian faith. It is not merely a suggestion, it is a command that flows from the heart of God Himself. The phrase "forgive as the Lord forgave you" reminds us that forgiveness is not optional, conditional, or based on how we feel. Instead, it is modeled after the very forgiveness God has extended to us through Jesus Christ.

"Be kind to one another, tenderhearted, forgiving one another, even as God in Christ forgave you." Ephesians 4:32 (KJV)

When God forgave us, He did so freely, completely, and unconditionally. He did not wait for us to deserve it, nor did He hold back portions of mercy for a later time. His forgiveness was full, wiping away our sins as far as the east is from the west. This divine example sets the standard for how we are to forgive others.

Forgiving as the Lord forgave us means:

It is an act of grace, not merit. People may never apologize, admit their wrong, or even recognize the pain they caused. But just as God forgave us while we were yet sinners, we extend forgiveness not because they earned it, but because grace demands it.

It brings freedom to the forgiver. Unforgiveness is a prison that chains the heart with bitterness, resentment, and pain. Releasing others does not excuse their behavior, it releases you from the burden of carrying it. Forgiveness allows healing to begin and opens the way for peace.

It reflects Christ to the world. Our ability to forgive mirrors the heart of God. When others see us forgiving what seems unforgivable, it becomes a testimony of Christ living within us. It shows that His love and Spirit are stronger than our human nature.

Forgiving as the Lord forgave you is not always easy. Sometimes, it feels impossible. But remember: God never asks us to do what He does not also empower us to do. His Spirit within us gives us the strength to release the hurt, surrender the pain, and walk in His peace.

Heavenly Father, thank You for the gift of forgiveness You have given me through Jesus Christ. Help me to remember the depth of Your mercy every time I struggle to forgive others. Teach me to extend grace as freely as You have extended it to me. Release me from the burden of bitterness and fill my heart with Your peace. May my forgiveness be a reflection of Your love, and may my life bring glory to Your name. In Jesus' name, I pray.

Amen and To God Be The Glory!

SEPTEMBER 30. - "DOING FREEDOM ~ LIKING HAPPINESS"

There is a simple yet profound truth in the phrase: *"Doing what you like is freedom; liking what you do is happiness."* Freedom and happiness are two deep longings of the human soul, and both are found in their purest form in God.

Freedom without direction can lead to emptiness. Happiness without foundation can be fleeting. But when freedom is aligned with God's will and happiness is rooted in His presence, both take on eternal meaning.

Doing what you like is freedom.

God created us with free will. We are not robots but living souls who can choose. Yet true freedom is not the ability to do anything without consequence, it is the ability to choose what is right without being enslaved by sin. Jesus said in John 8:36 (KJV): *"If the Son therefore shall make you free, ye shall be free indeed."* Freedom in Christ means we are no longer bound by guilt, shame, or the controlling power of sin. Instead, we are free to live in purpose, to walk in love, and to embrace the destiny God has placed before us.

Liking what you do is happiness.

Happiness is not merely found in the things we do, but in how we align our hearts with God in those things. You can be doing the simplest task, such as raising children, working a job, serving at church, or caring for someone in need, and still find joy if your heart delights in it as unto the Lord. Paul reminds us in Colossians 3:23 (KJV): *"And whatsoever ye do, do it heartily, as to the Lord, and not unto men."* When you like what you do because you recognize it as part of God's plan and an offering to Him, you will find lasting happiness, not just momentary pleasure.

The secret is not in chasing what feels good but in learning to see the goodness of God in what we are already doing. That shift in perspective transforms mundane responsibilities into meaningful opportunities, and fleeting satisfaction into enduring joy.

Heavenly Father, thank You for the gift of freedom through Jesus Christ. Help me to use my freedom not for selfish gain but to honor You in all I do. Teach me to find joy and contentment in the work of my hands, and to see each task as an act of worship. May my happiness not depend on circumstances but on the assurance that You are with me in every season of life. Lord, align my heart so that I not only do what pleases You but also learn to delight in it. In Jesus' name I pray, Amen and To God Be The Glory!

OCTOBER INTRODUCTION

As we enter into the month of October, we are reminded that the year is swiftly moving toward its close. The changing seasons reflect the rhythms of lifetimes of planting, times of growth, and times of harvest. For many, October symbolizes both reflection and preparation: looking back over what has been sown throughout the year and anticipating what still lies ahead. It is during this time that life often presses us with challenges. Questions about our future, burdens from our past, and trials in the present that test our endurance and faith.

Our devotional theme for this month is "Biblical Answers to Life's Pressing Problems." Every believer will face moments of uncertainty, hardship, or decision-making where human wisdom falls short. It is in these pressing times that the Word of God provides timeless guidance, divine comfort, and unshakable truth. God does not leave His children to navigate life's storms on their own; rather, He has given us His Word as a lamp to our feet and a light to our path (Psalm 119:105).

October reminds us that though the days grow shorter and the nights grow longer, God's promises remain steadfast and His presence constant. The same God who calmed the winds and waves still speaks peace into the storms of our lives. The same God who guided Israel through the wilderness still provides direction when our path feels uncertain. The same God who raised Jesus from the dead is still able to breathe life into situations that seem hopeless.

This month, as you engage with each devotional, let your heart be open to the Spirit's leading. Life's pressing problems are not designed to crush you but to push you closer to Christ. Every trial you face is an opportunity to see God's wisdom, strength, and faithfulness revealed in new and powerful ways.

"Come unto me, all ye that labour and are heavy laden, and I will give you rest. Take my yoke upon you, and learn of me; for I am meek and lowly in heart: and ye shall find rest unto your souls. For my yoke is easy, and my burden is light." Matthew 11:28–30 (KJV)

Heavenly Father, we thank You for bringing us into a new month filled with Your mercy and grace. As we step into October, we ask that You prepare our hearts to receive wisdom from Your Word. Lord, when life's problems weigh us down, remind us to come to You for strength, peace, and direction. Teach us to see trials not as barriers but as pathways to deeper trust in You. May this month's devotionals draw us nearer to Your truth and equip us to face every challenge with faith and courage. We surrender this month to Your hands, believing that You will work all things together for our good. In Jesus' mighty name we pray, Amen and To God Be the Glory!

OCTOBER 1. - "LETTING GO AND LETTING GOD"

There comes a time in every believer's journey when the weight of life becomes too heavy to carry alone. Problems pile up, pain lingers, and worries press on our minds like storm clouds refusing to move. It is in these moments that God whispers to us: "Be still and know that I am God" (Psalm 46:10 KJV).

Letting go is not a sign of weakness, it is an act of faith. When we say, "Dear God, today I'm letting go of my problems and asking You to handle them," we are choosing to place our trust in the One who knows the end from the beginning. He alone holds the power to turn problems into testimonies, burdens into blessings, and trials into triumphs.

When we let go of our hurt and ask God to heal us, we acknowledge that true healing comes from Him. Emotional wounds may linger far longer than physical ones, but God promises to bind up the brokenhearted (Psalm 147:3). His love is a balm that reaches the deepest parts of our pain.

When we release our worries and ask for God's blessing, we are walking in obedience to His Word. Philippians 4:6 reminds us: "Be careful for nothing; but in every thing by prayer and supplication with thanksgiving let your requests be made known unto God." The result of this surrender is peace ~ peace that passes all understanding (Philippians 4:7).

Letting go doesn't mean giving up. It means exchanging our weakness for God's strength, our confusion for His wisdom, and our stress for His peace. It is the ultimate surrender, one that places us right in the center of His will.

Heavenly Father, today I release into Your hands everything that has been weighing me down. I let go of my problems and ask You to work them out according to Your perfect plan. I let go of my hurt and ask You to heal me completely, body, mind, and spirit. I let go of my worries and trust You to bless me with peace, provision, and favor. Help me to rest in You, knowing that You are faithful to carry me through. In Jesus' name, Amen and To God Be The Glory!

OCTOBER 2. - "THERE IS NO SCRIPT FOR PRAYER ~ IT MUST COME FROM THE HEART"

Prayer is one of the most intimate, powerful, and personal ways we connect with God. Too often, people feel discouraged, thinking they don't know the "right words," the "right posture," or the "right timing." But the truth is simple: there is no wrong way to pray. If you're talking to God, you're doing it right.

Prayer isn't about perfect words, it's about a sincere heart. God doesn't require eloquence; He requires honesty. A whispered "Lord, help me" carries as much weight in heaven as a beautifully composed prayer spoken aloud. What moves God is not the style but the sincerity.

The Bible assures us of this truth: "Likewise the Spirit also helpeth our infirmities: for we know not what we should pray for as we ought: but the Spirit itself maketh intercession for us with groanings which cannot be uttered." Romans 8:26 (KJV)

This scripture tells us that even when we don't have the words, God still hears us. The Holy Spirit steps in, translating our sighs, tears, and unspoken thoughts into heavenly petitions. That means prayer is less about performance and more about presence ~ being present with God.

Whether you pray in the morning or the middle of the night, whether you are on your knees or driving in your car, whether your prayer is two words or two pages, God is listening. What matters most is that you are turning to Him, acknowledging your dependence, and trusting His love.

When you pray, know that you are never doing it "wrong." The Father delights in hearing His children's voices. Just like a parent cherishes every conversation with their child, whether simple or deep, so does God cherish every word from you.

Heavenly Father, thank You for reminding me that prayer is not about perfection but about connection. Teach me to come before You with boldness, sincerity, and faith, knowing that You hear me no matter how I express myself. Help me release the fear of "doing it wrong" and embrace the truth that You delight in every word I lift up to You. Thank You for the gift of prayer, for Your listening ear, and for Your unfailing love. In Jesus' name, I pray.

Amen and To God Be The Glory!

OCTOBER 3. - "BREAKING GENERATIONAL CURSES"

There comes a time in every family where someone must stand in the gap and say, "This stops with me." Cycles of brokenness, addiction, poverty, abuse, anger, and spiritual bondage can pass from generation to generation, but through Christ, we have the power to declare that those chains are broken. What "runs in the family" does not have to run through you. You are chosen to be the one who stands as a barrier against darkness and a bridge toward blessing.

The world may look at your bloodline and see patterns that seem unbreakable, but God looks at you and sees a vessel of deliverance. His Word reminds us in Galatians 3:13 (KJV): "Christ hath redeemed us from the curse of the law, being made a curse for us." Through the cross, Jesus didn't just save our souls; He gave us authority to cancel every curse assigned against us. That means the anger your father carried does not have to define your future. The addictions your mother battled do not have to become your testimony. The generational sickness, debt, or spiritual oppression that marked your family line can end the moment you choose to surrender your life fully to Christ and walk in His truth.

But breaking generational curses requires more than words, it requires faith, prayer, and obedience. It requires renewing your mind daily with the Word of God and choosing different actions than those who came before you. It means refusing to entertain the enemy's lies and standing firm in God's promises. When you declare, "It ran in my family until it ran into me," you are declaring war on the enemy and aligning yourself with the victory Christ already won.

Do not be discouraged if resistance comes. Breaking chains is not easy ~ it shakes the atmosphere. But remember, you are not standing in your own strength; you are standing in the authority of Jesus Christ. You may be the first in your family to walk in freedom, but because of your stand, generations after you will walk in blessing.

Heavenly Father, I thank You for the redeeming power of the blood of Jesus Christ. I declare that every generational curse, every cycle of brokenness, and every spiritual chain that has run through my family ends with me today. Lord, give me strength to walk in Your Word, wisdom to make new choices, and courage to stand firm when the enemy tries to bring the past into my present. I believe that through You, my family line will be marked with freedom, blessing, and favor. Let my life be the turning point for generations to come. In Jesus' name I pray.

Amen and To God Be The Glory!

OCTOBER 4. - "GOD'S GRACE IS SUFFICIENT ~ AND I'M GRATEFUL"

There are seasons in life when we come face-to-face with our weaknesses, limitations, and trials. It may be a thorn in our flesh, a battle we've prayed for God to remove, or a season that feels unbearable. In those moments, we are tempted to believe that we are not enough, that we cannot withstand what life has placed before us. But the truth of God's Word reminds us that we don't have to be enough, because His grace is.

The Apostle Paul understood this deeply. He pleaded with God three times to take away his thorn, but God's response was not removal, it was revelation. The Lord told him: "And he said unto me, My grace is sufficient for thee: for my strength is made perfect in weakness. Most gladly therefore will I rather glory in my infirmities, that the power of Christ may rest upon me." 2 Corinthians 12:9 (KJV)

This scripture is not just a comforting verse; it is a promise and a lifeline. God's grace is not limited, nor does it run dry. It is sufficient, completely adequate, abundantly enough, and always present for every circumstance we face. Where our strength ends, His begins. Where our ability falls short, His power takes over.

Grace does not always mean the absence of pain or struggle. Instead, it means the presence of God's power in the midst of it. His grace sustains us when we are weary, lifts us when we stumble, and carries us when we feel like giving up. It teaches us dependence, reminding us that victory comes not by our own strength but by leaning fully on Him.

So, when you feel overwhelmed, weak, or inadequate, remember that God is not asking you to do it on your own. He is asking you to rest in His sufficiency. His grace is greater than your weakness, His mercy is stronger than your failure, and His love is deeper than your fear.

Heavenly Father, I thank You for the sufficiency of Your grace. Even in my weakness, Your strength is made perfect. Forgive me for the times I have tried to carry life's burdens on my own, forgetting that Your power is what sustains me. Lord, teach me to rest in Your grace and to find joy in knowing that I am never alone. When trials come and my strength is gone, remind me that Your grace will carry me through. I choose to trust in You today and every day. In Jesus' mighty name, I pray. Amen and To God Be The Glory!

OCTOBER 5. - "GIVE YOURSELF PERMISSION TO WALK AWAY"

There are moments in life when God gives us discernment, an inner nudge, a whisper in our spirit, or a "bad vibe" that signals something is not aligned with His will for us. Too often, we silence that voice and push forward because of guilt, fear, or a sense of obligation. But the truth is, not everything or everyone is meant to walk with us into the next season of our journey.

Walking away doesn't always mean weakness, it can also mean wisdom. Scripture tells us, "Do not be deceived: Bad company corrupts good character" (1 Corinthians 15:33, NIV). If God warns us through discernment, it is not to harm us but to protect us. Sometimes what feels like a "bad vibe" is actually the Holy Spirit's way of saying, "This is not for you. Turn away."

When you continue to remain in environments that drain your spirit, diminish your peace, or lead you away from God's path, you are giving space to the enemy's influence. God's Word encourages us to guard our hearts, for out of it flow the issues of life (Proverbs 4:23). Protecting your heart may require walking away from conversations, relationships, or opportunities that do not align with God's truth.

Trust what you feel when the Spirit is guiding you. That discomfort may be your shield. That uneasiness may be your protection. God did not call you to live bound by toxic cycles, but to walk in freedom and peace.

Walking away in obedience to God's prompting is not rejection, it's redirection. It means you value His presence more than the temporary comfort of clinging to what feels familiar. Give yourself permission today to walk away from anything that steals your peace, clouds your joy, or pulls you from His presence.

Heavenly Father, I thank You for the gift of discernment and the gentle ways You warn me when something or someone is not right for my spirit. Give me the courage to walk away from anything that disrupts the peace You have placed within me. Help me to trust Your leading, even when it feels uncomfortable, and to embrace the freedom You provide through obedience. Strengthen me to protect my heart, honor Your wisdom, and walk boldly in Your will. In Jesus' name, Amen and To God Be The Glory!

OCTOBER 6. - "WALKING IN GOD'S POWER~LOVE~AND A SOUND MIND"

"For God hath not given us the spirit of fear; but of power, and of love, and of a sound mind." 2 Timothy 1:7 (KJV)

Fear is one of the greatest weapons the enemy uses to keep God's people bound. Fear paralyzes, blinds, and keeps us from stepping into the fullness of who God has called us to be. Yet, in this powerful verse, Paul reminds Timothy, and us, that fear does not come from God. If it doesn't come from Him, then we don't have to accept it.

God replaces fear with three unshakable gifts:

Power ~ This is not ordinary human strength but divine empowerment through the Holy Spirit. It is the same power that raised Jesus from the dead (Romans 8:11). With this power, you can stand boldly, overcome trials, and break chains that once held you captive.

Love ~ Fear often causes isolation, mistrust, and bitterness. But God pours His perfect love into our hearts (Romans 5:5), and perfect love casts out fear (1 John 4:18). Love equips us to forgive, to walk in unity, and to serve without fear of rejection.

A Sound Mind ~ In a world full of confusion, anxiety, and lies, God gives His children peace, clarity, and stability of thought. A sound mind means you can rest in His promises, think according to His Word, and discern truth from deception.

When fear whispers, "You can't," God's Spirit shouts, "Yes, you can because I am with you." When the enemy says, "You're not enough," God's Word declares, "My grace is sufficient." And when life feels overwhelming, God steadies your heart and mind with His unchanging truth.

Child of God, the next time fear tries to creep in, declare this scripture aloud. Stand tall, not in your strength, but in the Spirit of the Lord who equips you with power, fills you with love, and guards your mind with His peace.

Heavenly Father, I thank You for not giving me a spirit of fear but of power, of love, and of a sound mind. Strengthen me to stand firm in Your promises and to walk in boldness, knowing that fear has no place in my life. Let Your perfect love drive out every doubt, every anxiety, and every lie of the enemy. Guard my heart and mind with Your peace and help me to live as a testimony of Your strength and grace. In Jesus' mighty name I pray.

Amen and To God Be The Glory!

OCTOBER 7. - "GOD WILL FIGHT YOUR BATTLES ~ REPAY EVIL WITH GOOD"

Life often presents us with painful moments when others speak against us, mistreat us, or deal with us unfairly. Our natural response is to defend ourselves, retaliate, or return insult for insult. But as children of God, we are called to a higher standard, one that reflects the very heart of Christ.

The phrase reminds us: When someone speaks against you, speak well of them. When you are mistreated, treat them well. Repay evil with good, and God will fight your battles. This is not weakness; it is strength rooted in the Spirit of God.

Jesus Himself modeled this when He was mocked, falsely accused, and beaten. Instead of lashing out, He prayed, "Father, forgive them, for they know not what they do" (Luke 23:34). His response wasn't to return evil for evil, but to extend mercy and compassion in the face of cruelty.

Paul echoes this principle in Romans 12:17–19 (KJV): "Recompense to no man evil for evil. Provide things honest in the sight of all men. If it be possible, as much as lieth in you, live peaceably with all men. Dearly beloved, avenge not yourselves, but rather give place unto wrath: for it is written, Vengeance is mine; I will repay, saith the Lord."

When you choose to bless those who curse you, treat well those who mistreat you, and repay evil with good, you invite God into the battle. And when God fights for you, the victory is certain. Your response of grace disarms the enemy, silences accusations, and demonstrates the power of God's love.

This doesn't mean you ignore injustice or pretend pain doesn't exist, it means you trust God enough to let Him handle what you cannot. You remain in peace, guarding your heart from bitterness, while God works behind the scenes to turn the situation in your favor.

So today, instead of fighting back with your own strength, choose to rise above. Speak well of those who slander you. Extend kindness to those who mistreat you. And leave the outcome in the hands of the One who never loses a battle.

Heavenly Father, I thank You for being my defender and my shield. When others speak against me, give me the strength to speak blessings instead of curses. When I am mistreated, please help me to respond with kindness, love, and grace. Guard my heart from anger and bitterness and remind me that vengeance belongs to You alone. Teach me to trust You to fight my battles, knowing that You will always bring justice in Your perfect timing. May my life reflect the love of Christ, even toward those who oppose me. In Jesus' name I pray.

Amen and To God Be The Glory!

OCTOBER 8. - "STAND WITH THE WINNER ~ THE LORD"

There is a truth that every child of God must hold close to their heart: no matter what weapon the enemy forms against you, it will not prosper (Isaiah 54:17). When people rise up against you, when schemes are plotted, when lies are spoken, and when opposition tries to surround you, it is not truly them you are wrestling against it, it is the spirit operating through them. The apostle Paul reminds us in Ephesians 6:12 that "we wrestle not against flesh and blood, but against principalities, against powers, against the rulers of the darkness of this world, against spiritual wickedness in high places."

The enemy may try to use people to discourage you, frustrate you, or tear you down. But here is the encouragement: the devil in them cannot beat the God in you. The Spirit of the living God resides in you. Greater is He who is in you than he who is in the world (1 John 4:4). That means no demonic influence, no manipulative spirit, and no hidden agenda can override the power of God that flows through your life.

When others come against you, remember you don't have to fight with carnal weapons of anger, bitterness, or revenge. Instead, you stand firm in the authority of God, clothed in His armor, speaking His Word, and resting in His promises. The God in you is your shield, your defender, and your vindicator. And because God is undefeated, you are already walking in victory.

Let this truth strengthen your spirit today: The devil may roar, but he cannot devour what God has sealed. The enemy may try to shake your faith, but your foundation is unmovable in Christ. The devil in them may try to intimidate you, but the God in you has already conquered him.

"Ye are of God, little children, and have overcome them: because greater is he that is in you, than he that is in the world." 1 John 4:4 (KJV)

Heavenly Father, I thank You for the assurance that the power within me is greater than any power that rises against me. Lord, help me to remember that my battle is not with people, but with the enemy behind the scenes. Strengthen my faith, sharpen my discernment, and clothe me with Your armor daily. I declare that no devil, no scheme, and no weapon can overcome the God who lives in me. I walk in victory, I stand in authority, and I rest in Your promises. In Jesus' mighty name, Amen and To God Be The Glory!

OCTOBER 9. - "TRUST GOD'S PROCESS OF TRANSFORMATION"

Life has a way of placing us in seasons that feel crushing, pressing, or hidden in darkness. But often, what feels like destruction is actually the beginning of transformation. Consider the grape, its sweetness is locked inside until it is crushed. Only then does it become wine, something richer and more valuable. Diamonds form in the deep earth under intense heat and pressure. Olives are pressed hard before the oil flows. And seeds, though small and seemingly forgotten, must spend time in darkness before they break forth with new life.

This imagery reminds us that God does not waste pain, pressure, or seasons of waiting. What we see as breaking, He sees as building. What we call darkness, He calls preparation. The crushing is not meant to destroy you, but to bring forth what He has placed inside you. The pressure is not to overwhelm you, but to shape you into something that reflects His glory. The pressing is not punishment, but a process to release your anointing. The hidden seasons are not rejection, but incubation for growth.

Scripture tells us in 2 Corinthians 4:8-9 (KJV): "We are troubled on every side yet not distressed; we are perplexed, but not in despair; persecuted but not forsaken; cast down, but not destroyed."

Paul understood that life's crushing seasons do not mean abandonment by God, they mean transformation is taking place. Just as wine, diamonds, oil, and seeds go through their processes to become what they were destined to be, so must we. God is working in the unseen, turning our trials into testimonies and our pressure into purpose.

So, when you feel crushed, remember, sweetness is being released. When you feel pressed, know that anointing is coming forth. When you feel buried in darkness, trust that new life is about to break through. Transformation takes time, but God is faithful to complete the work He started in you. Trust His process, for He sees the end result even when you cannot.

Heavenly Father, thank You for reminding me that every crushing, pressing, and hidden season is part of Your divine process. Help me to trust You when I cannot see the outcome. Teach me to lean not on my own understanding but on Your perfect plan. When I feel overwhelmed by pressure or lost in darkness, let me remember that You are shaping me, strengthening me, and preparing me for greater purpose. I surrender my pain, my struggles, and my waiting seasons into Your hands. May my life reflect Your glory. In Jesus' mighty name I pray, Amen and To God Be The Glory!

OCTOBER 10. - "PUT YOUR TRUST IN JESUS"

When Jesus attended the wedding at Cana, He performed His first recorded miracle by turning ordinary water into extraordinary wine (John 2:1–11). This was not just a display of power but a revelation of His nature: to take the ordinary, the insufficient, and the disappointing, and transform it into something greater, something overflowing with purpose and joy.

Many of us find ourselves in seasons where life feels bitter, empty, or dry. Perhaps it's suffering through loss, hardship, betrayal, or uncertainty. In those moments, it is easy to believe that joy is out of reach. Yet, the same Savior who transformed water into wine is still at work today. He specializes in transformation. What seems wasted, broken, or too far gone in our eyes can become the very vessel of His glory and our breakthrough.

Suffering has a way of drawing us into deeper dependence on Christ. It brings us to the end of ourselves, just as the empty jars at the wedding brought the servants to depend on Jesus. When we hand over our pain, confusion, and hurt, Jesus doesn't just leave us with what we had; He gives us more and better. The wine He created at Cana was said to be of the highest quality was saved for last. That's what He does with our lives. He saves His best for those who trust Him, even when it looks like the supply has run out.

"You have turned my mourning into dancing; you have loosed my sackcloth and clothed me with gladness." Psalm 30:11 (ESV)

Heavenly Father, I thank You that You are the God of transformation. Just as You turned water into wine, I believe You can turn my suffering into joy, my mourning into dancing, and my pain into purpose. Help me to trust You in the process, even when all I see are empty jars. Teach me to surrender my heart fully, knowing that You always bring beauty out of ashes. Strengthen me with hope and remind me that Your best is never behind me but ahead. In Jesus' mighty name, I pray.

Amen and To God Be The Glory!

OCTOBER 11. - "TRANSFORMATION OVER INFORMATION"

The phrase "God doesn't always make His will clear because He values our being transformed more than our being informed" is a deep reminder that our walk with God is not simply about receiving answers but about becoming more like Him in the process.

So often, we long for clarity: "Lord, just show me the path. Just tell me what to do." But God, in His wisdom, sometimes withholds the specifics. Why? Because if He only gave us the blueprint, we might rush ahead, execute His plan in our own strength, and miss the shaping, molding, and refining that comes in the waiting.

The Christian life is not just about knowing where to go but about becoming who He has called us to be. Transformation happens in the tension between not knowing and choosing to trust anyway. It happens in the stretching of our faith, the surrender of our will, and the daily walk of obedience when the roadmap is unclear.

The Apostle Paul reminds us in Romans 12:2 (KJV): "And be not conformed to this world: but be ye transformed by the renewing of your mind, that ye may prove what is that good, and acceptable, and perfect, will of God."

Notice Paul doesn't say we are transformed by knowing every detail of God's will. Instead, transformation comes by the renewing of our minds, by leaning into God, depending on His Spirit, and allowing Him to shift us from the inside out. As we are transformed, we find ourselves walking in His will, even if we didn't have the entire picture from the start.

God's silence is never neglect. His lack of clarity is often an invitation into deeper intimacy and trust. The end goal is not just that we know His will but that we become His will in action. By being living reflections of His heart, His love, and His truth.

Heavenly Father, I thank You that You are a wise and loving God who cares more about who I am becoming than what I simply know. Teach me to trust You in the seasons where Your will feels unclear. Renew my mind, reshape my heart, and transform me into the likeness of Christ. Help me not to be anxious for answers but to rest in Your presence, knowing that You are guiding me step by step. May my transformation bring You glory, and may my life be a living testimony of Your faithfulness. In Jesus' name I pray, Amen and To God Be The Glory!

OCTOBER 12. - "HOW OFTEN DO YOU TELL GOD HE IS THE GREATEST ~ HOW OFTEN"

When we think about prayer, our minds often rush to our needs, struggles, and desires. We are quick to bring our petitions before God, and rightly so, for His Word invites us to cast all our cares upon Him because He cares for us (1 Peter 5:7). But prayer is more than just asking; it is also about adoration, thanksgiving, and worship.

How often do you pause in your prayer life to simply praise God? How often do you stop asking and start bragging on Him? Think about it: when was the last time you just sat in His presence and poured out words of adoration, not for what He has done, but simply for who He is?

The Psalmist reminds us in Psalm 145:3 (KJV): "Great is the Lord, and greatly to be praised; and his greatness is unsearchable."

This verse reveals a truth beyond comprehension. God's greatness cannot be measured, cannot be fully described, and cannot be contained. He is the greatest thing in the universe, yet He chooses to dwell in our hearts and hear our voices.

Imagine how our relationship with God would deepen if we made praise the foundation of our prayer life. Instead of rushing through a list of requests, what if we lingered to declare, "Lord, You are the greatest thing in my universe. You are my life, my hope, my joy, my strength, my everything."

This kind of prayer transforms us. It shifts our focus from our problems to His power, from our lack to His abundance, from our brokenness to His wholeness. Praise unlocks peace, renews faith, and builds intimacy with God. When we learn to praise more than we petition, we discover that many of our worries fade in the light of His glory.

So, how often? How often will you choose to set aside your list of needs and simply lift up His name? How often will you brag on Him to others, not just in prayer but in daily life? How often will you proclaim to the world and your own heart that Jesus is not just important He is everything? Let today be a day where you declare with confidence: He is the greatest thing in my universe!

Heavenly Father, You are worthy of all praise, honor, and glory. Too often I come to You with my requests but forget to exalt You for who You are. Forgive me for the times I have taken Your greatness for granted. Lord, You are the Alpha and the Omega, my provider, my healer, my peace, and my salvation. You are the greatest thing in my universe, and nothing compares to You. Teach me to praise You more, to worship You in spirit and in truth, and to let my lips and my life reflect how incredible You truly are. In Jesus' name, I pray.

Amen and To God Be The Glory!

OCTOBER 13. - "HOW MANY SCARS IS ENOUGH"

Love is one of the greatest gifts God has given humanity, but when misplaced, it can also be one of the greatest traps. There are times in life when we have excused wounds, pain, and even betrayal, simply because the one causing the hurt was someone we deeply loved or trusted. The scars we carry are often not only physical but emotional and spiritual marks of moments when we allowed others to cut us, not once, but repeatedly, because our love blinded us to the truth.

The Word of God warns us about this kind of blindness. Proverbs 27:6 says: "Faithful are the wounds of a friend; but the kisses of an enemy are deceitful." Notice the distinction, there is a difference between a wound meant for correction out of love and the repeated cuts inflicted by those who use our love as a weapon against us. A true friend, or one who genuinely loves us, may hurt us temporarily with truth, but never with intentional destruction. An enemy disguised as love will continue to harm while covering it up with charm, excuses, or promises.

How many times have we explained away mistreatment, told ourselves "They didn't mean it," or clung to the hope that their love would one day change? That is how scars accumulate. But God did not design us to live chained to toxic cycles. Christ came to set us free, not just from sin, but from anything and anyone that seeks to destroy the abundant life He promised.

We must learn that love does not mean tolerating abuse. Love does not mean continually justifying betrayal. Love does not mean handing the knife back to the very one who wounded us. Real, godly love brings healing, not harm; peace, not chaos; protection, not constant scars.

If you are carrying wounds today, know this: Jesus also bears scars. But His scars are different. His came from love that sacrificed itself to save, not love that destroy to control. His scars bring healing, restoration, and freedom. And in Him, your scars can also become testimonies, not of what someone did to you, but of how God brought you through it.

Heavenly Father, I thank You for opening my eyes to the truth of love. Forgive me for the times I allowed scars to be justified by misplaced affection or fear of letting go. Heal every wound that was caused by the hands of those I trusted. Teach me to love as You love, purely, without pain, without manipulation, and without fear. Help me set boundaries that protect the temple of my heart and guide me to relationships that reflect Your grace and truth. May my scars be a reminder not of my weakness, but of Your strength in my life. In Jesus' name, Amen and To God Be The Glory!

OCTOBER 14. - "I AM WHO I AM"

"I am who I am, like me, love me, take me, leave me. Know that I am a true friend to the end and ask for nothing in return except two things: don't hurt me or use me."

At the heart of this phrase is authenticity and loyalty. It speaks of being genuine, not hiding behind masks or living for the approval of others. It's a declaration of identity, rooted in the truth that God created us uniquely and wonderfully. We are not called to be copies of someone else, but to live out the fullness of who we are in Christ.

The words also highlight friendship, a friendship that is faithful, sacrificial, and true. True friends don't demand perfection; they walk with you through valleys and celebrate with you on mountaintops. A true friend doesn't hurt or use but encourages and uplifts. Yet sometimes we give this kind of love and loyalty, and others do not return it. That pain can be deep. But even then, God promises healing and reminds us that He will never leave us or betray our trust.

Scripture teaches us: "A friend loves at all times, and a brother is born for adversity." – Proverbs 17:17 (KJV)

This means that real friendship is not conditional, it doesn't fade when times get tough. Likewise, being true to who God made you to be means standing firm in your values. You may not always be accepted by everyone, but you are loved and fully accepted by God.

When you live authentically, loving deeply while setting boundaries against being hurt or used, you reflect the very heart of Christ. Jesus Himself was the truest friend and faithful even unto death on the cross. He asks us to mirror that kind of love, but also to walk in wisdom, protecting the heart He has entrusted to us.

Heavenly Father, thank You for making me in Your image and for reminding me that I don't have to change who I am to be loved. Help me to walk in authenticity, to give the gift of true friendship, and to cherish those You place in my life. Guard my heart against those who would hurt or use me and give me discernment to know who is truly for me. May I always reflect the loyalty and love of Christ to others, being a friend who uplifts, supports, and encourages. In Jesus' name I pray.

Amen and To God Be The Glory!

OCTOBER 15. - "FORGIVING MY PAST SELF"

There are moments when we look back on our younger selves and cringe at the choices we made, the words we spoke, or the paths we took. It is easy to become our own harshest critic, replaying mistakes and holding onto shame. But the truth is, God does not condemn us for our past, He redeems it.

When we say, "I have some issues with my past self, but she was young, and I forgive her," we are choosing to release the grip of self-condemnation and embrace God's mercy. Forgiveness is not just for others; it's also for us. If we cannot forgive ourselves, we may unknowingly block the freedom Christ already secured for us.

Paul reminds us in 2 Corinthians 5:17 (KJV): "Therefore if any man be in Christ, he is a new creature: old things are passed away; behold, all things are become new."

Your past self may have stumbled, fallen, and made decisions that brought pain, but she was also learning, growing, and surviving. The beautiful thing about God's grace is that He does not waste our past. Instead, He transforms it into a testimony of His love and power. Every wrong step you took has the potential to guide your present and bless your future.

Forgiving your past self is an act of grace that mirrors how God forgave you. Just as He does not hold your sins against you, you must not keep punishing yourself for being human. By extending compassion to your younger self, you are stepping into freedom, healing, and wholeness.

Heavenly Father, thank You for Your endless mercy and forgiveness. I release the weight of my past and forgive myself for the mistakes I made when I did not know better. Thank You for taking my brokenness and using it for Your glory. Teach me to walk in the freedom of being a new creation in Christ, no longer bound by guilt, but renewed by grace. Help me to see my past self with compassion and my present self with hope. In Jesus' name, I pray.

Amen and To God Be The Glory!

OCTOBER 16. - "MONEY ~ DOES IT MAKE THE MAN"

Money is one of the greatest tests of the human heart. It reveals what we treasure, what we trust in, and where we place our identity. The phrase "if you are nothing without money, you shouldn't have it" speaks directly to the truth that wealth should never define who we are. If our value, our confidence, and our sense of worth only exist when our pockets are full, then money has become our master instead of our servant.

The Bible warns us about the dangers of attaching our identity to riches. In Luke 12:15 (KJV), Jesus said: "Take heed, and beware of covetousness: for a man's life consisteth not in the abundance of the things which he possesseth." True life is not measured by bank accounts, possessions, or material gains, it is measured by our relationship with God, our character, and our eternal inheritance in Christ.

Wealth is not evil in itself; it is a tool. It can be used for good or misused for destruction. But when someone feels "nothing" without it, money has taken the place of God in their heart. That's dangerous, because it means that their joy, peace, and purpose are tied to something temporary instead of eternal.

God wants us to know who we are in Him, the chosen, beloved, redeemed, and valuable beyond measure. When we are secure in Christ, money cannot control us, whether we have much or little. Paul declared in Philippians 4:12-13 that he learned how to be content in all situations: "I know both how to be abased, and I know how to abound: everywhere and in all things I am instructed both to be full and to be hungry, both to abound and to suffer need. I can do all things through Christ which strengtheneth me."

This is the mindset of freedom: knowing that you are somebody not because of what you have, but because of who you belong to. If money comes, use it for God's glory. If it goes, remain steady in faith. For if you are nothing without it, you shouldn't have it, because your worth is not in riches, but with the One who gives life.

Heavenly Father, I thank You for being the source of my true worth. Forgive me for the times I have tied my identity to wealth, possessions, or status. Teach me to place my trust only in You. Help me to steward money wisely but never allow it to master my heart. Lord, make me rich in faith, rich in love, and rich in good works, so that no matter what I have or don't have, I remain content in You. Keep me grounded in Christ, for He is my greatest treasure. In Jesus' name I pray.

Amen and To God Be The Glory!

OCTOBER 17. - "NEVER FORGET HOW FAR THE LORD HAS BROUGHT YOU"

There are moments in life when we get so focused on what's next, what's missing, or what we wish was different, that we forget to look back and reflect on how far God has brought us. The journey may not have been easy, but if you take a moment to pause, you'll see evidence of His faithfulness in every chapter of your life.

Think about the times you didn't know how you would make it, yet you did. Remember the pain you thought would never end, but healing came. Consider the doors that were closed, only for God to open new ones you never saw coming. You are not where you started. And you are not alone.

God doesn't bring us out just to leave us. He leads, He carries, and He builds us through every trial. When you remember how far you've come, your faith for the future grows stronger. Gratitude replaces fear. Hope silences doubt.

"Bless the Lord, O my soul, and forget not all his benefits." Psalm 103:2 (KJV)

Father, I thank You for every step of the journey. When I look back, I see Your hand guiding me, protecting me, and providing for me. Help me to never forget how far You've brought me. Let gratitude fill my heart and fuel my trust in You for what's ahead. Keep me anchored in remembrance and full of praise. In Jesus' name I pray.

Amen and To God Be The Glory!

OCTOBER 18. - "IF MY PEOPLE PRAY"

The phrase "If My People Pray" carries both a divine invitation and a divine condition. It comes directly from God's heart, reminding us that prayer is not just a ritual but a covenantal response that moves heaven on our behalf.

In 2 Chronicles 7:14 (KJV), the Lord declares: "If my people, which are called by my name, shall humble themselves, and pray, and seek my face, and turn from their wicked ways; then will I hear from heaven, and will forgive their sin, and will heal their land."

This scripture shows us that God is attentive to the prayers of His people, but He requires sincerity, humility, and repentance. Prayer is not merely reciting words, it is a surrender of the heart. When God's children cry out, He promises to respond with forgiveness, healing, and restoration.

Many times, we may feel powerless in the face of the world's problems, family struggles, or personal battles. Yet God says the key is within His people, not governments, systems, or riches, but His praying people. Revival, breakthrough, and transformation begin in the prayer closet. When we bow our knees, we stand tall in victory.

Just think: prayer unlocks doors that no man can shut. Prayer heals wounds too deep for medicine. Prayer brings peace in the storm, strength in weakness, and light in the darkest valley. God is not waiting for perfect people ~ He is waiting for a praying people.

So let us rise up in faith, lay down pride, and approach His throne boldly. When His people pray, heaven responds, chains break, and blessings flow.

Heavenly Father, I thank You for the privilege and power of prayer. Forgive us for the times we have been too busy, distracted, or self-reliant to call on Your name. Today, we humble ourselves before You. We seek Your face, repent of our sins, and ask that You heal our hearts, our families, our communities, and our land. Lord, help us to be steadfast in prayer, trusting that You are faithful to hear and to answer. Stir within us a hunger to seek You daily and faith to believe that our prayers make a difference. In Jesus' mighty name we pray, Amen and To God Be The Glory!

OCTOBER 19. - "I AM NOT LIKE EVERYONE ELSE ~ I'M JUST ME"

The phrase, "I am not like everyone else. I don't pretend to be. I don't want to be. I am me," is a powerful declaration of identity. In a world that constantly pressures us to conform, blend in, and strive for acceptance, it takes courage to embrace who God has uniquely created us to be.

The truth is, God never intended for us to be carbon copies of one another. He knit us together in our mother's womb, shaping us with intention, precision, and purpose (Psalm 139:13–14). Each of us carries a divine imprint, our gifts, our voice, our personality, our story. Trying to be like someone else robs the world of the beauty of who God made us to be.

Paul reminds us in Romans 12:2 (KJV): "And be not conformed to this world: but be ye transformed by the renewing of your mind, that ye may prove what is that good, and acceptable, and perfect, will of God."

When you choose to say, "I am me," you are really saying, "I am who God created me to be." That is not arrogance, it is humility, because it acknowledges the Creator's design over society's expectations. The world may label you as "different," but heaven calls you set apart. Your difference is your anointing. Your uniqueness is your calling card. Your authenticity is your testimony.

Do not shrink to fit where God has called you to stand out. Do not dilute your light to make others comfortable in their darkness. When you embrace yourself as God designed you, you give others permission to embrace who they are as well.

So today, stand boldly and declare: "I am not like everyone else, and that's because God didn't make me to be like everyone else. I am His masterpiece."

Heavenly Father, I thank You for creating me uniquely and purposefully. Forgive me for the times I compared myself to others or doubted my worth. Teach me to fully embrace the person You have designed me to be and to walk confidently in my calling. Help me to remember that my difference is not a flaw, but a reflection of Your intentional design. May my life glorify You as I live authentically and boldly in the identity You have given me. In Jesus' name I pray.

Amen and To God Be The Glory!

OCTOBER 20. - "BELIEVE ~ BE PATIENT ~ NEVER GIVE UP

The journey of faith isn't always a straight path. At times, it winds through valleys of waiting, climbs hills of doubt, and crosses rivers of weariness. Yet, through it all, God is at work shaping our character, building our endurance, and preparing blessings that far exceed what we imagined.

Believing is the foundation. Faith is where it begins. When we believe in God's promises, we position ourselves to receive His goodness. Scripture says, "Without faith, it is impossible to please God." (Hebrews 11:6 NIV). Faith opens the door, but it is patience and perseverance that keep us walking through it.

Patience is where our trust is refined. Waiting on God doesn't mean nothing is happening, it means everything is happening behind the scenes in God's perfect timing. Our timelines may be rushed, but God's timing is always right. Those who wait on Him are never disappointed because they learn to hope for something eternal, not temporary.

And perseverance? That's the mark of spiritual maturity. It means holding on when your hands feel weak. It means continuing to pray when you haven't seen results. It means, trusting when you can't trace God. The best things, such as breakthroughs, answered prayers, restored relationships, divine callings are given to those who refuse to quit.

God is not ignoring your effort. He sees your quiet obedience, your late-night prayers, your sacrifices, and your tears. He honors your faith and is working out all things—even the hard, even the hidden—for your good. You may not see the fruit yet, but if you keep believing, stay patient, and refuse to give up, the harvest will come.

"Let us not become weary in doing good, for at the proper time we will reap a harvest if we do not give up." Galatians 6:9 (NIV)

Father God, I thank You for being faithful through every season of my life. Strengthen my faith when I doubt, increase my patience when I grow restless, and give me endurance when I feel like giving up. Help me to trust Your timing and not rush ahead of Your plan. Teach me to hold on when things get hard, and to keep my eyes on You when I grow weary. I believe that good things are coming, that better things are being prepared, and that the best is still ahead. I surrender my timeline to Yours and ask You to help me walk in faith until the harvest comes. In Jesus' name I pray, Amen and To God Be The Glory!

OCTOBER 21. - "A LIFE THAT TOUCHES OTHERS"

"As I live each day, I make a difference and touch one heart, one mind, one soul. In hope to bring a smile, laughter, comfort and hope into the lives of others. To all those reading this, may all your dreams come true, and your prayers be answered. Love, peace and happiness today and every day."

Each day God gives us is not just time on a clock but an opportunity to impact eternity through the lives we touch. Our words, actions, and presence can plant seeds of hope, healing, and encouragement in the hearts of others. Even the smallest act of kindness, a smile, a listening ear, or a word of prayer, can become the very thing that turns someone's day around or even draws them closer to Christ.

In a world filled with discouragement, division, and brokenness, God calls His children to be carriers of love, peace, and joy. When you live each day intentionally, with a heart willing to serve, you become a vessel of God's grace. You may not realize the ripple effect of your actions, but heaven does. Sometimes, the comfort you give is the very answer to someone's prayer. The laughter you share may lift a heavy burden. The hope you plant may be the spark that keeps someone from giving up.

Jesus said in Matthew 5:16 (KJV): "Let your light so shine before men, that they may see your good works, and glorify your Father which is in heaven."

Your light is not meant to be hidden; it is meant to shine into the lives of those who are hurting and searching. And as you shine, the glory always points back to God.

So, live today with purpose. Live tomorrow with intention. And let every day be a testimony of love, peace, and happiness through Christ.

Heavenly Father, thank You for the gift of each day. Help me to live with purpose, to touch hearts, uplift minds, and encourage souls. May my life reflect Your love in a way that brings comfort, joy, and hope to others. Teach me to shine my light so that others may see You through me. Lord, bless every reader of this devotional and may their dreams align with Your will, and may their prayers be answered according to Your perfect plan. Fill their hearts with love, peace, and happiness today and always. In Jesus' name I pray. Amen and To God Be The Glory!

OCTOBER 22. - "FROM MY LIPS TO GODS' EARS ~ WISHING YOU A BLESSED DAY"

There is a beautiful saying: "From my lips to God's ears." It reminds us that every word we speak to the Lord in sincerity reaches His throne. When we open our mouths in prayer, in gratitude, or even in tears, heaven is not deaf to our cries. Our Father bends His ear toward His children, cherishing every word we lift up in faith.

As the new day dawns, we recognize that each sunrise is an invitation from God, an opportunity to begin again. The moment our feet hit the floor, our lips can declare gratitude: "Thank You, Lord, for this beautiful new day." Each day is not only a continuation of our life's journey but also a new page that God Himself writes with His mercy and grace.

When we pray for strength, wisdom, joy, and protection, we are aligning our hearts with God's will. He knows the battles we face, the decisions we must make, and the trials that may come. But He also provides the strength to overcome, the wisdom to discern, the joy to endure, and the covering of His protection that no enemy can penetrate.

Scripture reminds us of this powerful truth: "The eyes of the Lord are on the righteous, and His ears are attentive to their cry." Psalm 34:15 (NIV)

Every word we speak from a sincere heart, whether whispered in the quiet of dawn or cried out in the depths of night is heard. Our lips do not utter in vain, because the God who formed us delights in communing with us. And when our words of gratitude, praise, and petition rise, He responds with blessings, guidance, and peace.

So today, let your words be faith-filled. Let your lips be instruments of gratitude and prayer. For what begins from your lips reaches the very ears of Almighty God.

Heavenly Father, from my lips to Your ears, I lift up my heart in gratitude today. Thank You for the gift of life, the blessing of a new day, and the opportunity to walk in Your purpose. I ask You for strength to face challenges, wisdom to make the right choices, joy to keep my spirit lifted, and protection over myself and my loved ones. May this day not only be wonderful but truly blessed, filled with Your presence in every step I take. In Jesus' name I pray, Amen and To God Be The Glory!

OCTOBER 23. - "LIVING WITH JOY IN THE PRESENT MOMENT"

The phrase reminds us of a powerful truth: "Never think hard about the past and bring tears. Don't think more about the future. It brings fears. Live this moment with a smile. It brings cheers."

How often do we find ourselves shackled by yesterday's regrets or tomorrow's uncertainties? The past can weigh us down with sorrow, shame, or missed opportunities. The future can grip us with anxiety, worry, and "what ifs." But God's Word reminds us that neither the past nor the future is where our true strength lies, our strength is in God's presence right here and right now.

Jesus Himself taught this principle in Matthew 6:34 (KJV): "Take therefore no thought for the morrow: for the morrow shall take thought for the things of itself. Sufficient unto the day is the evil thereof."

Worrying about tomorrow only steals the joy of today. Dwelling on the past only reopens old wounds. But choosing to smile in the present moment and trusting that God is with us, brings peace and joy to our hearts.

Living with a smile is not about pretending life is perfect. It is about faith. It is about believing that God has already forgiven your past, that He holds your future securely, and that His Spirit is walking with you now. When you live in this truth, you can rejoice in the moment, even through trials.

Paul said in Philippians 4:4 (KJV): "Rejoice in the Lord alway: and again I say, Rejoice." This isn't just advice, it's a lifestyle. Rejoicing brings cheer to your spirit and becomes a witness of God's goodness to others.

So today, I release the tears of the past. Refuse the fears of the future. Smile in this moment, because God is here. And where God is, there is fullness of joy.

Heavenly Father, thank You for reminding me that my past is forgiven and my future is in Your hands. Help me not to be weighed down by what has already happened, nor to be consumed by what may come. Teach me to trust You fully in this present moment. Fill my heart with peace, my face with a smile, and my spirit with joy that overflows into the lives of others. I choose to rejoice in You today, Lord, for You are my strength, my hope, and my salvation. In Jesus name I pray, Amen and To God Be The Glory!

OCTOBER 24. - "A GOD-LIKE HEART"

When we pause and reflect on the goodness of God, it is overwhelming to realize that His heart beats with love and care for us. Gratitude naturally flows when we recognize that we belong to a God without limitation. A God whose power knows no boundaries, whose hand is never shortened, and whose resources never run dry.

Think of it: you are not in the hands of chance, fate, or man's opinion. You belong to the Almighty. He is able to do mighty things for you, in you, and through you. His blessings are not rationed or scarce, they are abundant, overflowing, and beyond comprehension. What He is able to do, He is also willing to do for His children. His heart is not reluctant, nor does He hold back. Instead, His love overflows in generosity, pouring out provisions, mercies, and blessings that cannot be measured.

The Apostle Paul captures this truth beautifully in Ephesians 3:20 (KJV): "Now unto him that is able to do exceeding abundantly above all that we ask or think, according to the power that worketh in us."

God's blessings extend beyond what our arms can embrace, beyond what our minds can comprehend, and beyond what our hearts can contain. His love reaches into the deepest parts of our lives, touching our wounds, lifting our spirits, and covering us with grace. His generosity is boundless, and His provisions flow from His very heart of love.

This truth should stir gratitude within us. Gratitude that we are chosen, that we are covered, and that we are loved by a God whose heart beats endlessly for us. Gratitude that we can rest not in our strength, but in His measureless supply. Gratitude that we are never left empty, for His love continually fills and refills us.

Heavenly Father, I truly thank You for Your boundless love and limitless generosity. I stand in awe of Your heart that flows with blessings and grace beyond what I can understand. Fill me with gratitude each day as I remember that I belong to You. The God of abundance, the God of love, the God without limitation. Help me to live with confidence, knowing that what You are able to do, You are willing to do in my life. Let Your blessings touch me, cover me, and overflow through me to others. In Jesus' name I pray.

Amen and To God Be The Glory!

OCTOBER 25. - "IN ONE WORD ~ BLESSED"

There are moments in life when one word can capture the depth of our heart's condition. Today, that word is blessed. It doesn't need a long explanation, because being blessed is not only about circumstances but about God's presence, His promises, and His peace in our lives.

The psalmist declares: "Blessed is the man that trusteth in the Lord, and whose hope the Lord is." Jeremiah 17:7 (KJV)

To be blessed means to walk in the assurance that no matter what storms rage around us, God's hand is upon us. It is knowing that even when life presses hard, His Spirit strengthens us. Being blessed is not about what we have in the natural, but who we belong to in the spiritual.

One word, blessed, reminds us that God has already given us everything we need for life and godliness (2 Peter 1:3). It tells us that the cross secured our victory, and the resurrection sealed our hope. When we feel blessed, we are testifying that our joy comes not from man but from the Lord, who daily loads us with benefits.

So, let your one word today be blessed. Walk in it, speak it, believe it, and live it out. For if God calls you blessed, no one can curse you, and no trial can rob you of His favor.

Heavenly Father, I thank You for blessing me beyond measure. Even when I cannot see the full picture, I know that Your hand is on my life. I declare today that I am blessed because I trust in You. Strengthen me to walk in that blessing daily, and let my life reflect Your goodness. Keep me rooted in Your Word and unshaken by life's storms. In Jesus' name, I pray.

Amen and To God Be The Glory!

OCTOBER 26. - "THE BEAUTY THAT LAST FOREVER"

The world often measures beauty by outward appearance. Faces without blemish, bodies without flaws, and images that meet temporary standards of perfection. Yet, Scripture teaches us that true beauty is not found in what the eye can see but in what radiates from within, the heart and soul. Physical beauty fades with time, but the character, kindness, compassion, and love that flow from a Christ-centered heart endure and leave an eternal mark on others.

Think of the people who have impacted your life most deeply. Rarely is it because of how they looked; instead, it is because of how they made you feel, how they extended grace in your time of need, how they spoke words of encouragement, or how they stood beside you when others walked away. In the end, we don't remember the most beautiful face and body; we remember the most beautiful heart and soul.

The Apostle Peter gives us timeless wisdom in 1 Peter 3:3–4 (KJV): "Whose adorning let it not be that outward adorning of plaiting the hair, and of wearing of gold, or of putting on of apparel; but let it be the hidden man of the heart, in that which is not corruptible, even the ornament of a meek and quiet spirit, which is in the sight of God of great price."

God values the inner person, at "the heart." A meek and quiet spirit, one clothed in humility, love, and grace, is of great price in His eyes. This is beauty that no wrinkle, scar, or passing of years can take away.

When we live with a heart anchored in Christ, we reflect His beauty. Our lives become testimonies of love, patience, forgiveness, and joy. That is what lingers long after we're gone. The world may forget our features, but it will never forget how we loved.

Heavenly Father, thank You for reminding me that true beauty is not found in outward appearance but in the heart and soul transformed by Your Spirit. Teach me to cultivate a heart of love, grace, and compassion, so that my life reflects Your beauty to those around me. Help me to leave behind not just memories of what I looked like, but a legacy of kindness, faith, and Christlike character. Let my inner beauty shine brighter than anything this world calls beautiful. In Jesus' name, I pray.

Amen and To God Be The Glory!

OCTOBER 27. - "IMPERFECT BUT IMPACTFUL"

The phrase "You don't inspire others by being perfect. You inspire them by how you deal with your imperfections" holds a profound truth about the Christian Walk. Many people believe that influence and inspiration come from appearing flawless, polished, and without struggle. But perfection is not what touches hearts, authenticity does. When people see you wrestle with your struggles yet still cling to God, they see real faith in action.

God never asked us to put on a mask of perfection. Instead, He asked us to trust Him in our weakness. Paul reminds us in 2 Corinthians 12:9 (KJV): "And he said unto me, My grace is sufficient for thee: for my strength is made perfect in weakness." Notice, it is not our perfection that glorifies God, but His strength shining through our weaknesses.

When you openly acknowledge your flaws, failures, and mistakes, you make room for God's grace to be displayed. Others are not moved by a life that appears untouchable, but by a life that is broken yet surrendered. Your scars can become testimonies. Your struggles can become lessons. Your journey filled with imperfections can show others that if God can use you, He can use them too.

Think of Peter, who denied Jesus three times, yet went on to be a bold preacher of the Gospel. Think of David, who committed grave sins, yet was still called "a man after God's own heart." Think of Paul, who once persecuted the church, but became one of its greatest apostles. None of them inspired others because they were perfect, they inspired because of how God transformed them in the middle of their imperfections.

So, don't hide what God has healed. Don't bury what God has redeemed. Share your testimony. People need to see how God's grace carries you daily. That's what brings hope, not perfection, but perseverance in Christ.

Heavenly Father, I thank You that I do not have to be perfect to be used by You. Thank You for loving me in my weakness and for showing Your strength through my imperfections. Help me to walk in authenticity, to share my struggles with honesty, and to glorify You in the way I lean on Your grace. May my life be a testimony that inspires others not because I have it all together, but because You hold me together. In Jesus' name I pray.

Amen and To God Be The Glory!

OCTOBER 28. - "GUARDING YOUR HEART AGAINST BETRAYAL"

Judas Iscariot is proof that you could sit in a dynamic church with an amazing pastor and still become a friend of the devil if your heart is not 100% committed to Christ.

Judas Iscariot walked with Jesus Himself. He heard the greatest Teacher who ever lived, witnessed miracles that shook the very foundations of darkness, and was entrusted with responsibility among the twelve disciples. Yet, even in the presence of the Living Word, Judas's heart remained divided. Instead of surrendering fully to Christ, he allowed greed, pride, and hidden sin to take root. Ultimately, he opened the door for Satan to enter and became the betrayer.

This is a sobering reminder that spiritual proximity does not equal spiritual intimacy. Being in church, listening to powerful preaching, or even serving in ministry will not save us if our hearts are not fully yielded to Jesus. Judas proves that it is possible to look the part outwardly but be spiritually disconnected inwardly.

The devil thrives where there is compromise. A divided heart creates an entryway for deception, and before long, we may find ourselves trading eternal treasures for temporary gain. True discipleship requires more than attendance, knowledge, or association, it requires surrender, daily obedience, and a heart set fully on Christ.

The Bible warns us: "This people draweth nigh unto me with their mouth, and honoureth me with their lips; but their heart is far from me." Matthew 15:8 (KJV)

The greatest safeguard against becoming a "friend of the devil" is a life completely yielded to Christ, mind, body, and spirit. We must continually examine ourselves and ask, "Lord, do I truly belong to You, or am I merely standing near You?" A heart surrendered is a heart protected.

Heavenly Father, I come before You with humility, acknowledging that without You I am nothing. Guard my heart from deception and from the subtle traps of the enemy. Remove every trace of pride, greed, or compromise that would distance me from You. Lord, I don't just want to be near Your presence, I want to abide in You fully. Teach me to walk in obedience, to live with integrity, and to remain faithful even when temptations come. Keep me steadfast, so that I may never betray the One who saved me. In Jesus' mighty name, I pray.

Amen and To God Be The Glory!

OCTOBER 29. - "STRENGTH IS QUIET TEARS"

A strong person is not the one who doesn't cry. A strong person is one who is quiet and she has tears for a moment, and then picks up and keeps going.

Many people think strength means never showing weakness, never shedding a tear, or never admitting when the weight of life feels heavy. But the truth is, tears do not disqualify you from strength, they prove that you are human and still fighting. Crying is not a sign of defeat, but rather a release that allows you to breathe again, stand again, and move forward again.

When Hannah was barren, the Bible says she wept bitterly before the Lord in the temple (1 Samuel 1:10). Her tears did not make her weak. Instead, they became the very vehicle through which she poured her heart out to God, and in her brokenness, God remembered her. Even Jesus Himself wept (John 11:35). If the Son of God was not too strong to cry, then we too can release our tears without shame.

True strength is not found in the absence of tears, it is found in the ability to rise after the tears. Strength means you can bow down in pain for a moment, but you refuse to stay there. It means you let your tears fall, but you don't let them drown you. It means you wipe your eyes, lift your head, and walk forward by faith, knowing that God is walking with you.

The psalmist declared, "Weeping may endure for a night, but joy cometh in the morning" (Psalm 30:5, KJV). This is the promise of God: your tears may visit you, but they are temporary guests. Strength is found in holding on through the night with the hope that morning is on the way.

Beloved, you may have cried yourself to sleep at times. You may have silently carried pain that others could never see. But if you are still standing, still pressing, still moving forward, then you are stronger than you think. For every tear you've shed, God has kept a record (Psalm 56:8). And for every tear that falls, He sends grace to lift you up again.

Heavenly Father, I thank You for reminding me that my tears do not make me weak. They are part of my healing, part of my strength, and part of my journey. Lord, when I feel weighed down and overwhelmed, help me to release my pain into Your hands. Give me the courage to rise again after I've wept, and the faith to keep moving forward no matter what. Thank You for Your promise that joy will always follow sorrow, and that You are with me through every valley and every tear. In Jesus' name, Amen and To God Be The Glory!

OCTOBER 30. - "THE ART OF SAYING NO"

There is great strength and wisdom in learning to say no. Many of us struggle with this because we want to please people, avoid conflict, or appear "nice." Yet, the inability to say no often leads to exhaustion, frustration, and even compromise of our values.

The phrase reminds us: Learn the art of saying no. Don't lie. Don't make excuses. Don't overexplain yourself. Just simply decline. This is not a license to be harsh or unkind, but an invitation to embrace honesty, boundaries, and integrity.

When Jesus taught, He emphasized the importance of truthfulness in communication: "But let your 'Yes' be 'Yes,' and your 'No,' 'No.' For whatever is more than these is from the evil one." Matthew 5:37 (NKJV)

This scripture reveals that anything beyond a simple, truthful response opens the door for dishonesty or manipulation. God calls us to walk in truth, not in half-truths, excuses, or over-explanations. A plain yes or no spoken with love and clarity is enough.

Saying no can be one of the healthiest things you do for your spiritual, emotional, and physical well-being. It protects you from overcommitting, keeps you aligned with God's will, and allows you to give your best yes where He truly wants you. Every time you say no to something that doesn't serve God's purpose, you are saying yes to His plan for your life.

Think about Jesus: He didn't heal every person in Israel, attend every event, or meet every demand placed on Him. Instead, He was intentional, guided by the Father's will. Likewise, we are called to discern when to say yes and when to lovingly but firmly say no.

Heavenly Father, thank You for the wisdom of simplicity and truth. Help me to walk in honesty, never hiding behind excuses or unnecessary explanations. Give me the strength to say no when needed, and the discernment to know when to say yes. Teach me to set healthy boundaries that honor You and protect the purpose You've placed in me. May my words reflect integrity, and may my life be a testimony of obedience and balance. In Jesus' name, I pray.

Amen and To God Be The Glory!

OCTOBER 31. - "LIVING IN INTEGRITY AMID MISUNDERSTANDING"

"You can't control how others interpret your actions or words. Everyone perceives things based on their current situation and mindset. Just keep acting with honesty, love, and a good heart."

It's a universal truth: no matter how carefully we speak or how lovingly we act, others may misunderstand us. People see life through the lens of their own experiences, emotions, and biases. Sometimes, even our best intentions are misinterpreted, and this can be discouraging.

Yet, the calling of a believer is not to live for the approval or understanding of others but to reflect God's character in all we do. Proverbs 3:3-4 reminds us: "Let not mercy and truth forsake thee: bind them about thy neck; write them upon the table of thine heart: So shalt thou find favour and good understanding in the sight of God and man." (KJV)

Notice the order here: first mercy and truth. Our priority is to act rightly, to live with integrity, to love genuinely. If we anchor our words and actions in honesty, kindness, and love, we leave the judgment of perception to God.

Living with a good heart doesn't guarantee that everyone will understand or agree with us, but it guarantees that we are walking in alignment with God's will. When criticism or misunderstanding comes, it is not a reflection of your character, but often a reflection of the other person's perspective or current state of heart.

Remember, the Apostle Paul said in Galatians 1:10: "For am I now seeking the approval of man, or of God? Or am I trying to please man? If I were still trying to please man, I would not be a servant of Christ."

Your responsibility is simple: keep living with honesty, integrity, and love. The results, the perceptions, and the opinions belong to God to manage.

You cannot control the world's perception, but you can control your heart, your intentions, and your actions. Let honesty, love, and a good heart be your standard, and leave the rest to God.

Heavenly Father, thank You for Your perfect wisdom and understanding. Help me to live in integrity, speaking truth and acting with love, even when others misinterpret my actions or words. Teach me to rely on Your approval rather than seeking the validation of people. Protect my heart from discouragement and help me to continue walking in honesty, compassion, and faithfulness. May my life reflect Your goodness, and may Your favor be upon me even when misunderstandings arise. Guide my words, guard my heart, and strengthen my resolve to act rightly, trusting You for the outcome. In Jesus' name, I pray,

Amen and To God Be The Glory!

NOVEMBER INTRODUCTION

As we step into the month of November, we are often reminded of the changing seasons, both in nature and in our lives. The leaves fall, the days grow shorter, and there is a sense of reflection in the air. Similarly, life presents us with moments of transition, challenges, and pressing problems that seem to weigh heavily on our hearts. In times like these, it is easy to feel overwhelmed, anxious, or uncertain about the path ahead. Yet, Scripture assures us that God is not indifferent to our struggles; He is actively engaged in providing wisdom, guidance, and peace that surpasses human understanding.

This devotional is designed to help you navigate life's trials with a spirit anchored in faith. Each day, you will encounter biblical insights, reflections, and prayers that address common yet critical challenges. Whether they concern relationships, finances, health, spiritual growth, or emotional well-being. The goal is simple: to remind you that God's Word is alive and powerful, offering practical and divine solutions to the problems you face today.

As we journey through November, let us remember that our God is not only a problem-solver but also a refuge for the weary. When life's burdens feel too heavy, He provides strength. When confusion clouds our judgment, He provides clarity. And when fear threatens to consume us, He provides courage. This month's devotional invites you to pause, reflect, and allow God's Word to transform your perspective, renew your hope, and equip you to face life's pressing problems with confidence and faith.

"Cast all your anxiety on him because he cares for you." 1 Peter 5:7 (NIV)

Heavenly Father, as I enter this month, I surrender all my worries, fears, and challenges into Your hands. Teach me to trust You more deeply, to rely on Your wisdom, and to walk boldly in faith even when life feels uncertain. Help me to see Your solutions clearly and to embrace Your peace that surpasses all understanding. Strengthen my heart, renew my spirit, and guide me through every pressing problem I may face. Let Your Word be my anchor, and Your presence my constant comfort.

In Jesus' name, I pray, Amen and To God Be The Glory!

NOVEMBER 1. - "GUARDING THE BALANCE OF YOUR LIFE"

There is a deep truth in the phrase: "If you allow people to make more withdrawals than deposits in your life, you will be out of balance and in the red. Know when to close the account."

Life is much like a spiritual bank account. God has entrusted us with time, strength, love, peace, and wisdom. Each day, we give and receive, people pour into us through encouragement, kindness, and prayer, and at times they also withdraw from us through needs, demands, and conflicts. But if we constantly allow others to pull from us without healthy boundaries or replenishment from God, we will find ourselves spiritually bankrupt.

Even Jesus understood the importance of balance. Scripture tells us in Luke 5:16 (KJV): "And he withdrew himself into the wilderness and prayed." After ministering to the crowds, healing the sick, and teaching, Jesus often stepped away to recharge in the presence of His Father. He did not let people's constant demands drain Him to the point of weakness, He knew when to withdraw and when to pour out.

In the same way, we must discern when relationships or environments are taking more than they are giving. If the "withdrawals" of stress, manipulation, or negativity outweigh the "deposits" of encouragement, love, and growth, then it is time to set Godly boundaries. This doesn't mean you stop loving or praying for people, it means you guard your spirit so that you can remain effective and fruitful in the Kingdom.

Remember, you are not called to live in constant depletion. You are called to live in overflow. Jesus said in John 10:10 (KJV): "I am come that they might have life, and that they might have it more abundantly." Abundance cannot exist where imbalance and emptiness rule.

So, know when to close the account. Know when to stop allowing unhealthy patterns and toxic withdrawals. Fill yourself daily in God's presence and surround yourself with people who pour back into you with love, prayer, and encouragement. In doing so, you will remain balanced, strong, and full of the Spirit to continue the work God has called you to do.

Heavenly Father, I thank You for being the source of my strength, peace, and joy. Help me to discern when I am giving too much of myself without being replenished. Teach me to set boundaries in wisdom, not in bitterness. Lord, show me how to surround myself with people who uplift and encourage, and above all, help me to daily withdraw from the well of Your Spirit, where there is no lack. Keep me balanced, strong, and in alignment with Your will. In Jesus' name, I pray. Amen and To God Be The Glory!

NOVEMBER 2. - "LESSONS IN THE HARD PLACES"

Life is a classroom, and often the hardest lessons do not come from ease but from trial. Every challenge we face, every sting of disappointment, every wave of frustration, and every storm of fear carries within it an invitation from God: an invitation to grow, to deepen, and to be transformed into the likeness of Christ. The situations we most resist are often the very ones shaping us into who God has called us to be.

Anything that annoys you is teaching you patience. Annoyances are small tests of the spirit. They reveal what is still unsettled within us. Instead of responding in anger, God calls us to embrace patience, remembering that patience is not weakness but strength under control. "But let patience have her perfect work, that ye may be perfect and entire, wanting nothing" (James 1:4 KJV).

Anything that abandoned you is teaching you to stand on your own two feet. People may walk away, circumstances may shift, but God never leaves. Their absence teaches us dependence on the One who said, "I will never leave thee, nor forsake thee" (Hebrews 13:5 KJV). In their leaving, you discover that your foundation must be Christ alone, not the approval or presence of man.

Anything that angers you is teaching you forgiveness and compassion. Anger unchecked can destroy, but anger surrendered to God transforms into compassion. Through forgiveness, you free yourself, not just the offender. Jesus Himself prayed, "Father, forgive them; for they know not what they do" (Luke 23:34 KJV).

Anything that has power over you is teaching you to take your power back. Bondage to fear, addiction, or control reveals where we've given the enemy authority. But in Christ, we reclaim our freedom. "If the Son therefore shall make you free, ye shall be free indeed" (John 8:36). Taking your power back means submitting to God's authority first and resisting all that would enslave you.

Anything you hate is teaching you unconditional love. Hatred breeds bitterness, but when surrendered, it becomes a doorway into deeper love. God calls us to love not only those who love us but also those who oppose us. "But I say unto you, Love your enemies, bless them that curse you, do good to them that hate you, and pray for them which despitefully use you" (Matthew 5:44 KJV).

Anything you fear is teaching you courage to overcome. Fear whispers defeat, but courage stands on God's promises. Courage is not the absence of fear but moving forward in faith despite it. "For God hath not given us the spirit of fear; but of power, and of love, and of a sound mind" (2 Timothy 1:7 KJV).

Anything you cannot control is teaching you how to let go. Control belongs to God alone. When life spins outside our grasp, He calls us to surrender, trusting Him with every outcome. "Casting all your care upon him; for he careth for you" (1 Peter 5:7 KJV).

Each trial, whether big or small, is not wasted. They are steppingstones meant to build us, refine us, and push us into the fullness of who God created us to be. We must learn to think, grow, and prosper in every season, for the Lord uses all things, good or bad for our good and His glory (Romans 8:28).

Heavenly Father, I thank You for the lessons hidden in the challenges of life. Teach me patience in the face of irritation, strength when I feel abandoned, forgiveness when I am angered, and freedom when I feel powerless. Help me to respond with love when hatred arises, to walk in courage when fear surrounds me, and to release control into Your capable hands. Lord, transform every trial into a tool for my growth and every setback into a setup for my prosperity in You. May I always remember that in Christ, I am victorious. In Jesus' name I pray, Amen and To God Be The Glory!

NOVEMBER 3. - "EVERY REJECTION OPENS THE DOOR TO GOD'S REDIRECTION"

"The People Who Tried To Bury You Didn't Know You Were A Seed"

Rejection is one of the most painful experiences a person can go through. Whether it comes from people, opportunities, relationships, or dreams, rejection can pierce deeply and make us question our worth or our future. But as believers, we must remember that rejection does not have the final say in our lives. Instead, it is often the very thing God uses to position us for something greater.

The truth is this: every rejection is an open door to God's redirection. When one door closes, God is guiding us toward another one that leads to His perfect will for our lives.

Think of Joseph in Genesis. He was rejected by his own brothers, sold into slavery, and unjustly imprisoned. Each of those painful rejections could have broken him, but they were all steps in God's plan to redirect him toward his destiny, to become a ruler in Egypt and save many lives during famine. What seemed like defeat was divine positioning.

We also see this truth in Acts 16:6-10. Paul and his companions were "kept by the Holy Spirit from preaching the word in the province of Asia" and "the Spirit of Jesus would not allow them" to enter Bithynia. To some, that may have felt like rejection—but it was God's redirection. Instead, Paul received a vision of a man in Macedonia calling for help, leading to the gospel spreading into Europe.

God sees what we cannot see. Sometimes He closes a door because He knows it will lead to destruction. Sometimes He redirects us because His plan is bigger than what we are asking for. What feels like loss today may actually be protection, preparation, or promotion for tomorrow.

So, when rejection comes, don't despair. Don't let bitterness take root. Instead, trust that God is working behind the scenes. Every "no" you receive from people is God's way of saying, "Trust Me, I have something better in store."

"And we know that all things work together for good to them that love God, to them who are the called according to his purpose." Romans 8:28 (KJV)

Heavenly Father, I thank You for being the Author and Finisher of my life. Lord, when I face rejection, help me not to see it as the end but as a redirection toward something greater You have planned for me. Remove the sting of disappointment and replace it with faith and expectation. Teach me to trust Your timing, Your wisdom, and Your perfect will. Align my steps with Your divine purpose and let me never miss the blessings that You are guiding me to. I declare that every rejection is working for my good, because You are always in control. In Jesus' name, I pray.

Amen and To God Be The Glory!

NOVEMBER 4. - "LIFE IS SHORT ~ ENJOY IT"

Life is but a vapor fleeting, fragile, and unpredictable. James reminds us in James 4:14 (KJV), "For what is your life? It is even a vapour, that appeareth for a little time, and then vanisheth away." With this truth in mind, how we choose to live and who we choose to surround ourselves with, matters greatly.

The phrase "life is short, spend time with people who make you laugh and feel loved" is a gentle yet powerful reminder that our days are not endless. Since time is precious, God calls us to steward it wisely. Laughter, joy, and love are not trivial, they are God's gifts that refresh our souls and remind us of His goodness.

When we spend time with people who lift us up, who encourage us, who love us with sincerity, and who bring laughter into our lives, we are experiencing a reflection of God's love through His people. Proverbs 17:22 tells us, "A merry heart doeth good like a medicine: but a broken spirit drieth the bones." Joy is medicine to the soul, and it comes alive in the company of those who genuinely care for us.

God never designed us to walk through life in isolation. Jesus Himself surrounded Himself with His disciples, shared meals with friends, and wept and rejoiced with others. If He, being the Son of God, modeled the importance of companionship, how much more should we seek relationships that nurture, encourage, and draw us closer to God?

Let us, then, live intentionally. Let us treasure the laughter shared at the dinner table, the warmth of a friend's embrace, the encouragement of a prayer partner, and the love of family. These are not small things; they are sacred gifts that echo eternity.

Heavenly Father, I thank You for the gift of life and the people You have placed in it. Teach me to number my days so that I may live with wisdom and purpose. Help me to surround myself with those who encourage, uplift, and love me as You do. Fill my life with joy and laughter that reflects Your goodness. Guard my heart from negativity and from relationships that pull me away from Your peace. Lord, let me be a source of laughter and love for others as well. May every moment I live bring glory to Your name. In Jesus' name, Amen and o God Be The Glory!

NOVEMBER 5. - "SPEND YOUR TIME ON THOSE WHO LOVE YOU UNCONDITIONALLY"

Life is a gift from God, and with that gift comes the precious treasure of time. Every moment we spend is a moment we can never get back. That's why it is so important to be wise in how we use our time and who we give it to. The phrase, "Spend your time on those who love you unconditionally. Don't waste it on those who only love you when the conditions are right for them," is a reminder of the value of God-centered relationships.

The world is full of conditional love. Love that says, "I'm here for you only when it benefits me," or "I'll stand with you as long as things are easy." This kind of love is unstable, unreliable, and ultimately draining. It is not rooted in God's truth. But unconditional love reflects the heart of God, who loves us not because of what we can give Him, but because of who He is.

Scripture tells us: "A friend loves at all times, and a brother is born for adversity." Proverbs 17:17 (KJV)

This verse shows us that true, godly love does not change with the seasons of life. A real friend loves in the sunshine and in the storm. They don't disappear when you're broken, struggling, or no longer useful to them. Instead, they walk with you through adversity because their love is anchored in commitment, not convenience.

Jesus Himself modeled unconditional love. He washed the feet of His disciples, including Judas who betrayed Him. He forgave Peter who denied Him. He loved us while we were yet sinners (Romans 5:8). His example teaches us not to waste our time desperately chasing after those who give us only partial, conditional affection, but to instead invest in relationships that mirror His love. Relationships that build us up, strengthen our walk with God, and draw us closer to His presence.

Spending time with those who love you unconditionally is not about selfishness, it's about stewardship. God calls us to guard our hearts (Proverbs 4:23). When we pour into people who genuinely love us, we grow in strength, joy, and encouragement. But when we give ourselves to those who only show up when it's convenient, we leave ourselves open to unnecessary hurt and distraction from God's purpose.

So today, ask yourself: Am I investing in relationships that reflect God's love? Am I chasing after people who only love me when it's convenient, or am I cherishing those who love me at all times? Your time is too precious to waste, invest it wisely, and always keep Christ at the center of your love.

Heavenly Father, thank You for showing me what true, unconditional love looks like through Your Son, Jesus Christ. Teach me to discern between those who only love me for what I can offer and those who love me with a heart that reflects Yours. Help me to spend my time wisely, investing in relationships that honor You and build me up in faith. Give me the courage to let go of conditional relationships that drain me, and the wisdom to cherish the people who truly love me at all times. May my own love reflect Yours, faithful, steadfast, and unconditional. In Jesus' name, I pray.

Amen and To God Be The Glory!

NOVEMBER 6. - "LOVE YOURSELF A LITTLE EXTRA RIGHT NOW"

Life has a way of pulling us in many directions. Sometimes you're carrying responsibilities no one knows about, fighting battles in silence, and trying your best just to keep going. On the outside, you smile and keep moving, but on the inside, your heart is weary. This is why it's so important to love yourself a little extra right now.

God did not create you to be hard on yourself. He did not call you to perfection, He called you to progress. He knows every unseen struggle, every quiet tear, and every effort you make even when no one acknowledges it. That's why you must give yourself grace, because God Himself extends grace to you daily.

When you stumble, remember that God says His strength is made perfect in your weakness (2 Corinthians 12:9). When you feel like no one sees your effort, know that God does. and He is a rewarder of those who diligently seek Him (Hebrews 11:6). Loving yourself is not prideful; it is honoring the God who made you, understanding that you are His workmanship (Ephesians 2:10).

So today, instead of criticizing yourself, speak life over yourself. Instead of replaying failures, thank God for your growth. Instead of pushing past exhaustion without rest, pause and breathe in God's peace. You are doing your best, and that is enough in the eyes of the One who created you. Love yourself a little extra, because you are deeply loved by God.

"Come unto me, all ye that labour and are heavy laden, and I will give you rest." — Matthew 11:28 (KJV)

Heavenly Father, thank You for loving me beyond my flaws and failures. Thank You for seeing the burdens I carry that others cannot see. Help me to extend grace to myself the way You extend grace to me. Teach me to rest in You and to walk in the truth that I am enough because I am Yours. Strengthen me to keep moving forward with faith, peace, and confidence in Your love. In Jesus' name I pray.

Amen and To God Be The Glory!

NOVEMBER 7. - "WHY LOYALTY COST MORE THAN IT GIVES"

There are times in life when our loyalty has kept us bound in places where common sense should have led us to walk away. Loyalty is a beautiful trait, it reflects faithfulness, steadfastness, and commitment. But when it is misplaced, it can become a chain instead of a blessing. Many of us have stayed in relationships, friendships, jobs, or situations not because they were healthy, but because our heart said "I can't give up on them yet" while our spirit whispered, "This is not where you belong."

Loyalty to people or things that drain us is not the loyalty that God calls us to. Scripture reminds us that our first loyalty must always be to Him: "Do not be misled: 'Bad company corrupts good character.' 1 Corinthians 15:33 (NIV)

Sometimes, loyalty is disguised as love, but if it keeps you in bondage, it is not love, it is a trap. Common sense, guided by the Holy Spirit, will often show us red flags. Yet, because of loyalty, we silence that still small voice, hoping things will change. But God does not want us tied to things that hinder our growth or stifle our purpose.

The truth is this: misplaced loyalty can blind us, but God's wisdom opens our eyes. If loyalty has kept you in situations where common sense should have taken you out, it is time to shift your loyalty back to God. He is the one who will never fail, never misuse your love, and never take your faithfulness for granted.

Sometimes walking away is not betrayal, it's obedience. Sometimes letting go is not weakness, it's wisdom. And sometimes, choosing yourself with God is the most loyal decision you can ever make.

Father, I thank You for being the One I can always be loyal to without fear of being misused or broken. Lord, forgive me for the times I stayed in places where You were telling me to move, simply because I confused loyalty with obedience. Teach me to discern when my loyalty is misplaced and give me the courage to walk away when necessary. Let my heart always be tied to You above all else, because You are faithful and true. Order my steps, Lord, and help me stand in wisdom, not bondage. In Jesus' name I pray. Amen and To God Be The Glory!

NOVEMBER 8. - "CARING IS ENOUGH"

The world often teaches us that influence and significance come through brilliance, wealth, beauty, or perfection. Many people strive for these things, believing they are the only ways to leave an impact. Yet, God's Word reminds us that His kingdom operates on a completely different standard.

To make a difference in someone's life, you don't have to shine with human accolades you simply have to care. A listening ear, a kind word, a warm smile, or a helping hand can carry more eternal weight than riches, titles, or outward beauty.

Scripture says: "And above all things have fervent charity among yourselves: for charity shall cover the multitude of sins." 1 Peter 4:8 (KJV)

Love expressed through genuine care has the power to heal, restore, and inspire. Jesus demonstrated this throughout His ministry. He didn't seek to impress with worldly power, but with compassion. He fed the hungry, touched the untouchable, wept with the grieving, and spoke hope into the hopeless.

Think of the Good Samaritan (Luke 10:25–37). He was not identified as rich, brilliant, or perfect. In fact, he was an outsider, someone least expected to help. Yet what made him different was his compassion, he cared. And that care changed the course of another man's life.

When we show genuine care, we reflect the very heart of Christ. Our simple acts of kindness become vessels of God's love. You may never know the full extent of the difference you make, but rest assured, heaven records it.

So today, don't disqualify yourself because you feel inadequate, unworthy, or imperfect. You don't need to be all the things the world says. Just care. Care deeply, care genuinely, and care consistently—and God will use you in mighty ways.

Heavenly Father, thank You for reminding me that I don't need to be perfect to make a difference. Teach me to care as Jesus cared, with love that is sincere and without condition. Open my eyes to those around me who are hurting, lonely, or in need of encouragement. Help me to be Your hands and feet, showing compassion in both small and great ways. May my life reflect Your love and may every act of kindness point others back to You. In Jesus' name, I pray.

Amen and To God Be The Glory!

NOVEMBER 9. - "A LIFE THAT INSPIRES"

The phrase "I want to inspire people. I want someone to look at me and say because of you I didn't give up" carries a beautiful weight of purpose. It is not just about living for yourself but living in such a way that your light ignites hope in others. Our lives were never meant to be lived in isolation; they are designed to reflect God's glory and to strengthen those who walk beside us.

When we endure trials and keep pressing forward, people are watching even if we don't realize it. Our perseverance becomes a testimony that whispers to someone else, "If she can make it, so can I. If God sustained him, He can sustain me too."

The apostle Matthew said it this way: "Let your light so shine before men, that they may see your good works, and glorify your Father which is in heaven." Matthew 5:16 (KJV)

Your faith, resilience, and determination to keep moving forward are not just for your own growth. They are seeds of inspiration for someone who is on the verge of giving up. Each time you choose to trust God instead of collapsing under pressure, you create a living example of hope. Each time you rise after falling, you show others that their story isn't over either.

The world needs people who will not just survive their storms but thrive in them, pointing to the strength of God as their anchor. You never know whose life may be changed because they saw your endurance, your kindness, your unshakable faith, or your refusal to quit.

So, live boldly. Live faithfully. Live in such a way that your life becomes a sermon without words, a daily inspiration that proves God's power is real.

Heavenly Father, thank You for giving me the strength to endure and the courage to rise when life tries to push me down. Lord, help me to live in such a way that my life becomes a testimony of Your faithfulness. Let my light shine so brightly that others find hope and refuse to give up because they see You working through me. Use my journey, my struggles, and my victories as an inspiration that points people back to You. In every step I take, may Your name be glorified. In Jesus name I pray, Amen and To God Be The Glory!

NOVEMBER 10. - "FROM BROKEN PIECES TO A MAJOR COMEBACK"

Life does not always read like a fairy tale. Many of us carry chapters in our stories that we wish we could tear out and rewrite. Broken pieces from past mistakes, terrible choices made in moments of weakness, and ugly truths that we would rather hide can often weigh heavily on our hearts. Yet, in the hands of God, what once looked like a tragedy becomes the setup for a powerful testimony.

When we surrender those broken pieces to Him, He reshapes them into something beautiful. What the enemy meant to destroy us with becomes the very thing God uses to lift us up. Our comeback is not a result of our strength or wisdom, but of His grace, mercy, and unending love. Through Christ, our story does not end with our failures, it ends with redemption.

This is the reason we can walk in peace. Peace is not the absence of trouble but the presence of God in the middle of it. Grace is what saved us from what we deserved, and it's what continues to carry us forward. Your story is not defined by the brokenness of yesterday but by the comeback that God is writing today.

"And we know that all things work together for good to them that love God, to them who are the called according to his purpose."
Romans 8:28 (KJV)

Heavenly Father, I thank You for taking the broken pieces of my life and turning them into a testimony of Your love and grace. Thank You for not giving up on me when I made terrible choices and for covering me when the truth of my past seemed unbearable. Lord, help me to walk in the peace You've given me and never forget the power of the comeback You orchestrated in my life. May my story bring hope to others and glorify Your name. In Jesus' mighty name, Amen and To God Be The Glory!

NOVEMBER 11. - "THIS PLACE IS NOT WHERE MY STORY BEGAN OR WHERE IT WILL END"

"GOD IS STILL WRITING MY STORY"

"Being confident of this very thing, that he which hath begun a good work in you will perform it until the day of Jesus Christ." Philippians 1:6 (KJV)

Every journey has a beginning, but that beginning does not define the entire story. You may live here now, but your story began elsewhere. That beginning is not just a geographical place, it represents your roots, your upbringing, your early struggles, and the foundation that God has laid for your life.

Where you were born may have been where the first chapters of your life were written. Where lessons were learned, mistakes were made, and victories were won. But God never intended for your story to remain in the first chapter. He moves us, grows us, and sometimes even uproots us, to show that His plans for us are not confined to where we started.

Where you are now represents where God has positioned you for your current season. Just because your story began somewhere else does not mean God is finished with you where you are now. The God who started writing your story in one place is still the Author of your life today, and He is adding new chapters of grace, growth, and purpose.

Sometimes we look back and wonder why we had to start where we did, or why our journey included certain painful places. But every beginning, every transition, and every destination is part of God's divine penmanship. Your birthplace may have shaped you, but it does not limit you. Your current location may challenge you, but it cannot contain you. God is still writing, and His promises are unfolding daily.

Remember this: where you began was never meant to be where you ended. God uses our roots to give us strength and our new seasons to bring us into His promises. The same God who was with you back then, is with you now. He will be with you wherever life leads.

Heavenly Father, I thank You for my beginnings and for every step of the journey You have brought me through. Thank You for reminding me that where I started does not define where I am going, because You are the Author of my life. Help me to embrace my current season with faith and courage, knowing that You are still writing my story. Let my life be a testimony of Your faithfulness from beginning to end. In Jesus' name I pray, Amen and To God Be The Glory!

NOVEMBER 12. - "LIFE IS TOO SHORT ~ MAKE THE MOST OF EVERYDAY"

"Rejoice evermore. Pray without ceasing. In everything give thanks: for this is the will of God in Christ Jesus concerning you." 1 Thessalonians 5:16-18 (KJV)

Life is a precious gift, a fleeting journey filled with moments that cannot be reclaimed. Too often, we get caught up in arguments, disagreements, and the pursuit of things that, in the end, hold little eternal value. The Lord calls us to a higher perspective, and that is to focus on gratitude, love, and joy.

When we choose to count our blessings, we shift our hearts from frustration to contentment. A simple smile, a word of encouragement, or a hug shared with a loved one carries more significance than any argument ever will. Life is too short to waste on negativity, and every day presents an opportunity to pour love into the lives of those who stand faithfully by us.

The Bible reminds us to rejoice always, pray continually, and give thanks in every circumstance. These instructions are not just religious rituals; they are lifelines to joy and peace. When we embrace gratitude, trivial conflicts that once seemed so important lose weight in the balance of things. When we choose love over anger, peace replaces strife. When we make the most of every day, we honor God by living fully, intentionally, and joyfully.

Let today be a day where you intentionally smile, speak words of encouragement, and treasure every moment with your friends and family. Life is a series of fleeting moments, and the time we spend nurturing love and joy becomes the legacy we leave behind.

Heavenly Father, I truly thank You for the gift of life and for the people You have placed in my journey. Help me to see beyond petty arguments and conflicts and to focus on the blessings You have given me. Teach me to love generously, to smile sincerely, and to make the most of every day. Fill my heart with gratitude and peace, so that my life may reflect Your joy and glory. Let me be a light to my family, friends, and all whom I encounter. May every action I take honor You and bring life, hope, and love to others. In Jesus' name, I pray.

Amen and To God Be The Glory!

NOVEMBER 13. - "STANDING ON THE PROMISE OF GOD'S PRESENCE"

"There shall not any man be able to stand before thee all the days of thy life: as I was with Moses, so I will be with thee: I will not fail thee, nor forsake thee." Joshua 1:5 (KJV)

When Joshua was called to lead the children of Israel after the death of Moses, the task before him was daunting. He was stepping into the shoes of a great leader and was about to lead people into an unknown land filled with enemies, challenges, and obstacles. In that moment, God spoke a powerful promise that has carried generations of believers: "I will not fail thee, nor forsake thee."

This verse reminds us of two powerful truths:

God's Power is Greater Than Any Opposition. The Lord tells Joshua, "There shall not any man be able to stand before thee all the days of thy life." That same assurance is ours today. No weapon formed against you shall prosper (Isaiah 54:17). Enemies may rise, challenges may come, but none can overthrow the power and authority of God at work in your life.

God's Presence is Constant and Unfailing Notice God did not promise Joshua a problem-free journey, but He did promise His presence. "As I was with Moses, so I will be with thee." That same presence that parted the Red Sea, brought water from the rock, and rained manna from heaven was now with Joshua and is with us today through Christ Jesus. We do not walk alone.

God's Faithfulness Does Not Change. "I will not fail thee, nor forsake thee." This is the heartbeat of God's covenant love. People may fail us, plans may fail, but God never does. Hebrews 13:5 repeats this same promise: "I will never leave thee, nor forsake thee." His word is unshakable, His character unchanging, and His love unending.

When life feels overwhelming, when fear whispers that we are not enough, remember this: The God who was with Joshua is the same God who is with you. Stand firm in His word, for His presence is your strength, His promise is your confidence, and His power is your victory.

Heavenly Father, I thank You for the promise of Your unfailing presence. Just as You were with Joshua, be with me in every season of my life. Strengthen my faith when I feel weak, remind me of Your word when I feel afraid, and guide my steps when the way before me seems uncertain. I trust that no enemy, no trial, and no weapon can stand against me because You are with me. Lord, never let me forget that You will not fail me nor forsake me. In Jesus' mighty name, I pray.

Amen and To God Be The Glory!

NOVEMBER 14. - "RAISE THE RENT AND KICK THEM OUT"

The phrase "Don't let negative and toxic people rent space in your head. Raise the rent and kick them out" is a reminder that our minds are precious real estate. What we allow to settle in our thoughts has the power to shape our attitudes, decisions, and ultimately our destiny. If we continuously give room to the words, actions, or presence of negative and toxic people, we allow them to take authority over something God has called us to guard, our hearts and minds.

The truth is that negativity thrives when we give it permission. Toxic voices, whether through people or lingering memories of hurt, try to convince us we are less than what God says we are. They drain our energy, steal our joy, and attempt to suffocate our hope. But the Word of God is clear: "Above all else, guard your heart, for everything you do flows from it." (Proverbs 4:23, NIV)

Guarding your heart and mind requires boundaries. You cannot stop people from speaking against you, but you can stop their words from taking residence inside of you. Just as a landlord decides who gets to live in their property, you have authority over what thoughts you allow to settle in your spirit. If someone is toxic, they have a way of always tearing you down, sowing doubt, or stirring confusion. Then it's time to "raise the rent" by strengthening your standards through God's Word.

When you raise the rent, you're saying: I will not tolerate lies where God has spoken truth. I will not entertain fear where God has promised peace. I will not harbor bitterness where God commands forgiveness. This isn't about pride or pushing people away, it's about protecting the God-given peace of your mind and spirit.

The Apostle Paul reminds us: "Do not be conformed to this world but be transformed by the renewing of your mind." (Romans 12:2, KJV)

Renewing your mind means you're constantly evicting the clutter of negativity and replacing it with God's truth. Instead of fear, you speak faith. Instead of bitterness, you extend forgiveness. Instead of self-doubt, you declare God's promises. That's how you raise the rent. By refusing to live on the world's terms and choosing instead to fill your head with the eternal truths of God.

So today, examine who or what you've been giving free rent to in your thoughts. Is it someone's criticism, a toxic relationship, or a lie you've been repeating to yourself? Whatever it is, evict it. Replace it with God's promises. And watch peace, joy, and strength return to your heart.

Heavenly Father, thank You for reminding me that my mind and heart are valuable and belong to You. Forgive me for the times I have allowed toxic thoughts or people to take up space in my spirit. Teach me to raise the rent by lifting up Your Word above every lie, every doubt, and every negative influence. Fill me with discernment to know when to let go, courage to set boundaries, and wisdom to keep my heart guarded. I declare that my mind is renewed daily by Your Spirit and that peace, joy, and love will dwell within me. In Jesus' mighty name I pray.

Amen and To God Be The Glory!

NOVEMBER 15. - "DON'T BE DEFINED BY OTHERS"

Life is full of voices from family, friends, coworkers, even strangers on the internet. Everyone seems to have something to say about who you are, what you should be doing, or how you should live. Opinions are everywhere, and if we are not careful, we can begin to internalize those opinions until they become labels that weigh us down. But as children of God, we must remember: our worth, our identity, and our purpose are not determined by what people think, but by what God has already declared over us.

The truth is that people's opinions are often rooted in their own experiences, insecurities, or limited understanding of who you are. They may call you "not enough," "a failure," or "too broken to be used." But God calls you chosen, beloved, redeemed, forgiven, and victorious. You were fearfully and wonderfully made (Psalm 139:14), and no one else's words can cancel what God has spoken over your life.

When you allow yourself to be defined by others, you are handing over your identity to voices that cannot see the full picture. But when you choose to align yourself with God's Word, you anchor your heart in truth that cannot be shaken. Opinions change, circumstances change, but God's Word never changes.

The Apostle Paul put it clearly in Galatians 1:10 (KJV): "For do I now persuade men, or God? or do I seek to please men? for if I yet pleased men, I should not be the servant of Christ." Paul recognized that living for human approval is a trap. Our calling is higher, it is to serve Christ, to walk in the identity He has given us, and to fulfill the purpose He has designed for us.

Beloved, don't let someone else's limited view box you in. Don't let their negative words take root in your spirit. Stand on the truth of who God says you are. You are more than a conqueror through Christ. You are the head and not the tail. You are set apart for His glory.

Let your heart rest in this: people may have opinions, but only God has the final say.

Heavenly Father, I thank You that my identity is not found in the shifting opinions of others but in the unshakable truth of Your Word. Help me to silence the lies and labels that the world tries to put on me and instead embrace who You created me to be. Remind me daily that I am Your child, chosen, redeemed, and loved beyond measure. Give me courage to walk boldly in my God-given identity and to live for Your approval above all else. In Jesus' name, I pray. Amen and To God Be The Glory!

NOVEMBER 16. - "NEVER JUDGE SOMEONE BASED ON A SEASON"

Life is made up of seasons. Some were filled with struggle, some with waiting, and others with breakthroughs. Yet one of the greatest dangers we face is judging someone based on the season they are currently in. What we see today is not the end of their story. God is always at work, shifting, moving, and aligning things for His glory and our good.

David's story reminds us of this truth. One season, he was a forgotten shepherd boy, overlooked even by his own family. But in the next season, God exalted him to be the King of Israel (1 Samuel 16). Ruth, a foreign widow gleaning leftovers in the fields, was later elevated to own those same fields through God's divine arrangement (Ruth 2–4). Mordecai, who once sat humbly outside the king's gate, was later honored with royal authority inside the palace (Esther 6:10–11).

These examples testify that our God is a God of divine turnaround. The same hands that hold the universe also hold your seasons. When we judge others by their present condition, we risk underestimating the power of God's favor and timing in their lives. Today's struggle might be tomorrow's testimony. Today's "not enough" may become tomorrow's abundance.

Scripture: "To everything there is a season, and a time to every purpose under the heaven." Ecclesiastes 3:1 (KJV)

This verse reminds us that every season, whether waiting, weeping, or winning, has purpose. God wastes nothing. His timing is perfect, and His favor is unearned but freely given. He is the God of unmerited favor, who turns ashes into beauty, mourning into dancing, and valleys into mountaintops.

Heavenly Father, thank You for being the God of all seasons. Help me not to judge others by where they are now but to see them through the lens of Your promises. Teach me patience in my own season, knowing You are always at work behind the scenes. Lord, I trust that You can turn my trials into triumphs, my waiting into winning, and my pain into purpose. Strengthen my faith to believe in Your divine timing and help me to rejoice not only in my own breakthroughs but also in the victories of others. I declare today that You are the God of turnaround, the God of unmerited favor, and the God who writes the final chapter of my life. In Jesus' name, I pray.

Amen and To God Be The Glory!

NOVEMBER 17. - "NEVER LET THE PAST IMPRISON YOU"

The phrase "never be a prisoner of your past, it was just a lesson not a life sentence" carries a deep truth that echoes throughout the Word of God. Many of us have made mistakes, walked down dark paths, or endured experiences that left scars. The enemy loves to chain us to those memories, reminding us of failures and shortcomings to make us believe that our past defines our worth. But in Christ, our past is not our prison, it is our teacher.

Paul reminds us in Philippians 3:13-14 (KJV): "Brethren, I count not myself to have apprehended: but this one thing I do, forgetting those things which are behind, and reaching forth unto those things which are before, I press toward the mark for the prize of the high calling of God in Christ Jesus."

Notice Paul's determination: he doesn't ignore that he had a past. He once persecuted Christians, but he refuses to let it chain him down. Instead, he sees his past as a testimony of God's grace and uses it as fuel to press forward toward God's calling.

Your past is not a life sentence because Jesus Christ already paid the price for your freedom. What once was bondage has now become a platform for testimony. That broken relationship, that failure, that season of rebellion, or that painful loss does not dictate your destiny. God uses the lessons of the past to strengthen your faith, sharpen your character, and prepare you for the future.

When you hold onto regret, shame, or guilt, you give the past power it doesn't deserve. But when you surrender it to God, He turns it into wisdom, growth, and victory. You are not who you were, you are who God says you are: redeemed, forgiven, and free.

Heavenly Father, I thank You for being a God of mercy and grace. Thank You for reminding me that my past is not a prison but a lesson. Help me to release regret, shame, and guilt, and to embrace the freedom that Christ purchased for me on the cross. Teach me to walk forward with confidence, pressing toward the purpose You have for me. May my testimony of redemption bring hope to others who feel trapped by their past. I declare today that I am no longer bound. I am free, I am forgiven, and I am walking into the future You have designed for me. In Jesus' name, Amen and To God Be The Glory!

NOVEMBER 18. - "THE POWER OF ONE SMALL PRAYER"

Scripture: "The effectual fervent prayer of a righteous man availeth much." James 5:16 (KJV)

In the quiet moments of life, it's easy to feel that our prayers are too small, too insignificant, or too simple to matter. We may think that a short whisper, a silent plea, or a heartfelt "God help me" can't possibly make a difference in the grand scheme of things. Yet, the Word of God reminds us that it's not the quantity or the eloquence of our words that reach Heaven, but the sincerity of our hearts.

"Never underestimate the power of one small prayer." These words carry profound truth. God does not measure our devotion by the length of our prayers or the flowery language we use. He looks deeper into the heart, the intentions, the faith that underlies every word we utter. A single, honest prayer, spoken in humility and trust, has the power to shift circumstances, bring peace to our souls, and draw us closer to God.

Consider the story of Hannah in 1 Samuel 1. In her deep sorrow, she poured out her heart before God with a simple, desperate prayer for a child. She didn't need an audience, elaborate words, or a grand ceremony. She simply prayed. And God heard her. He answered her prayer, not because of the beauty of her words, but because of the authenticity and faith in her heart.

Your small prayer can do more than you realize. It can break strongholds, heal relationships, and bring clarity to confusion. When life feels overwhelming, when the world seems too heavy to carry, remember: one heartfelt prayer is powerful. It's a conversation with the Creator of the universe, and He is attentive to every syllable, every sigh, and every tear.

Let this truth guide you: God values your heart over your speech. He honors your faith, even when it's expressed in the simplest terms. Never doubt that your prayer, no matter how small or brief, carries eternal weight.

Heavenly Father, thank You for always hearing me, even when my words are few or imperfect. Lord, teach me to pray with a sincere heart, trusting that You see, know, and understand every burden I carry. Help me never to underestimate the power of even the smallest prayer and strengthen my faith to come to You boldly and honestly. May my heart always be aligned with Your will, and may Your presence fill me with peace, knowing that You are listening and working on my behalf. In every moment, Lord, let my prayers draw me closer to You and bring glory to Your name I pray, Amen and To God Be The Glory!

NOVEMBER 19. - "LEARN TO ACCEPT BOTH TRUTHS"

People Will Fail You, And You Will Fail People: Learn To Accept Both Truths

"Bear ye one another's burdens and so fulfill the law of Christ."
— Galatians 6:2 (KJV)

Life is a tapestry of relationships of friends, family, coworkers, and even strangers. Each connection holds the potential for joy, support, and love. But it also carries the reality of human imperfection. People will fail you. Sometimes their words will wound, their actions will disappoint, or their presence will be absent when you need them most. And in the same breath, you will fail others, unintentionally or otherwise. The truth is, no human being is perfect. We are all "work" in progress, learning as we go.

Understanding and accepting these truths frees you from bitterness and unrealistic expectations. When someone disappoints you, it is not necessarily an act of malice; often it is a reflection of their own struggles, limitations, or circumstances. Likewise, your own missteps do not define you permanently, they are opportunities to grow, seek forgiveness, and improve.

The Bible reminds us to bear one another's burdens. This does not mean excusing wrongdoing, but it does mean extending grace and understanding, recognizing that failure is part of the human experience. Accepting the imperfection in others and in ourselves creates space for compassion, patience, and reconciliation.

Embracing these truths also builds resilience. When you accept that people will fail you, you no longer rely on them to provide your ultimate peace, security, or happiness. Instead, you turn to God, who is faithful and unchanging. Your expectations shift from perfection to empathy, from control to trust in God's guidance.

Remember: learning to accept human failure is not a license for passivity; it is an invitation to practice patience, forgiveness, and humility. It's also a call to self-reflection to acknowledge your own failures, to seek forgiveness, and to strive toward being a source of grace for others. Embrace human imperfection with grace. Learn from it, grow from it, and extend God's love despite it.

Heavenly Father, thank You for Your unending patience and grace. Help me to accept that people will fail me, just as I will fail others. Teach me to respond with forgiveness, understanding, and love, rather than bitterness or anger. Strengthen my heart to extend grace when it is needed and to humbly admit my own shortcomings. May Your Spirit guide me to walk in empathy and compassion, reflecting Your love in every relationship. Guard me against disappointment turning into despair, and remind me that my ultimate security is found in You alone. In Jesus' Name, I pray, Amen and To God Be The Glory!

NOVEMBER 20. - "NO WEAPON FORMED AGAINST ME SHALL PROSPER"

"No weapon that is formed against thee shall prosper; and every tongue that shall rise against thee in judgment thou shalt condemn. This is the heritage of the servants of the Lord, and their righteousness is of me, saith the Lord." Isaiah 54:17 (KJV)

Life has a way of presenting trials that seem overwhelming. People who speak falsely against us, circumstances that appear stacked against us, and accusations that sting with the weight of injustice. Yet, as children of God, we are not left defenseless. Isaiah 54:17 boldly declares that no weapon formed against us shall prosper. The power of this verse is immense: it assures us that every attack, whether verbal, spiritual, or situational, is under the sovereign control of God.

The statement continues with even greater assurance: "every tongue that rises up against thee in judgment thou shalt condemn." This is a declaration of divine vindication. Those who rise against you, speaking lies or spreading false accusations, are not beyond the reach of God's justice. In His perfect timing, God Himself will bring every false accuser before His throne. The Lord has preordained that they will face a court where truth reigns supreme, and where their deceit will be exposed.

Beloved, it is essential to recognize that God's protection is both proactive and reactive. Not only does He shield you from the attacks that reach you, but He also assures you the privilege of seeing justice done, as He allows you to witness the downfall of those who have sought your harm. This is not vengeance born of anger, it is divine justice, a reflection of God's righteousness and perfect timing.

When we understand this truth, fear loses its grip. Anxiety over what others say or do diminishes because we are confident in the ultimate authority of God. Instead of reacting with bitterness or revenge, we can stand firm, knowing that every weapon raised against us is nullified, and every false tongue will be silenced in His court.

Heavenly Father, I thank You that no weapon formed against me shall prosper. I thank You for the assurance that every lie spoken against me will be judged by Your righteous hand. Strengthen my heart, Lord, to stand firm and unwavering in faith, even when accusations rise and enemies speak falsely. Help me to trust Your perfect timing, knowing that You will bring justice in Your court and vindicate me according to Your word. Let me remain steadfast, walking in peace and confidence, knowing that Your protection surrounds me and Your righteousness covers me. I decree that every plan of the enemy against my life is nullified in the mighty name of Jesus.

Amen and To God Be The Glory!

NOVEMBER 21. - "RESTORING HONOR AND REVERENCE"

"There once was a time the president was honored, police were respected, newborns were treasured, and the elderly were revered. Let's bring that back, can we?"

The longing for days when respect, honor, and reverence were not just ideals but lived realities is something many of us feel deeply. Society often changes, and sometimes, values that were once foundational seem to fade. But as believers, we are called to be beacons of light and agents of transformation, restoring dignity where it has been lost.

Scripture reminds us in Romans 13:7 (KJV): "Render therefore to all their dues: tribute to whom tribute is due; custom to whom custom; fear to whom fear; honour to whom honour."

This verse calls us to live intentionally, showing honor and respect to those God has placed in authority, to those who serve our communities, to the vulnerable, and to the wisdom of age. It is not about blind obedience or societal expectation. It is about reflecting the heart of God in our daily actions.

Respect begins in the heart. When we honor others, we acknowledge the image of God in them. When we treasure the young and uphold the elderly, we cultivate a society grounded in love, dignity, and divine order. Even when the world seems to drift from these values, we, as children of God, can model them. By doing so, we set the stage for revival, both in families and communities.

Let us also remember that restoration begins with prayer. We cannot rely solely on society to bring back honor, respect, and reverence; we must actively seek God's guidance and influence others by our example.

Heavenly Father, we thank You for the gift of life and the order You have established in society. Lord, awaken in us hearts of honor, respect, and reverence. Help us to treasure the young, uphold those who serve, and honor those in authority according to Your Word. Let our actions reflect Your heart and inspire others to return to a culture of love, dignity, and reverence. Restore what has been lost, Lord, and let Your kingdom values shine through us. In all that we do, may we glorify You and bring Your light to a world in need. In Jesus name I pray, Amen and To God Be The Glory!

NOVEMBER 22. - "REALIZING YOUR WORTH"

Once You Realize What You're Worth, Nothing Can Stop You

One of the greatest struggles many believers face is recognizing their true worth in Christ. The world constantly throws labels, insults, and unrealistic standards at us, attempting to diminish our value and make us feel less than who we really are. But the truth of God's Word tells us otherwise. Our worth is not determined by people, circumstances, or failures. It is anchored in Christ, sealed by His blood, and declared by His Word.

When you realize what you are worth in the eyes of God, everything changes. You stop settling for less than God's best. You stop allowing the enemy's lies to control your mind. You stop tolerating relationships, habits, and situations that tear you down. You begin to walk with a confidence that cannot be shaken, because your worth is no longer tied to opinions but rooted in God's eternal truth.

The Scripture declares: "I will praise thee; for I am fearfully and wonderfully made marvellous are thy works; and that my soul knoweth right well." – Psalm 139:14 (KJV)

David understood that his value was not in what men said about him but in how God created him. You were handcrafted by God Himself, designed with purpose, beauty, strength, and destiny. When you see yourself as God sees you, you won't allow anyone or anything to make you feel unworthy.

Realizing your worth doesn't mean arrogance; it means confidence in God's design and plan for your life. It means walking in authority, knowing that you are chosen, loved, redeemed, and equipped. Once you know your worth, nothing can stop you—not fear, not rejection, not failure, and not even the enemy himself. Because when God is for you, who can be against you? (Romans 8:31).

Heavenly Father, I thank You for creating me in Your image and for declaring that I am fearfully and wonderfully made. Help me to see myself as You see me—not through the lens of my mistakes or the opinions of others, but through the truth of Your Word. Teach me to walk in the confidence of my worth, knowing that I am loved, chosen, and redeemed by You. Strengthen me to reject the lies of the enemy and to boldly embrace the destiny You have set before me. Lord, I declare that once I realize my worth in You, nothing and no one can stop me from fulfilling my purpose. In Jesus' mighty name I pray.

Amen and To God Be The Glory!

NOVEMBER 23. - "TEARS OF THE SOUL"

The most painful tears are not the ones that fall from your eyes and cover your face. They're the ones that fall from your heart and cover your soul. Eye-tears are visible. Others can see them, wipe them, or ask what's wrong. But heart-tears are invisible. They flow in silence, in the deep places of your being where words cannot reach. These are the tears that come from betrayal, loss, disappointment, and the weight of unanswered questions. They are the tears that no tissue can dry because they do not stain the skin, they stain the soul.

David knew this kind of pain. In Psalm 34:18 (KJV), we read: "The Lord is nigh unto them that are of a broken heart; and saveth such as be of a contrite spirit." This verse is God's assurance that even when the world cannot see or understand the tears of your heart, He does. The Lord is near to those who cry silently in their spirits. He bends low to hear the whispers of your soul, the cries that never leave your lips.

The truth is, heart-tears often feel unbearable because they seem unending. They linger long after your eyes are dry. But here's the hope: God bottles every tear whether visible or hidden (Psalm 56:8). None go unnoticed. In His presence, there is healing for the wounds that no one else can see. The tears of your soul are not wasted; they water the ground where God will bring forth strength, growth, and a deeper faith.

When your soul feels drenched in pain, remember: God is closer than the tears themselves. He doesn't just wipe them away, He transforms them into testimonies. The tears that fall from your heart may feel like they're drowning you now, but in God's hands, they will become rivers of restoration and wells of joy.

Heavenly Father, You see the tears no one else can see. You know the pain that runs deeper than words and the weight that presses on my soul. Lord, I give You my hidden tears, the ones that no one else understands. Heal the broken places in my heart and restore my spirit with Your peace. Remind me that every tear I shed is seen and treasured by You. Turn my sorrow into strength and let my testimony shine brighter than my pain. I trust You to bring healing, hope, and renewal. In Jesus' name I pray.

Amen and To God Be The Glory!

NOVEMBER 24. - "SOME PEOPLE ARE JUST A CHAPTER ~ NOT THE ENTIRE STORY

Life is filled with relationships, some lasting a lifetime, and others for only a season. Sometimes, we desperately want certain people to stay with us through the entire journey, but God, in His infinite wisdom, knows they were only meant to play a role in a chapter, not the whole book. This truth can be painful, but it is also freeing, because God's plan for our lives is purposeful and complete, even when it doesn't align with our desires.

Think of Joseph in the book of Genesis. He had brothers who betrayed him, a master who trusted him but later imprisoned him, and fellow prisoners who forgot him. Yet every relationship, whether hurtful or supportive, was part of a chapter that carried Joseph toward his destiny, to save a nation and his own family. Had Joseph clung to bitterness or longed for those who had left or harmed him, he would have missed the greater plan God was writing in his life.

The Bible reminds us in Ecclesiastes 3:1 (KJV): "To everything there is a season, and a time to every purpose under the heaven." Some people are meant to teach us lessons, others to help us grow, and still others to show us the way forward. But not everyone is meant to stay forever. Releasing them with grace allows us to step into the next season God has prepared.

We must learn to trust God with the pen of our lives. When He turns the page, it's not to erase what was, but to build upon it. The chapter may close, but the story continues, and with God as the Author, the ending will always be filled with hope and purpose.

Heavenly Father, thank You for being the Author and Finisher of my faith. Help me to trust Your wisdom when people leave my life, knowing that every chapter has its purpose. Give me peace when I want to hold on and courage to let go when it is time. Teach me to value the lessons of each season and to keep my eyes fixed on You, the One who writes my story with love and intention. May my heart remain soft, free of bitterness, and full of gratitude for what was, and hopeful for what is to come. In Jesus' name I pray.

Amen and To God Be The Glory!

NOVEMBER 25. - "THE POWER OF PERSISTENCE AND CONSISTENCY"

"If you are persistent, you will get it. If you are consistent, you will keep it."

In life, there are many dreams, goals, and promises that God places in our hearts. Often, the difference between those who see them fulfilled and those who let them slip away lies in two powerful virtues: persistence and consistency.

Persistence is the determination to push through obstacles, to keep knocking when doors seem closed, and to continue sowing even when the ground looks dry. Persistence is rooted in faith that God will honor the labor, the tears, and the prayers you pour into the vision He has given you. Without persistence, many would give up right before their breakthrough.

Consistency, on the other hand, is what sustains the blessing once it arrives. Too many times, people achieve something great through persistence but fail to remain consistent in their stewardship. Consistency requires discipline, daily devotion, and commitment to doing the right things repeatedly even when the excitement fades. It is not enough to reach a blessing; we must remain faithful to keep and multiply it.

The Bible says in Galatians 6:9 (KJV): "And let us not be weary in well doing: for in due season we shall reap, if we faint not." This verse speaks to persistence, to keep sowing, keep praying, keep obeying. But it also speaks to consistency, don't grow weary in well-doing, keep pressing forward, and the harvest will not only come, but it will remain.

God Himself models both persistence and consistency. He persistently pursued us in love, even when we strayed, and He consistently provides new mercies every morning (Lamentations 3:22-23). If we are to live like Him, we must embrace both.

So, keep pressing forward with persistence to obtain the promises of God. And once He blesses you, stay consistent in prayer, in obedience, and in your walk with Him, so that what He has entrusted to you will remain and bear fruit.

Heavenly Father, I thank You for reminding me of the importance of persistence and consistency. Help me to be persistent in pursuing the vision You have placed in my heart, and never to give up, no matter the obstacles. Once I obtain what You have promised, give me the strength and discipline to remain consistent, so that I may be a faithful steward of every blessing You entrust to me. Teach me to walk daily in Your will, to persevere in faith, and to remain steadfast in obedience. In Jesus' mighty name I pray.

Amen and To God Be The Glory!

NOVEMBER 26. - "A HEART OVERFLOWING WITH GRATITUDE ~ THANKSGIVING BLESSINGS"

Thanksgiving is more than a holiday; it is a posture of the heart. Gratitude shifts our perspective from what we lack to the abundance of blessings God has already poured into our lives. In a world filled with challenges, it is easy to focus on what went wrong, what we lost, or what we are still waiting on God to do. Yet the Bible reminds us to "give thanks in all circumstances; for this is God's will for you in Christ Jesus" (1 Thessalonians 5:18, NIV).

Notice that the scripture does not say to give thanks for all circumstances, but in them. Life is not always kind, and trials can feel overwhelming, but our thanksgiving is rooted not in our situation, but in our Savior. Gratitude acknowledges God's goodness even when life is hard. It is an act of worship that tells the Lord, "I trust You, even here."

Thanksgiving realigns our spirit. When we begin to recount God's blessings starting with His provision, His protection, His faithfulness, His mercy, His unchanging love, our hearts grow lighter, and our faith grows stronger. Gratitude unlocks peace, fuels hope and draws us closer to the heart of God.

This Thanksgiving, let us not only enjoy the fellowship of family, the warmth of food, and the joy of gathering, but let us also pause to intentionally thank God for the gift of life, the strength to endure, the grace that saves us, and the eternal hope we have in Christ Jesus.

Heavenly Father, on this Thanksgiving, I bow my heart before You with gratitude. Thank You for waking me up this morning, for the breath in my lungs, and for the strength to keep moving forward. Thank You for family, for friends, for shelter, for provision, and for the countless blessings I often take for granted.

Lord, I also thank You for the trials that shaped me, for the tears that drew me closer to You, and for the storms that proved You are my anchor. Teach me to always find reasons to give thanks, even when life feels heavy. Help me to live with a grateful heart every day, not just in this season.

Most of all, I thank You for Jesus, the greatest gift of all, who gave His life that I might live eternally with You. May my gratitude overflow into kindness, generosity, and love toward others. In Jesus' mighty name I pray, Amen and To God Be The Glory!

NOVEMBER 27. - "LOVING YOURSELF GOD'S WAY"

The journey of love begins within. Often, we are taught to love others, but sometimes we forget that the commandment to "love your neighbor as yourself" (Mark 12:31) assumes we first love ourselves. True, godly love for self isn't rooted in arrogance or selfishness, it's rooted in seeing ourselves the way God sees us.

"Loving yourself starts with liking yourself."

When you like yourself, you accept who God created you to be. You stop comparing yourself to others and start embracing the unique gifts and qualities the Lord has given you. God did not make a mistake when He formed you in your mother's womb (Psalm 139:13–14).

"Which starts with respecting yourself."

Respect is an acknowledgment of worth. When you respect yourself, you set boundaries, make decisions that honor God, and refuse to settle for less than what He has promised you. Respect means you will no longer compromise your values just to gain approval, because you already have the approval of your Heavenly Father.

"Which starts with thinking of yourself in a positive way."

Your thoughts shape your life. Proverbs 23:7 reminds us, "For as he thinketh in his heart, so is he." When your mind is filled with negativity, lies, and doubt, you rob yourself of peace. But when you renew your mind with God's Word (Romans 12:2), you begin to walk in confidence, joy, and strength. Thinking positively about yourself isn't empty self-talk, it's agreeing with what God already says about you.

When you think of yourself in a positive, godly way, it will lead to respect. When you respect yourself, you'll begin to truly like who you are. And when you like yourself, you can fully love yourself the way God intended without guilt, shame, or comparison. That love will naturally flow outward to others, fulfilling the commandment of Christ.

"I will praise thee; for I am fearfully and wonderfully made: marvellous are thy works; and that my soul knoweth right well." Psalm 139:14 (KJV)

Heavenly Father, thank You for creating me in Your image and for loving me unconditionally. Help me to see myself as You see me as precious, valuable, and chosen. Teach me to think positively about myself according to Your Word, to respect myself by walking in integrity, to like myself for who I am, and to love myself with the same grace You extend to me daily. May this love overflow into how I treat others, reflecting Your light in all I do. Strengthen me, Lord, to never forget my worth in You. In Jesus' Name, I pray.

Amen and To God Be The Glory!

NOVEMBER 28. - "GUARDING OUR WORDS AND OUR LOYALTIES"

The phrase "Don't tell me what they said about me until you can tell me what you said" cuts deep into the heart of loyalty, truth, and accountability. It is easy for people to repeat gossip, carry half-truths, or highlight the words of others without ever acknowledging their own role in the conversation. But God calls His children to a higher standard, a standard of honesty, integrity, and peace.

In moments when someone comes to you with what "they said," the real test is not in the words of others, but in how you responded. Did you defend, correct, or stand for truth? Or did you remain silent and let the negativity spread? Our silence can sometimes be just as harmful as agreement. True friendship, and even more, true discipleship, requires us to speak life when others speak death, and to protect the dignity of others rather than tearing them down.

The Bible reminds us: A perverse person stirs up conflict, and a gossip separates close friends." Proverbs 16:28 (NIV)

Gossip thrives when people refuse to confront it. But the person of wisdom and integrity doesn't just reject gossip; they actively choose to build others up. Instead of joining the chorus of negativity, you need to become a shield, a voice of truth, compassion, and defense.

So, the next time someone comes to you with "they said," remember this: the real measure of their heart is found in what they said back. Did they defend you? Did they shut the door to slander? Or did they let your name be tarnished for the sake of fitting in? God is calling us all to be the kind of people who defend others in their absence, not just compliment them in their presence.

Heavenly Father, teach me to be a person of truth and loyalty. Help me to shut the door on gossip and stand firm in defending those who are not present to speak for themselves. Give me the courage to use my words to heal and not to harm, to protect and not to expose myself in ignorance. Lord may my tongue always be a vessel of Your love, and may my heart never be entangled in the snares of gossip. Help me to remember that I will give an account for every word I speak. Let my words honor You and uplift others. In Jesus' name, I pray.

Amen and To God Be The Glory!

NOVEMBER 29. - "THE STRENGTH AND ANOINTING OF THE LORD"

The Word of God assures us in Psalm 89:21: "My hand will sustain him; surely my arm will strengthen him." This is a divine reminder that we do not stand in our own strength but in the mighty hand of God. His sustaining hand doesn't just lift us up temporarily, it holds us securely, guides us purposefully, and strengthens us continually. When life feels overwhelming, it is His everlasting arms that keep us from falling.

The psalmist continues in Psalm 92:10: "But my horn you have exalted like that of a wild ox; I have been anointed with fresh oil." Here we see the evidence of God's empowerment. The "horn" in Scripture symbolizes strength, authority, and victory. Like a wild ox, untamed and powerful, God grants His children resilience and might beyond human limitation. The fresh oil poured upon us is the anointing of the Holy Spirit, renewing us, refreshing us, and setting us apart for His purpose.

Together, these scriptures testify of God's intimate involvement in the lives of His people. He sustains us when we are weak, strengthens us when we feel faint, exalts us when we are overlooked, and anoints us with power to fulfill His calling. This is not just about enduring; it is about thriving under the overflow of His Spirit.

When the enemy seeks to wear us down, God sustains. When doubt whispers, God strengthens. When trials strip us of dignity, God exalts. And when dryness threatens to consume us, His oil of gladness and fresh anointing revives us. What a faithful God we serve!

"But you, LORD, are a shield around me, my glory, the One who lifts my head high."

Psalm 3:3

Heavenly Father, I thank You for Your sustaining hand and Your mighty arm that strengthens me daily. Thank You for exalting me above my circumstances and anointing me with fresh oil from Your Spirit. When I feel weary, remind me that Your strength is made perfect in my weakness. Help me to walk boldly, not in my own power, but in the authority and anointing You have placed upon my life. May my life continually glorify You as I stand in the strength of Your hand. In Jesus' name I pray, Amen and To God Be The Glory!

NOVEMBER 30. - "MOTIVATION AND GOOD HABITS"

Motivation is What Gets You Started. Habit Will Keep You Going.

Motivation is powerful, it sparks the beginning of something new. It is that inner fire, that burst of energy, that makes us say, "I can do this." But the truth is, motivation alone is not enough to carry us through the storms, trials, or even the daily routines of life. Feelings come and go, energy rises and falls, but habits, those consistent, disciplined actions rooted in faith are what anchor us.

In our spiritual walk, motivation may push us to pray, read the Word, or attend church, but it is the habit of consistently seeking God that sustains us. Jesus Himself set the perfect example. Scripture tells us that "very early in the morning, while it was still dark, Jesus got up, left the house and went off to a solitary place, where he prayed" (Mark 1:35, NIV). This was not an occasional act driven by emotion, it was His holy habit.

When we build godly habits, such as prayer, studying Scripture, worship, forgiveness, and service, we strengthen our spiritual muscles. Over time, these habits shape our character and bring stability when motivation fades. Habits rooted in God's Word become the foundation that carries us when we feel weary, discouraged, or unmotivated.

Think of it like planting seeds: motivation may plant the seed, but habit waters it daily until the fruit grows. The Apostle Paul reminds us, "Let us not become weary in doing good, for at the proper time we will reap a harvest if we do not give up" (Galatians 6:9, NIV).

So today, ask yourself: Are you depending only on bursts of motivation, or are you cultivating habits that will keep you steadfast? Motivation may get you started, but it is godly discipline, daily habits anchored in Christ that will keep you going until you finish the race.

Heavenly Father, thank You for the gift of new beginnings and the spark of motivation that moves us forward. But Lord, help me not to rely only on my feelings or bursts of energy. Teach me the power of discipline, of consistent godly habits that keep me rooted in You. Strengthen me to seek You daily in prayer, in Your Word, and in obedience. Let my habits be aligned with Your will so that I may persevere through every season of life. In Jesus' name I pray, Amen and To God Be The Glory!

DECEMBER INTRODUCTION

December – Finding Light in the Season of Reflection

As the year draws to a close, December often brings a unique mix of emotions. For some, it is a season of celebration, joy, and anticipation for new beginnings. For others, it can be a time of reflection, sorrow, or unanswered questions about life's journey. Regardless of where you find yourself, this month invites us to pause, reflect, and intentionally seek God's wisdom for the challenges we face. Life does not pause for the calendar, and neither do the problems we encounter, but God's Word offers timeless guidance, comfort, and clarity for every situation.

In this December devotional, we will focus on discovering biblical answers to life's pressing problems from the weight of disappointment and fear to the struggles of relationships, finances, and personal purpose. Each devotional is designed to help you draw nearer to God, uncover His solutions, and apply His principles to real-life situations. The goal is not only to provide encouragement but also to empower you with practical, faith-filled steps so that you can navigate challenges with confidence, hope, and peace.

As we approach the end of the year, remember that every problem carries a lesson, every challenge holds an opportunity for growth, and every situation is an invitation to deepen your trust in God. His Word remains a lamp to our feet and a light to our path, guiding us through darkness and uncertainty.

"Trust in the Lord with all your heart, and lean not on your own understanding; in all your ways acknowledge Him, and He shall direct your paths." Proverbs 3:5-6 (NKJV)

Heavenly Father, as we journey through this final month of the year, we come before You with open hearts and minds. Lord, help us to release the burdens we carry and to trust fully in Your wisdom and guidance. Illuminate our paths with Your Word, grant us discernment in times of uncertainty, and fill us with peace as we face the challenges before us. Teach us to rely on Your promises, embrace Your solutions, and walk boldly in faith, knowing that You are with us in every situation. Thank You for Your unending love, grace, and provision. May this devotional month draw us closer to You and prepare us to step into the new year renewed, empowered, and victorious. In Jesus name, we pray. Amen and To God Be The Glory!

DECEMBER 1. - "THE POWER OF PLANTING A SEED"

In our walk with Christ, we sometimes feel an urgency to make others see and understand the truth of God's Word immediately. We speak, we plead, and we explain, but the reality is this: no matter how passionately we share the message, we cannot force someone to receive what their heart is not yet prepared to embrace. Spiritual growth, like natural growth, has its seasons.

Jesus spoke often about the power of seeds. In 1 Corinthians 3:6-7 (KJV), Paul reminds us, "I have planted, Apollos watered; but God gave the increase. So then neither is he that planteth anything, neither he that watereth; but God that giveth the increase." This scripture teaches us that our responsibility is not to make the seed grow, but to faithfully plant and sometimes water. The life-giving power belongs to God alone.

Planting a seed may seem small or insignificant in the moment. Whether it's a kind word, a prayer whispered over someone's life, a testimony shared, or simply living out Christ's love in front of them. Yet, what we plant in faith may one day take root in the soil of their heart. We may never see the full fruit of what God does with that seed, but we can trust His timing and His Spirit to bring it to life.

Think of the farmer: he cannot make the seed sprout overnight. He plants it in hope, waters it diligently, and trusts God for the growth. Likewise, when we share the Word of God, we are not responsible for the harvest, only for the faithfulness of planting. Even if the person seems uninterested, hardened, or resistant, the seed of God's truth has been deposited, and in the right season, it can break through.

So let us not grow discouraged when our words are not immediately received. What feels like rejection today may become a testimony tomorrow. What feels like wasted effort may one day bear fruit that impacts generations. Never underestimate the power of a seed planted in faith.

Heavenly Father, thank You for entrusting us with the privilege of planting seeds of Your Word in the lives of others. Remind us that our role is to share in obedience and love, not to control the outcome. Help us to be patient, faithful, and consistent, knowing that You are the one who brings the increase. May every seed we plant through our words, our actions, and our prayers, take root in Your timing and bear fruit for Your kingdom. Give us peace when we do not see results right away and strength to keep sowing in faith. In Jesus' name we pray, Amen and To God Be The Glory!

DECEMBER 2. - "PURPOSE IN THE PAIN"

Nothing that touches our lives slips past the sovereignty of God. Even the seasons that leave us questioning, "Why this? Why now?" are woven into His divine plan. Everything God allows, whether it's a blessing that fills our hearts with joy or a trial that brings us to our knees, comes with a purpose.

Sometimes, we mistake hardship for abandonment, but in reality, it can be God's greatest tool for transformation. The deep valleys teach us to lean on His strength, the mistakes remind us of our need for His grace, and the wounds carve out compassion for others. What feels like loss can become the soil where spiritual growth takes root.

Joseph's life is a testimony to this truth. Betrayed by his brothers, sold into slavery, and wrongfully imprisoned, he endured years of suffering. Yet, looking back, Joseph declared to his brothers: "But as for you, ye thought evil against me; but God meant it unto good" Genesis 50:20 (KJV)

Our greatest errors can become lessons that anchor us in humility. Our deepest pain can become the very tool God uses to shape us into someone stronger, wiser, and more compassionate. In His hands, nothing is wasted.

If you are walking through a painful chapter right now, remember, God is not finished with your story. Every detail, even the parts you wish you could erase, can be redeemed for your good and His glory.

Heavenly Father, I truly thank You for being the Master Potter, shaping me even through my mistakes and my pain. Help me to trust that everything You allow has purpose, even when I don't understand it. Use every tear, every failure, and every hardship to mold me into the person You've called me to be. Give me faith to see beyond the present moment and hope to believe in Your redemptive plan. In Jesus' name I pray, Amen and To God Be The Glory!

DECEMBER 3. - "THE FOOL AND THE PRUDENT"

"A fool despiseth his father's instruction: but he that regardeth reproof is prudent." Proverbs 15:5 (KJV)

When we read Proverbs 15:5, we find a sharp contrast between two kinds of people: the fool and the prudent. The fool rejects instruction, especially from a father or one in authority, while the prudent heart receives correction and grows from it. This proverb is not only about the parent-child relationship but also about how we respond to guidance, wisdom, and correction from God and others in authority over us.

A fool despises instruction because pride blinds the heart. Pride whispers, "I don't need advice. I already know best." But wisdom teaches us that correction is not punishment, it is protection. Instruction is not rejection, it is redirection. God places voices of authority, whether parents, mentors, pastors, or even His Word, in our lives to help us avoid pitfalls and grow into maturity.

The prudent person does not view reproof as an attack but as a gift. Correction may sting in the moment, but it saves us from greater pain later. Just as a loving parent disciplines a child to keep them safe, so God disciplines His children to keep them on the right path. Hebrews 12:11 reminds us, "Now no chastening for the present seemeth to be joyous, but grievous: nevertheless, afterward it yieldeth the peaceable fruit of righteousness unto them which are exercised thereby."

To despise instruction is to close the door to growth. To embrace it is to open the door to wisdom. Every reproof received humbly is an opportunity for transformation. The prudent learn not just from their own mistakes but from the counsel of others.

Let us ask ourselves: when God corrects us through His Word, or when someone He has placed in our lives gives us instruction, how do we respond? Do we become defensive, offended, and resistant? Or do we pause, listen, and allow God to refine us? The difference determines whether we walk the path of foolishness or wisdom.

Heavenly Father, I thank You for Your Word that corrects, instructs, and guides me. Forgive me for the times I have rejected wisdom and despised correction out of pride. Help me to have a teachable heart, one that welcomes reproof and instruction with humility. Give me discernment to recognize Your voice, whether through Scripture, through those You place in my life, or through the conviction of the Holy Spirit. May I grow in prudence and walk daily in Your wisdom. Keep me from the path of foolishness and lead me into the peaceable fruit of righteousness. In Jesus' name, I pray.

Amen and To God Be The Glory!

DECEMBER 4. - "PRUNE THOSE LIMBS FOR PEACE AND GROWTH"

In life, relationships can either nurture us or drain us. Some people uplift, encourage, and bring us closer to God's purpose, while others create confusion, manipulation, and discouragement. The phrase reminds us: "Avoid people who mess with your head, people who say things to upset you, people who want you to make them a priority but won't do the same for you, people who don't apologize. You don't need these kinds of people. Avoid them. Prune those names."

This is not about arrogance or unforgiveness. It is about stewardship of your spirit, your peace, and your destiny. The Bible teaches us to use discernment in our relationships. Proverbs 13:20 (KJV) says, "He that walketh with wise men shall be wise: but a companion of fools shall be destroyed." The people we walk with influence our thoughts, our peace, and even our spiritual growth.

Jesus Himself modeled this principle. He loved all, but He did not give equal access to all. He preached to the multitudes, sent out the seventy, discipled the twelve, but allowed only three (Peter, James, and John) into His most intimate moments. Why? Because access matters. Not everyone deserves a front-row seat in your life. Some must be loved from a distance.

Pruning is not easy. It requires courage to let go of unhealthy ties and wisdom to discern who is not aligned with God's will for your life. Some people thrive on drama, manipulation, or selfishness. They drain you without pouring back. They wound with words but refuse to repent. God does not want you to remain entangled in such cycles. Instead, He calls you to guard your heart (Proverbs 4:23) and pursue peace (Romans 12:18).

When you prune relationships that hinder, you make room for divine connections—people who will walk with you, encourage you, and sharpen you in the Lord. Remember, even a garden cannot bear fruit if weeds are not pulled out. God sometimes calls us to prune in order to grow.

Heavenly Father, I thank You for wisdom and discernment in my relationships. Teach me to recognize those who are not healthy for my spirit and give me the strength to release them in love. Help me to guard my heart, to walk with wise and godly people, and to prune away what hinders my peace and growth. Surround me with those who uplift me, honor You, and encourage me to fulfill my purpose. Lord, I surrender my relationships to You and ask for Your guidance in every connection. In Jesus' name, Amen and To God Be The Glory!

DECEMBER 5. - "BEING STUCK WHERE YOU DON'T BELONG IS PAINFUL"

Growth is Painful, Change is Painful, but Nothing is as Painful as Staying Stuck Somewhere You Don't Belong

Growth is never comfortable. It stretches us, challenges us, and forces us to leave behind what feels safe and familiar. Change can be even more unsettling, because it often requires letting go of people, places, or habits that no longer align with God's plan for our lives. Yet as difficult as both growth and change may be, the deepest pain comes from remaining stuck in a place God never intended for us to stay.

Many times, fear keeps us bound, fear of the unknown, fear of rejection, or fear of failure. But God did not call us to live in stagnation. He calls us forward, from glory to glory, and from faith to faith. When we resist His leading, we remain trapped in cycles that drain our spirit and rob us of His best. Staying stuck can look like holding onto toxic relationships, clinging to old mindsets, or refusing to step into new opportunities because they feel uncertain.

The children of Israel faced this same struggle. Though they were delivered from slavery in Egypt, many longed to return to what was familiar rather than endure the painful process of transition toward the Promised Land. Their fear of the wilderness blinded them to the fact that staying in Egypt was far more painful than moving forward with God.

Scripture reminds us: "Forget the former things; do not dwell on the past. See, I am doing a new thing! Now it springs up; do you not perceive it? I am making a way in the wilderness and streams in the wasteland." Isaiah 43:18-19 (NIV)

God is not content with us staying stuck. He wants us to walk in His purpose, even if it requires painful pruning, stretching, and transformation. The discomfort you feel in growth is temporary, but the fruit it produces is eternal. Staying in a place where you don't belong may feel easier in the short term, but it only leads to emptiness and regret.

Today, let this be a reminder that every tear, every struggle, and every uncomfortable step you take in the process of change is God positioning you for His greater plan. Trust Him enough to move forward.

Heavenly Father, I thank You for loving me too much to let me stay stuck where I don't belong. Even when growth feels painful and change feels overwhelming, I know You are shaping me for greater things. Give me the courage to release what no longer serves Your purpose in my life and the faith to step into the unknown with You. Strengthen me to trust that the pain of growth is far less than the pain of disobedience or stagnation. Help me to see Your "new thing" springing forth in my life and to walk boldly into it. In Jesus' name, Amen and To God Be The Glory!

DECEMBER 6. - "THE SPIRIT WHO INTERCEDED FOR US"

"And he that searcheth the hearts knoweth what is the mind of the Spirit, because he maketh intercession for the saints according to the will of God." Romans 8:27 (KJV)

There are moments in life when words fail us. Times when the burdens are so heavy, the pain so deep, or the confusion so strong that we do not know what to say in prayer. In these moments, God does not leave us helpless or unheard. Romans 8:27 reminds us of the powerful truth that the Spirit of God steps in and intercedes on our behalf.

The verse begins with the assurance that "He that searcheth the hearts"that is, God Himself ~ He knows the depths of our inner being. Even when we cannot articulate our struggles, God searches the heart. He knows not only what we are going through but also what we need. He understands the silent cries, the unspoken fears, and the hidden battles.

But what makes this truth even more profound is that the Spirit aligns our unformed prayers with the will of God. Sometimes, what we ask for may not be what is best for us, but the Spirit intercedes in such a way that our requests are brought into harmony with the Father's perfect plan. This means that every prayer, even the ones prayed with trembling lips or a weary heart, is refined by the Spirit and presented in a way that pleases God.

This is a source of great comfort. It means we are never praying alone. It means our weaknesses in prayer are covered by divine strength. It means that even when we don't know the words to say, heaven hears the Spirit's intercession on our behalf.

So today, rest in this assurance: You are not unheard. You are not forgotten. The Spirit Himself is interceding for you, and the Father who knows all things is working it out according to His will and for your good.

Heavenly Father, I thank You that even when I don't have the words to express my heart, You know me fully. Thank You for the gift of Your Spirit who intercedes on my behalf. Lord, help me to trust that every prayer I lift is heard and perfected according to Your will. Teach me to rest in the confidence that I am never alone in prayer, and that Your Spirit is working all things together for my good and Your glory. Strengthen my faith and give me peace as I wait on Your perfect timing. In Jesus' name, I pray.

Amen and To God Be The Glory!

DECEMBER 7. - "SAVED BY A THREAD"

Life has a way of bringing us to places where our strength feels spent, our hope seems dim, and our grip on faith feels as fragile as a single thread. Yet, in those moments, what we are holding on to matters more than how tightly we can hold. If the thread you're clinging to is the hem of Christ's garment, then even your weakest grasp connects you to His limitless power.

In Mark 5:25–29, we read about the woman with the issue of blood. For twelve long years, she suffered, tried every earthly solution, and spent all she had without finding relief. She was not only physically broken but emotionally and spiritually weary. Yet, she believed: "If I may touch but His clothes, I shall be whole." Her faith was not in her own strength but in the healing virtue that flowed from Jesus. And with the touch of a trembling hand, power went out from Him, and she was made whole.

This story teaches us that when we are hanging on by a thread, it is not the size of our faith but the source of our faith that makes the difference. A small touch on the hem of His garment carried enough power to change a life forever. Likewise, your weakest prayer, your faintest cry, and your weary grip are still mighty when connected to Jesus.

Sometimes God allows us to come to the end of ourselves so that we learn to cling to Him alone. That "thread" is not the last strand of your strength, it is the beginning of His. The hem of His garment represents both access and humility. You may not feel strong enough to stand tall in faith, but even bowed down in desperation, reaching for His hem is enough.

So, when you feel like you are unraveling, don't let go of that thread. If it's the hem of His garment, healing, restoration, and breakthrough are already flowing your way.

"For she said, If I may touch but His clothes, I shall be whole. And straightway the fountain of her blood was dried up; and she felt in her body that she was healed of that plague." Mark 5:28–29 (KJV)

Heavenly Father, I thank You that even in my weakest moments, I am never without hope when I am holding onto You. Lord, when life feels heavy and my strength is gone, help me to reach out in faith, even if all I can grasp is the hem of Your garment. Teach me to trust not in my own ability but in Your power that never fails. Just as You healed the woman who touched You in faith, I ask that You bring healing, restoration, and peace into my life. Strengthen me to hold on, and remind me that as long as I am clinging to You, I cannot fall. In Jesus' name, Amen and To God Be The Glory!

DECEMBER 8. - "RAIN ONLY MATTERS IF THERE ARE SEEDS IN THE GROUND"

When it rains, it is a blessing. It nourishes the soil, refreshes the land, and brings forth growth. Yet, the rain only truly benefits those who have taken the time to plant seeds. A farmer who has sown nothing can watch the rain come and go, but it produces no harvest for him. Spiritually, this is a powerful truth: the blessings of God's outpouring are most evident in the lives of those who have sown in faith, obedience, prayer, and perseverance.

The Bible says in Galatians 6:7–9 (KJV): "Be not deceived; God is not mocked: for whatsoever a man soweth, that shall he also reap.

For he that soweth to his flesh shall of the flesh reap corruption; but he that soweth to the Spirit shall of the Spirit reap life everlasting.

And let us not be weary in well doing: for in due season we shall reap, if we faint not."

The rain of God's favor, His provision, His anointing, and His opportunities is constant. But it is only meaningful to those who have seeds. Whether seeds of faith, generosity, love, or diligence in the ground. If you've prayed, fasted, believed, served others, and walked faithfully with God, then the rain that falls will cause those seeds to sprout and bring forth a harvest.

If, however, there are no seeds in the soil, the rain may refresh the land, but it won't produce fruit. That is why we must continually plant through obedience, acts of kindness, service, and prayer. Every seed matters. Every seed carries potential. And when the heavens open and the rain comes, those who have trusted God with their sowing will rejoice in the abundance of the harvest.

So, do not despise the small seeds you plant today. Your prayers, your sacrifices, your acts of faith may seem hidden in the soil, but God sees. And when His rain comes, you will reap more than you imagined, because He is the Lord of the harvest.

Heavenly Father, thank You for being the God who sends the rain in due season. Help me to be diligent in sowing seeds of faith, love, obedience, and righteousness into the ground of my life. Teach me not to grow weary in well-doing, but to trust that every seed planted in You will bring forth a harvest. Lord, prepare me for Your outpouring, and let the rain of Your Spirit cause my seeds to grow into a testimony of Your goodness. In Jesus' mighty name I pray.

Amen and To God Be The Glory!

DECEMBER 9. - "PRIORITIZING PEACE AND REST IN GOD"

There's nothing wrong with taking a break from everything and concentrating on yourself. We live in a world that constantly demands more from us, our time, our energy, our hearts. Many of us feel the weight of responsibility for others, trying to fix what is broken around us, soothe every conflict, and carry every burden. But God never asked us to carry the whole world on our shoulders, that role belongs only to Him.

Jesus Himself modeled the importance of stepping away to rest. The Bible tells us in Mark 6:31 (KJV): "And he said unto them, Come ye yourselves apart into a desert place, and rest a while: for there were many coming and going, and they had no leisure so much as to eat." Even Jesus, the Son of God, recognized the need for solitude, rest, and time to recharge in the presence of the Father.

When we neglect our own well-being, we run on empty and eventually burn out. Trying to please everyone and fix everything not only drains us but also takes away from the peace God intends for us to enjoy. Remember: peace of mind is not selfish, it is stewardship. You are responsible for caring for the vessel God has given you.

Prioritizing your happiness and peace of mind is not about ignoring others, but about creating balance. It is about recognizing that you cannot pour into others if you are running dry. God wants you to rest in His presence, to allow Him to restore your soul, and to remind you that the joy of the Lord is your strength, not the approval or happiness of others.

So, pause. Breathe. Take that break. Lay your burdens at the feet of Jesus and let Him carry what you cannot. True peace and happiness are found when you release control and allow God to be God in your life.

Heavenly Father, I thank You for reminding me that it is okay to rest. Lord, I release the pressure of always trying to fix, please, and carry everything on my own. Teach me to make my peace and happiness in You a priority, so that I may be refreshed and renewed. Help me to trust You with what is broken and to rest in Your presence without guilt or fear. Fill me with Your joy, restore my soul, and remind me daily that my peace comes from You alone. In Jesus' name, I pray.

Amen and To God Be The Glory!

DECEMBER 10. - "MY EMERGENCY CONTACT IS JESUS"

There are moments in life when loneliness tries to weigh us down. When forms ask for an "emergency contact" and the reality of our singleness stares us in the face. But what if we shift our perspective? What if, instead of seeing it as a lack, we see it as an opportunity to declare our absolute dependence on God?

The phrase, "I am so single that when you ask for an emergency contact, I put down Jesus," is more than just humor, it's a profound truth. Jesus is not only our Savior but also our ultimate First Responder. Before family, before friends, before anyone else can show up, He is already present. He is "a very present help in trouble" (Psalm 46:1 KJV).

When everyone else may fail to answer the call, Jesus never misses it. He doesn't have voicemail, He doesn't put us on hold, and He doesn't screen our cries. Psalm 50:15 (KJV) reminds us: "Call upon me in the day of trouble; I will deliver thee, and thou shalt glorify me." He is not just our emergency contact; He is our constant companion.

Being single does not mean being alone, because God has promised, "I will never leave you nor forsake you" (Hebrews 13:5 KJV). So, whether you are filling out paperwork, facing trials, or simply longing for companionship, you can rest knowing Jesus is on call 24/7. His line is never busy. His response time is immediate. His help is perfect.

Let this truth encourage you: you may not have a spouse to write down or family nearby, but you have the King of Kings watching over you. And if Jesus is your emergency contact, then you are always safe, always loved, and always covered.

Father, I thank You that I am never truly alone. In moments where life reminds me of my singleness or my lack of human support, help me to remember that You are my ever-present help. You are my protector, my provider, and my comforter. Teach me to lean on You not just in emergencies but in every moment of my life. Let my heart rest in the assurance that I can call on You and You will answer. Strengthen me with Your presence and help me rejoice in the gift of having You as my ultimate contact, companion, and covering. In Jesus' name, I pray.

Amen and To God Be The Glory!

DECEMBER 11. - "THERE IS NO SUCH THING AS A HOPELESS SITUATION"

Life often brings us moments where the weight of circumstances feels unbearable. There are times when everything seems to be falling apart, relationships strained, finances depleted, health declining, or doors of opportunity slamming shut. In those moments, it is easy to label the situation as hopeless. Yet as children of God, we must remember there is no such thing as a hopeless situation when God is involved.

The truth is, every single circumstance in your life can change in an instant because God is sovereign, powerful, and faithful. What seems like the end for you is just the beginning of what God is about to do. He specializes in turning dead ends into new beginnings and impossibilities into testimonies.

Think of Joseph in the pit and prison, forgotten by men but never forgotten by God. What looked like a hopeless life of slavery became the very pathway to the palace. Think of the Israelites standing before the Red Sea, hemmed in by Pharaoh's army. Humanly speaking, their situation was impossible, but God split the waters and made a way where there was no way.

When we face situations that appear hopeless, God is not asking us to figure out the "how." He is asking us to trust His ability, timing, and purpose. What looks final to you is never final with Him. Circumstances may shift, people may walk away, resources may dry up—but God remains the unchanging source of miracles.

"For with God nothing shall be impossible." Luke 1:37 (KJV)

This verse reminds us that no matter the difficulty, God's power has no limits. What seems unchangeable is only waiting for His divine touch.

Heavenly Father, I thank You that no situation in my life is beyond Your reach. When I feel trapped by circumstances, remind me that You are the God of the impossible. Strengthen my faith to trust You even when I cannot see a way forward. Turn every dead end into a testimony of Your power and love. I declare that my life, my family, my health, and my future are in Your hands, and in You there is always hope. In Jesus' mighty name I pray.

Amen and To God Be The Glory!

DECEMBER 12. - "WHY THEY DON'T ASK YOUR SIDE"

Some people never ask for your side of the story because the version they heard fits the narrative they've already chosen to believe. Their opinion of you is shaped not by truth, but by what aligns with how they want to feel about you. This can be painful, especially when your name is spoken against, your character is misunderstood, and your heart is judged unfairly.

But the Word of God reminds us that the opinions of people do not define our worth or identity, God does. In moments where voices rise against us, we can rest in the assurance that He knows the whole story. He sees beyond the gossip, the assumptions, and the one-sided narratives.

"No weapon that is formed against thee shall prosper; and every tongue that shall rise against thee in judgment thou shalt condemn. This is the heritage of the servants of the LORD, and their righteousness is of me, saith the LORD." Isaiah 54:17 (KJV)

This verse is a promise that the tongues rising against you, whether through lies, slander, or half-truths, will not prevail. The truth may not always be revealed in the way we expect, but God's justice will always stand. Instead of spending our strength trying to defend ourselves in every situation, we can entrust our reputation to the One who is the ultimate Judge and Defender.

When people don't care to hear your side, remember this: Jesus Himself was falsely accused, mocked, and misunderstood. Yet He remained silent before His accusers, entrusting His vindication to the Father. That same God who vindicated Christ will also vindicate you in due season.

Heavenly Father, I come before You with a heart that has been misunderstood and sometimes misjudged by others. Lord, You know the truth, for You see all and hear all. Help me to rest in the confidence that my identity is not found in the opinions of people but in who You say I am. Strengthen me to walk in love even when I am wronged and give me peace when my voice is not heard. I trust You to be my Defender, my Advocate, and my Deliverer. May every tongue that rises against me be silenced by Your truth, and may my life continue to reflect Your glory. In Jesus' name I pray, Amen and To God Be The Glory!

DECEMBER 13. - "THE LOVE YOU DESERVE"

The phrase "Someday someone will come into your life and love you the way you deserve to be loved" carries a weight of hope and healing. Many hearts have been broken, used, or undervalued. At times, we may wonder if true love, that kind of godly, selfless, patient, and kind love, will ever find us. But the truth is, God Himself has already set the standard of love, and He will not allow His children to settle for less than what He has ordained.

The love you deserve is not rooted in fleeting emotions or shallow desires. It is anchored in respect, sacrifice, and spiritual alignment. God's Word tells us: "Love is patient, love is kind. It does not envy, it does not boast, it is not proud. It does not dishonor others, it is not self-seeking, it is not easily angered, it keeps no record of wrongs." 1 Corinthians 13:4–5 (NIV)

This is the kind of love God desires for you, not one that manipulates, wounds, or diminishes your worth. While waiting for this love, remember that God is preparing both you and the one He has chosen. Sometimes, the delay is not denial but a season of refinement where He heals the wounds of your heart, teaches you your worth, and draws you closer to His own love.

Never forget that you are already loved beyond measure by Christ, who gave His life for you. His love defines you, not the absence of someone's affection. When you rest in His love, you become whole, and in His perfect timing, He will bring the right person who reflects that same Christ-like love.

Heavenly Father, thank You for reminding me that I am deeply loved and valued in Your eyes. Teach me to rest in Your perfect love while I wait for the one You have prepared for me. Guard my heart from settling for less than what You have ordained. Heal every wound from the past and fill me with patience, trust, and hope. When the right time comes, let the love that enters my life mirror Your unconditional love. The kind of love that's pure, patient, and kind. Until then, help me walk in contentment, joy, and confidence in You. In Jesus' name, Amen and To God Be The Glory!

DECEMBER 14. - "WHEN YOU ACTUALLY MATTERS"

In our fast-paced world, people are often "too busy." Schedules fill up, responsibilities pile high, and priorities shift daily. Yet the truth remains: when you actually matter to someone, they will always make time for you. Love shows itself not in empty words, but in consistent action. Real care doesn't hide behind excuses or half-truths, it shows up, it makes room, and it chooses you even in the busiest of seasons.

This principle is a reflection of God's character toward us. Though He governs the entire universe, He never neglects His children. His ear is always open to our prayers, His presence never too far to reach, and His love never too distracted to attend to our needs. The Psalmist reminds us of this unshakable truth: "The Lord is near to all who call on him, to all who call on him in truth." Psalm 145:18 (KJV)

Notice the scripture doesn't say God might be near or will sometimes be near. It says He is near ~ always. Unlike people who may grow tired, forget, or make excuses, God makes time for us without fail. This teaches us what genuine love looks like: it's present, it's truthful, and it shows up consistently.

In our relationships with others, we must learn to discern between those who value us in truth and those who only speak with empty intentions. True connection doesn't require begging for someone's time, chasing after their attention, or accepting their excuses. When people truly care, they will make room in their lives just as God always makes room for us.

So, as God models perfect faithfulness, let us also strive to reflect Him in how we treat others. Let us show up with love, honesty, and effort, making time for the ones who matter without excuses.

Heavenly Father, thank You for always making time for me. Even when the world seems busy and people fall short, You are a constant source of love, care, and presence. Help me to recognize the value of genuine relationships and give me wisdom to discern who truly matters in my life. Teach me to love as You love, faithfully, honestly, and without excuses. Strengthen me to give time and effort where You desire me to, and to release what does not align with Your will. I thank You that Your presence is always near, and I rest in Your unfailing love. In Jesus' name I pray, Amen and To God Be The Glory!

DECEMBER 15. - "SOMETIMES HAPPINESS IS JUST DOING YOU"

"Sometimes Happiness Looks Like Staying Home, Minding Your Business, Telling People No, and Just Doing You"

Life often pressures us to be constantly busy, surrounded by people, and saying "yes" to everyone's requests. But true happiness is not found in pleasing the world, it is found in living with peace, balance, and wisdom. Sometimes happiness looks like slowing down, staying home, minding your own business, telling people "No", and simply being who God created you to be.

God did not design us to carry everyone else's burdens at the expense of our own well-being. The Bible reminds us in 1 Thessalonians 4:11-12 (KJV): "And that ye study to be quiet, and to do your own business, and to work with your own hands, as we commanded you; That ye may walk honestly toward them that are without, and that ye may have lack of nothing."

This scripture teaches us the blessing of simplicity and peace. Studying to be quiet means we learn to value stillness and contentment rather than chaos. Minding our own business keeps us from unnecessary drama and distraction. Saying "no" when needed helps us guard our mental, emotional, and spiritual health. And choosing to "just do you" means walking authentically in the calling God has given, without being pressured by the opinions of others.

Even Jesus often withdrew from the crowds to spend time in solitude and prayer (Luke 5:16). If the Savior Himself knew the importance of stepping back and recharging, how much more should we? Happiness is not always about what we gain or who we please, but about protecting the peace God has given us.

So, if happiness for you today looks like resting, minding your business, setting boundaries, and simply being at peace in God's presence and embracing it. That is not selfishness; it is wisdom.

Heavenly Father, thank You for reminding me that peace is a gift from You. Teach me to find joy in simplicity, to be content in stillness, and to set healthy boundaries without guilt. Help me to mind my own business, to guard my heart, and to walk in wisdom. May my happiness come not from the approval of others but from the assurance that I am living in alignment with Your will. Give me strength to say "no" when I need to, and courage to rest when my soul requires it. In all things, let me honor You in my choices and my peace.

Amen and To God Be The Glory!

DECEMBER 16. - "SOMEONE WHO WILL BE THER FOR US"

Sometimes in life we just need someone who will be there for us. Someone who will listen. Someone who will understand. God created us with a need for connection both with Him and with one another. While independence has its place, true strength often comes when we lean on those God has placed in our lives. In our hardest moments, what we long for is not always a solution, but the presence of someone who will sit with us, hear us, and remind us that we are not alone.

The beautiful truth is that God Himself is that constant Someone. Scripture reminds us: "Cast all your care upon Him; for He careth for you" (1 Peter 5:7, KJV). The Lord not only hears and listens to us, but He deeply cares for the burdens we carry. He doesn't brush aside our pain, nor does He grow weary of our tears. Instead, He listens, He understands, and He comforts us with His peace that surpasses understanding.

At the same time, God often sends people into our lives to be His hands and feet. A true friend, a mentor, or even a kind stranger can be used by the Lord to lend an ear, to offer comfort, or to simply sit in silence beside us. Ecclesiastes 4:9–10 tells us: "Two are better than one, because they have a good reward for their labour. For if they fall, the one will lift up his fellow: but woe to him that is alone when he falleth; for he hath not another to help him up."

So, when we feel weary, let us not isolate ourselves in silence. Instead, let us remember that God has promised to always be with us, and that He often provides people who reflect His love. And let us, in turn, be willing to be that listening ear and compassionate heart for someone else. Sometimes, the greatest ministry we can give is simply to be present.

Heavenly Father, thank You for being the One who always listens, who always understands, and who never leaves us. Lord, in times when I feel overwhelmed, help me to cast my cares upon You, trusting that You care for me deeply. Thank You also for the people You have placed in my life who encourage me, comfort me, and remind me of Your love. Teach me to be that same listening ear and caring presence for others, so that through my life, Your compassion can be shown. In Jesus' name I pray. Amen and To God Be The Glory!

DECEMBER 17. - "STANDING IN OUR TRUTH"

There are moments in life when silence speaks louder than words. Sometimes, standing in your truth is more important than speaking it. Words can be twisted, misunderstood, or even ignored, but a life lived in alignment with God's truth carries an undeniable power. When your actions reflect the convictions of your heart, they testify more strongly than any speech ever could.

The Bible tells us in Matthew 5:16 (KJV): "Let your light so shine before men, that they may see your good works, and glorify your Father which is in heaven." Notice that Jesus doesn't say, "Let them hear your words," but rather, "let them see your good works." Sometimes, the greatest witness is not what we say but how we live.

Standing in your truth means remaining firm in who God has called you to be, regardless of whether you are applauded or criticized. It is choosing integrity over popularity, faithfulness over convenience, and obedience over compromise. Speaking can be easy, living the truth consistently is harder, but far more powerful.

Think of Daniel in Babylon. He didn't loudly proclaim his devotion to God when commanded to eat from the king's table or bow to idols. Instead, he simply stood firm in his truth, and he lived by God's commands. His silent obedience spoke volumes and eventually brought glory to God.

When you stand in your truth, rooted in Christ, you show the world that your faith is not just words, it is life. You may not always need to explain yourself. Sometimes, your steady walk, your unwavering faith, and your consistent love for others speak more than your lips ever could.

Heavenly Father, thank You for being the God of truth and integrity. Teach me to live in such a way that my life reflects Your Word, even when I do not speak it aloud. Give me strength to stand firm in my convictions, courage to walk in obedience, and wisdom to know when to speak and when to remain silent. May my actions glorify You and draw others closer to Your light. In Jesus' name, I pray.

Amen and To God Be The Glory!

DECEMBER 18. - "COMING OUT STRONGER"

If Jonah came out of the great fish, Daniel came out of the lions' den, and Lazarus came out of the tomb, then surely you will come out of your problems. God's Word is full of testimonies of His mighty deliverance. These stories remind us that no situation is too overwhelming for our God.

Jonah's time in the belly of the fish was dark and confining, yet it was also a place of preparation, prayer, and transformation. Daniel's night in the lions' den could have been his end, yet God shut the mouths of the lions, showing His supernatural protection. Lazarus lay in a tomb for four days, a seemingly hopeless situation, yet the same God who gave life to the dead called him forth with a powerful voice.

Your problems, no matter how deep, dark, or daunting, are not beyond God's reach. He is the same yesterday, today, and forever. What feels like a tomb, a den, or a belly of a fish in your life is only temporary. Your breakthrough is on the horizon. Trust that God is working behind the scenes, turning your trials into testimonies. Hold on, pray fervently, and never doubt that you too will emerge victoriously.

Remember: deliverance does not always come immediately, but it is certain when you trust in God. Your challenges are not the end, they are the setup for your breakthrough. Stand firm in faith, speak life over your situation, and believe that just as God brought His servants out, He will bring you out stronger, wiser, and victorious.

"Call unto me, and I will answer thee, and show thee great and mighty things, which thou knowest not." Jeremiah 33:3 KJV

Heavenly Father, I thank You for being my refuge and my strength. Lord, I stand on Your promises today, knowing that no problem is too great for You. Just as You delivered Jonah, Daniel, and Lazarus, I trust You to deliver me from the trials that seek to overwhelm me. Give me patience in waiting, faith in the unseen, and courage to keep moving forward. Let my story be a testimony of Your greatness and mercy. I praise You for the breakthrough that is already on its way. In Jesus' mighty name, I pray.

Amen and To God Be The Glory!

DECEMBER 19. - "FROM MY LIPS TO GOD'S EARS ~ A PRAYER OF HOPE"

"Dear Lord, when I stand at the beginning of a new day, bless me with the wisdom to see the best of things to come, wisdom to make good decisions, and most of all, faith that You are walking with me every step of the way."

Every morning presents us with a choice: to approach the day with fear or with faith. Too often, the weight of yesterday or the uncertainties of tomorrow can cloud our vision, making us doubt God's promises. Yet, Scripture reminds us that hope is not wishful thinking; it is rooted in the unwavering character of God.

When we speak words of hope and lay our desires before God, we are participating in a divine dialogue. The phrase "From my lips to God's ears" is not merely poetic, it is an acknowledgment that God hears, understands, and acts on behalf of His children. In declaring a prayer of hope, we are aligning our hearts with God's will, asking Him to transform our perspective and guide our steps.

The wisdom we seek each day is twofold. First, the wisdom to see the best in things to come allows us to remain optimistic even in uncertainty. Romans 15:13 encourages this mindset: "Now may the God of hope fill you with all joy and peace in believing, that you may abound in hope by the power of the Holy Spirit." (Romans 15:13, KJV)

Second, the wisdom to make good decisions reminds us that God equips those who seek His guidance. Every choice, no matter how small, is an opportunity to reflect His wisdom in our lives.

Finally, faith is the anchor that sustains us. Trusting that God is walking with us every step of the way allows us to face trials with courage, knowing that we are never alone. Even when circumstances appear bleak, faith reminds us that God's plans are perfect and His timing impeccable.

Today, speak your hope aloud. Whisper it in your heart. Write it down. Let it be a declaration that shapes your day, guides your decisions, and reinforces your trust in God's constant presence.

Heavenly Father, I lift my voice and my heart to You. As I begin this new day, fill me with Your wisdom to see the good that lies ahead. Teach me to make decisions that honor You and strengthen my faith to trust Your presence with every step I take. Guard my heart from doubt and fear and remind me that Your plans for me are always good. May Your hope shine in me and through me, touching everyone I encounter today. Thank You, Lord, for hearing my prayer and for walking with me faithfully.

Amen and To God Be The Glory!

DECEMBER 20. - "YOU CAN GIVE KNOWLEDGE ~ BUT YOU CAN'T MAKE THEM THINK"

"TRUTH REQUIRES CHANGE"

We live in a world overflowing with information. Knowledge is abundant, wisdom is rare, and understanding is even rarer. You can share facts, guidance, and truth with someone, but the decision to apply that knowledge and truly think through its implication's rests solely with them.

The phrase, "you can give a person knowledge, but you can't make them think," carries a sobering truth: awareness alone does not guarantee transformation. Some people resist truth because it confronts their comfort zones or challenges ingrained habits. Change requires effort, humility, and a willingness to face uncomfortable realities.

As believers, we are called to speak truth in love and plant seeds of wisdom. Yet, we must also accept that not everyone will respond. God does not force understanding on anyone. The heart of man must be willing, and that willingness often comes only when a person encounters the consequences of ignoring truth.

This devotion reminds us to guard our own hearts. Let us pursue knowledge but let us pursue thinking and understanding even more. Let us not be satisfied with knowing God's Word superficially. Let the truth penetrate, convict, and transform our hearts, so that we reflect His wisdom in our daily lives.

Remember: you cannot force change in someone else, but you can be a living testimony of what change through God's truth looks like. Your life may inspire them to think, to reconsider, or to take steps toward transformation.

"The heart is deceitful above all things, and desperately wicked: who can know it?" Jeremiah 17:9 (KJV)

Heavenly Father, I thank You for the gift of knowledge and the wisdom that comes from You. Lord, I ask that You help me not just to know Your Word, but to understand it, meditate on it, and apply it in every area of my life. Teach me patience for those who resist truth and give me the grace to be a reflection of Your wisdom. May my life shine as a testimony, encouraging others to seek understanding and transformation through You. Lord, help me remember that true change begins in the heart, and that Your Spirit alone can guide a willing heart to think, repent, and grow. In all things, let Your truth reign in me. In Jesus name I pray, Amen and To God Be The Glory!

DECEMBER 21. - "RECOGNIZING TRUE ENEMIES AND GOD' FAITHFULNESS"

Life often presents us with challenges that disguise themselves in subtle forms. Sometimes our enemies are not obvious people or events, but intangible forces that creep into our minds and hearts: anxiety that paralyzes, depression that clouds joy, procrastination that stalls our progress, complacency that dulls our ambition, negativity that poisons our thoughts, even seemingly harmless fun or enticing ideas that lead us astray. These are tactics of the enemy, attempting to pull us away from God's plan, peace, and purpose.

Yet in the midst of these disguised enemies, there is a powerful truth we must hold on to: God is always good, faithful, loving, patient, kind, truthful, and welcoming. His presence is constant, His guidance unchanging, and His love unfailing. While the enemy seeks to deceive and distract, God provides clarity, strength, and wisdom.

When anxiety threatens to overwhelm you, remember that God's peace surpasses all understanding (Philippians 4:7). When depression whispers lies of hopelessness, God reminds you of His promises and purpose for your life. When procrastination or complacency sets in, His Spirit equips you with discipline and determination. Every force that seems to oppose you is no match for the goodness and faithfulness of your Creator.

This devotion calls us to discern carefully between what is temporary, deceptive, or destructive, and what is eternal, truthful, and life-giving. Align yourself with what God attributes. His love and kindness, His patience and truth, and you will recognize the difference between the enemy's schemes and God's purposes. Your victory is not in avoiding trials, but in standing firm in the knowledge that God's character never fails.

"We are not ignorant of his devices." 2 Corinthians 2:11 (KJV)

Heavenly Father, thank You for being the constant in a world full of distractions and hidden enemies. Help me to discern the tactics of the enemy, whether they appear as anxiety, depression, procrastination, or even seemingly harmless distractions. Teach me to cling to Your goodness, faithfulness, love, patience, kindness, truth, and welcoming nature. Strengthen me to stand firm in Your promises and to trust that nothing can separate me from Your care. Guard my heart and mind, Lord, and let Your light guide me through every challenge. I receive Your peace, Your wisdom, and Your strength today and every day. In Jesus' name, I pray.

Amen and To God Be The Glory!

DECEMBER 22. - "DISCERNMENT IN FRIENDSHIP"

"Not everyone who shakes hands with you has good intentions. Some of your friends are agents of hell, and they are just buying time. May God help you know your enemies, in Jesus' name."

Friendships and relationships are gifts from God, but not every person who appears friendly is truly on your side. The enemy often disguises himself as a friend, presenting what seems good, kind, or trustworthy, only to manipulate, harm, or derail God's plans for your life. Proverbs 27:6 reminds us, "Faithful are the wounds of a friend; but the kisses of an enemy are deceitful." Some people will smile with you, shake hands with you, and speak words of encouragement, all the while harboring intentions that could destroy your peace, purpose, or testimony.

The Bible teaches us the importance of wisdom and discernment. Psalm 141:4 (NIV) says, "Do not let my heart be drawn to what is evil, to take part in wicked deeds with those who are evildoers; do not let me eat their delicacies." God desires that we remain vigilant, prayerful, and discerning, even in relationships that seem harmless. Our spiritual eyes must be open to recognize deception, not to live in paranoia, but to guard our hearts and protect the calling God has placed on our lives.

Being discerning does not mean withdrawing from all relationships, but it means testing the motives of those around you and seeking God's guidance. True friends build you up, encourage righteousness, and pray for your success. False friends, on the other hand, may subtly attempt to lead you astray. God promises in 1 John 4:1 (KJV), "Beloved, believe not every spirit, but try the spirits whether they are of God: because many false prophets are gone out into the world."

Let us pray for wisdom, discernment, and protection. Ask God to reveal the hearts of those around you and grant you the courage to distance yourself from harmful influences. Trust in the Lord, for He will surround you with those who truly care for your soul and your destiny.

Heavenly Father, I thank You for Your unfailing love and protection. Lord, give me the discernment to see the hearts of those around me. Help me recognize friends who are genuine and those whose intentions are not aligned with Your will. Deliver me from deceit, manipulation, and hidden agendas. Surround me with people who build me up and draw me closer to You. Lord, may Your Spirit guide my choices in friendships and relationships. Guard my heart and protect my purpose. I declare that no weapon formed against me shall prosper, and no enemy, seen or unseen, shall have power over me. In Jesus' mighty name, I pray.

Amen and To God Be The Glory!

DECEMBER 23. - "HOW WOULD YOU DEFINE THE POOREST PERSON"

The Poorest Person is Not One Without Money, It's the One Without God

In the world, we often measure wealth by money, possessions, or status. Society applauds those with material success and often equates lack of finance with poverty. But the truth is far deeper and far more spiritual: the poorest person is not the one without money, it is the one without God.

Without God, a person may have riches yet feel empty, restless, or without purpose. Life may seem shallow, relationships may feel hollow, and no achievement can bring lasting peace. Conversely, a life with God is rich beyond measure. Even in the simplest circumstances, a person walking with God experiences true joy, eternal hope, guidance, and an inner contentment that the world cannot give or take away.

Scripture reminds us of this truth in Psalm 16:11 (KJV): "Thou wilt shew me the path of life: in thy presence is fulness of joy; at thy right hand there are pleasures for evermore."

Here, the psalmist reveals that the ultimate wealth lies in the presence of God. When we are connected to Him, we are spiritually full, emotionally fulfilled, and eternally secure. No amount of earthly treasure can compare to the riches found in His love, His guidance, and His unchanging faithfulness.

Let us remember that possessions can be lost, status can fade, but God's presence is eternal. Our richest moments are not measured by what we have in our hands, but by the peace, joy, and assurance in our hearts through Him. To be without God is to be spiritually impoverished, no matter what the world may see.

Heavenly Father, thank You for the immeasurable treasure of Your presence. Help me to seek You above all things, to cherish You more than wealth or status, and to remain anchored in Your love. Teach me to find joy, contentment, and purpose in You, even when the world praises material riches. Guard my heart against the lie that money or possessions define my worth. May my life be a testimony of Your richness and grace, and may I never forget that true wealth is found in You alone.

Amen and To God Be The Glory!

DECEMBER 24. - "RECOGNIZING OUR BLESSINGS"

"Give thanks in all circumstances; for this is the will of God in Christ Jesus for you." 1 Thessalonians 5:18 (ESV)

As the holiday season approaches, life often becomes a whirlwind of activity from shopping, planning, preparing, and attending events. It can be easy to get caught up in the busyness, forgetting the deeper significance of this season. But there is a simple yet profound practice that can bring peace and perspective: pausing to reflect on our blessings.

Even in moments of struggle, when life seems overwhelming, there are countless reasons to rejoice. God has been faithful. He has carried us through trials, sustained us in moments of weakness, and surrounded us with people who love and uplift us. Surviving the impossible is not just a testament to our strength, it is a testimony of God's grace working through our lives.

During this season, take a moment to look around. Consider the people who have touched your life with love, encouragement, and support. Recall the times when circumstances seemed hopeless, yet somehow, God's hand guided you to a better place. Even small victories, moments of joy, and daily provisions are reminders of His goodness.

Gratitude is more than a fleeting feeling; it is a choice. Choosing to focus on what we have rather than what we lack transforms our perspective. It shifts our hearts from complaint to praise and strengthens our faith. Saying "God is good" is not just a ritual, it is a declaration of trust in the One who has been with us through it all.

Let this holiday season be a time to reflect deeply, to be intentional about gratitude, and to rejoice in the countless ways God has blessed your life.

Heavenly Father, I thank You for Your unending goodness and mercy. I thank You for carrying me through trials I never thought I could survive. I thank You for the people You have placed in my life to love, encourage, and support me. Lord, help me to always recognize my blessings, even in the midst of challenges. Teach me to live a life of gratitude and to trust in Your plans. May my heart be filled with joy and my spirit overflow with thanksgiving, not just during this holiday season, but every day of my life.

Amen and To God Be The Glory!

DECEMBER 25. - "O HOLY NIGHT ~ CHRIST THE SAVIOR IS BORN"

The phrase "Oh Holy Night, Christ the Savior is born" captures the most sacred and transforming moment in all of human history. The night when heaven touched earth in the person of Jesus Christ. That night was not ordinary; it was holy, sanctified by the presence of God wrapped in human flesh. The long-awaited Messiah had finally come, fulfilling prophecy and bringing hope to a weary world.

When Jesus was born in Bethlehem, the angels announced His arrival to humble shepherds, declaring, "For unto you is born this day in the city of David a Saviour, which is Christ the Lord" (Luke 2:11 KJV). This was not just the birth of a child, but the unveiling of God's redemption plan for mankind.

That holy night reminds us that God stepped into our darkness with His light. The Savior did not come in the splendor of a palace but in the lowliness of a manger, showing that His glory is revealed in humility and His power perfected in weakness. Christ's birth marks the beginning of our salvation journey, the doorway to forgiveness, reconciliation, and eternal life.

Whenever we reflect on "Oh Holy Night," we are invited to pause and worship. It is a call to kneel before the Savior in awe and gratitude, just as the shepherds and wise men did. It is a reminder that hope was born, peace entered the world, and love became flesh among us.

Let us carry that holy night in our hearts every day. Just as the heavens declared His glory at His birth, our lives should now declare His glory through our faith, obedience, and worship.

For unto us a child is born, unto us a son is given and the government shall be upon his shoulder: and his name shall be called Wonderful, Counsellor, The mighty God, The everlasting Father, The Prince of Peace." Isaiah 9:6 (KJV)

Heavenly Father, we thank You for the gift of Your Son, Jesus Christ, who was born on that holy night to bring salvation to the world. We stand in awe of Your love and mercy, for You sent the Light into our darkness and gave us hope when we were hopeless. Lord, help us to never take this gift for granted. May our hearts continually rejoice in the birth of our Savior and live in the light of His presence. Strengthen our faith, deepen our worship, and guide us to share this good news with others. In Jesus' mighty name we pray.

Amen and To God Be The Glory!

DECEMBER 26. - "THIS IS THE TIME OF YEAR TO JUST STOP AND TAKE A PAUSE"

Life has a way of keeping us busy, sometimes far too busy. The demands of work, family, and daily responsibilities often fill every hour of our schedule, leaving little space to breathe, reflect, or simply be. But there comes a moment, especially at certain seasons of the year, when God calls us to pause. A pause is not wasted time, it is a divine invitation to rest in His presence, to realign our hearts, and to regain the strength needed to continue our journey with purpose.

Taking a pause does not mean giving up. It means recognizing that our strength alone cannot carry us, and that the One who sustains all things longs to refresh our spirit. When we pause, we shift our focus from the noise of life back to the peace of Christ. It's in the stillness that we hear His whisper most clearly. It's in the silence that He reminds us of His promises.

The psalmist reminds us of this truth: "Be still and know that I am God: I will be exalted among the heathen, I will be exalted in the earth." Psalm 46:10 (KJV)

This scripture is not merely about physical stillness but spiritual surrender. When we stop striving and simply acknowledge that God is in control, peace enters our hearts. A pause gives us space to reflect on how far God has brought us, to release what we cannot control, and to rest in His unfailing love.

So, in this time of year, whether it be a season of change, of celebration, or even of hardship, just remember that God is inviting you to take a holy pause. To breathe. To reset. To trust. In that pause, you will find renewal, clarity, and the strength to keep moving forward in His will.

Heavenly Father, I thank You for the gentle reminder to stop and take a pause. In the busyness of life, I sometimes forget that my soul needs rest in You. Teach me to be still in Your presence and to listen for Your voice. Help me to release the burdens I cannot carry and trust fully in Your plan. May this season of pause draw me closer to You and refresh my spirit with peace, clarity, and strength. In Jesus' name, I pray.

Amen and o God Be The Glory!

DECEMBER 27. - "THIS LITTLE LIGHT OF MINE ~ I'M GONNA LET IT SHINE"

The phrase "This little light of mine, I'm gonna let it shine" is more than a children's song, it is a declaration of faith and a call to action. Light has always been a powerful symbol throughout Scripture. In Genesis, God's very first creative command was, "Let there be light" (Genesis 1:3 KJV). In John's Gospel, we are reminded that Jesus is "the true Light which gives light to every man coming into the world" (John 1:9 NKJV). And when we embrace Christ, His light doesn't just dwell in us, it radiates outward, touching those around us.

As we celebrate the birth of Christ this holiday season, we are reminded of the words of Jesus: "You are the light of the world. A city that is set on a hill cannot be hidden. Neither do people light a lamp and put it under a bowl. Instead, they put it on its stand, and it gives light to everyone in the house. In the same way, let your light shine before others, that they may see your good deeds and glorify your Father in heaven." Matthew 5:14–16 (KJV)

The birth of Christ was the ultimate arrival of light into a dark and broken world. Shepherds saw the glory of God in the skies. Wise men followed the star that illuminated their path to the newborn King. Angels declared peace on earth and good will toward men. Every part of the nativity story is drenched in light, symbolizing hope, redemption, and the unshakable presence of God.

So, when we say "This little light of mine, I'm gonna let it shine," we are making a choice this season not just to celebrate with decorations, gifts, and songs, but to live in such a way that others encounter the brilliance of Christ through us. Our words, our actions, our generosity, and even our attitudes can shine brighter than any Christmas lights strung on a tree.

Let this season be marked by light that is not dim, hidden, or flickering, but bright, pure, and immaculate. A light that reflects the holiness of Christ. A light that shines in our homes, in our communities, and even in places where darkness tries to linger.

The world doesn't need another decoration to admire, it needs living testimonies of Christ's birth. It needs people who shine so brightly that others are drawn, not to us, but to the Savior who was born in Bethlehem and is alive forevermore.

Heavenly Father, thank You for sending Jesus, the Light of the world, into the darkness of our lives and our world. As we celebrate His birth this holiday season, may our lives reflect His light, bright, immaculate, and unwavering. Help us not to hide our light, but to let it shine in every place You position us. Use us to bring warmth where there is coldness, hope where there is despair, and love where there is bitterness. Let our light be a living testimony that points back to Christ, our Savior and Redeemer. In Jesus' name we pray, Amen and To God Be The Glory!

DECEMBER 28. - "THE BLESSING OF LOW MAINTENANCE FRIENDS"

Life can be full of busyness from work, family, responsibilities, unexpected trials, and seasons of silence. In the midst of it all, there are those rare and precious friendships that don't demand constant attention to survive. These are the low-maintenance friendships, the ones where you may not speak for months, but when you reconnect, it feels like no time has passed. The bond is still strong, the love still genuine, and the understanding still deep.

Such friendships are rooted not in convenience but in authenticity. They are a gift from God, a reminder that true love and loyalty do not fade with distance or time. Scripture reminds us: "A friend loves at all times, and a brother is born for adversity." Proverbs 17:17 (KJV)

Notice the verse doesn't say a friend loves only when present or only when convenient. It says at all times. Genuine friendships carry the strength of unconditional love and grace. Just like God's love for us, true friends remain connected at the heart even when circumstances keep us apart.

Low-maintenance friends are living testimonies of patience, grace, and maturity. They don't keep score of unanswered calls or delayed texts. They understand seasons of life. And when you meet again, it's as if time has been bridged by love. These friendships mirror the way Christ treats us by never counting the distance but always welcoming us back with open arms.

If you are blessed with such friends, cherish them. Pray for them. Thank God for them. And strive to be that kind of friend yourself, as steady, understanding, forgiving, and filled with unconditional love.

Heavenly Father, thank You for the gift of true friendship. Thank You for those low-maintenance friends who love us through every season, no matter the distance or silence. Lord, help us to cherish them, to pray for them, and to show them the same grace and understanding they give us. Teach us to be faithful friends who reflect Your love and patience. May every reconnection remind us of the beauty of bonds rooted in You. In Jesus' name, Amen and To God Be The Glory!

DECEMBER 29. - "WILL YOU PUT ON THE FULL ARMOR OF GOD"

When you wake up each morning, there is a decision to be made: Will you walk into the day clothed in your own strength, or will you be fully armed in the power of God? The Apostle Paul reminds us in Ephesians 6:11 (KJV): "Put on the whole armor of God, that ye may be able to stand against the wiles of the devil."

The devil is strategic, he studies weaknesses, waits for tired moments, and seeks to exploit vulnerabilities. But when you put on the full armor of God, you representing truth, righteousness, peace, faith, salvation, and the Word of God and you are no longer fighting in your own ability. Instead, you are covered by Christ Himself.

Think of what it means when you are clothed in the armor of God:

The belt of truth secures you against lies and deception.

The breastplate of righteousness guards your heart from corruption.

The shoes of peace steady your walk, no matter the chaos around you.

The shield of faith extinguishes every fiery dart of doubt, fear, or temptation.

The helmet of salvation covers your mind with the assurance of eternal life.

The sword of the Spirit equips you with the living Word of God to strike down the enemy.

When you put it all on, you are making a bold declaration: "Devil, you cannot come against me without first going through Jesus Christ." And that is a battle you can never lose because Jesus has already won.

This armor isn't optional, it's essential. Without it, you're exposed. With it, you're untouchable, not because of who you are, but because of who fights for you. To be clothed in the armor of God is to stand in the power of Christ's victory at the cross.

So today, as you step into life's challenges, ask yourself: Will I put on the full armor of God? If your answer is yes, then know that no matter what the enemy tries, he will always be met with the strength and authority of Jesus.

Heavenly Father, thank You for providing me with spiritual armor to withstand the attacks of the enemy. Help me to daily clothe myself with Your truth, righteousness, peace, faith, salvation, and Word. Remind me that in Christ I am already victorious, and that no weapon formed against me shall prosper. Let the enemy see not me, but Jesus standing before him. In Your strength, I will not fear. In Jesus' mighty name, Amen and To God Be The Glory!

DECEMBER 30. - "THE BATTLES NOT YOURS IT'S THE LORDS"

"And he said, Hearken ye, all Judah, and ye inhabitants of Jerusalem, and thou king Jehoshaphat, Thus saith the LORD unto you, Be not afraid nor dismayed by reason of this great multitude; for the battle is not yours, but God's." 2 Chronicles 20:15 (KJV)

Life often feels like a battlefield. Sometimes the enemy seems too strong, the mountain too high, or the storm too violent to endure. In these moments, fear can grip our hearts and doubts can flood our minds. But in 2 Chronicles 20:15, God reminds His people that the fight does not rest on our human strength or wisdom. The victory belongs to Him.

King Jehoshaphat and the people of Judah were facing a vast army they could not defeat on their own. Instead of relying on weapons or strategy, Jehoshaphat turned to prayer and fasting. God answered with a powerful assurance: "Be not afraid nor dismayed for the battle is not yours, but God's."

This is more than encouragement; it's a command to trust. God does not want His children paralyzed by fear or overwhelmed by the enemy's size. He wants us to rest in His power and sovereignty. The Lord fights for those who call upon Him, and His strength has no limits.

When we face battles, whether spiritual attacks, health crises, broken relationships, or financial struggles, we must remember that our role is obedience, faith, and praise. The Lord will do the fighting, and His victory will bring glory to His name.

So today, lay your burdens at His feet. Stop carrying the weight of a battle that was never yours to fight in the first place. Stand still, worship, and watch what God will do on your behalf.

Heavenly Father, I thank You that the battle is not mine, but Yours. When fear tries to grip me and discouragement surrounds me, help me to stand firm in faith, knowing You are my Defender, my Deliverer, and my Strength. Teach me to trust You completely and not lean on my own understanding. Fight for me, Lord, and let my life be a testimony of Your power and faithfulness. In Jesus' mighty name I pray.

Amen and To God Be The Glory!

DECEMBER 31. "FOR GOD BLESSES US TO BE A BLESSING TO OTHERS ~ IF ONLY WE WOULD"

ROBERTA HECK MINISTIRES STRIVES FOR UNITY AND FELLOWSHIP

"Behold, how good and how pleasant it is for brethren to dwell together in unity!" Psalm 133:1 (KJV)

Unity is one of the greatest gifts God has given His people. Where there is unity, there is peace. Where there is peace, there is strength. Psalm 133 reminds us that unity is not only pleasant to the soul but also precious to the heart of God. It is in unity that His blessings flow.

At Roberta Heck Ministries, we believe that God blesses us so that we can, in turn, be a blessing to others. When we walk in harmony with one another, we reflect the very nature of Christ, who prayed for His disciples to be one just as He and the Father are one (John 17:21). This is the essence of fellowship and choosing to set aside differences, extending love, and embracing one another as members of God's family.

Unity is not always easy; it requires humility, forgiveness, and grace. But it is in striving together that we grow stronger. Our ministry is committed to cultivating an atmosphere of fellowship, where people are uplifted, encouraged, and reminded that they are not alone. We believe that harmony among God's people allows His Spirit to work freely, healing hearts, restoring relationships, and bringing communities closer to Him.

When God's people unite, the world witnesses His love in action. And when His love is revealed through unity, blessings are multiplied, not only in the ministry but in every life we touch.

"And let us consider one another to provoke unto love and to good works: Not forsaking the assembling of ourselves together, as the manner of some is but exhorting one another: and so much the more, as ye see the day approaching." Hebrews 10:24–25 (KJV)

Heavenly Father, we truly thank You for the beauty of unity and the strength found in fellowship. Lord, help us at Roberta Heck Ministries to walk in harmony, seeking peace and pursuing love in all we do. May we be a reflection of Your heart, blessing others as You have blessed us. Strengthen our bonds as brothers and sisters in Christ and let our unity bring glory to Your name. May everything we strive for be rooted in love, guided by Your Spirit, and centered on Your will. In Jesus' name, we pray.

Amen and To God Be The Glory!

If our devotional impacted your life please leave us a review on Amazon.com.

God Bless!

www.ingramcontent.com/pod-product-compliance
Lightning Source LLC
Chambersburg PA
CBHW070310240426
43663CB00038BA/1294